Multilingualism and History

CW01623510

We often hear that our world "is more multilingual than ever before," but is it true? This book shatters the familiar cliché and shines the light on the millennia-long history of multilingualism as a social, institutional, and demographic phenomenon. Its fifteen chapters, written in clear, accessible language by prominent historians, classicists, and sociolinguists, span the period from the third century BC to the present day, and range from ancient Rome and Egypt to medieval London and Jerusalem, from Russian, Ottoman, and Austro-Hungarian Empires to modern Norway, Ukraine, and Spain. Going against the grain of traditional language histories, these thought-provoking case studies challenge stereotypical beliefs, foreground historic normativity of institutional multilingualism and language mixing, examine the transformation of polyglot societies into monolingual ones, and bring out the cognitive and affective dissonance in present-day orientations to multilingualism, where 'celebrations of linguistic diversity' coexist uneasily with the creation of 'language police.'

ANETA PAVLENKO is Research Professor at the Center for Multilingualism at the University of Oslo, Norway. She has authored more than a hundred articles and ten books on various aspects of multilingualism, including *The Bilingual Mind and What It Tells Us about Language and Thought* (Cambridge University Press, 2014), and has lectured widely in North America, Europe, and Asia. She is Past President of the American Association for Applied Linguistics and winner of the 2006 BAAL Book of the Year award, the 2009 TESOL Award for Distinguished Research, the 2021 AAAL Research Article award and the 2023 AAAL Distinguished Scholarship and Service Award.

Multilingualism and History

Edited by

Aneta Pavlenko

University of Oslo

CAMBRIDGE
UNIVERSITY PRESS

CAMBRIDGE
UNIVERSITY PRESS

Shaftesbury Road, Cambridge CB2 8EA, United Kingdom

One Liberty Plaza, 20th Floor, New York, NY 10006, USA

477 Williamstown Road, Port Melbourne, VIC 3207, Australia

314–321, 3rd Floor, Plot 3, Splendor Forum, Jasola District Centre, New Delhi – 110025, India

103 Penang Road, #05–06/07, Visioncrest Commercial, Singapore 238467

Cambridge University Press is part of Cambridge University Press & Assessment, a department of the University of Cambridge.

We share the University's mission to contribute to society through the pursuit of education, learning and research at the highest international levels of excellence.

www.cambridge.org
Information on this title: www.cambridge.org/9781009236263

DOI: 10.1017/9781009236287

First published 2023
First paperback edition 2025

A catalogue record for this publication is available from the British Library

Library of Congress Cataloging-in-Publication data
Names: Pavlenko, Aneta, 1963- editor.
Title: Multilingualism and history / edited by Aneta Pavlenko, University of Oslo.
Description: Cambridge ; New York, NY : Cambridge University Press, 2023. | Includes bibliographical references and index.
Identifiers: LCCN 2022032516 (print) | LCCN 2022032517 (ebook) | ISBN 9781009236256 (hardback) | ISBN 9781009236263 (paperback) | ISBN 9781009236287 (epub)
Subjects: LCSH: Multilingualism–History. | LCGFT: Essays.
Classification: LCC P115 .M85 2023 (print) | LCC P115 (ebook) | DDC 306.44/6–dc23/eng/20220810
LC record available at https://lccn.loc.gov/2022032516
LC ebook record available at https://lccn.loc.gov/2022032517

ISBN 978-1-009-23625-6 Hardback
ISBN 978-1-009-23626-3 Paperback

Contents

Figures

Contributors

Gesine Argent, University of Edinburgh

Yasmine Beale-Rivaya, Texas State University

Jan Fellerer, University of Oxford

Benjamin C. Fortna, University of Arizona

Susan Gal, University of Chicago

Pia Lane, Center for Multilingualism, University of Oslo

Rachel Mairs, University of Reading

Anastasia Maravela, University of Oslo

Alex Mullen, University of Nottingham

Aneta Pavlenko, Center for Multilingualism, University of Oslo

Jonathan Rubin, Bar-Ilan University

Zorana Sokolovska, University of Fribourg and University of Teacher Education Lucerne

Roland Willemyns, Vrije Universiteit Brussels

Laura Wright, University of Cambridge

Acknowledgments

Editing, like writing, can be a lonely process, and I am immensely grateful to everyone who made it less so, above all to Alexandre Duchêne and Pia Lane, who initially joined me as coeditors on this project and took part in the drafting of the book proposal and the process of peer review. I deeply regret the fact that both decided to step down for personal reasons. A major inspiration behind this project was the workshop on the history of ideas on multilingualism organized by Alexandre Duchêne and Raphael Berthele in November 2014 in Fribourg, and I am thankful to both of them for the intellectually stimulating conversations we had. I am also grateful to the Center for Multilingualism at the University of Oslo for supporting the round table on "Multilingual practices from antiquity to the present day," co-organized by Pia Lane and myself, which brought (nearly) all of the contributors together for exciting discussions in April 2019.

To maintain academic rigor we relied on numerous academic colleagues around the world who generously donated their time and expertise to one of the most crucial yet least visible and appreciated academic tasks – peer review. For their prompt and insightful feedback on individual chapters, thank you to all the contributors who doubled as internal reviewers and to a stellar group of external reviewers: Constanze Ackermann-Boström (Umeå University), Frederick Anscombe (Birkbeck College, University of London), Cyril Aslanov (The Hebrew University of Jerusalem), Mark Bai Li (University of Oxford), Elisabeth Barakos (University of Hamburg), James Clackson (University of Cambridge), Juan Camilo Conde Silvestre (University of Murcia), James Costa (Sorbonne Nouvelle), Martin Durrell (University of Manchester), Halvor Eifring (University of Oslo), Robert Evans (University of Oxford), Hilary Footitt (University of Reading), Victor Friedman (University of Chicago), Michael Gorham (University of Florida), Madoka Hammine (Meio University), Monica Heller (University of Toronto), Francis Hult (University of Maryland), Olesya Khanina (Institute of Linguistics, Russian Academy of Sciences), Nils Langer (University of Flensburg), Li Wei (Institute of Education, University College London), Pedro Mantes

España (University of Cordoba), Hannah McElgunn (University of British Columbia), Laura Morreale (Georgetown University), Maya Muratov (New York University), Kari Aga Myklebost (the Arctic University of Norway), Jan Henrik Nilsson (Lund University), Aleksandra Oszmiańska-Pagett (Wyższa Szkoła Języków Obcych, Poznań) Arietta Papaconstantinou (University of Reading), Christine Philiou (University of California, Berkeley), David Porter (Yale University), Denys Pringle (Cardiff University), Vladislav Rjéoutski (German Historical Institute, Moscow), Lara Ryazanova-Clarke (University of Edinburgh), Karène Sanchez Summerer (Leiden University), Yuri Slezkine (University of California, Berkeley), Bernardino Cardoso Tavares (University of Luxembourg), Jacob Thaisen (University of Oslo), Sofia Torallas Tovar (University of Chicago), Nikolai Vakhtin (European University at St. Petersburg), Wim Vandenbussche (Vrije University, Brussels), Estelle Ingrand Varenne (University of Poitiers), Marja Vierros (University of Helsinki), Greg Woolf (University of California, Los Angeles), and Xinqiu Guan (Old Dominion University).

A virtual collaboration throughout the COVID pandemic, a contested US election, and, in the last weeks of this project, a devastating war in my homeland has been an unsettling and sometimes surreal experience. I am all the more grateful to the contributors for their willingness to undergo the intense editing process, the patience with which they responded to my endless queries, and the warmth of the exchanges on topics that had nothing to do with this volume. It was a pleasure and an honor to work with such an outstanding group of scholars and human beings.

1 Multilingualism and Historical Amnesia: An Introduction

Aneta Pavlenko

> We have pushed Humpty Dumpty off the wall and watched him shatter into thousands of little bits and pieces; and we have descended on the pieces and broken them down into progressively smaller bits and pieces. But we cannot put him together again because we find it much easier to analyze than to synthesize.
>
> (Wright, 1982, p. 24)

Academic interest in multilingualism had waxed and waned throughout the twentieth century, but by the time I started a doctoral program in linguistics in 1992, researchers had articulated central questions (e.g., Fishman, 1965), written several introductions (e.g., Grosjean, 1982), and established the key lines of inquiry: bilingual brain, bilingual development, bilingual education, language policy, code-switching, and language contact, maintenance, and shift. By the time I defended my dissertation, the disparate lines of inquiry had come together as a field that coalesced around a dedicated publisher, Multilingual Matters; the first International Symposium on Bilingualism, organized in 1997 by Li Wei; the *International Journal of Bilingualism*, launched in 1997 by Li Wei, and *Bilingualism: Language and Cognition*, founded in 1998 by François Grosjean and his colleagues. At the time, no one could have predicted the explosive growth of the field. Today, no one knows how many professional journals there are and how many meetings on different aspects of multilingualism are held at any given point.

What's more, research on multilingualism was never confined to the four founding disciplines: linguistics, psychology, education, and anthropology. The influx of immigrants in the West and concerns about their integration raised interest in the history of linguistically diverse societies. The landmark collection by Adams et al. (2002) and Adams' magisterial *Bilingualism and the Latin Language* (2003) inspired a plethora of publications on bi- and

For their insightful comments on the various drafts of this chapter, I am deeply grateful to Ágoston Berecz, Joshua Brown, Robert Evans, Jan Fellerer, François Grosjean, Alex Mullen, Sebastian Muth, Ingrid Piller, Bernard Spolsky, and, especially, Anastasia Maravela, who, with an eagle eye, read both the first and the final draft.

multilingualism in antiquity (e.g., Bowman et al., 2021; Clackson et al., 2020; Elder & Mullen, 2019; Jonker et al., 2021; Mullen, 2013; Mullen & James, 2012; Papaconstantinou, 2010; Smelik, 2013); Trotter's (2000) pioneering collection was followed by numerous studies of medieval multilingualism (e.g., Bloemendal, 2015; Classen, 2016; Jefferson & Putter, 2013; Pahta et al., 2018; Rubin, 2018); while Evans (2004) and Burke (2004) turned the tide in the study of linguistic diversity in early modernity and the Austro-Hungarian, Russian, and Ottoman Empires (e.g., Fortna, 2010; Gallagher, 2019; Gilbert, 2020; Judson, 2006; Murre-van den Berg et al., 2020; Offord et al., 2018; Prokopovych et al., 2019; Tosi, 2020; Wolf, 2015).

The problem is that the twain rarely meet. Some historical studies, uninformed by recent research on multilingualism, are content to signal "multilingualism was here": they offer intriguing glimpses of language-mixing in ancient inscriptions and medieval manuscripts but fail to ask probing questions and fit their findings in the larger scheme of things. Sociolinguists, on the other hand, are cognizant of complexities of multilingualism but suffer from historical amnesia (Spolsky's (2009) historical sensibility is an exception rather than the rule). The purpose of this introduction – and of the volume at large – is to bring together these research strands.

I will begin by outlining the myths and misconceptions that inspired my own interest in the history of multilingual societies and, eventually, the round table at the Center for Multilingualism in Oslo and the volume you have in your hands. Then, I will place the chapters in context by discussing the paradoxes and contradictions of historical multilingualism in six institutional domains: administration, courts of law, religion, army, education, and public signage. In the last section, I will consider the picture emerging from recent work. The opposite of what we have come to believe, this picture undermines the sense of contemporary exceptionalism and opens up space for historically informed narratives and avenues of pursuit.

1.1 Academic Ignorance Pacts: The Joys and Dangers of Fragmented Conversations

Concerns about compartmentalization aren't new in academia. In March 1980, H. Curtis Wright, Professor of Library and Information Sciences at Brigham Young University, gave a heartfelt talk at a conference on Libraries and Culture, arguing that we have little chance of solving larger puzzles if we insist on breaking academic conversations into progressively smaller bits. I wonder if his naked frustration sounded misplaced to the meeting attendees, secure in their connections through dusty libraries and print journals that landed in their mailboxes with a predictable thud. Today, their world seems positively quaint to academics who access rare editions online and converse with colleagues around the globe from the comfort of their cozy dens. Wright's (1982) fears, however, sound more resonant as technological advances accelerate centrifugal forces that create new academic connections but also new divides.

Psychologists, political scientists, economists, and sociologists are debating the decline of central questions in their disciplines, split into isolated academic tribes, with their own agendas, meetings, and publications, and so are scholars in communication science, "said to be more fragmented and hyper-specialized than ever before, producing an increasing number of small, niche research topics that lack intellectual coherence as a whole" (Song et al., 2020, p. 310). Cross-disciplinary divides elicit their own concerns. Evans (2004, p. 2) roasted historians for "neglect of the language issue," Edwards (1994, pp. 206–207) and Burke (2004) chided sociolinguists for neglect of history, and Fishman (1991) bemoaned mutual contempt between sociolinguists and sociologists:

> After three decades, sociolinguistics has remained just as it was: a province of linguistics and anthropology, and a rather provincial province at that. The greatest loser by far in this 'reciprocal ignorance' pact is the sociolinguistic enterprise. (p. 132)

In the sociolinguistics of multilingualism, his unflinching description still rings true. Despite its self-avowed multidisciplinarity, the field of multilingualism is undermined by ignorance pacts and the interplay between centripetal and centrifugal trends. The reasons are easy to understand. We all enjoy being with colleagues who share our jargon, rationales, conventions, and the politics of citation and review. As many of this volume's contributors found out, explaining to other academics what we do, how we do it, why our methods should be trusted, what we think of footnotes, and where our findings fit is an exasperating task. And while interdisciplinary collaboration is encouraged in academia, we all know the downsides: the need to master 'other' literatures when we can barely keep up with the flood of publications in 'our own' area, the risk that publications in 'other' journals would be invisible to 'our own' colleagues, and plain methodological distrust. Ethnographers are skeptical about the value of statistics and experiments, psychologists scoff at "pretentiousness and barren verbiage" in sociolinguistics (Edwards, 2012, p. 38), and no one but historical sociolinguists attends talks about code-switching in medieval sermons and manuscripts. Even when there is goodwill, the pressure to write and publish leaves us with little time to think, listen, and read.

What we don't often talk about are the dangers of fragmented conversations. In the field of multilingualism, the ever-narrowing circles of academic exchanges and peer review have led to slipping scholarly standards, the creation of journals that look suspiciously like self-publishing, the formation of echo chambers where no claim is too ridiculous to print, and the proliferation of new subfields, such as 'superdiversity' and 'material culture of multilingualism,' innocent of all knowledge accumulated in the fields of archaeology, classics, history, and epigraphy. At the heart of this unilateral ignorance pact is a conviction that historical knowledge – and the disciplines that engage with it – have little relevance to multilingualism of the digital age.

The conviction isn't new – history has been given short shrift since the inception of the field. When invoked, the historical narrative begins, pace Anderson (1991), with the formation of ideologically monolingual nation-states. *The Routledge Handbook of Multilingualism*, for instance, opens with the nineteenth-century national movements and identifies the period after World War II as the time when "the role of language in nation-building and in the organization of citizenship took on new salience in public and academic discourse" (Martin-Jones et al., 2012, pp. 2–3). So does *The Cambridge Handbook of Language Policy*, where 'history of the field' begins with the rise of the nineteenth-century nation-states (Jernudd & Nekvapil, 2012).

Peeking through this narrow – and undeniably Western European – lens, study after study traces progress from the rigid national language paradigms to the unbridled diversity of our own world, which, we are told, is more multilingual than ever before or, in more elegant terms, is taking *the multilingual turn*: "Multilingualism in all its forms has taken center stage in the communicative environments of late modernity" (Jacquemet, 2018, p. 379). The differences between our multilingualism and its shabby predecessors are outlined in a recent bold manifesto:

> In the first place, multilingualism in its present form has become an inherent and crucial property of society. This is in contrast to previous multilingual arrangements in the world, which although important too were far from being as central as they are now. . .. The multilingualism of the past was largely circumstantial, unevenly spread between groups and individuals. Being multilingual at that time was important for reaching specifically limited (but not unimportant) aims: multilingualism did not determine the development of humanity. . .. Today, multilingual practices comply with the current state of the world and new patterns are deployed anywhere from small groups to international, transnational corporations. In addition to the essential task of human communication, multiple languages have become inherent to the core undertakings of humankind, such as industry and business, medicine and earth sustainability activities, politics and state development, education and arts. (Aronin, 2020, pp. 20–21)

The assertion is theorized by Lo Bianco (2020), an expert on language policy, who contrasts past and present on three dimensions – dispersion, density, and practical challenge:

> Today, there are fewer non-multilingual societies than at any time since the spread of nation-state ideologies premised on the idea that national unity required linguistic uniformity. In addition to population movements, this represents the defeat of extreme monolingual nation-making practices and of aggressive assimilation practices.

This greater dispersion of multilingual contexts is so extensive that we can speak of a near universality of the phenomenon of demo-multilingualism, or language diversity at the population level. In addition to spread, we can also observe greater density of multilingualism, involving intensity and depth, so that multilingual configurations merge with a proliferating number of semiotic systems and forms of difference and identity in single polities. The third characteristic of multilingualism today resides in the depth and persistence of the practical challenge that multiple languages and multilingual citizenries pose to public administration, education and commercial life. (pp. 42–43)

Together, Aronin (2020) and Lo Bianco (2020) make explicit four tenets that undergird a lot of recent scholarship in the field:

- **Modern multilingualism presents a greater challenge:** In the past, it was "largely circumstantial" (Aronin, 2020), while today we witness "the practical challenge that multiple languages and multilingual citizenries pose to public administration, education and commercial life" (Lo Bianco, 2020, p. 43); for similar arguments, see Geldof (2018, pp. 52–53).
- **Modern multilingualism is quantitatively different:** Language diversity at the population level is greater, more dense, and dispersed than ever before (Lo Bianco, 2020) and, according to some, is best understood as *superdiversity* (Arnaut et al., 2016; Canagarajah, 2017; Creese & Blackledge, 2018).
- **Modern multilingualism is qualitatively different:** Globalization gave rise to 'increasingly unbounded' transidiomatic practices, where speakers transcend the boundaries of named languages and blend semiotic resources into unprecedentedly complex forms (see Jacquemet, 2018; Lo Bianco, 2020, p. 41).
- **Modern language policies are more tolerant:** We are witnessing "the defeat of extreme monolingual nation-making practices and of aggressive assimilation practices" (Lo Bianco, 2020) in favor of more linguistically tolerant policies.

The absence of pertinent references makes it hard to decide what, if any, historical data the authors draw on to reach these conclusions. Fortunately, studies of historical multilingualism, based on material evidence spanning millennia, make it easy to put the claims to the test and to form a more informed opinion about the uniqueness of the modern-day 'multilingual challenge.'

1.2 'The Multilingual Challenge' through History: Paradoxes and Contradictions

Multilingualism can be examined through a variety of lenses, including that of a single manuscript, but to make claims about multilingual societies scholars need to consider *language management* (Spolsky, 2009), defined here as explicit efforts to regulate the choice of languages and scripts in institutional domains and communication with the public. These norms and accommodations may vary greatly across domains and a full picture of a single society requires a systematic analysis of practices in the international, institutional, and private spheres. We won't go that far. Since claims about 'the multilingual challenge' have focused on the public domain, I will skirt the private sphere and international commerce and diplomacy, where multilingualism has been traditionally par for the course, and focus on six institutional domains: (1) administration; (2) courts of law; (3) religion; (4) army; (5) education; and (6) public signage.

These domains will be considered in nine focal settings, some of which are also featured in the chapters: Ptolemaic Egypt (see also Chapter 2); the Roman Empire (Chapters 2, 3, and 4); Norman Sicily; medieval England (Chapter 5); medieval Castile; the Grand Duchy of Lithuania and the Polish-Lithuanian Commonwealth; Pennsylvania; the Austro-Hungarian Empire (Chapter 10); and the Russian Empire (Chapters 8 and 9). Clustered in Europe, with forays to Africa and North America, these choices are selective, not exhaustive, and the same can be said about the case studies in the volume at large. To put forth a compelling argument and illustrate it with examples of different approaches to language management, I chose the best-documented settings from the Graeco-Roman world, the Middle Ages, and the early modern empires.

The data comes from published studies, primary sources, and, in the case of the Grand Duchy of Lithuania, Russian Empire, and Pennsylvania, from my own ongoing archival research. Like all historical evidence, the data on language management and institutional practices is constrained by the vagaries of survival and, in the case of premodern multilingualism, the fragmentary nature of much of the evidence and dissociation from its original contexts, authors, and addressees, which places limitations on scholarly understanding and interpretation (Pavlenko & Mullen, 2015). Nevertheless, it is sufficiently informative to revise the claims made about premodern and modern multilingualism and to articulate an alternative vision of the field.

1.2.1 "The Kingdom with One Language Is Weak and Fragile": Multilingual Administrations

The chapters by Maravela, Mullen, and Wright highlight the normativity of bi- and multilingual bureaucracies and documents in, respectively, Ptolemaic and Roman Egypt and medieval England. Of course, the Ptolemies were not the first to preside over a bilingual administration (cf. Jonker et al., 2021). Prior to the takeover by Alexander the Great and his self-appointed successor Ptolemy I, Egypt was part of the multiethnic Persian Empire whose officials eschewed Persian in favor of Aramaic, the lingua franca of the east. Nevertheless, thanks to its obsession with record-keeping and dry sands, perfect for preservation of writing on papyri and potsherds, Ptolemaic Egypt is the world's first fairly well-documented state and, by definition, the first well-documented bilingual society – no other kingdom boasts such a wealth of official records, trial proceedings, business contracts, marriage certificates, and tax receipts (Bagnall, 2009a; Manning, 2010, pp. 6–10). The Ptolemies also make an intriguing case. As Macedonian Greeks, they were proud speakers of the language of Homer, averse to learning 'barbarian tongues',[1] but in the countryside everyone spoke Egyptian, creating a knotty problem: How do you rule the people whose language you don't speak and don't care to learn?

To foster Greek literacy among Egyptian scribes, Ptolemy I dangled a promise of social mobility and offered tax exemptions to teachers of Greek (Clarysse & Thompson, 2006). The incentives worked. The scribes learned Greek, just as they learned Aramaic under the Persians, and his successors presided over a bilingual administration, where the upper echelon worked in Greek and local officials conducted bilingual auctions, issued tax receipts in Demotic Egyptian, and wrote reports in synthetic bureaucratese that fused Greek recording practices with an Egyptian calendar and measurements (Bagnall, 2009a; Manning, 2010, 2019; Vierros, 2012). What made the Ptolemies unique was their uncanny ability to promote Hellenization, without suppressing Egyptian, and to incentivize bilingualism, without becoming bilingual themselves.

Romans maintained the Greek bureaucracy with one exception: birth certificates, military diplomas, and wills of Roman citizens in Egypt were issued in Latin (cf. Maravela, Mullen, this volume). To encourage Greek in private transactions, authorities expanded the number of Greek notary offices in the hinterland and required the deposition of Demotic contracts in Alexandria – a complication Egyptians wished to avoid. By the end of the first century AD, even private correspondence between Egyptians was in Greek, while Demotic disappeared from sales deeds, contracts, and tax receipts (Yiftach-Firanko, 2009). In one of the greatest paradoxes of our multilingual history, Romans Latinized their western provinces (cf. Mullen, this volume) and Hellenized Egypt more successfully than the Ptolemies ever did.

Medieval Norman conquerors faced an added problem: their own vernacular had no written tradition. In England, they started out with English charters but then switched to Latin. The only Romance documents known from the Norman era are a grant of land to the Knights Hospitaller (1140) and a draft

[1] 'The language of Homer' appears here in a metaphoric sense. In the literal sense, this mixture of different forms of Greek was not spoken by the Ptolemies. What's more, their native dialect, Macedonian Greek, was looked down upon by Athenians and other Greeks. The medium of the Ptolemaic administration was the most prestigious variety – Attic Greek (Maravela, this volume).

returned by mistake during Henry II's inquest of sheriffs in 1170 (Clanchy, 2013). The error reveals multilingualism behind the Latin façade: the kings articulated their wishes in Romance, the clerks transformed them into formulaic Latin, and public criers read the texts in Latin and *patriae lingua* [native tongue], that is, Romance and regional varieties of English. The towering monument to this multilingual bureaucracy is the first English census – the *Domesday Book*. To survey his lands, resolve ownership debates, and fix the rates of tax, in 1085 King William dispatched representatives to all the shires to collect *verdicts*, oral testimonies on property. The *Domesday Book* names five interpreters, *latimers*, but they may have been a fraction of the total interpreter corps that collected the *verdicts* in English, Romance, and, on one occasion, Welsh, and translated them into Latin (Clanchy, 2013; Tsurushima, 1995).

In southern Europe, Normans captured Greek-speaking Calabria and Arab Sicily. Balarm (Palermo), taken over in 1072, became the first Muslim city to be (re-)conquered by Christians. To rule his motley crew, King Roger II adopted a novel solution (for medieval Europe, that is): a trilingual administration. Arabic documents, issued by the royal chancery, followed Islamic notary manuals; Greek charters adopted Byzantine conventions; and Latin *diplomata* conformed to the patterns of the papal chancery and the Duchy of Normandy (Johns, 2002; Metcalfe, 2003). The choice of language depended

Fig. 1.1 Trilingual royal chancery in Palermo, with Greek, Saracen (Arabic), and Latin scribes. Illustration from the manuscript by Petrus de Ebulo, *Liber ad honorem Augusti*, c. 1194 AD. Bürgerbibliothek, Bern. Codex 120 II, f.101 r. Public domain.

on the issuing authority. Many charters were composed in Greek but the fiscal administration, created on the model of Fatimid Cairo, operated in Arabic, and Norman barons needed translators to figure out what the paperwork said. Royal ministers Christodoulos and George of Antioch were fluent in Greek and Arabic, Matthew of Salerno spoke all three chancery tongues, and the kings – or the scribes writing on their behalf – signed charters in Greek, Latin, or with a flourish of an Arabic motto-signature, *'alāma* (Johns & Jamil, 2004). Missing in chancery action was the mother tongue of the Norman Franks.

Lithuanian dukes faced a similar challenge: most of the territory of their Grand Duchy – today's Lithuania, Belarus, and parts of Ukraine, Russia, Poland, and Moldova – was populated by Rusyns and their native Lithuanian wasn't a written tongue. To communicate with their subjects, the dukes adopted *ruthenicum* [Ruski] as their chancery language and *Ruska Pravda* as their law code.[2] The first Lithuanian coins, minted in Vilnius in 1386, had a Cyrillic legend *Kniaz' Iaga*, Duke Jogaila, and the chancery, founded in 1392 by Grand Duke Witold, employed two teams of scribes: Rusyn scribes issued domestic charters in Ruski and corresponded with Muscovy, while Polish clerks issued Latin charters to Catholic churches and corresponded with Rome in Latin and the Teutonic Order in German (Grusha, 2015; Kosman, 1971). To repopulate his lands and benefit from foreign expertise, Duke Witold welcomed German colonists and Armenian, Jewish, and Tatar settlers from Crimea. The Burgundian envoy to his court, Guillebert de Lannoy, was surprised by the vibrant diversity of the town of Troki (modern Trakai), with its mix of Saracen Tatars, "Germans, Lithuanians, Rusyns, and a great quantity of Jews, each group speaking its own tongue" (de Lannoy, 1840, p. 25). Tatar scribes were also on hand: when de Lannoy was ready to leave, Witold equipped him with safe-conducts in Ruski, Latin, and Tatar.

King István I of Hungary (1000–1038) also welcomed colonists and advised his son that *unius linguae uniusque moris regnum imbecille et fragile est* [the kingdom with one language and one custom is weak and fragile] (Evans, 2004, p. 3).[3] To rule the kingdom, inhabited by Magyars, Slavs, and German colonists, the kings relied on Latin. From the eleventh to the mid-nineteenth century, Latin would serve as the language of bureaucracy, parliamentary debates, and interaction with foreigners, and many a visitor would be surprised by village notaries using Latin as "the language of office and business throughout Hungary" (Beudant, 1823, p. 21). Only in 1844 was Magyar

[2] 'Ruski' is the name used in the Grand Duchy of Lithuania but not a conventional linguistic term. Belarusian, Ukrainian, and Russian linguists variously call the language Old Belarusian, Old Ukrainian, Western Russian, or Lithuanian Russian, while Western linguists favor the artificial label *Ruthenian*, derived from the Latin *ruthenicum*. To convey local perceptions and blurry boundaries between Slavic vernaculars, I decided to keep the authentic term.

[3] Modern historians doubt the royal authorship of the admonition.

declared official – to the great disappointment of Croatian deputies who filibustered in Latin to no avail (Almási & Šubarić, 2015).

In the Russian Empire, Peter I and his successors adopted a territorial approach to language management: Baltic provinces were administered in German, Finland in Swedish, and Poland in Polish until the advent of Russification reforms (Kappeler, 2001; Pavlenko, 2011a). Peter I also invited foreign colonists, many of them German speakers. Together with Baltic Germans from Livland, Kurland, and Estland, the new arrivals played an important part in the imperial administration, modeled on the Swedish and Prussian counterparts, with the colleges named in a Germanic manner *Iustits*, *Kommerts*, *Politsei*. Each college had a German interpreter on staff and the documents, including the all-important *Table of Ranks* (1722), were published in both tongues, enriching Russian with countless German titles (Dahmen, 2015).

In the Austro-Hungarian Empire, the 1867 *Ausgleich*, Compromise, created the Dual Monarchy that embodied the tension between competing visions of language and power. The 1868 Nationalities Act of the Kingdom of Hungary reinforced the status of Magyar and made language equality conditional:

> This equality of rights, insofar as it applies to the several languages in use in this country, may be modified by special dispositions only so far as these comport with the unity of the state, the practical necessities of government, and the administration of justice (translated in Maxwell, 2009, p. 26).

In contrast, in Cisleithania – most of today's Austria, Czech Republic, and Slovenia, as well as parts of Italy, Romania, Poland, Croatia, Montenegro, and Ukraine – Article 19 of the 1867 Constitution declared all languages equal, with no one obliged to learn additional tongues:

> All the state's ethnic groups [*Volksstämme*] are equal, and each has an inviolable right to preserve and cultivate its nationality and language. The state recognizes the equality of all languages current in a region within schools, administration and public life. In those lands which are home to various ethnic groups, the institutions of public education shall be organized in such a way that each of these groups receives the means to be educated in its own language, without being forced to learn a second regional language (Article 19, *Reichsgesetzblatt*, translated in Wolf, 2015, p. 42).[4]

Then, the two monarchies took diverging paths. Hungary unrolled a Magyarization campaign, while in Austria, the central government functioned in German and regional bureaucracies employed bi- and multilingual civil servants who worked in German and official regional languages,

[4] The provision about not being obligated to learn a second language was added under the pressure of influential Bohemian deputies, concerned that German speakers in Bohemia might be forced to learn Czech (Judson, 2019).

Fig. 1.2 100 Austro-Hungarian krona (1912), obverse. Public domain.

Landessprache – Italian, Slovenian, Croatian, Czech, Romanian, Ruski, and Polish (Berecz, 2021a; Prokopovych et al., 2019; Wolf, 2015; see also Fellerer, this volume). The two-faced nature of the Dual Monarchy is captured on its banknotes that feature Magyar on the Hungarian side and ten languages on the Austrian side (Csernicskó & Beregszászi, 2019) (Fig. 1.2). Gal (2011), an expert on the history of language ideologies and practices in the Austro-Hungarian empire, has long argued that "the conventional, *monolingual* image of European linguistic nationalism that is evident in the scholarship of our day misrepresents the European past" (p. 31). The banknote illustrates the point starkly: modern scholars see the single-language side and miss the polyglot side.

1.2.2 Linguistic Diversity in the Courts of Law

Court records, argues Fellerer (this volume), offer a unique window into the workings of bi- and multilingualism in daily life. This is especially true for premodern polities distinguished by *legal pluralism*, a coexistence of multiple systems of normative law, often practiced in different tongues (Ando, 2016; Czajkowski et al., 2020).

In Egypt, Ptolemy II sanctioned one court for Greek speakers, another one for Egyptians, plus the royal court that heard cases in Greek on an ad hoc basis; Jews, granted self-governing privileges, had their own courts and an option to appeal to Greek judges, which they often exercised (Bagnall & Derow, 2004;

Manning, 2010, 2019; Yiftach-Firanko, 2009). The language of legal documents was subject to choice. Greek was favored in petitions to high officials, wills, and transactions with high sums and Demotic Egyptian preferred in marriage contracts, property deeds involving Egyptian inheritance laws, and contracts for small sums drawn on the cheap (Vandorpe & Waebens, 2009; Vierros, 2012). Greek courts accepted translated evidence but judges were inconvenienced by Demotic deeds. In 146 BC, Ptolemy VI decreed that Demotic contracts should be registered in the official archives with a summary in Greek and in 118 BC, Ptolemy VIII curtailed consolidation of power in Greek hands and made the language of the contract the deciding factor in the choice of the court (for the texts of the decrees, see Bagnall & Derow, 2004).

In Sicily, Norman conquerors preserved the status quo ante, allowing Muslims, Greeks, and Jews to follow their own laws (Metcalfe, 2003). So did King Alfonso VI in Tulaytula (Toledo), (re-)conquered from Muslims in 1085. Eager to gain support of the city's influential Arabic-speaking Christians, *Mozarabs*, Alfonso VI offered them self-governing privileges, *fueros*; later on similar privileges were extended to Castilians, Franks, Muslims, and Jews (for Spanish texts, see Garcia-Gallo, 1975). Taxation was organized on the Castilian model, but in other domains Mozarabs were ruled by their own *alcalde*, mayor, and followed their traditional Visigothic code, *Liber Iudiciorum*, mixed with customary Islamic law (Moreno, 2012).

This wasn't the only code they preserved. For two centuries after the Christian takeover, Mozarabs, Muslims, and Jews maintained Arabic and relied on documents that followed Islamic notary manuals, complete with the traditional opening *bismillah al-rahman al-rahim*, "In the name of Allah, the Merciful, the Compassionate" (Beale-Rivaya, 2012; Beale-Rivaya & Busic, 2018; Moreno, 2012; Witcombe, 2018). Their transactions with the Catholic church were also recorded in Arabic, as seen in the nearly 1,200 charters of land sales, donations, leases, property rentals, and wills preserved in the archives of the Cathedral of Toledo and the convent of San Clemente. The choice is not as surprising as it seems: the documents were meant for Mozarab courts, where judges dealt easily with pre- and post-conquest Arabic deeds and offered an extra layer of protection in civil proceedings by requiring witnesses to confirm the validity of their signatures (for the documents, see González Palencia, 1926–1930; for discussion see Beale-Rivaya, 2012; Moreno, 2012; Witcombe, 2018).

Legally homogeneous settings weren't exempt from linguistic challenges. In medieval English courts, judges and pleaders – often good Englishmen, with names like Denham, Howard, King, Huntingdon, Heyham, and Westcote, and a fondness for English proverbs – listened to testimony in Romance/French and English, made pleas in French, composed writs in Latin, and had proceedings recorded in Latin by trilingual clerks (Brand, 2000; Woodbine, 1943). In 1285, one author justified writing a treatise on law in Romance by the fact that the pleas were *in romanis verbis, et non in latinis, pronunciatur* (Woodbine, 1943, p. 428).

XXXVII

Fig. 1.3 Dublin Court of Exchequer at work. The Red Book of the Exchequer. Reproduced by permission of the National Archives.

One such proceeding, discussed by Kerby-Fulton (2015), is illustrated in a picture from an office manual, composed in Ireland circa 1420 (Fig. 1.3). To total up the accounts at the royal accounting office, the Exchequer, the clerks gathered around a table covered with a checkered cloth with moveable

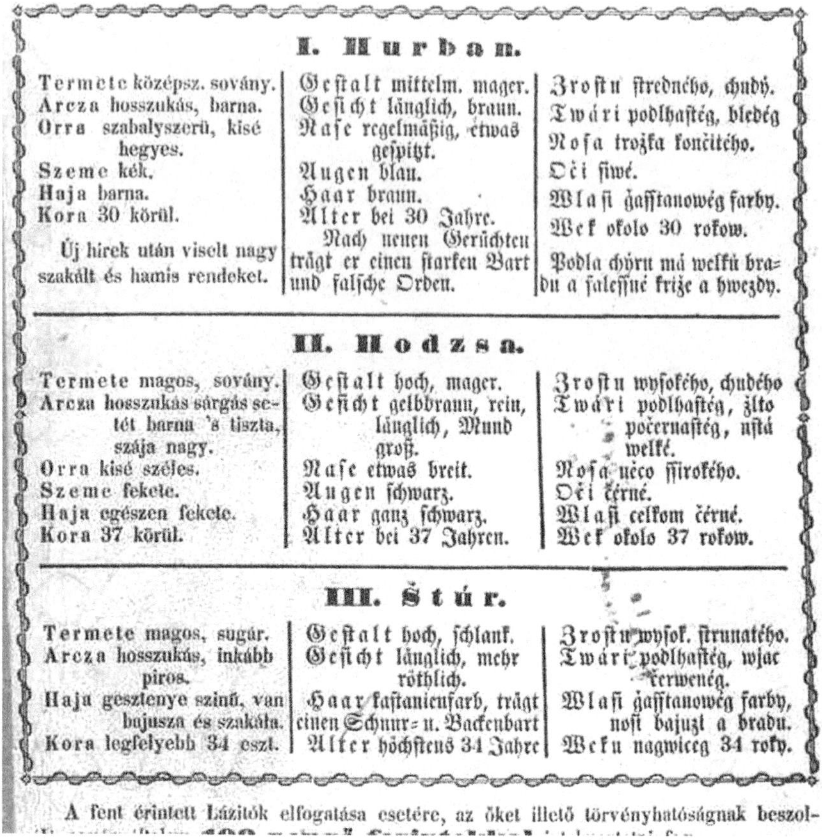

I. Hurban.

Termete középsz. sovány.	Geſtalt mittelm. mager.	Zroſtu ſtredného, chudý.
Arcza hosszukás, barna.	Geſicht länglich, braun.	Twári podlhaſtég, bledég
Orra szabalyszerü, kisé hegyes.	Naſe regelmäßig, etwas geſpitzt.	Noſa trozka končitého.
Szeme kék.	Augen blau.	Oči ſiwé.
Haja barna.	Haar braun.	Wlaſi gaſſtanowég farby.
Kora 30 körül.	Alter bei 30 Jahre.	Wek okolo 30 rokow.
Új hirek után viselt nagy szakált és hamis rendeket.	Nach neuen Gerüchten trägt er einen ſtarken Bart und falſche Orden.	Podla chýrn má welkú bradu a faleſſné križe a hwezdy.

II. Hodzsa.

Termete magos, sovány.	Geſtalt hoch, mager.	Zroſtu wyſokého, chudého
Arcza hosszukás sárgás setét barna 's tiszta, szája nagy.	Geſicht gelbbraun, rein, länglich, Mund groß.	Twári podlhaſtég, žlto počernaſtég, uſtá welké.
Orra kisé széles.	Naſe etwas breit.	Noſa něco ſſirokého.
Szeme fekete.	Augen ſchwarz.	Oči černé.
Haja egészen fekete.	Haar ganz ſchwarz.	Wlaſi celkom černé.
Kora 37 körül.	Alter bei 37 Jahren.	Wek okolo 37 rokow.

III. Štúr.

Termete magos, sugár.	Geſtalt hoch, ſchlank.	Zroſtu wyſok. ſtrunatého.
Arcza hosszukás, inkább piros.	Geſicht länglich, mehr röthlich.	Twári podlhaſtég, wjac čerwenég.
Haja gesztenye szinü, van bajusza és szakála.	Haar kaſtanienfarb, trägt einen Schnur= u. Backenbart	Wlaſi gaſſtanowég farby, noſi bajuzl a bradu.
Kora legfelyebb 34 eszt.	Alter höchſtens 34 Jahre	Weku nagwiceg 34 roky.

A fent érintett Lázitók elfogatása esetére, az őket illető törvényhatóságnak beszol-

Fig. 1.4 Trilingual arrest warrant (1848). Slovak National Museum. Public domain.

counters – a medieval version of the spreadsheet. The piteous little figure at the bottom is the hapless sheriff being audited and on the right are the three suitors pleading on his behalf. Seated on the left are three magistrates, headed by the judge identified as Sharpe on his sleeve and at the back is a row of clerks, including the Chief Remembrancer (checking on his pen) and the Clerk of the Pipe (preparing a writ). Speech bubbles reveal that everyone is speaking French: the magistrates exclaim *Voyr dire*, the suitors protest *Chalange*, and the usher is announcing the adjournment of the court: *A demain*. The Clerk of the Pipe, meanwhile, is performing routine translation, composing a Latin writ.

In modern times, the challenges didn't subside. The complexity of law enforcement in the Habsburg Empire is well illustrated by the trilingual warrant issued in May 1848 for Slovak activists Jozef Hurban, Michal Hodža, and Ľudovít Štúr (Fig. 1.4). Issued by commissioner Beniczky in

Magyar, German, and Czech, the warrant is signed with three versions of the commissioner's first name – Lajos, Ludwig, and Ludewjt. Missing in action is the activists' native Slovak, treated as a dialect of Czech (Komora, 2015, p. 87; for discussion of linguistic diversity in the courtrooms of Dualist Hungary (1867–1918), see Berecz, 2021b).

A single language didn't solve the problem – instead it necessitated reliance on court interpreters, as seen in sixteenth-century Spain (Sarmiento-Pérez, 2016), seventeenth-century France (Cohen, 2016), and colonial Pennsylvania, where William Penn made English official in court:

> And be it further Enacted by the Authority aforesaid that all pleadings Processes and records in Court shall be Short and in English and in an Ordinary and plaine Character that they may be Esily read & understood and Justice Speedily administered (*Great Law of Pennsylvania*, 1682).[5]

The founding father of Pennsylvanian court interpreting was Penn's real estate agent, a multilingual Swede named Lasse Cock. In 1683, Cock interpreted at the trial of a Swedish woman, Margaret Mattson, accused of putting spells on her neighbors' cows – the jury found Margaret guilty of having a fame as a witch but innocent of the actual deeds (*Minutes of the Provincial Council of Pennsylvania,* 1683–1700, pp. 94–96). In the eighteenth and nineteenth centuries, the influx of German immigrants brought in a new twist: court proceedings in German. In 1876, German-born journalist Ludwig Wollenweber was greatly surprised by the ease with which judges and lawyers in the city of Reading conversed in the local variety of German, Pennsylvania Dutch. "The proceedings naturally occurred in English," he reported,

> but since most of the residents of Berks County, especially those from outside of Reading, can express themselves more clearly in German than in English, even if they have been born here, plaintiffs, respondents and witnesses often prefer to be examined in German (translated in Louden, 2016, p. 251).

This wasn't an isolated case. In Harrisburg in 1907 "a witness spoke High German, Judge Thomas Capp spoke the Pennsylvania Dutch of Lebanon County, and Senator John E. Fox, the defendant's counsel, spoke the Pennsylvania Dutch of Dauphin County" (Louden, 2016, p. 251). And in Allentown in 1904, proceedings in the mysterious murder of Mabel Bechtel were "carried on in the 'Pennsylvania Dutch' dialect, which was understood not only by the judge, jury and lawyers, but by most of the spectators in the crowded courtroom" (*New York Times*, January 22, 1904). The only ones in need of interpreters were the journalists. "The continued use of German as the household language, for three or four generations," grumbled *The Washington*

[5] www.phmc.state.pa.us/portal/communities/documents/1681-1776/great-law.html

Times reporter, "tends to isolation from the world, non-comprehension of its affairs and a conservatism which might as well be called pig-headed" (January 24, 1904). The critique is familiar to us but the acceptance of foreign language testimony is not – nowadays in the USA, bilingual jurors are struck down by peremptory challenges or instructed to attend only to English interpreting.

1.2.3 Sacred Tongues

Maravela's chapter focuses on religious settings, a vantage point essential in historic inquiry because *religious pluralism* was the second linchpin of peaceful coexistence and so was the diversity of sacred tongues. Savvy Ptolemies, eager to secure support from Egyptian priests, pretended to worship sacred animals, gave land grants and donations to temples, and safeguarded the rights of Egyptians, Greeks, and Jews to worship as they wished (Manning, 2010, 2019). Appreciative of royal protections and subventions, the priests reciprocated by learning Greek and using it to offer oracular advice, interpret dreams, and issue bilingual decrees that stressed Ptolemaic legitimacy and bestowed divine honors on pharaohs-kings. Burials followed the faith and the language of choice of the deceased, but there were also those who hedged their bets with paired tombstones in Greek and Egyptian addressed to all gods (Manning, 2019).

The Roman elite was also fond of bilingual tombstones, where Latin texts named the deceased and celebrated their accomplishments and verses in Greek signaled – one last time! – their erudition and wit (Noy, 2000). Immigrants added their own flourishes to linguistic diversity in the graveyard: The earliest Jewish cemetery of Rome, the Monteverde catacomb, yielded 155 epitaphs in Greek (76 percent) and 49 in Latin, Hebrew, and Aramaic (24 percent) (Abrecht, 2020; on multilingual tombstones, see also Mullen & James, 2012). The scarcity of Hebrew hints at attrition of the Holy Tongue among the Jews. Even in Syria Palaestina, formerly Roman Judea, by the late second century AD, the readings of the Torah were accompanied by Aramaic translations. The practice angered Rabbi Yehuda HaNasi, aka Judah the Prince: "Why Aramaic in the land of Israel? Either the holy tongue or Greek!" (Bava Kamma 83a, translated in Smelik, 2013, p. 92).

Medieval societies also furnish examples of religious-linguistic pluralism. In Norman Sicily, Count Roger de Hauteville forbade his Catholic priests to proselytize among his Muslim troops and let his new subjects keep their mosques, churches, and synagogues (Metcalfe, 2003). His widow, Countess Adelaide, followed in his footsteps: the oldest paper document in Europe is a letter from Adelaide, written in 1109 in Arabic and Greek, which asks Muslim officials of Enna to protect the Greek abbey of San Filippo di Fragalà (Booms

(a)

(b)

Fig. 1.5 (a) Quranic mottos in the church of Santa Maria dell'Ammiraglio, Palermo. Photo by the author, April 2017. (b) Medallion with formulaic wishes of fortune and prosperity in Arabic in the Samuel ha-Levi (El Tránsito) synagogue, Toledo. Photo by the author, September 2019.

& Higgs, 2016). And when her son, Roger II, was crowned as king in 1130, religious hymns were sung in Greek and Latin and royal symbols engraved in three tongues. The obverse of the gold coins praised "King Roger, sublime and powerful, by the grace of Allah" in Arabic and the reverse declared "Jesus Christ conquers" in Greek. The monetary reforms of the 1140s added silver ducats with a Latin motto *Iesus Christus regnat in aeternum* (Booms & Higgs, 2016; Metcalfe, 2003).

Roger II's courtiers followed suit. When his minister George of Antioch built a church of Santa Maria dell'Ammiraglio, he added a column with Quranic mottos (Fig. 1.5a). And when the mother of the royal priest

Grisandus passed away in 1148, she was commemorated with a marble plaque: in the center was the Greek cross and the letters IC XC NI KA [Jesus Christ is victorious], invoking the resurrection and the victory of Norman Christians, and on the sides inscriptions in Latin, Greek, Arabic, and Arabic in Hebrew script (Houben, 2013; Zeitler, 1996).

Similar spirit reigned in post-conquest Toledo, where King Alfonso VI married a Muslim princess, declared himself the Emperor of Two Religions, and had a daughter who married Roger II of Sicily. In 1156, relatives of a Mozarab parishioner of the church of Santas Justa y Rufina commissioned a tombstone with two inscriptions: the Arabic one began with a *bismillah* "In the name of Allah, the Merciful, the Compassionate" and the Latin one with "In the name of our Lord Jesus Christ" (Dodds et al., 2008). Kufic inscriptions also had other functions, the first of which was to convey respect: when Toledan Jews built a new synagogue in 1357, they added medallions with formulaic wishes of fortune and prosperity in Kufic script (Fig. 1.5b). The second was to proselytize. From 1172 to 1214, King Alfonso VIII minted golden dinars in Arabic (no Latin!) that declared him 'the Emir of the Catholics' and 'the Imam of the Christian faith' and promised that "Whoever believes and is baptized will be saved" (Ecker, 2004) (Fig. 1.6).

The most 'inclusive' arrangement can be seen today in the Cathedral of Seville on the tomb of Fernando III, the leader of the 'Reconquista' and a self-proclaimed King of Three Religions. Commissioned in 1252 by Fernando's son, King Alfonso X the Wise, the grandiose tomb is flanked by epitaphs in Latin, Castilian, Arabic, and Hebrew, each with appropriate names (Hispania, España, Al-Andalus, Sefarad) and calendar dates (from the birth of Christ in Latin; from 38 BC, the beginning of *Pax Romana*, in Castilian; from Mahomet's flight from Mecca in Arabic; and from the creation of the world in Hebrew). And while one

Fig. 1.6 Maravedi of Alfonso VIII, minted in 1191 AD. Classical Numismatic Group. Wikimedia, CC license 2.5.

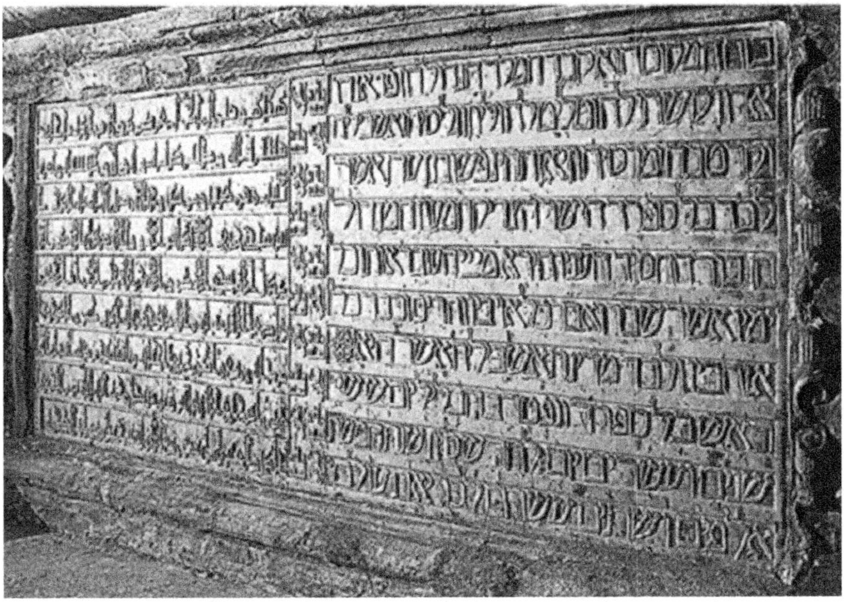

Fig. 1.7 Arabic and Hebrew on the tomb of Fernando III, Cathedral of Seville. Wikimedia.

doubts that Muslims were enamored of the conqueror-king, the display was good politics and the discordant verbal note was neither Arabic nor Hebrew but the upstart Castilian (Dodds et al., 2008; Nickson, 2015).

In contexts where the faithful had trouble understanding the sacred tongue, religious authorities turned to interpreting, as in Palestinian synagogues (Smelik, 2013), bilingual sermons, as in medieval English churches (Fletcher, 2013), and the mixing of languages and scripts, as in sixteenth-century Castile, where crypto-Muslims copied the Quran in *Aljamiado*, Arabicized Romance in Kufic script (García-Arenal, 2015).

Similar practices are documented in the Polish-Lithuanian Commonwealth. Established in 1569 as the union of Poland and the Grand Duchy of Lithuania, in 1573 the Commonwealth adopted the Warsaw Confederation Act that granted religious freedoms to all: Catholic, Lutheran, and Orthodox churches, Tatar mosques, and Rabbinic and Karaite synagogues. What worried the Armenian priests, Jewish rabbis, and Tatar imams was attrition of sacred tongues among their young men, fluent only in Slavic vernaculars. To preserve the sanctity of worship, they translated religious texts but retained the sacred scripts. The Armenians of Lwów, for instance, translated the Psalter into their native Kypchak in Armenian script – published in 1618 it is now celebrated as the first Kypchak book in print (Garkavets, 2002). Tatar imams composed *tafsirs*, the Quran with interlinear Slavic translations, and *kitabs*, idiosyncratic anthologies, whose Arabic façade concealed a blend of four tongues: religious passages, penned in Arabic and Ottoman Turkish, and translations and comments in Ruski and Polish (Akiner, 2017; Kulwicka-Kamińska & Łapicz, 2015).The oldest extant Slavic translation of the Quran is the Minsk Tafsir (1686), whose medium is variously described as 'Polish with elements of Belarusian' or vice versa, but cannot be named with certainty because of its Arabic script. In the territories that later became Belarus, locals mixed Ruski and Polish in speech and in writing distinguished the two by script, Cyrillic vs Latin. When such speech is transliterated in Arabic, scholars lack reliable means to decide which is which. As a consequence, both Poland and Belarus claim credit for the first Slavic Quran (Kulwicka-Kamińska & Łapicz, 2015).

In Russia, Peter I promoted a limited version of religious tolerance (minus the Jews). The monument to his vision is St. Petersburg's Nevsky Prospect, where, within steps of each other, we find a Russian Orthodox cathedral, a Dutch church, a German Lutheran church Petrikirche, an Armenian church, and Russia's oldest Catholic church that offered services in German, Italian, Polish, and French. In the nineteenth century, a celebrity visitor, Alexandre Dumas-père, dubbed the Nevsky *la rue de tolérance*. By the twentieth century, the city also housed one of Europe's largest synagogues (opened in 1893) and a beautiful Tatar mosque (1913), facing the Fortress of Peter and Paul. Unlike in Europe today, construction of the mosque elicited no protests nor heated debates (on Muslim St. Petersburg, see Bekkin, 2021; Bekkin & Tagirdzhanova, 2016).

1.2.4 A Multilingual Army: A Boon or a Bane?

Mairs' chapter draws attention to multilingualism of the military enterprise. For the ancients, linguistic diversity in the army was a double-edged sword. Carthaginians, wrote Greek historian Polybius (1.67.2–9), hired Libyan, Iberian, Celtic, Ligurian, and Greek troops in hopes they wouldn't band in dissent. Yet in doing so, they placed generals at the mercy of interpreters and sowed confusion and distrust in the camp. Ptolemy IV, noted Polybius, also relied on an interpreter to address the Egyptian phalanx of his troops, while the Roman army of his era, the second century BC, was commendable for its linguistic homogeneity. Later on, Romans would prove Polybius wrong – the imperial army would be both victorious *and* diverse (on linguistic diversity and interpreting in the Roman army, see Felice, 2019; Mairs, this volume; Peretz, 2006).

The second driver of multilingualism in the army was the language of the enemy. In England, at the start of the Hundred Years war the parliament decreed

> que tout seigneur, baron, chevalier et honnestes hommes de bonnes villes mesissent cure et dilligence de estruire et aprendre leurs enfans la langhe françoise par quoy il en fuissent plus able et plus coustummier ens leurs gherres.

[that all lords, barons, knights and honest men of good towns should exercise care and diligence to teach their children the French language in order that they might be more able and better equipped in their wars.] (Froissart, 1867, p. 419)

To drum up support for his unpopular war, Edward III told the parliament in 1344 and again in 1346 that Philip IV of France was striving to destroy the English language. Ironically, the only record of these warnings is in French. In another paradox of our multilingual history, the reigns of Edward III (1327–1377) and Richard II (1377–1399) were the height of the anti-French propaganda and the heyday of administrative French. At the end of the war, the English knew more French than before, thanks to military campaigns in France (on languages and the Hundred Years war, see Butterfield, 2009; on multilingualism in the English army, see Curry et al., 2010).

The third driver of multilingualism in the military was the need for foreign expertise. In the fledgling army of Peter I, Prussian and Saxon officers used German as the language of command: in 1698 an eyewitness noted that "German colonels trained [Russian] soldiers every day in German" (Dahmen, 2015, p. 26). Russian military code was published in both languages (Fig. 1.8) and army titles, like *fel'dfebel'* [sergeant] or *unter-offitser* [corporal], had a distinct Germanic ring. Peter's navy favored English and Dutch: Vice Admiral

Fig. 1.8 Russia's bilingual military code, second edition, 1737. Public domain.

Cornelius Cruys was a Dutch-speaking Norwegian and the *Naval Statute* was issued in 1720 in Russian and *Hollands*. As time went by, borrowings from Dutch – *matros* [sailor], *shturman* [navigator], *kajuta* [cabin], *trap* [rope ladder], *verf'* [shipyard], and *shvabra* [mop] – became everyday Russian words.

In the Austro-Hungarian army, on the other hand, diversity turned into a liability. The army's *Kommandosprache* was German, and each recruit was required to learn eighty or so commands, such as "March!" and "Open fire!" The training of new recruits, however, was in their native Serbo-Croatian, Czech, German, Magyar, Italian, Polish, Romanian, Ruski, Slovak, and Slovene, and if 20 percent of the regiment shared a native tongue, it became one of the official *Regimentsprache* (Evans, 2004; Prokopovych et al., 2019; Scheer, 2016; Wolf, 2015). In the summer of 1914, 142 regiments were monolingual (31 in German), 162 bilingual, 24 trilingual, and a few quadrilingual. Officers were required to learn their soldiers' tongues, with the help of multilingual handbooks – a requirement that posed challenges in peace time and was nearly impossible at the front. A career officer, August von Urbanski, recalled getting a battalion that

> consisted of about 50 per cent Czechs, 20 per cent Germans, 20 per cent Poles and 10 per cent Italians. Half of the Czechs were able to speak German, while almost no Poles spoke it. The Italians spoke Italian and German, while our Greek spoke only broken Czech. . .. They even don't understand each other. The company leader speaks only German. I failed to talk to the Czechs. They always answered: no German, Pan Hetman. Only after several days when I used some Czech words – the only ones I knew – they started to talk to me in broken German. (translated in Scheer, 2016, pp. 70–71)

To communicate, commanding and medical staff relied on interpreters, on gestures, on English and French as the lingua francas, and on multilingual booklets and forms (Fig. 1.9). Yet communication wasn't the only challenge

Leicht verwundet	verwundet	schwer verwundet	krank	schwer krank
könnyen megsebesült	megsebesült	bajos megsebesült	beteg	bajos beteg
lehce raněn	raněn	těžce raněn	nemocen	těžce nemocen
lekko raniony	raniony	ciężko raniony	chory	ciężko chory
легко ранений	ранений	тяжко ранений	хорий	тяжко хорий
leggiermente ferito	ferito	gravemente ferito	ammalato	grave ammalato
lako ranjen	ranjen	teško ranjen	bolestan	teško bolestan
lahko ranjen	ranjen	težko ranjen	bolan	težko bolan
uşor rânit	rânit	greu rânit	bolnav	greu bolnav

Reserve-Spital des

Fig. 1.9 Multilingual communication form for doctors and wounded soldiers in the Austro-Hungarian army (Scheer, 2017). Public domain.

at the front – officers also needed a sense of the soldiers' loyalties and moods. "It was very difficult," recalled officer Ernst Horsetzky, "to try and grasp the thinking of everyone in a multilingual army and explore their true sentiments" (translated in Scheer, 2016, p. 74). Polybius, it appears, did have a point after all.

1.2.5 Bilingual Education and the Diffusion of Knowledge

Rubin's and Argent's chapters draw attention to education and intercultural contacts as a site of language learning and the diffusion of knowledge. The origins of bilingual education are commonly traced to elite and scribal schooling in the Near East (Griffith, 2015). In the Old Babylonian scribal program, the Eduba [Tablet House], dated to 2,000–1,600 BC, Akkadian-speaking students were instructed in Sumerian, a non-Semitic language that had not been spoken for centuries but was seen as the proper conduit for traditional texts. Thousands of clay tablets found at Nippur, Ur, Sippar, and Kish show that at the upper level, Eduba pupils were encouraged to be "radically bilingual, constantly switching back and forth, even within the same text, between Sumerian and Akkadian" (Griffith, 2015, p. 9). By 500 BC, scribes were taught in Akkadian and Aramaic but translanguaging was still par for the course, as seen in a Babylonian tablet displayed at the British Museum under a label "A classroom experiment." Imprinted on the clay tablet is an exercise that required future scribes to use the traditional cuneiform syllabic signs of Akkadian to express the sounds of Aramaic.

In Rome, where Greek was quintessential for social mobility, we find bilingual education for the upper class (Cribiore, 2001; Mullen, this volume). Not everyone ended up as fluent as Cicero who peppered his letters with Greek verse, but Homer's *Iliad* was as familiar to educated Romans as Shakespeare is in the English-speaking world. Moreover, while royal libraries often held books in multiple tongues (cf. König et al., 2013), Romans created bilingual *public* libraries. Julius Caesar, reports Suetonius (*Iul.* 44.2), charged Varro with opening public libraries with works of Latin and Greek. The idea came to naught but a decade after Caesar's death, his follower Gaius Asinius Pollio used the spoils of a successful campaign in Illyria to rebuild the Hall of Freedom, *Atrium Libertatis*, and to endow it with a bilingual library, adorned with Greek art. Emperor Augustus added bilingual libraries on the Palatine and in the Porticus of Octavia and Vespasian in the Temple of Peace (Dix & Houston, 2006). As patrons, the emperors had the privilege to add manuscripts and an obligation to replace damaged scrolls. When a fire wrecked Rome's libraries, tells Suetonius (*Dom.* 20), Emperor Domitian restored them at enormous expense, procuring copies of texts from all over and sending scribes to Alexandria to make fresh copies of important manuscripts.

In the Middle Ages, kings saw rare books as a point of pride and sponsored translation projects and new works. In Palermo, Roger II commissioned al-Idrisi to write a description of the known world (in Arabic) and Doxopatrios to pen the *History of the Five Patriarchates* (in Greek) (Houben, 2013). In Castile, Alfonso X assembled a team of Castilian, Italian, and Jewish scholars to produce a Castilian compilation of world history, updated astronomical tables, treatises on law, and translations of the Visigothic Code and the Talmud (Goldstein, 2009; O'Callaghan, 1993). And in Baghdad, Abbasid rulers sponsored translations of Greek works of philosophy, medicine, mathematics, physics, and astrology that preserved Hellenistic scholarship for the Western world and enriched it with Arab discoveries (Gutas, 1998). In the twelfth century, itinerant scholars rediscovered these riches in Castilian libraries, mastered Arabic, and translated them into Latin with the help of multilingual Mozarabs, Muslims, and Jews (Burnett, 2001). Copied and recopied in the monasteries and Latin-medium universities in England, Italy, and France, these translations brought the ideas of Greek, Muslim, and Jewish scholars to the wider world.

Modernization of Russia – and Russian – also proceeded on borrowed words. Peter I encouraged the import of foreign texts and turned a blind eye to enlightened plunder: 2,000 German volumes appropriated in Mitau and Riga during the Northern War became the foundation of Russia's first public library opened in St. Petersburg in 1714 (Dahmen, 2015). The tsar also initiated a monumental translation project: having sent many Russian youths to study abroad, on return Peter I directed them to translate manuals on modern technologies (Cracraft, 2004). In the absence of adequate Russian terms, it was a nearly impossible task – one translator, unable to deliver, slashed his wrists in distress. Others muddled along, with the help of foreign associates – Englishman Henry Farquharson, Scot Jacob Bruce, and Peter's African godson, Abraham Gannibal, who trained as a military engineer in France (posterity remembers him as Pushkin's great-grandfather and forgets that he was also a talented engineer, translator, and Tallinn's first – and so far only – Black mayor). As time went by, grammars, dictionaries, and translations created on Peter's orders filled linguistic gaps with neologisms, foreign loans, and calques.

The children of the Russian elite were taught in German, Russian, and French (cf. Argent, this volume), but university lectures were mostly in Russian, until Alexander I reopened the German-medium University of Dorpat (modern Tartu) (1801) and the Polish-medium University of Wilna (Vilnius) (1803) and founded the University of Warsaw (1816). Non-Russian primary education thrived because the government was opposed to assimilation of pagan nomads, Muslims, and Jews treated as 'aliens' (Pavlenko,

2011a). The Jewish statute of 1804, for instance, sanctioned Jewish schools, provided they taught some Russian, Polish, or German. And when Tatar missionaries sparked a wave of apostasy from Orthodoxy in the Volga region, an 1870 decree sanctioned transitional bilingual education that began in the pupils' mother tongues and then shifted to Russian with the mother tongue as an aid (Dowler, 2001).

In Austria in 1870–1871, 9 percent of the schools taught in two, three, or four languages and switching between tongues was a daily routine for teachers and students alike (Wolf, 2015). And in Pennsylvania, in 1839 the State House of Representatives decreed that

> in districts or primary districts whose citizens speak the *German* language, the directors shall establish schools in which the exercises shall, if suitable teachers can be procured, be either wholly or in part conducted in that language as said citizens may desire. (*Report of the Superintendent of Common Schools*, 1839, p. 18)

From then on, 'the German question' would stir controversy in the state, yet some schools remained bilingual until the advent of World War I (Donner, 2008).

In the twentieth century, multilingual schooling reached its height in the USSR, where titular republics offered parents a choice of (a) schools with titular languages (e.g., Latvian) as the medium and select subjects in Russian, (b) schools with Russian as the medium and select subjects in titular languages, and (c) schooling in Russian and minority languages (Pavlenko, 2013). When the USSR collapsed, Latvia, where Russians constituted 42.5 percent of the population, tried to close all Russian schools but the accession to the European Union forced Latvian authorities to keep some open: to save face, the authorities rebranded bilingual schools from the sites of occupation to symbols of multiculturalism (Pavlenko, 2011b; Silova, 2006).

1.2.6 Multilingual Public Signage

Public displays in multiple languages are well documented in the ancient world (Adams, 2003; Bowman & Crowther, 2020; Bowman et al., 2021; Jonker et al., 2021; Mullen & James, 2012). The most famous is the Memphis decree of 196 BC, aka the Rosetta Stone, inscribed in Hieroglyphic Egyptian, Demotic Egyptian, and Greek. Other bilingual decrees that came to light in Egypt since the discovery of the Rosetta Stone show that the priests favored their own tongue: Greek text was relegated to the bottom, to the back or to the sides, and sometimes omitted altogether, despite explicit orders to inscribe three texts (Bagnall & Derow, 2004; Bowman et al., 2021; Cole, 2015). The Middle Ages left their own multilingual legacy, from trilingual inscriptions of the Norman kings in Palermo to the tomb of Fernando III in Seville.

Fig. 1.10 (a) Russian-German sign for Pochtovaya Street installed in 1768. Dvortsovaya naberezhnaya 34, St. Petersburg. Photo by the author, September 2018. (b) Restored German-Czech street sign, Prague. Photo courtesy of Matyaš Viktora, June 2020.

The Enlightenment brought in an urban innovation – street signs. In St. Petersburg, where many immigrants spoke German, the first plaques were bilingual (Fig. 1.10a), courtesy of Catherine the Great, who wrote to her chief of police:

> Order that, at the end of every street and alley, signs are to be attached bearing the name of that street or alley in the Russian and German languages; if any streets and alleys are as yet unnamed – please name them. (May 8, 1768; translated in Franklin, 2019, p. 158)

By the turn of the twentieth century, many cityscapes were vibrantly diverse: Ottoman cities featured street signs in French and in Turkish in Arabic script (Strauss, 2011); Prague displayed German-Czech plaques (Fig. 1.10b); Sarajevo authorized signs in Latin, Cyrillic, and Arabic scripts (Berecz, 2019); businesses, from St. Petersburg to Philadelphia, advertised their wares in multiple tongues (Fig. 1.11; see also Fortna's and Pavlenko's chapters); and Warsaw, Tallinn, and Helsinki added imperial Russian (Fig. 1.12a). This isn't to say that everyone was charmed by linguistic diversity in the public space. While imperial officials and foreign visitors welcomed familiar languages, for Poles, Estonians, and Finns, Russian was an unwelcome reminder of who was in charge; Czechs and Slovenes were eager to remove German; and Saxon towns of Transylvania resented the imposition of Magyar (Berecz, 2019).

In the wake of World War I, Istanbul, St. Petersburg, and Philadelphia scaled back on the visibility of 'foreign' tongues, but in the city called Pressburg in German and Pozsony in Magyar trilingual signage was at its peak (Fig. 1.12b). Founded by German colonists, Pressburg-Pozsony had served as Hungary's royal seat (1536–1783), coronation town (until 1830),

(a) (b)

Fig. 1.11 Multilingual signage at the turn of the twentieth century:
(a) St. Petersburg: Nevsky 20, home of *St Petersburger Zeitung*, the German bookstore and library of Andreas Isler, and the *Grand Magasin de Paris*.
(b) Philadelphia: Christian Street 821, home of Banca Frank di Berardino that doubled as an Italian travel agency and a telegraph office. Public domain.

(a) (b)

Fig. 1.12 (a) Street sign in Swedish, Finnish, and Russian from the early twentieth century, Helsinki. Photo courtesy of Ekaterina Protassova, June 2020. (b) Street sign in Slovak, German, and Magyar from the 1920s, Bratislava. Photo by the author.

and home of the Hungarian parliament (until 1848). Following the collapse of the Dual Monarchy, in April 1919 the city was renamed Bratislava and declared the capital of Slovakia, part of the newly formed Czechoslovakia. And since the population of Bratislava was almost evenly split between Germans (36.3 percent), Slovaks (32.9 percent), and Magyars (29 percent), municipal authorities issued a decree to create trilingual signs but "in such a way that the Slovak language is in the first place and the inscription in a non-Slovak language is not bigger than the Slovak text" (translated in Bugge, 2004, p. 223).

1.3 Toward a History of Multilingual Societies

1.3.1 The Ubiquity of Multilingual Administrations

Historic studies of institutional and societal multilingualism allow us to discard the four tenets listed in the opening of this chapter and to replace them with the findings to date. The first key finding is the ubiquity of 'the multilingual challenge': all conquerors, empire builders, and rulers who welcomed foreign colonists had to deal with linguistic diversity of their populations. The second finding is the ubiquity of the multilingual response. To communicate with their linguistically diverse subjects, rulers selected languages well suited for administrative purposes and, in the best-case scenario, familiar to the people they ruled (if not, town criers translated decrees into local vernaculars). Rulers' mother tongues took a back seat to efficiency and image: decrees in the languages of the addressees were more effective in conveying orders, and multilingual inscriptions projected power, dominance, and strength. The cornerstones of language management were the hierarchies of prestige, where the top tier was occupied by *Kultursprache*, like Latin, Arabic, or Greek, and the bottom tier by vernaculars, ignored by chanceries, like Romance in Norman Sicily, Lithuanian in the Grand Duchy, or Magyar in the Kingdom of Hungary. These hierarchies resulted in five types of administrative language choices:

(a) The conquerors' *mother tongue*, as seen in the Roman West (Mullen, this volume);
(b) A *lingua franca*, as seen in the Persian Empire, where the elite eschewed Persian in favor of chancery Aramaic; in the Roman East, administered in Greek (Maravela, Mullen, this volume); in Indonesia, where the Dutch favored Malay (Willemyns, this volume); or in Hungary, where Latin bureaucracy persisted until 1844 (Almási & Šubarić, 2015);
(c) *Language(s) of the subjugated populations*, as seen in Norman Sicily and the Grand Duchy of Lithuania, where the conquerors' own vernaculars lacked tradition and prestige, or in the Mongol Empire, where the khans realized that orders in Mongolian in Uyghur script went unread and changed the chancery tongues: in Iran to Persian and in the Golden Horde, inhabited by Turkic tribes, to Kypchak, the lingua franca of the East (Abzalov, 2008; Akiner, 2017);
(d) *Bi- and multilingual arrangements* that combined the languages of the rulers and the ruled, as in Ptolemaic Egypt (Maravela, this volume) or the language of the rulers and lingua francas, as in eighteenth-century Russia, where decrees appeared in Russian, German, and French;

(e) *Hierarchical multilingual arrangements* with the dominant language and titular, regional, or minority tongues, as in Habsburg Austria (Prokopovych et al., 2019) or the USSR, where by 1938 primary education was offered in more than seventy languages (Pavlenko, 2013).

And since nowadays institutional multilingualism is firmly linked to 'social inclusion' and 'tolerance,' it is tempting to project this view backward and to congratulate enlightened Norman kings and Lithuanian dukes on their progressive views. Yet to do so would be an anachronistic mistake. 'Tolerance' refers to reluctant acceptance of the phenomena one dislikes, deems undesirable, and has the power to eradicate. In the context of religion, for instance, the idea of tolerance becomes relevant with the rise of monotheistic faiths. When it comes to languages, 'tolerance' is a fairly modern lens. For most of history, linguistic diversity was a fact of life, not a benevolent choice.

1.3.2 The Birth of Linguistic Intolerance

The third finding is that the dogmatic view of linguistic nationalism as a post-1789 phenomenon, recycled in our textbooks and handbooks, displays "a certain present-minded arrogance" (Davies, 2004, p. 569) and is off by several centuries. The oldest policy that tells people what to speak and *not* to speak – or at least the oldest one I know of to date – are the Statutes of Kilkenny (1366) directed by Edward III at English settlers going native in Ireland:

> now many English of the said land forsaking the English language, fashion, mode of riding, laws and usages, live and govern themselves according to the manners, fashion, and language of the Irish enemies; and also have made divers marriages and alliances between themselves and the Irish enemies aforesaid; whereby the said land and the liege people thereof, the English language, the allegiance due to our lord the King, and the English laws there, are put in subjection and decayed... it is ordained and established, that every Englishman use the English language, and be named by an English name, leaving off entirely the manner of naming used by the Irish... and if any English, or Irish living amongst the English, use the Irish language amongst themselves, contrary to this ordinance, and thereof be attaint, that his lands and tenements, if he have any, be seized into the hands of his immediate lord, until he come to one of the Places of our lord the King, and find sufficient surety to adopt and use the English language, and then that he have restitution of his said lands (translated in Berry, 1907, pp. 431, 435).

The Statutes are strikingly modern in equating language with loyalty, creative in the penalties for Irish use, and a bit self-defeating in the fact that they were articulated in French.

A century and a half later, King Fernando of Aragon and Queen Isabel of Castile forged a new path, with a nudge from a linguist, Antonio de Nebrija, whose Castilian grammar opened with a glib motto: *que siempre la lengua fue compañera del imperio* [that language always accompanied the empire]. The idea would be put to practice in the New World but the people Nebrija had in mind were closer to home – in Granada, surrendered on January 2, 1492 by its last Muslim king. In the prologue to his grammar, Nebrija listed French and Italian traders among the addressees but singled out "the enemies of our faith, who now have the need to know the Castilian language" (translated in Armillas-Tiseyra, 2016, p. 204).

The surrender of Granada inspired Fernando and Isabel to create a purely Christian Spain. Their first step was the Alhambra decree that ordered the Jews of Castile and Aragon to convert or leave by July 31. The Muslim community – large, armed, and essential for the local economy – was left alone until 1499, when Francisco Jiménez de Cisneros, the archbishop of Toledo and the primate of Castile, arrived in Granada and, with his usual fanatic zeal, turned the Great Mosque into a church, mass baptized 3,000 Muslims in one day, and in October of 1501 oversaw a bonfire of confiscated Arabic books (Gilbert, 2020; Harvey, 2005; Pick, 2004). In 1502, the Edicts of Conversion ordered the Muslims of Castile and León to accept baptism or leave. To help new converts, nicknamed *Moriscos*, remain Christian, the authorities decided to eliminate the language of the Quran. "We order," declared the 1526 Edict of Granada,

> that from now on none of them, nor their children, nor any other person of theirs, speak in Arabic or write anything in Arabic, and that they all speak the Spanish language. (translated in Giménez-Aguibar & Wasserman Soler, 2011, p. 235)

With the help of 80,000 ducats, Morisco leaders negotiated a forty-year period of grace. Once it expired, King Philip II had no mercy. The royal decree, published on January 1, 1567, revoked the legal validity of Arabic documents and ordered Moriscos to replace Arabic with Castilian in three years on the threat of jail (first offense) and exile (second offense):

> We decree and order that after three years, that they be counted starting from the day in which our letter is published and promulgated in the aforementioned city of Granada, a period of time given to them so that they may learn to speak and write in our Castilian language, which they call *Aljamia*, none of the aforementioned newly converted of the kingdom of Granada, either man or woman, can speak, read, or write in the aforementioned Arabic language, either in their house, outside, in public, or in secret. (translated in Giménez-Aguibar & Wasserman Soler, 2011, p. 241)

In another innovative touch, in 1575 Philip II ordered Toledan officials to raze all Kufic inscriptions and install Latin plaques. His successor Philip III went one better – in 1609, he issued a decree of expulsion of Moriscos. By 1614, the authorities deported 300,000 'enemies of Christian faith,' many of them devoted Christians who spoke only Castilian (Harvey, 2005). For me, this is the turning point in the history of linguistic nationalism and language policy (see also Spolsky, 2009, p. 153). Spanish kings weren't the first to scrape words from stone, tell their subjects what *not* to speak, or expel undesirable 'others.' Their innovation lies in using the time-tested methods of inscription razing, book burning, and deportation to eradicate the enemy tongue with the help of a linguist, the Inquisition, the church, and, ultimately, the fleet.

1.3.3 Un-diversifications of the Twentieth Century

"Whoever is growing up today in cities like Brussels or Antwerp, Rotterdam or Amsterdam, Paris or Marseille, London or Birmingham, Berlin or Frankfurt – just to mention European cities – can scarcely imagine how little ethnic-cultural diversity there was in the middle of the 20th century," professes Belgian politician-academic Geldof (2018, p. 43). In contrast, today "in cities such as Brussels, Rotterdam, Amsterdam or The Hague, migrants and people with foreign-born parents... make up a bit more than half of the population" (Geldof, 2018, p. 45). This demographic change is linked by the author to twentieth-century migrations:

> Contemporary superdiversity and the present-day population of Western Europe builds largely upon the migrations and migration policies implemented since the Second World War. ... After post-war reconstruction had been completed, Europe enjoyed a period of unparalleled economic prosperity.... From 1950 on, Western European countries therefore sought foreign workers, either from their former colonies such as Suriname and South East Asia or from Poland and Southern Europe, focusing upon Italian, Greek, Spanish and Portuguese migrants. (Geldof, 2018, pp. 43–44)

I won't dwell too much on the shrunken definition of 'Europe' whose 'unparalleled economic prosperity' never extended to those of us growing up in its Central and Eastern parts, and since misery loves company, I welcome the news that Italy, Spain, Greece, and Portugal aren't entirely 'Western' either. I also don't dispute the number of migrants in London and Rotterdam. What concerns me is the willful blindness with which migrations of the twentieth century are reduced to labor migration, the disregard of the reasons post-war Berlin, Frankfurt, and Amsterdam were deprived of the joys of diversity (could it be the Holocaust?), and the stubbornness with which a Western European lens is applied to Europe as a whole and sometimes to the world at large.

Historical studies complicate the picture: migration and language contact are common already in antiquity (cf. Clackson et al., 2020), while the distinguishing feature of the twentieth century is the relentless 'unmixing of peoples' in the memorable words of the British Foreign Minister Lord

Curzon. In 1923, Curzon headed the Military and Territorial Commission that signed the peace treaty of Lausanne. The treaty granted Turkey immunity for crimes committed between 1914 and 1922, including Armenian, Assyrian, and Greek genocide, and approved a Turkish–Greek population exchange. Privately, Curzon deemed it "a thoroughly bad and vicious solution for which the world will pay a heavy penalty for a hundred years to come" (Barutciski, 2003, p. 25). Publicly, the Lausanne treaty set the international legal precedent for expulsions and deportations in the service of greater good. Fortna's pivotal chapter in this volume traces the transition from multilingualism to monolingualism in post-Ottoman Turkey. Here, I will illustrate the unmixing through changes in the ethnolinguistic makeup of three cities: Russian St. Petersburg, post-Ottoman Alexandria, and Slovak Bratislava, formerly Austro-Hungarian Pressburg-Pozsony (for other examples, see Pavlenko's chapter).

In 1771, Scottish classicist William Richardson wrote in a letter from the Russian capital:

> It is said that, except Constantinople, no city in Europe contains a greater variety of strangers than St Petersburg. In London and Paris you have Europeans of all nations; but you have not, additionally to these, different races of Tartars, Circassians, and Armenians. (Richardson, 1784/1968, p. 412)

In 1869, St. Petersburg population census found that 17 percent of the city's residents were foreigners: 7 percent were Germans, 2.7 percent Finns, 2.2 percent Poles, and the remaining 5 percent were split among Swedes, Estonians, Latvians, French, Dutch, English, Italians, Armenians, Tatars, and Jews (Duke, 2008). Linguistic diversity was higher since many citizens were of non-Russian descent and still spoke their *Muttersprache* at home. Following the 1917 revolution, this diversity – and multilingualism at large – were obliterated by out-migration, purges of suspect speakers of foreign languages, and deportations of Germans and Finns. Nowadays, ethnic Russians constitute 92.5 percent of the city's population, fluent Russian speakers are at 99.7 percent, and the cityscape reveals a uniformly Russian façade (Baranova & Fedorova, 2019; see also Pavlenko, this volume).

In Alexandria, ethnolinguistic mélange was at its height in the early twentieth century, with diverse communities connected by French. In 1927, the first post-Ottoman census found that residents with foreign passports – Greeks, Jews, Italians, French, Brits, Austrians, Germans, Cypriots, and Maltese – constituted 17.4 percent of the population (Mabro, 2004). As in St. Petersburg, linguistic diversity was much higher because many Ottoman Syrians, Lebanese, Palestinians, Jews, Armenians, Greeks, and Turks took advantage of the offer of Egyptian citizenship. It is only in the wake of the Arab–Israeli wars of 1948 and 1956 – when Jews were expelled and other foreigners were 'encouraged' to leave – that Alexandria acquired a truly Egyptian face.

Bratislava started out in 1919 with administration in Magyar, German, and Czechoslovak. Yet leaders of the Slovak People's party – Father Andrej Hlinka, Father Jozef Tiso, and lawyer Vojtech Tuka – disliked the constitutional term 'Czechoslovak' that didn't distinguish between Slovak and Czech. The party's official organ, *Slovák*, scorned Jews for refusing to embrace Slovak and reminded the party faithful that Slovak was purer than Czech. In 1937 Father Hlinka proposed a constitutional amendment that made Slovak the only official language in Slovakia. To popularize the idea, his officials printed 60,000 stickers with a motto *Na Slovensku po slovensky* [In Slovakia in Slovak language] and pasted them all over Bratislava (Bakke, 1999).

In 1938, Hlinka passed away, but Prague, shaken up by the Sudeten crisis, gave Slovakia its long-sought autonomy. On October 8, 1938, Father Tiso returned to Bratislava as a premier and gave a reassuring speech in Slovak, Magyar, and German (no Czech). Soon after, thousands of Czech officials and teachers were expelled. The guiding principle of the new Slovak leaders, reported in 1939 George Kennan, the Secretary of the American legation in Prague, "has been linguistic chauvinism in its most petty and shortsighted form" (Kennan, 1968, p. 25).

Following Tiso's meeting with Hitler, Slovakia was declared independent and placed under the protection of the Third Reich, making Father Tiso the only Catholic priest to head a European state other than the Vatican. The Prime Minister's post went to Tuka, the idol of the paramilitary Hlinka guard and the author of its slogan *Hitler, Hlinka, jedna linka* [Hitler, Hlinka, on the same track]. Then, Slovakization took a new turn. The remaining Czechs were expelled and the Jewish Question found a permanent solution: under the pretense of sending workers to the Third Reich, 58,000 Jews were deported to Nazi camps, with the help of the Hlinka guard (Ward, 2013). After the war, Tiso and Tuka were executed for crimes against humanity but in the midst of expulsions and extermination their dream of *Na Slovensku po slovensky* came true.

The Czechoslovak government also pitched in. In 1945, President Beneš signed decrees that stripped Germans and Magyars of their citizenship, property, and civil rights and declared them traitors and collaborators, guilty of the disintegration of the Czechoslovak state. By 1948, three million Germans were expelled from Czechoslovakia. Magyars, following a population exchange treaty, were transported to Hungary and resettled in the houses of deported Germans (Molnár & Szarka, 2010).[6] From 1950, Slovaks have been dominant

[6] Importantly, not all Magyars elected to leave. Today, Magyar is still spoken along southern borders and the Slovak government is criticized by Council of Europe experts for constraints placed on the use of Magyar as a minority language.

in Bratislava, rising from 32.9 percent to 90 percent of the population (Statistical Office of the Slovak Republic, 2012).

What we see through a post-imperial lens is the new international norm: two World Wars, the partitions of Palestine, Cyprus, and India, and the dissolution of Yugoslavia and the USSR were all accompanied by migrations of linguistic and ethnic unmixing (Brubaker, 1998). But when you read multilingualism textbooks and handbooks, like *The Routledge Handbook of Migration and Language* (Canagarajah, 2017), you won't find a single word about the twentieth-century expulsions, deportations, population transfers, ethnic cleansing, inter-ethnic warfare, and genocide that undiversified countless polyglot cities with the same ruthless efficiency with which their Catholic majesties and the Inquisition purified Spain between 1492 and 1614.

1.3.4 The Banal Normativity of 'Translanguaging'

Language-mixing in writing and speech has long been at the center of academic attention: at the first International Symposium on Bilingualism in 1997 all but one plenary were dedicated to code-switching. In the decades since, declares Jacquemet (2018), "the study of multilingualism in transnational communities has generated an impressive array of new terminology, from codemeshing... to translanguaging... to transglossic language practice, to explain the increasingly unbounded nature of communicative practices" (p. 379). The clunky terms are definitely new but the pretense that the 'increasingly unbounded' practices are also new and are explained, rather than labeled, by modish coinage puzzles me to no end. I am by no means the only one confounded by this development. Edwards (2012) notes offhand that

> those guilty of using these ugly terms have remarkably stannous ears, a particularly unhappy circumstance, surely, for those who are language scholars. On a particularly critical day, I might be tempted to suggest that those who write in this way have forfeited any claim on our serious attention. (pp. 34–35)

If anything, the fascination with code-switching on the part of language scholars (and every student in a bilingualism class!) says more about us than it does about multilingualism: we see the practice as transgressive in some way, akin to cross-dressing. Of course, we aren't the only ones to think so: in Rome, Cicero urged his son Marcus not to sprinkle his native tongue with alien words. But then again it was also embarrassing not to understand a reference in Greek and Cicero didn't always follow his own advice: the king of code-switching, he once crammed a short letter of recommendation to Caesar – whom he always tried to impress – with three Greek quotes from the *Odyssey*, three from the *Iliad*, and a fragment from the now lost play of Euripides (on Roman bilingual epistolography, see Elder & Mullen, 2019).

The fifth important finding is the banal normativity of script- and language-mixing in business records, private letters, and religious texts in many historical settings (Maravela, Mullen, Wright, Argent, Fortna; see also Pahta et al., 2018). Historical evidence also furnishes echoes of mixed speech in the classroom (e.g., Griffith, 2015), in church (e.g., Fletcher, 2013), and in the courts of law: One memorable character in the seventeenth-century court records of the Armenian community of Kamieniets-Podolsk is a belligerent youth who defied his elders with a mix of elaborate Turkic curses and Polish threats (Garkavets, 2002, pp. 940–943).[7] All this is to say that translanguaging, or whatever you prefer to call it, is unremarkable in and of itself.

What made it look transgressive was normalization of monolingual practices that restricted mixing of languages and scripts to the private domain. Nowadays, even studies of 'superdiversity' admit that the public sector is a linguistically unified marketplace (Sabaté-Dalmau, 2018) and fail to find translanguaging in the workplace (Nekvapil & Sherman, 2018). Paeans to 'increasingly complex' immigrant practices are at best virtue signaling and at worst a diversion from linguistic inequalities in public life (for a similar argument, see May, 2016).

1.3.5 Linguistic Tolerance: A Study in Affective and Cognitive Dissonance

The greatest innovations of modernity in the area of language management are the idea that each and every language can satisfy all needs ('one language fits all'), compulsory linguistic assimilation policies, and systematic erasure of 'undesirable' tongues.

In the Russian Empire, Polish-speaking territories were the first to feel the brunt of imperial Russification. After the Polish uprising of 1830–1831, Tsar Nicholas I closed Polish-medium universities and replaced Polish with Russian in the administration of the Western provinces and state-supported schools. Following the 1863–1864 Polish rebellion, Alexander II extended language reforms to Congress Poland, replacing Polish with Russian, first in administration and official press, and then in education and court proceedings; in Lithuania even the use of Polish during school breaks became a punishable offense and so did tombstones in languages other than Russian (Kappeler, 2001; Kryczynsky, 1937; Pavlenko, 2011a). In the 1880s, Alexander III expanded Russification to the Baltic provinces, with an aim to replace German with Russian as the language of administration, court proceedings, and secondary schools (Pavlenko, 2011a).

[7] Arrivals from Tatar Crimea, Armenians of Lviv and Kamieniets-Podolsk spoke Kypchak as their mother tongue.

In the USA, in 1917 the authorities unrolled their own anti-German campaign: Louisiana prohibited German teaching from elementary schools all the way to the university; in Iowa, Governor Harding issued the 'Babel proclamation' that banned sermons, instruction, public addresses, and "conversation in public places, on trains and over the telephone" in any language but English, and in South Dakota, several men and women were fined $10 to $25 for speaking 'the Teutonic tongue' in public and one manager paid $100 for allowing it in his store.[8] Then, in a striking legal development, fifteen states – Arkansas, California, Connecticut, Hawaii, Idaho, Indiana, Iowa, Louisiana, Nebraska, Nevada, Ohio, Oklahoma, Oregon, South Dakota, and Texas – made use of foreign languages in elementary schools a criminal offense, punishable with imprisonment (ranging from 10 days to 6 months) and fines (ranging from $25 to $100, approximately $315 to $1,260 in today's dollars). A second offense in Nevada and Oregon cost violators a year in county jail or a fine up to $1,000 (approximately $12,600).[9]

The severity of the nineteenth- and early twentieth-century Russification, Americanization, or Magyarization (cf. Berecz, 2021a) makes the assertion that we are witnessing "the defeat of extreme monolingual nation-making practices and of aggressive assimilation practices" (Lo Bianco, 2020, p. 42) intuitively appealing, despite the underwhelming integration of immigrant languages in the 'superdiverse' public space (King & Carson, 2016), the decision of the council of London's 'superdiverse' borough, Newham, to boost integration by slashing translation funding and removing all foreign language newspapers from the libraries (Nye, 2013), or a German public campaign that tried to compel immigrants to learn *Deutsch* (Fig. 1.13a).

When we turn to Eastern Europe, the argument loses its appeal. A quick look at the Council of Europe (CoE) experts' reports from Slovakia, Estonia, Latvia, Ukraine, or Lithuania, posted on the CoE website, reveals that aggressive assimilation practices are still alive and doing well. Estonia, for one, created a novel institution, the Language Inspectorate, aka 'language police,' to monitor the compliance with the state Language Law under the threat of fines and termination of employment. The Inspectorate, complained CoE experts, "continues to wield wide powers in the field of employment, including in particular verification of language proficiency and imposition of fines" (Advisory Committee on the Framework Convention for the Protection of National Minorities, 2015, p. 1). Public campaigns aimed at migrants in

[8] https://iowaculture.gov/history/education/educator-resources/primary-source-sets/immigration-regulation-response-and/babel-proclamation; "Fines imposed for speaking German," *Harrisburg Telegraph*, November 2, 1918.

[9] For collections of relevant laws, see Hood (1919), Lischka (1926).

(a) (b)

Fig. 1.13 (a) "Out with the language" / "I speak German," a German-medium campaign aimed at migrants in Germany, 2010–2011.[10] (b) "Untie your tongue" / "Learn the language – it's worth it," a Russian-medium campaign aimed at Russian speakers in Estonia, 2010. Public domain.

Germany and Russian speakers in Estonia are emblematic of the differences between East and West (Fig. 1.13).

The concluding chapters in this volume engage with the tension at the heart of present-day European multilingualism, where 'celebration of linguistic diversity' coexists uneasily with the establishment of official 'language police.' Sokolovska's analysis of CoE language debates shows that multilingualism in the abstract is easy to 'celebrate': Parliamentarians from Lithuania, Spain, Ukraine, and Ireland are all in favor of plurilingual repertoires. It is the individual constellations of languages and the embedded hierarchies of prestige that cause frustration and strife, evident in the complaint of Lithuania's representative about foreign investors who rely on English and never learn Lithuanian. The 'celebration of linguistic diversity,' promoted by CoE, argues Sokolovska, reproduces existing hierarchies under the guise of equality.

Lane's chapter draws attention to emotional consequences of another quintessentially modern practice, language revitalization, highlighting the shame, anxiety, and guilt experienced by those who speak their 'heritage' languages poorly

[10] www.languageonthemove.com/the-cult-of-personal-responsibility/

or not at all. Beale-Rivaya analyzes the reproduction of linguistic stereotypes in a popular form of Spanish public entertainment, the festival of Moors and Christians, while Pavlenko considers ways in which former polyglot cities appropriate ghost signs in dissonant languages, no longer spoken on city streets, to create a simulacrum of linguistic diversity and conceal the suppression of minority tongues. Together, the two chapters spotlight the contestation and commodification of historic multilingualism in the public space by political actors invested in certain visions of the national past. The purpose of this introduction – and the volume at large – is to show that such distortions of history are facilitated by the disregard of the past in multilingualism as an academic field.

1.3.6 The Field of Multilingualism and Historical Amnesia

The millennia-long history of institutional and societal multilingualism reveals that the claims of uniqueness of today's 'multilingual challenge' are patently false, deeply ignorant, and utterly absurd. To see multilingualism through the keyhole of the nineteenth-century Western European nation-states, twentieth-century labor migrations, and their twenty-first-century 'superdiverse' outcomes is to emulate a man who touched an elephant's ear and exclaimed, in the unforgettable words of John Godfrey Saxe, "Deny the fact who can, this marvel of an elephant is very like a fan!"

But then again every storyteller knows that their storyline depends on their point of view. There is even a name for shifting narrative perspectives – the Rashomon effect, after Kurosawa's classic film *Rashomon* (1950), where four witnesses retell 'the same' event differently to present themselves in the best possible light. Academic narratives are governed by the same principle. The history of multilingualism is often told from the perspective of ideologically monolingual – or bilingual – nation-states because that's where many influential scholars reside. The Whig history of progress from 'circumstantial' multilingualism of yesteryear to 'superdiversity' of the present-day is a self-serving enterprise that reinforces the established academic hierarchy and allows its adepts to 'defend' and 'celebrate' immigrant multilingualism and to brand their own work as new, superior, and distinct (cf. Pavlenko, 2019). The non-history also benefits the field at large by giving it a compelling raison d'être – exceptionality of today's 'multilingual challenge.'

Yet the causes of historical amnesia run deeper than academic fragmentation and conceit. While science is, or at least aims to be, objective and international, academic departments are housed in national universities that privilege national languages, literatures, and histories. Habsburg history, noted Evans (2004), has long suffered from the legacy of this tunnel vision, whereby "historiographical traditions have been defined and often hermetically sealed off by language, to yield narrow and exclusive interpretations" (p. 24). Normative multilingualism, until recently, fell through the cracks as no one's history.

The neglect is exacerbated by demands on academics' language skills. In the study of Ptolemaic Egypt, for instance, labor was traditionally divided between classicists focused on Greek (and some Latin) papyri and Egyptologists who studied Hieroglyphic, Hieratic, and Demotic texts (Bagnall, 2009b, pp. xvii–xviii). Both groups had their conferences and publications, and it is only recently that the interest in bilingualism inspired scholars to acquire additional expertise or work in teams. In other contexts, multilingual documents still gather dust in the archives. "It is ... one of the tragedies of early modern American history," bitterly complained German historian Wellenreuther (2005), "that so many of the [American] historians working in this field are unfamiliar with quaint European languages like Latin, French, Dutch and German" (p. vii).

Sociolinguists are prey to a different trend. A century ago, noted Piller (2016), German linguist Hugo Schuchardt comfortably addressed his international audience in German with quotes and references in Latin, Spanish, and French. In contrast, today linguistic diversity is celebrated in English Only, under the premise that a lingua franca levels the playing field. The purportedly democratic fashion has led to two paradoxical outcomes: (a) a privileged class of monolingual English-speaking sociolinguists who study multilingualism 'in translation,' with the help of research assistants, and (b) English-medium textbooks and handbooks with nary a non-English reference that render invisible – and irrelevant – publications in other tongues.[11]

This volume aims to dispel the fog of historical amnesia with studies that go against the grain of traditional language histories, challenge clichéd beliefs, foreground historic normativity of institutional multilingualism and language-mixing, examine the transformation of polyglot societies into monolingual ones, and bring out the dissonance in our orientations to linguistic diversity. Most crucially, it reinforces Judson's (2006, 2019) argument that linguistic diversity per se *does not* cause political conflicts – languages became implicated in strife following their politicization by nationalist activists and instrumentalization by populist demagogues.

Having worked at the intersection of psycholinguistics, sociolinguistics, and forensic linguistics for over two decades, I am fully aware of the challenges of interdisciplinary dialogs and advantages of staying put. Yet I also see big questions as an important centripetal force. My hope is to initiate a conversation about multilingual history in the longue durée and from multiple points of view, based on five ontological and epistemological assumptions:

[11] *The Routledge Handbook of Language and Superdiversity* edited by Creese and Blackledge (2018) is a good example. Its 536 pages contain 2,048 references, of these only 37 (1.8 percent) are in languages other than English. If you subtract the three chapters that contain an unusually high number of such references – namely, Geldof (2018), Nekvapil and Sherman (2018), and Sabaté-Dalmau (2018) – the total of foreign references drops to 8 (0.4 percent).

- '**languages**' are social and linguistic conventions whose institutional and perceptual realities, including their very names, vary across individuals, time, and place;
- '**multilingualism**' and '**monolingualism**' are idealized modern abstractions that serve as umbrella terms for a wide range of individual and social phenomena;
- **theoretical constructs**, such as 'official language policy,' 'minority languages,' 'linguistic imperialism,' 'linguistic tolerance,' and 'language rights,' central in discussions of modern multilingualism, are an anachronistic lens on the past – historical language management and ideologies require their own theories and terminology;
- **the timelines** of the rise of linguistic nationalism need reconsideration and so does the assumption of a uniform march to or from multilingualism – social phenomena labeled 'multilingualism' unfold and fold on different timelines in different contexts;
- **language scholars** aren't mere observers of linguistic powerplays – they are also actors who may assist in erasure of linguistic diversity (Wright and Gal, this volume) or experience the consequences of such erasure (Lane, this volume).

I am also fully aware that a single volume doesn't suffice. What we need are new theories of language management and ideologies (see also Mullen, this volume), comparative analyses of multilingual institutions and societies (for an example, see Mairs, this volume) and, above all, studies that push beyond the laxity of trendy terms to ask uncomfortable questions:

- How do we reconcile the traditional view of linguistic nationalism as one nation=one language with historic evidence of polyglot nationalism?
- Where does ethnolinguistic unmixing fit in the theories of language and migration?
- Are our notions of 'language equality' shaped by the legacy of linguistic nationalism?
- How does a struggle for 'language rights' morph from the fight for equality into the demand for exclusivity, paving the road for oppression of new 'linguistic minorities'?
- If multilingual institutions and 'language accommodations' equal social and political inclusion, why is it that Western democracies offer fewer such 'accommodations' than the former 'prisons of the nations,' like Cisleithania/Austria and the USSR?
- And if language conflicts are essentially about political and economic power, can language accommodations and access policies level the playing field?
- Is linguistic nationalism an idea we can ever un-practice and un-think?

I want to express deep gratitude to all contributors for their willingness to step over – or kick aside – the disciplinary boundaries to speak to a larger audience about what they do and how they do it and a fervent hope that the dialog between sociolinguists and historians will go on. I also hope that sociolinguists will be able to move beyond the empty cliché of "our world is more multilingual than ever before" and that future textbook authors and handbook editors will endow the field with a history of multilingual polities, overshadowed, at present, by the rise of ideologically monolingual nation-states. Until then, the big picture of multilingualism remains distorted, like the elephant, and, like Humpty Dumpty, cannot be reassembled with ease.

Bibliography

Primary Sources

Advisory Committee on the Framework Convention for the Protection of National Minorities (2015) *Fourth opinion on Estonia*, adopted on 19 March 2015. Strasbourg: Council of Europe.

Berry, H. (1907) *Statutes and ordinances and acts of the parliament of Ireland: Volume 1 King John to Henry V*. Dublin: Alexander Thom & Co.

Beudant, F. (1823) *Travels in Hungary in 1818*. Translated from French. London: Richard Phillips & Co.

De Lannoy, G. (1840) *Voyages et ambassades de Messire de Guillebert de Lannoy, 1399–1450*. Mons: Typographie d'Em. Hoyois, Libraire.

Froissart, J. (1867) *Oeuvres de Froissart publiées par M. le baron Kervyn de Lettenhove: Tome deuxième, 1322–1339*. Bruxelles: Comptoir Universel d'Imprimerie et de Librarie, Victor Devaux.

Garcia-Gallo, A. (1975) *Los fueros de Toledo* [Toledan charters]. Madrid: Instituto Nacional de Estudios Jurídicos.

González Palencia, A. (1926–1930) *Los mozárabes de Toledo en los siglos XII y XIII* [Mozarabs of Toledo in the 12th and 13th centuries]. Madrid: Instituto de Valencia de Don Juan.

Hood, W. (1919) *State laws relating to education*. Washington, DC: Government Printing Office.

Kennan, G. (1968) *From Prague after Munich: Diplomatic papers, 1938–1940*. Princeton, NJ: Princeton University Press.

Lischka, C. (1926) *Private schools and state laws*. Washington, DC: Bureau of Education.

Minutes of the Provincial Council of Pennsylvania (1683–1700). Minutes of the Provincial Council of Pennsylvania, from the organization to the termination of the proprietary government, containing the proceedings of Council from March 10, 1683 to November 27, 1700. Volume 1 (1852). Philadelphia: Jo. Severns & Co.

Report of the Superintendent of Common Schools (1839). Harrisburg.

Richardson, W. (1784) *Anecdotes of the Russian empire: in a series of letters, written a few years ago, from St Petersburg*. London: W. Strahan & T. Cadell.

Statistical Office of the Slovak Republic (2012) The 2011 Population and Housing Census. Retrieved at www.statistics.sk

Secondary Sources

Abrecht, R. (2020) An immigrant neighborhood in ancient Rome. *Urban History*, 47, 2–22.

Abzalov, L. (2008) Тюркский язык в официальном делопроизводстве Улуса Джучи в 13 столетии [Turkic language in the administration of Ulus Jochi in the 13th century]. *Ученые Записки Казанского Государственного Университета* [Proceedings of Kazan State University], 150, 8, 176–182.

Adams, J. N. (2003) *Bilingualism and the Latin language*. Cambridge: Cambridge University Press.

Adams, J. N., Janse, M., & S. Swain (eds.) (2002) *Bilingualism in ancient society: Language contact and the written text*. Cambridge: Cambridge University Press.

Akiner, S. (2017) Cultural hybridity in the religious literature of the Tatars of North-Eastern Europe. *The Slavonic and East European Review*, 95, 3, 401–428.

Almási, G. & L. Šubarić (eds.) (2015) *Latin at the crossroads of identity: The evolution of linguistic nationalism in the Kingdom of Hungary*. Leiden/Boston, MA: Brill.

Anderson, B. (1991) *Imagined communities: Reflections on the origins and spread of nationalism*. London/New York: Verso.

Ando, C. (2016) Legal pluralism in practice. In Du Plessis, P., Ando, C. & K. Tuori (eds.) *The Oxford Handbook of Roman Law and Society*. Oxford: Oxford University Press, pp. 283–295.

Armillas-Tiseyra, M. (2016) On language and empire: The prologue to Grammar of the Castilian language (1492). *Proceedings of the Modern Language Association of America*, 131, 1, 197–208.

Arnaut, K., Blommaert, J., Rampton, B. & M. Spotti (eds.) (2016) *Language and superdiversity*. New York/London: Routledge.

Aronin, L. (2020) Dominant language constellations as an approach for studying multilingual practices. In LoBianco, J. & L. Aronin (eds.) *Dominant language constellations: A new perspective on multilingualism*. Cham, Switzerland: Springer, pp. 19–33.

Bagnall, R. (cd.) (2009a) *The Oxford Handbook of Papyrology*. Oxford: Oxford University Press.

(2009b) Introduction. In Bagnall, R. (ed.) *The Oxford Handbook of Papyrology*. Oxford: Oxford University Press, pp. xvii–xxi.

Bagnall, R. & P. Derow (eds.) (2004) *The Hellenistic period: Historical sources in translation*. Oxford: Blackwell.

Bakke, E. (1999) *Doomed to failure? The Czechoslovak nation project and the Slovak autonomist reaction, 1918–1938*. Ph.D. dissertation, University of Oslo.

Baranova, V. & K. Fedorova (2019) 'Invisible minorities' and 'hidden diversity' in Saint-Petersburg's linguistic landscape. *Language and Communication*, 68, 17–27.

Barutciski, M. (2003) Lausanne revisited: Population exchanges and international law and policy. In Hirschon, R. (ed.) *Crossing the Aegean: An appraisal of the*

1923 compulsory population exchange between Greece and Turkey. New York/ Oxford: Berghahn Books, pp. 23–37.

Beale-Rivaya, Y. (2012) The written record as witness: Language shift from Arabic to Romance in the documents of the Mozarabs of Toledo in the twelfth and thirteenth centuries. *La Corónica*, 40, 2, 27–50.

Beale-Rivaya, Y. & J. Busic (eds.) (2018) *A companion to medieval Toledo: Reconsidering the canons*. Leiden/Boston, MA: Brill.

Bekkin, R. (2021) Соборная мечеть Санкт-Петербурга в фотографиях и открытках [The cathedral mosque of St. Petersburg in photos and postcards]. *Journal of Endangered Languages*, 19, 11, 336–346.

Bekkin, R. & A. Tagirdzhanova [Беккин, Р. & А. Тагирджанова] (2016) *Мусульманский Петербург: Исторический путеводитель* [Muslim St. Petersburg: Historical guidebook]. Moscow/St. Petersburg: Institute for African Studies.

Berecz, A. (2019) The language of street signs in Dualist Transylvania and the Banat. *Acta Universitatis Sapientiae, Philologica*, 11, 2, 23–36.

(2021a) Top-down and bottom-up Magyarization in multiethnic Banat towns under dualist Hungary (1867–1914). *European Review of History*, 28, 3, 422–440.

(2021b) Linguistic diversity and the court system in Dualist Hungary. *Multilingua*, 40, 3, 393–419.

Bloemendal, J. (ed.) (2015) *Bilingual Europe: Latin and vernacular cultures, examples of bilingualism and multilingualism c. 1300–1800*. Leiden/Boston, MA: Brill.

Booms, D. & P. Higgs (2016) *Sicily: Culture and conquest*. London: The British Museum.

Bowman, A. & C. Crowther (eds.) (2020) *The epigraphy of Ptolemaic Egypt*. Oxford: Oxford University Press.

Bowman, A., Crowther, C., Hornblower, S., Mairs, R., & K. Savvopoulos (eds.) (2021) *Corpus of Ptolemaic inscriptions. Part I Greek, bilingual and trilingual inscriptions from Egypt*. Oxford: Oxford University Press.

Brand, P. (2000) The languages of the law in later medieval England. In Trotter, D. (ed.) *Multilingualism in later medieval Britain*. Woodbridge, Suffolk: D.S. Brewer, pp. 63–76.

Brubaker, R. (1998) Migrations of 'ethnic unmixing' in the 'New Europe.' *International Migration Review*, 32, 4, 1047–1065.

Bugge, P. (2004) The making of a Slovak city: the Czechoslovak renaming of Pressburg/Pozsony/Prešporok, 1918–1919. *Austrian History Yearbook*, 35, 205–227.

Burke, P. (2004) *Languages and communities in early modern Europe*. Cambridge: Cambridge University Press.

Burnett, C. (2001) The coherence of the Arabic–Latin translation program in Toledo in the twelfth century. *Science in Context*, 14, 1–2, 249–288.

Butterfield, A. (2009) *The familiar enemy: Chaucer, language and nation in the Hundred Years war*. Oxford: Oxford University Press.

Canagarajah, S. (ed.) (2017) *The Routledge Handbook of Migration and Language*. London/New York: Routledge.

Clackson, J., James, P., McDonald, K., Tagliapetra, L., & N. Zair (eds.) (2020) *Migration, mobility and language contact in and around the ancient Mediterranean*. Cambridge: Cambridge University Press.

Clanchy, M. (2013) *From memory to written record: England 1066–1307*. Third ed. Malden, MA: Wiley-Blackwell.

Clarysse, W. & D. Thompson (2006) *Counting the people in Hellenistic Egypt*. Cambridge: Cambridge University Press.

Classen, A. (ed.) (2016) *Multilingualism in the Middle Ages and early modern age: Communication and miscommunication in the premodern world*. Berlin: Mouton De Gruyter.

Cohen, P. (2016) Torture and translation in the multilingual courtrooms of early modern France. *Renaissance Quarterly*, 69, 899–939.

Cole, E. (2015) *Interpretation and authority: The social functions of translation in ancient Egypt*. Ph.D. dissertation, UCLA.

Cracraft, J. (2004) *The Petrine revolution in Russian culture*. Cambridge, MA: Harvard University Press.

Creese, A. & A. Blackledge (2018) *The Routledge Handbook of Language and Superdiversity*. London/New York: Routledge.

Cribiore, R. (2001) *Gymnastics of the mind: Greek education in Hellenistic and Roman Egypt*. Princeton, NJ: Princeton University Press.

Csernicskó, I. & A. Beregszászi (2019) Different states, same practices: visual construction of language policy on banknotes in the territory of present-day Transcarpathia. *Language Policy*, 18, 269–293.

Curry, A., Bell, A., Chapman, A., King, A. & D. Simpkin (2010) Languages in the military profession in later medieval England. In Ingham, R. (ed.) *The Anglo-Norman language and its contexts*. York: York Medieval Press, pp. 74–93.

Czajkowski, K., Eckhardt, B. & M. Strothmann (eds.) (2020) *Law in the Roman provinces*. Oxford: Oxford University Press.

Dahmen, K. (2015) The use, functions, and spread of German in eighteenth-century Russia. *The Russian Review*, 74, 20–40.

Davies, R. (2004) Nations and national identities in the medieval world: An apologia. *Revue Belge d'Histoire Contemporaine*, 34, 4, 567–579.

Dix, K. & G. Houston (2006) Public libraries in the city of Rome: From the Augustan age to the time of Diocletian. *Mélanges de l'École française de Rome. Antiquité*, 118, 2, 671–717.

Dodds, J., Menocal, M. & A. Krasner Balbale (2008) *The arts of intimacy: Christians, Jews and Muslims in the making of Castilian culture*. New Haven/London: Yale University Press.

Donner, W. (2008) "Neither Germans nor Englishmen but Americans": Education, assimilation and ethnicity among nineteenth-century Pennsylvania Germans. *Pennsylvania History: A Journal of Mid-Atlantic Studies*, 75, 2, 197–226.

Dowler, W. (2001) *Classroom and empire: The politics of schooling Russia's eastern nationalities,* 1860–1917. Montreal/London/Ithaca: McGill-Queen's University Press.

Duke, S. (2008) Multiethnic St Petersburg: The late imperial period. In Goscilo, H. & S. Norris (eds.) *Preserving Petersburg: History, memory, nostalgia*. Bloomington: Indiana University Press, pp. 142–163.

Ecker, H. (2004) *Caliphs and kings: The art and influence of Islamic Spain*. New York: Hispanic Society of America.

Edwards, J. (1994) *Multilingualism*. London/New York: Penguin Books.

(2012) *Multilingualism: Understanding linguistic diversity*. New York/London: Continuum.

Elder, O. & A. Mullen (2019) *The language of Roman letters: Bilingual epistolography from Cicero to Fronto*. Cambridge: Cambridge University Press.

Evans, R. (2004) Language and state building: The case of the Habsburg monarchy. *Austrian History Yearbook,* 35, 1–24.

Felice, E.-M. (2019) *Multilingualism and language choice in the imperial Roman army*. Ph.D. dissertation, University of Oxford.

Fishman, J. (1965) Who speaks what language, to whom and when? *La Linguistique*, 2, 67–88.

(1991) Putting the 'socio' back into the sociolinguistic enterprise. *International Journal of the Sociology of Language*, 92, 127–138.

Fletcher, A. (2013) Written versus spoken macaronic discourse in late medieval England: The view from the pulpit. In Jefferson, J. & A. Putter (eds.) *Multilingualism in medieval Britain (c. 1066–1520): Sources and analysis*. Turnhout, Belgium: Brepols, pp. 137–151.

Fortna, B. (2010) *Learning to read in the late Ottoman Empire and the early Turkish Republic*. London: Palgrave Macmillan.

Franklin, S. (2019) *The Russian graphosphere, 1450–1850*. Cambridge: Cambridge University Press.

Gal, S. (2011) Polyglot nationalism: Alternative perspectives on language in 19th century Hungary. *Langage et société*, 136, 31–53.

Gallagher, J. (2019) *Learning languages in early modern England*. Oxford: Oxford University Press.

García-Arenal, M. (2015) The converted Muslims of Spain: Morisco cultural resistance and engagement with Islamic knowledge (1502–1610). In Tottoli, R. (ed.) *The Routledge Handbook of Islam in the West*. London/New York: Routledge, pp. 38–54.

Garkavets, A. (2002) *Кыпчакское письменное наследие, том 1. Каталог и тексты памятников армянским письмом* [Kypchak written legacy, volume 1 Catalog and texts of books in Armenian script]. Almaty: Desht-i-Kypchak.

Geldof, D. (2018) Superdiversity as a lens to understand complexities. In Creese, A. & A. Blackledge (eds.) *The Routledge Handbook of Language and Superdiversity*. London/New York: Routledge, pp. 43–56.

Gilbert, C. (2020) *In good faith: Arabic translation and translators in early modern Spain*. Philadelphia, PA: University of Pennsylvania Press.

Giménez-Eguibar, P. & D. Wasserman Soler (2011) *La mala algarabía*: Church, monarchy, and the Arabic language in 16th century Spain. *The Medieval History Journal*, 14, 2, 229–258.

Goldstein, B. (2009) Astronomy as a "neutral zone": Interreligious cooperation in medieval Spain. *Medieval Encounters*, 15, 159–174.

Griffith, M. (2015) Origins and relations to the Near East. In Bloomer, M. (ed.) *A companion to ancient education*. Malden, MA: John Wiley & Sons, pp. 7–25.

Grosjean, F. (1982) *Life with two languages: An introduction to bilingualism*. Cambridge, MA: Harvard University Press.

Grusha, A. (2015) *Документальная письменность Великого Княжества Литовского (конец XIV–первая треть XVI в.)* [Chancery writing in the Grand Duchy of Lithuania, end of the 14th–beginning of the 16th centuries]. Minsk: Belaruskaya navuka.

Gutas, D. (1998) *Greek thought, Arabic culture: The Graeco-Arabic translation movement in Baghdad and early 'Abbāsid society (2nd–4th/8th–10th centuries).* London/New York: Routledge.

Harvey, L. P. (2005) *Muslims in Spain, 1500 to 1614*. Chicago: The University of Chicago Press.

Houben, H. (2013) Between occidental and oriental cultures: Norman Sicily as a 'third space'? In Burkhardt, S. & T. Foerster (eds.) *Norman tradition and transcultural heritage: exchange of cultures in the 'Norman' peripheries of medieval Europe.* Burlington, VT: Ashgate, pp. 19–33.

Jacquemet, M. (2018) Sociolinguistic superdiversity and asylum. In Creese, A. & A. Blackledge (eds.) *The Routledge Handbook of Language and Superdiversity.* London/New York: Routledge, pp. 379–395.

Jefferson, J. & A. Putter (eds.) (2013) *Multilingualism in medieval Britain (c. 1066–1520): Sources and analysis.* Turnhout, Belgium: Brepols.

Jernudd, B. & J. Nekvapil (2012) History of the field: A sketch. In Spolsky, B. (ed.) *The Cambridge Handbook of Language Policy*. Cambridge: Cambridge University Press, pp. 16–36.

Johns, J. (2002) *Arabic administration in Norman Sicily: The royal diwan*. Cambridge: Cambridge University Press.

Johns, J. & N. Jamil (2004) Signs of the times: Arabic signatures as a measure of acculturation in Norman Sicily. *Muqarnas*, 21, 181–192.

Jonker, L., Berlejung, A., & I. Cornelius (eds.) (2021) *Multilingualism in ancient contexts: Perspectives from ancient Near Eastern and early Christian contexts.* Stellenbosch, South Africa: SUN PReSS.

Judson, P. (2006) *Guardians of the nation: Activists on the language frontiers of imperial Austria*. Cambridge, MA: Harvard University Press.

(2019) Encounters with language diversity in late Habsburg Austria. In Prokopovych, M., Bethke, C. & T. Scheer (eds.) *Language diversity in the late Habsburg Empire*. Leiden/Boston: Brill, pp. 12–25.

Kappeler, A. (2001) *The Russian Empire: A multiethnic history.* Translated by A. Clayton. London/New York: Pearson.

Kerby-Fulton, K. (2015) Competing Archives, Competing Languages: Office Vernaculars, Civil Servant Raconteurs, and the Porous Nature of French during Ireland's Rise of English. *Speculum*, 90, 3, 674–700.

King, L. & L. Carson (eds.) (2016) *The multilingual city: Vitality, conflict and change.* Bristol: Multilingual Matters.

Komora, P. (2015) *Ludovít Štúr (1815–1856), reformer of the Slovak society.* Bratislava: Slovak National Museum.

König, J., Oikonomopoulou, K. & G. Woolf (eds.) (2013) *Ancient libraries.* Cambridge: Cambridge University Press.

Kosman, M. (1971) Dokumenty wielkiego księcia Witolda [Documents of the Grand Duke Witold]. *Studia Zródloznawcze*, 16, 139–169.

Kryczynsky, L. (1937) *Historia meczetu w Wilnie* [A history of a Wilna mosque]. *Wrocław.*

Kulwicka-Kamińska, J. & Cz. Łapicz (2015) *Tefsir Tatarów Wielkiego Księstwa Litewskiego: Teoria i praktyka badawcza* [The Tafsir of the Tatars of the Grand Duchy of Lithuania]. Toruń.

Lo Bianco, J. (2020) A meeting of concepts and praxis: Multilingualism, language policy and the Dominant Language Constellation. In LoBianco, J. & L. Aronin (eds.) *Dominant language constellations: A new perspective on multilingualism.* Cham, Switzerland: Springer, pp. 35–56.

Louden, M. (2016) *Pennsylvania Dutch: The Story of an American Language.* Baltimore, MD: Johns Hopkins University Press.

Mabro, R. (2004) Alexandria 1860–1960: the cosmopolitan identity. In Hirst, A. & M. Silk (eds.) *Alexandria, real and imagined.* London/New York: Routledge, pp. 247–262.

Manning, J. (2010) *The last pharaohs: Egypt under the Ptolemies, 305–30 BC.* Princeton, NJ: Princeton University Press.

(2019) The Ptolemaic governmental branches and the role of temples and elite groups. In Vandorpe, K. (ed.) *A companion to Greco-Roman and late antique Egypt.* Hoboken, NJ: John Wiley and Sons, pp. 103–117.

Martin-Jones, M., Blackledge, A., & A. Creese (2012) Introduction: a sociolinguistics of multilingualism for our times. In Martin-Jones et al. (eds.) *The Routledge Handbook of Multilingualism.* London/New York: Routledge, pp. 1–26.

Maxwell, A. (2009) *Choosing Slovakia: Slavic Hungary, the Czechoslovak language and accidental nationalism.* London/New York: I.B. Tauris.

May, S. (2016) Language, imperialism, and the modern nation-state system: Implications for language rights. In Garcia, O., Flores, N. & M. Spotti (eds.) *The Oxford Handbook of Language and Society.* Oxford: Oxford University Press.

Metcalfe, A. (2003) *Muslims and Christians in Norman Sicily: Arabic speakers and the end of Islam.* New York/London: Routledge.

Molnár, I. & L. Szarka (2010) *Memories and reflections of the dispossessed: A collection of memoirs for the 60th anniversary of the Czechoslovak–Hungarian population exchange.* Komarom, Hungary.

Moreno, A. (2012) *Arabicizing, privileges, and liturgy in medieval Castilian Toledo: the problems and mutations of Mozarab identification (1085–1436).* Ph.D. dissertation, University of California Los Angeles.

Mullen, A. (2013) *Southern Gaul and the Mediterranean: Multilingualism and multiple identities in the Iron Age and Roman periods.* Cambridge: Cambridge University Press.

Mullen, A. & P. James (eds.) (2012) *Multilingualism in the Graeco-Roman worlds.* Cambridge: Cambridge University Press.

Murre-van den Berg, H., Sanchez Summerer, K., & T. Baarda (eds.) (2020) *Arabic and its alternatives: Religious minorities and their languages in the emerging nation states of the Middle East (1920–1950).* Leiden: Brill.

Nekvapil, J. & T. Sherman (2018) Managing superdiversity in multinational companies. In Creese, A. & A. Blackledge (eds.) *The Routledge Handbook of Language and Superdiversity: An Interdisciplinary Perspective.* London/New York: Routledge, pp. 329–344.

Nickson, T. (2015) Remembering Fernando: Multilingualism in medieval Iberia. In Eastmond, A. (ed.) *Viewing inscriptions in the late antique and medieval world.* Cambridge: Cambridge University Press, pp. 169–186.

Noy, D. (2000) *Foreigners at Rome: Citizens and strangers.* London: Duckworth/The Classical Press of Wales.

Nye, C. (2013) Naturalising Newham – radical plan to boost integration. *BBC.* Retrieved at www.bbc.com/news/uk-24146572

O"Callaghan, J. (1993) *The learned king: The reign of Alfonso X of Castile.* Philadelphia: University of Pennsylvania Press.

Offord, D., Rjeoutski, V., & G. Argent (2018) *The French language in Russia: A social, political, cultural and literary history.* Amsterdam: Amsterdam University Press.

Pahta, P., Skaffari, J. & L. Wright (eds.) (2018) *Multilingual practices in language history: English and beyond.* Berlin: Mouton De Gruyter.

Papaconstantinou, A. (ed.) (2010) *The multilingual experience in Egypt, from the Ptolemies to the Abbasids.* Burlington, VT: Ashgate.

Pavlenko, A. (2011a) Linguistic russification in the Russian Empire: peasants into Russians? *Russian Linguistics*, 35, 331–350.

(2011b) Language rights versus speakers' rights: on the applicability of Western language rights approaches in Eastern European contexts. *Language Policy*, 10, 37–58.

(2013) Language management in the Russian Empire, Soviet Union, and post-Soviet countries. In Bayley, R., Cameron, R. & C. Lucas (eds.) *The Oxford Handbook of Sociolinguistics.* Oxford: Oxford University Press, pp. 651–679.

(2019) Superdiversity and why it isn't: Reflections on terminological innovation and academic branding. In Schmenk, B., Breidbach, S. & L. Küster (eds.) *Sloganization in language education discourse: Conceptual thinking in the age of academic marketization.* Bristol: Multilingual Matters, pp. 142–168.

Pavlenko, A. & A. Mullen (2015) Why diachronicity matters in the study of linguistic landscapes. *Linguistic Landscape*, 1, 1–2, 114–132.

Peretz, D. (2006) The Roman interpreter and his diplomatic and military roles. *Historia: Zeitschrift für Alte Geschichte*, 55, 4, 451–470.

Pick, L. (2004) *Conflict and coexistence: Archbishop Rodrigo and the Muslims and Jews of medieval Spain.* Ann Arbor, MI: The University of Michigan Press.

Piller, I. (2016) Monolingual ways of seeing multilingualism. *Journal of Multicultural Discourses*, 11, 1, 25–33.

Prokopovych, M., Bethke, C. & T. Scheer (eds.) (2019) *Language diversity in the late Habsburg Empire.* Leiden/Boston: Brill.

Rubin, J. (2018) *Learning in a crusader city: Intellectual activity and intercultural exchanges in Acre, 1191–1291.* Cambridge: Cambridge University Press.

Sabaté-Dalmau, M. (2018) Multilingualism in migrant-tailored businesses: The case of telecommunications, multinationals and "ethnic" call shops. In Creese, A. & A. Blackledge (eds.) *The Routledge Handbook of Language and Superdiversity: An Interdisciplinary Perspective.* London/New York: Routledge, pp. 361–376.

Sarmiento-Pérez, M. (2016) Interpreting for the Inquisition. In Takeda, K. & J. Baigorri-Jalón (eds.) *New insights in the history of interpreting.* Amsterdam: John Benjamins, pp. 47–73.

Scheer, T. (2016) Habsburg Languages at War: "The linguistic confusion at the tower of Babel couldn't have been worse." In Walker, J. & C. Declercq (eds.) *Languages and the First World War: Communicating in a Transnational War*. London: Palgrave, pp. 62–78.

(2017) Linguistic strife in times of war. https://scilog.fwf.ac.at/en/humanities-and-social-sciences/6974/linguistic-strife-times-war

Silova, I. (2006) *From sites of occupation to symbols of multiculturalism: Reconceptualizing minority education in post-Soviet Latvia*. Greenwich, CT: Information Age Publishing.

Smelik, W. (2013) *Rabbis, language and translation in late antiquity*. Cambridge: Cambridge University Press.

Song, H., Eberl, J, & O. Eisele (2020) Less fragmented than we thought? Towards clarification of a subdisciplinary linkage in communication science, 2010–2019. *Journal of Communication*, 70, 310–334.

Spolsky, B. (2009) *Language management*. Cambridge: Cambridge University Press.

Strauss, J. (2011) Linguistic diversity and everyday life in the Ottoman cities of the Eastern Mediterranean and the Balkans (late 19th–early 20th century). *The History of the Family*, 16, 2, 126–141.

Tosi, A. (2020) *Language and the Grand Tour: Linguistic experiences of travelling in early modern Europe*. Cambridge: Cambridge University Press.

Trotter, D. (ed.) (2000) *Multilingualism in later medieval Britain*. Suffolk: D.S. Brewer.

Tsurushima, H. (1995) *Domesday Interpreters*. Anglo-Norman Studies, 18, 201–222.

Vandorpe, K. & S. Waebens (2009) *Reconstructing Pathyris' archives. A multicultural community in Hellenistic Egypt*. Brussel: Koninklijke Academie van België.

Vierros, M. (2012) *Bilingual notaries in Hellenistic Egypt: A study of Greek as a second language*. Brussel: Koninklijke Academie van België.

Ward, J. M. (2013) *Priest, politician, collaborator: Jozef Tiso and the making of fascist Slovakia*. Ithaca, NY/London: Cornell University Press.

Wellenreuther, H. (2005) Preface and acknowledgments. In Wellenreuther, C. & C. Wessel (eds.) *The Moravian mission diaries of David Zeisberger, 1772–1781*. University Park, PA: The Pennsylvania State University, pp. vii–viii.

Witcombe, T. (2018) Maurice and the Mozarabic charter: A cross-cultural transaction in early thirteenth-century Toledo. *Journal of Medieval Arabic Studies*, 10, 2, 234–256.

Wolf, M. (2015) *The Habsburg monarchy's many-languaged soul: Translating and interpreting, 1848–1918*. Translated by K. Sturge. Amsterdam/Philadelphia, PA: John Benjamins.

Woodbine, G. (1943) The language of English law. *Speculum*, 18, 4, 395–436.

Wright, H. C. (1982) Ancient burials of metallic foundation documents in stone boxes. *University of Illinois Graduate School of Library and Information Science Occasional Papers*, 157, 1–41.

Yiftach-Firanko, U. (2009) Law in Graeco-Roman Egypt: Hellenization, fusion, romanization. In Bagnall, R. (ed.) *The Oxford Handbook of Papyrology*. Oxford: Oxford University Press, pp. 541–560.

Zeitler, B. (1996) "Urbs felix dotata populo trilingui": Some thoughts about a twelfth-century funerary memorial from Palermo. *Medieval Encounters*, 2, 2, 114–139.

2 Greek Meets Egyptian at the Temple Gate: Bilingual Papyri from Hellenistic and Roman Egypt (Third Century BCE–Fourth Century CE)

Anastasia Maravela

The linguistic cohabitation of Egyptian and Greek in Egypt is one of the longest in the ancient world. It extends from the conquest of the country by a Greek army led by Alexander of Macedon (332 BCE) until sometime after the Arab conquest (641 CE). While throughout this time Egyptian remained the majority language, under the Ptolemies Greek became the linguistic vehicle for state administration, one of two languages used for the administration of justice, and the language privileged by the country's cultural elites. Greek retained its roles and prestige after Egypt's incorporation into the Roman Empire (30 BCE), while Egyptian came under hard pressure as a means of written communication and eventually transitioned to an alphabetic script based on Greek – a language we know as Coptic.

This chapter will present the sources and contexts of Greek–Egyptian bilingualism and will outline the main angles from which the phenomenon has been approached in research carried out at the interface of papyrology, Egyptology, linguistics, and ancient history. The core of the chapter presents a selection of case studies that give glimpses into the shifting relations between the two languages over time and exemplify typical bilingual settings and interactions, and the questions raised about them. Where possible, examples will be derived from the domain of religion, broadly defined. This vantage point appears advantageous for multiple reasons. An important reason is its potential to yield new perspectives that will complement the earlier studies and accounts of multilingualism in Egypt (e.g., Bagnall, 2021; Depauw, 2012; Fournet, 2009; Lieven, 2018; Papaconstantinou, 2010; Peremans, 1964, 1983; Rémondon, 1964; Rochette, 1996; Thompson, 2009; Torallas Tovar, 2010a,b; Torallas Tovar & Vierros, 2019; Vierros, 2012, 2014). Another reason is the key role that the Egyptian religious functionaries, priests, and temple-trained scribes played as part of the Ptolemaic administrative machine. This role, that facilitated greatly the Greek rule in Egypt, was contingent on bilingualism. A third, no less important, reason is that in the realm of religion the relative

I am grateful to the reviewers for constructive comments and to Aneta Pavlenko for important feedback, inspiring discussions, careful editorial work, and, not least, patience.

positions of the two languages were less given than in the other arenas in which they interacted. In fact, Egyptian was the conveyor of a venerable religious tradition that fascinated the Greek segment of the population and motivated cultural and linguistic transmission from Egyptian to Greek.

The fascination that the Egyptian religious and historical traditions could exert on Greeks is evidenced by the closing lines of a hymn inscribed on the forecourt gate of the temple of Isis-Thermouthis at Narmouthis (Medinet Madi) in the Arsinoite district (Fayum). It was one of four hymns in traditional Greek meters and diction that an otherwise unknown individual with the Egyptian-inspired Greek name Isidorus ('gift of Isis') dedicated sometime in the 80s BCE. The closing verses of the hymn comment on the incorporation in it of Egyptian lore, in particular of legends about Pramarres, the deified Middle Kingdom ruler Amenemhat III, founder of the Narmouthis temple:

> Having learned these things with certainty from men who research and record the past / and having myself inscribed and set them all up publicly, / *I translated* for the benefit of Greeks the power of a prince who was a god / since no other mortal possessed such power. (Hymn IV, 37–40 my translation and emphasis[1])

Isidorus advertises his mediating role in the transfer of knowledge from the Egyptian tradition to interested speakers of Greek. He takes pride in the linguistic competence that allows him to "translate" (*hermēneusa*) an Egyptian tradition and set it up in Greek linguistic and literary guise on the temple gate where it would be accessible to monolingual visitors. So great is Isidorus' linguistic self-consciousness that he even claims a share in the power attributed to the legendary god-king by dint of subtly disguised ambiguity: "No other mortal" in the last verse may refer both to Pramarres and the bilingual translator/poet.

By referring to his hymns as "translations," Isidorus expressly inscribed his act of linguistic and cultural mediation in a tradition pioneered circa two centuries earlier by the Egyptian priest Manetho. The historian Flavius Josephus informs us that in *Aegyptiaca*, a universal chronicle with the focus on Egyptian history and religious tradition intended for a Greek readership, Manetho undertook "to translate the Egyptian history from the sacred writings [i.e. writings in Hieroglyphic and Hieratic]."[2] This programmatic statement by Manetho, which Josephus presumably reported accurately, launched the tradition of communication and translation from Egyptian to Greek in the domain of religion but was not met with unanimous approval in Egyptian priestly circles (Rochette, 1995).

[1] An alternative translation can be found in Moyer (2016, p. 233).
[2] Josephus, *Against Apion* 1.26.

Isidorus was one of those who by virtue of their language skills facilitated the flow of religious ideas and traditions from Egyptian to Greek. His cultural adherence – since at that late phase of the Hellenistic period it makes little sense to speak of ethnic Greeks or ethnic Egyptians – and his precise association with the temple are uncertain. More significant is the location in which he chose to display his 'translation' – the gate of the Narmouthis temple (Moyer, 2016). As the inner space of Egyptian temples was accessible to priests only, the temple gate and the sacred way leading up to it were arenas of manifold activities (financial, judicial, civic, etc.) and hence a hub of interactions, linguistic and cultural, between inhabitants of diverse linguistic backgrounds (Clarysse, 2010a).

2.1 The Sources and Research Methods on Bilingualism in Hellenistic and Roman Egypt

The keys to unlocking Egypt's bilingual culture have been provided by papyri, inscriptions, and graffiti in the two languages. The study of these source texts gathered pace after Napoleon's campaign (1798–1801) and the decipherment of Hieroglyphs by Champollion (1822). The inscription on which this milestone development relied, the 'Rosetta stone,' is a bilingual/three-script document in Egyptian (Hieroglyphic and Demotic) and in Greek, with a religious background. It records the decree by which the congregation of the Egyptian priests at Memphis (196 BCE) conferred honours on Ptolemy V Epiphanes for benefactions to the temples and his love of Egypt and its people (Bowman et al. 2021, no. 126). Its role in the decipherment of Egypt's earliest writing system is emblematic of the role played by documentary evidence (papyri, inscriptions, etc.) in illuminating Egypt's bilingual culture. The authoritative statement of the Egyptian priests also foregrounds the significance of religion and its practitioners in Greek–Egyptian linguistic interactions.

Papyri and inscriptions host a wide variety of written text types: literary and official texts, as well as texts that document life in the Greco-Egyptian society in its different phases and aspects at various social levels. Official and private correspondence, petitions and declarations to authorities, private agreements, court proceedings, handbooks of magic and applied spells, medical treatises and prescriptions, school texts, hymns, prayers, oracular questions, horoscopes, mummy labels, and funerary inscriptions are only a sample of the text types represented among this rich source material.

The textual corpus is sufficiently wide-ranging in space and time and socioculturally diverse to offer a cross-section of language use and interactions under Greek and Roman rule. However, this rich body of evidence also poses challenges. A serious challenge is that the research basis consists exclusively of written texts. The perspectives thus gained pertain largely to language use in written communication; in certain cases, what we get is views on biliteracy (Mairs, 2012). On the other hand, as some of the case studies discussed below demonstrate, oral communication is not entirely out of sight. Some texts allow assumptions or raise questions about the language(s) of the oral interactions preceding or following the production of a written text. Moreover, the chance survival of the material and the uncertainties surrounding the provenance of texts that have emerged by way of the antiquities trade entail that our view of the linguistic tableau in Hellenistic and Roman Egypt is bound to remain partial. By far the most conspicuous gap concerns the linguistic environment in the capital, Alexandria. As the papyri from the city have perished due to the humid climate in the Nile delta, reconstruction of the linguistic mosaic in that major urban center relies on the limited number of texts from Alexandria recovered elsewhere, the inscriptions from the city, and linguistic perspectives embedded in literary texts. Finally, a balanced evaluation of Greek–Egyptian bilingualism requires publication of more source texts in Demotic and, not least, collaboration between experts in Greek and in Demotic papyrology so that complete studies of bilingual texts can be produced to complement the perspectives gained by some recent milestone publications (Mairs & Martin, 2008–2009; Renberg & Naether, 2010; Vandorpe & Vleeming, 2017).

To understand Greek–Egyptian bilingualism/biliteracy, scholars examine (a) the content of the relevant texts, (b) their language, and/or (c) material and graphic aspects. Information about the circumstances in which the text was produced, the persons mentioned, their relations and activities, as well as references to written or oral communication in Greek or Egyptian have allowed researchers to identify typical bilingual settings and intermediaries. The grammar of the text (spelling and morpho-syntactical variation, semantic shifts, nonstandard expressions) indicate the degree of a scribe's familiarity with Greek or Egyptian and disclose first language (L1) influence. The script and/or scribal implements used, and the relation between the language(s) and structure of a text also contribute insights on linguistic competences.

The evidence that occupies center stage in the study of Greek–Egyptian bilingualism includes (a) bilingual documents, written partly in Greek and partly in Egyptian and (b) bilingual archives, that is, assemblages of documents that pertain to an individual or a group (typically, a family) that comprise documents in Greek, in Egyptian and/or bilingual documents. Monolingual texts are not devoid of interest either, especially when they contain mentions of code-switching, oral interpretation, (in)ability to write or communicate orally in Greek or in Egyptian, or when they display language use typical for bilinguals (peculiar spellings, calques, expressions translated literally, etc.). Translations, explicitly presenting themselves as such or identifiable on other grounds, indicate the social sectors in which bilingual professionals were active. In the case of Egyptian and Greek pride of place is held by religious settings, notarial offices, and the law courts.

Accordingly, the prevailing approaches to Egyptian–Greek language contact have been sociohistorical and sociolinguistic, with greater or lesser emphasis on either element or a balanced combination. The former approach has been pioneered in studies of bilingualism by Egyptologists, papyrologists, and ancient historians with a particularly active research tradition in the Low Countries (Clarysse, Peremans, Pestman, Rochette, Vandorpe, and others). Adams' (2003) monograph examining the contacts between Latin and indigenous languages within the Roman Empire has stimulated a flood of sociolinguistic studies of language interactions within the empire and beyond (e.g., Adams et al., 2002; Mullen & James, 2012; Vierros, 2012). Finally, important insights into the interplay between scribal traditions and language choice have been generated by studies informed by the principles of material philology (Cromwell & Grossman, 2017).

2.2 Case Studies

2.2.1 Dreams of Bilinguals

Among the earliest and most interesting bilingual papyri from Hellenistic Egypt is a private letter in Greek, below which the sender has added a dream narrative in Demotic (Renberg & Naether, 2010). The papyrus has been assigned to the latter half of the third century BCE, that is, within a century or so from the Greek conquest. The letter was sent from a man called Ptolemaios to a friend called Achilles. The sender's name was associated with the Macedonian-Greek dynasty, while the recipient has the name of the legendary protagonist of Homer's *Iliad*. Achilles may have resided in the Arsinoite district (Fayum), an area densely populated with Greek settlers. The correspondents may have been either descendants of the settlers or Hellenized Egyptians (Prada, 2013; Renberg & Naether, 2010). Parts of the letter are lost or obscure, but this is what can be gleaned from what remains. Ptolemaios informs his friend about a dream he had, that apparently concerns Achilles. The formulation that connects the letter with the dream narrative reads as follows:

> *[I]t also (?) seemed good to me that I should fully inform you about the dream, so that you will know in what way the gods know you. I have written below in Egyptian, so that you will know precisely.* When I was about to go to sleep, I wrote two short letters, the one concerning Taunchis the daughter of Thermouthis, the other concerning Tetimouthis the daughter of Taues, who is the daughter of Ptolemaios. And yet one more [letter] exiting I placed . . . [the text breaks off]. (translated in Renberg & Naether, 2010, pp. 51, 54, my emphasis)

In the conclusion of the letter Ptolemaios exhorts Achilles to "pour a drink for [/anoint] yourself, in which manner *I too celebrated a fine day*." He introduces the Demotic dream narrative thus: "I saw myself in a dream in the following way: I am standing at the doorway of the sanctuary. A priest is sitting there, and many people are standing beside him." The narrative is concluded with the reassurance, issued either by the narrator (Ptolemaios) or by the priest who figures in it: "Psais, <the> great god, *knows your name*, I recognized (?) it in my heart. The good order, may it be known" (translated in Renberg & Naether, 2010, p. 54, my emphasis).

Before commenting on the language and contents of this remarkable document, it is worth noting that Ptolemaios writes both the Greek and the Demotic sections with a reed pen, the writing implement of Greek scribes, instead of switching to the rush pen traditionally used by scribes of Demotic (Kidd, 2013; Tait, 1988). He thus adheres to a new scribal fashion, that of writing Demotic with a reed pen, that emerged at around the time when the letter was written and that has been associated with bilingual scribes trained in both traditions (Clarysse, 1993). Ptolemaios' Greek is competent and free from spelling errors. It has two remarkable features: (a) verbal echoes of the administrative jargon (*diasaphēsai* [to fully inform you]; *hypegrapsa* [I have written below]) and (b) expressive Egyptianisms, the most remarkable of which is the expression "I celebrated a fine day" (*hēmeran kalēn ēgagon*). It is unattested in Greek and is considered to be a translation of the Egyptian phrase *ir hrw nfr*, which designates celebration and (often uncontrolled) festivity occasioned by a religious festival (Renberg & Naether, 2010; Prada, 2013). In my view, a more accurate description of this expression is as a combination of Greek loan translation of the Egyptian "good/fine day" (*hrw nfr = hēmeran kalēn)* with the Greek verb used in the phrase "celebrate a religious festival" (*agō heortēn)*. Ptolemaios' transposition of an Egyptian religious concept into Greek produces a syntactically and semantically innovative fusion of the two languages.

The expression "in what way the gods know you," which is not idiomatic in Greek either, is likely to have an Egyptian background too. Even if no precise equivalent can be offered in Egyptian, it is echoed in the expression "Psais ... *knows your name*" in the Demotic part and reflects the Egyptian belief that dreams convey messages about the attitude of the gods and therefore offer the opportunity to humans to influence the divine will (Renberg & Naether, 2010). In sum, the graphic and linguistic picture of the document reveals the impact of advanced bilingualism with linguistic innovations in both directions. This would have been the result of substantial contact with both languages, which would have been achieved either through scribal training and administrative work, as indicated by other features in the language of the letter, or through a mixed family background.

As to the relation between the language in which the dream was conveyed (Egyptian) and the language in which Ptolemaios usually dreamed, the issue is complicated since the dream reported was in all likelihood an incubated dream, that is, a dream induced by sleeping in a temple with the purpose of divination. In Egypt and other ancient cultures, the messages conveyed by divinatory dreams were encoded in puns or word plays, the 'keys' to which were found in dream interpretation manuals. The code-switch for the dream conveys above all the Egyptian religious frame within which dream interpretation was sought, not necessarily the primary dreaming language of Ptolemaios himself, whatever his ethnic or cultural identity and his L1 may have been (Kidd, 2011; Prada, 2013). In any case, encoding and comprehension of puns indicates advanced proficiency in Egyptian.

Half a century or so later, in the much better documented setting of the Serapeum at Saqqâra, the necropolis west of Memphis, we come across a pair of bilingual siblings who also recorded their own and others' dreams in Greek and Demotic (Legras, 2011; Thompson, 2012; Wilcken, 1927). The two brothers were offspring of a Macedonian soldier-settler. The older brother, Ptolemaios, spent twenty years (ca. 172–152 BCE) in voluntary confinement at the precinct of Astarte/Ishtar. Ptolemaios' dreams were recorded in Greek (Lewis, 1986). This is hardly surprising given his insistence on his Greek identity in petitions concerning disputes he had with Egyptians. More perplexing is that he recorded in Greek dreams of individuals with Egyptian names, to wit the young woman Taues and the man Nektembes. Their dreams contain first-person sequences, that is, we hear the dreamer narrate her/his dream and report her/his own words and the words of others, as for example, in Taues' dream: "I wished to turn back; I was saying that *all these many together are nine*. They said: '*yes, you are released; you may go*.' It is late for me" (translated in Lewis, 1986, pp. 81–82, my emphasis).

This discontinuity raises a question: Would a native speaker of Egyptian dream in Greek or did Taues communicate her dream to Ptolemaios in Egyptian and he translated it into Greek to submit to one of the Greek dream-interpreters at the Serapeum (Renberg, 2017)? We know that Taues and her twin sister needed the brothers' writing services to compose petitions in Greek, but we do not know whether she had oral communication skills in Greek. If she had, it is not inconceivable that she had dreams in Greek since comparative studies show that bilingual dreaming does not require a high level of second language (L2) proficiency (Sicard & de Bot, 2013). At any rate, most of the communication between the twin sisters and the Macedonian brothers, Ptolemaios and Apollonios, is likely to have been in Egyptian.

Similar questions are raised by two Demotic dream records attributed to Apollonios (Botti, 1941; Bresciani et al., 1978; Legras, 2011). Did Apollonios, who wrote mostly in Greek, dream in Egyptian? Or did Demotic priest-scribes translate his dreams from Greek? The former option is a strong probability as some of the linguistic traits of Apollonios' Greek reflect the influence of Egyptian (Vierros, 2021). It is all the more interesting that a double identity is negotiated in one of these dreams: "Second [dream]. A man sings: *Apollonios in Greek, Peteharenpi in Egyptian is the one who knows this*" (after Quack, 2008, p. 373, my emphasis). The speaker identifies Apollonios in Greek and then gives the Egyptian equivalent of his name (Peteharenpi means 'the one who Horus of Buto [Greek equivalent: Apollo] has given'). The double identification of Apollonios almost certainly nods to the practice of 'polyonymy,' that is, the use of double names by individuals. Research into this social practice in Hellenistic Egypt suggests that its popularity rose steadily from the second century BCE and that one of the most common name combinations was that of corresponding theophoric names – one Greek, the other Egyptian (Coussement, 2016). There is no evidence that Apollonios had a double name in real life, but the dream at least holds out this possibility for him.

Awareness of Greek–Egyptian linguistic and theological equivalents is attested by another papyrus copied by Apollonios. It contains the Greek version of a piece of Egyptian historical fiction, *Nectanebos' Dream*, or *The Prophecy of Petesis* (Ryholt, 2002; Wilcken, 1927, pp. 369–374). The multiple Egyptian formulae reflected in the Greek text leave no doubt that we are faced with a translation that discloses the linguistic and theological adaptations of the Egyptian hypotext when it supplies the Egyptian word for the boat that transports god Onuris ("a papyrus boat, called *rōmps* in Egyptian, came to anchor at Memphis") and the Greek equivalent of this divine figure ("called Onuris in Egyptian and Ares in Greek").

The large archive of ostraca, also from Saqqâra, that belonged to the funerary priest Ḥor of Sebennytos, furnishes a comparable view of the language competence of a mobile Egyptian religious functionary active in the same sanctuary at around the same time (ca. 167/6–147 BCE). Ḥor had held a lower-class priestly office at Isiopolis (Delta) before moving to Saqqâra to give his services to the ibis-cult associated with Thoth, the god of writing. Ḥor's written record – oracular dreams pertaining to contemporary events apparently communicated to the king, personal dreams, petitions, memoranda, and hymns – is almost exclusively in Demotic (Jennes, 2019; Ray, 1976). Sole exceptions are drafts of a dream oracle from Hermes Trismegistos addressed to the country's rulers (Ray, 1976, pp. 1–6). The Greek of these drafts is "execrable" (according to Ray), with major problems of syntax and semantics and at least one sequence in draft B depends directly on Egyptian (Ray, 1976, p. 3). Ḥor's writings indicate that he operated in a Egypto-centric universe in contrast to the linguistically mixed world of Ptolemaios and his younger brother Apollonios. It is noteworthy that the only two references to a language/script in Ḥor's writings concern Egyptian: "speaking the words of the Egyptian(s)" and "I gave it to him (in) writing of the Egyptian(s)" (Ray, 1976, pp. 5, 112). Hor turned to Greek only when he needed to pass his message across to the Greek-speaking authorities at the highest level. Even then, and despite the faultless spelling, the Greek text went through several drafts to reach a syntactically functional state – which indicates a low level of competence in and minimal active use of this language.

2.2.2 Egyptians in Contact with Greek: Bilingual Archives

There is virtually no chance that we will manage to form an accurate picture of communication in the army, in the markets, and on the streets where Greek and Egyptian speakers mixed on a daily basis. We are better placed when it comes to notarial offices, vital nodes of language contact, where oral discourse of the transacting parties was translated into written text in one language, the other, or both.

Egyptian notary offices were traditionally attached to a temple and notarial deeds contained the clause that the notary "writes in the name of the priests of . . ." (Chaufray & Wegner, 2016; Zauzich, 1968). Scribal training took place under the auspices of temples. Scribes often held priestly office and priests held multiple scribal titles that reflected their administrative tasks (Arlt, 2008; Muhs, 2005). As a result of a policy of expanding the network of Greek notary (agoranomic) offices and making the registration of Demotic legal instruments mandatory from 146/5 BCE, the volume of business at temple notary offices shrank and so did temple income (Pestman, 1985a).

Greek notarial offices recruited bilingual scribes. Some were members of the established Egyptian families of temple-trained scribes, who used Greek names when acting as agoranomic notaries and Egyptian names in their private transactions (Pestman, 1978; Vandorpe, 2011; Vierros, 2012). The proficiency of Greek notarial scribes in Demotic has been proven for the early Roman Arsinoite district (Fayum) where, even in strongholds of Egyptian cults (Tebtynis, Soknopaiou Nesos), the Demotic titles of notary scribes reveal their identity with the known 'Greek' notaries (Muhs, 2005). Their bilingualism and ability to serve Greek and Egyptian clients alike probably played a part in the success of the Greek notarial offices, especially in areas with dense Egyptian populations (Vandorpe, 2011).

Bilingual papyrological archives of funerary priests spanning from the second century BCE to the early first century CE indicate that in these circles Greek was used for the mandated liaisons with the authorities or in connection with disputes referred to Greek magistrates or Greek courts (Clarysse, 2010b). Petitions to higher authorities were in Greek. This is exemplified nicely by a series of appeals for protection addressed to Ptolemy X Alexander I by another of the funerary priests active at Saqqâra, Peteesis, son of Chonouphis at 99–98 BCE (Thompson, 2012; Wilcken, 1927, pp. 453–472). Greek was also the language of transactions involving state revenues. This is evidenced by the tax receipts and an agreement regulating dues in connection with mummification rights, all in Greek, in the archive of the undertakers of Apollonos polis, Cynopolite district (Clarysse, 2007, 2010b).

Translations of documents from Demotic were made in the context of disputes referred to Greek magistrates or Greek courts, the popularity of which grew steadily among Egyptians. When in 117 BCE the funerary priest Horos was caught up in a dispute over the ownership of a house in Great Diospolis (Thebes/Luxor), his lawyer produced a Greek translation of the sale agreement, originally drawn up in Demotic, to support his client's claim to the property (Bagnall & Derow, 2004, pp. 218–225). Other translations of Egyptian documents into Greek in this and other archives were also made for use in court. Even documents without known context – but with the tag "translated [from Egyptian]" – are likely to have been produced in connection with legal battles (Vandorpe & Vleeming, 2017).

Thompson (2012) has stressed the contribution of legal engagements to Hellenization in Egypt. To illustrate the point, she analyzed the use of Greek by Peteesis' descendants at Saqqâra: When in 89 BCE Peteesis' son, Chonouphis, made out a loan to an Egyptian by the name Peteimouthes, the agreement was drawn up in Greek. Peteesis' granddaughter Thaues-Asklepias, whose Greek alias commemorates her father's association with the great Asklepieion near Memphis, had her Demotic marriage agreement registered in a Greek notarial office and referred the case against her husband for failure to comply with the terms to a Greek court. This option became available to Egyptians from 118 BCE when a royal decree connected the language of the documents with the court that would hear a potential dispute (Pestman, 1985b). Nevertheless, this generation's turn to Greek was not wholesale, since in 78 BCE the funerary revenues of Peteesis' homonymous grandson were stipulated in a Demotic agreement. The determining factor for the use of Greek by practitioners of the Egyptian religion was possibly pragmatism and the need for some sense of security, perhaps connected with the view of Greek courts as more powerful and the enforcement of their decisions as more efficient. In contrast, transactions pertaining to matters of traditional religion (mummification) and involving fellow Egyptians relied on Demotic.

Geographical situation within the country and the ethnic composition of the population in the area must have made a difference too. While the descendants of the Egyptian Peteesis at Saqqâra gravitated toward Greek two centuries after the inception of the Greek rule, language use in the family of the Greek cavalry officer Dryton at Pathyris south of Thebes apparently moved in the opposite direction in the mid-second century BCE. Dryton drew up three wills in Greek and even copied Greek poetry. His second wife, Apollonia-Senmonthis, had her private financial agreements drawn up mostly in Greek after 136 BCE when a Greek notary office opened at Pathyris. However, the next generation in the family turned to Demotic in their private affairs (loans, marriage contracts, divorce agreements). Only their petitions and some tax receipts are in Greek. The fact that their mother's family and the families of their spouses were firmly embedded in their Egyptian milieu and its legal preferences and traditions, as well as the location of Pathyris far from the more Hellenized parts of Egypt possibly played a role in the family's linguistic choices (Clarysse, 2010b; Vandorpe, 2002, 2014; Vierros, 2008).

The written trail of Dryton's family raises complex questions about oral, reading, and writing competences. It is possible that family members spoke both languages, but this is less certain of the female members. Dryton and his son Esthladas wrote passable Greek, but the former's competence in Demotic may have been limited. Since he received at least one letter in Demotic, Dryton may have had reading competence in Egyptian too (Vandorpe, 2002). Alternatively, he may have resorted to a notarial or other scribe who read it for him, as he and his family members did when they drew up notarial or private agreements in Egyptian. It is highly unlikely that Apollonia-Senmonthis was literate in any language since her husband wrote her accounts in Greek. This is even more certain for their daughters. The lack of private letters by or to the female members of the family could be an indication of illiteracy. This would be compatible with what we know about the education of women and what we know of this Egyptian-dominated community in which Dryton had difficulties getting hold of people literate in Greek to witness his will – instead he resorted to witnesses subscribing in Egyptian, three of them local priests (Vandorpe, 2014).

2.3 Egyptian in the Roman Period: From 'Collective Agraphia' to a Greek-Inspired Script

2.3.1 Speaking Egyptian, Writing 'Greek'

The position of Demotic as a language of private legal documents was critically affected by a set of requirements for contractually validated agreements that took effect in the late Ptolemaic/early Roman period (Depauw, 2012; Lewis, 1993). Signatures in the witnesses' chosen language were replaced by subscriptions of the transacting parties in Greek (Muhs, 2005). We encounter a hybrid practice in the documents from the archive of Satabous, a priest at Soknopaiou Nesos (Arsinoite district), drawn up at different points during the first hundred years of Roman rule (Hoogendijk & Feucht, 2013).

In 11 CE Satabous bought a house from a priest by the Greek name Chairemon. The agreement was drawn up at the Greek notary office at the village where the seller resided. The body of the agreement is in Demotic, followed by a summary of contents (registration note) in Greek, the declaration of the seller in Greek, and the declaration of the buyer in Demotic (Muhs, 2014, pp. 113–115). This bilingual arrangement suggests that Greek notary offices incorporated linguistic services formerly available through temple notaries. The graphic and material features of this impressive document confirm this idea. The Demotic sections are written with a reed pen, a writing implement associated with the Greek scribal tradition, while the overlap of the papyrus sheet-joins (right over left) reflects the direction of writing in Greek. This and other documents from the archive are transitional from a linguistic viewpoint too. By the end of the first century CE Demotic ceased to be used for notarial documents and other document types, such as tax receipts (Vandorpe & Clarysse, 2008). As priests in a stronghold of the Egyptian religion, Satabous and his descendants continued using bilingual legal documents and some of them (Satabous and his eldest son Herieus) subscribed in Egyptian, be it due to illiteracy in Greek or as a statement of identity. On the other hand, bilingual and Hellenized members of the Egyptian priesthood like Chairemon or the Kronion-Isidora family at Tebtynis (Hickey, 2012; Muhs, 2005) were far better adapted to the new climate created by the promotion of Greek by the Roman administration.

As Greek gained in prominence and Demotic was increasingly confined to the religious sphere (temple libraries, internal temple affairs, funerary industry), scribal competence in Demotic declined. This resulted in a state of "collective agraphia" (Fournet, 2020, p. 4) as the Egyptian-speaking majority was left with the sole option of using Greek for all types of written communication, including private correspondence. Very few letters in Demotic are extant after the late first century CE (Bagnall, 1993, 2021; Depauw, 2006). Thus, larger segments of the population became familiar with Greek – some for professional reasons and some with the aid of bilingual intermediaries (scribes or readers). This is illustrated by the note that prefaces a letter in Greek from the mid-second century CE. The letter was sent by a man called Ptolemaios to his mother, Zosime, and his sister, Rhodous. The addressees must have been illiterate in Greek since an added message instructs an anonymous intermediary: "You, whoever you are, who are reading the letter, make a small effort and translate to the women what is written in this letter and communicate it to them" (Bülow-Jacobsen & McCarren, 1985, pp. 78–79). The use of the technical term for translation (*methermēneuō*) indicates that the sender envisages the linguistic transposition of the message, apparently into Egyptian, which would have been the language spoken by the two women despite their nice Greek names.

Some of the phonological features of Ptolemaios' Greek, especially the confusion /e – o/ in unstressed syllables, testify to the influence of Egyptian phonology on his spelling. Studies of phonological and morpho-syntactical variation in the rich corpus of papyrus documents have demonstrated the value of an individualized sociolinguistic approach to language variation in documents, one that differentiates between internal developments in Greek and crosslinguistic influence (Bentein, 2015; Dahlgren & Leiwo, 2020; Leiwo, 2010, 2017; Stolk, 2017; Vierros, 2012, 2021). Features that indicate Egyptian influence on written Greek have been identified already in the third century BCE archives (Clarysse, 1993, 2010c; Evans, 2012). For a society in which the connection between language use and ethnic identity is not straightforward, the challenge is to distinguish between variation arising from (a) imperfect L2 command, (b) L2 influence on L1 in Greeks with prolonged exposure to Egyptian and (c) language contact phenomena. With the passage of time, Egyptian-influenced features manifested themselves in written Greek at all levels (Torallas Tovar, 2010b). Some researchers have even argued that from the second century CE an 'Egyptian variety' of Greek is discernible, at least on the phonological level, with stress-induced vowel reductions as its prime indicator (Dahlgren, 2016).

Linguistic influence of Greek on Egyptian appears modest before the adoption of the Coptic script. Greek loanwords in Demotic fall into certain, semantically specialized, groups: titles (for gods, kings, officials), derivatives of proper names, and terminology pertaining to the administration, the army, and economic life (Clarysse, 1987). These overlap to a large extent with realms of social life in which Greek held a dominant position. The picture changes dramatically with the emergence of the Coptic script. After this turning point the presence of Greek loanwords in Egyptian (now collected in the *Database and Dictionary of Greek Loanwords in Coptic*; see also Grossman et al., 2017) becomes all-pervasive. This puzzling development, which cannot have arisen from the slim basis of Greek loanwords in written Demotic, has received two complementary explanations: (a) that Greek loanwords were part of the oral repertory of Egyptians to a far greater extent than the written record indicates and (b) that the priest-scribes of Demotic filtered out Greek in an act of linguistic purism (Ray, 1994). An idiosyncratic corpus of second/third century CE texts on potsherds (ostraca) from the Narmouthis temple area indirectly confirms the first part of this explanation. They preserve coherent Demotic texts with syntactically integrated Greek legal and administrative words. This unique corpus of bigraphic texts takes us back to the domain of religion and the various activities under its auspices (administrative, educational, and scholarly) that harboured bilingualism and convergence.

2.3.2 *Egyptian 'Meets' Greek: Graphic Convergence*

During the Roman period the personnel of Egyptian temples was caught between competing pressures: on the one hand, the preservation of the indigenous religious-literary culture and the forms of writing in which it had been encoded and, on the other, adaptation to a new linguistic environment with increasing societal bilingualism. The temple libraries from Tebtynis and Soknopaiou Nesos testify that for the first two centuries of the Roman rule Egyptian priests and scribes held on to tradition. However, transactions with Roman authorities were carried out entirely in Greek. The shift of language of the popular 'oracular question tickets' to Greek may signal adaptation to the linguistic preferences of the clientele that sought this form of divination (Ripat, 2006). Part of the temple personnel must have been Greek-speaking, since Greek versions of internal temple manuals were in circulation, such as the translation of *The Book of the Temple* preserved on a papyrus now split between Oslo and Washington, P.Oslo I 2 + P.Wash.Univ. II 71 (Messerer, 2017, no. 10).

Increasing osmosis with Greek was presumably a propelling factor toward a milestone in the history of Egyptian, the development of the alphabetic script known as 'Coptic,' which proceeded in parallel with gradual abandonment of the traditional scripts for Egyptian. As late Demotic is close to Coptic, the rupture is not linguistic but graphic. The Coptic script, the earliest full-fledged specimens of which are assigned to the third century CE, is based on the Greek alphabet with six additional graphemes derived from Demotic for the Egyptian phonemes for which the Greek alphabet offered no satisfactory equivalents (Depauw, 2012; Fournet, 2020; Quack, 2017; Stadler, 2008). During a protracted transitional phase that starts in the late first century CE diverse graphic experiments, not necessarily connected to each other, evidence attempts to encode Egyptian using the Greek alphabet enhanced with Demotic-derived symbols. They are subsumed under the highly reductive term 'Old Coptic' (Love, 2016).

The uses to which the 'Old Coptic' script systems were put, and the types of texts encoded, provide clues about the circles that may have pioneered the graphic fusion of Egyptian and Greek. 'Old Coptic' scripts were used either for 'phonetic glossing' or to encode substantial, coherent texts (Quack, 2017). 'Phonetic glossing' refers here to annotations scribbled above text sequences written in older forms of Egyptian (Hieroglyphic, Hieratic). They serve the purpose of phonetic clarification, spelling out the vowels that were not noted in these script systems. Phonetic glossing appears in a broad spectrum of liturgical, literary, and ritual texts. It is also in evidence on Narmouthis potsherds in the form of inline transliterations of nouns, mostly divine names, also given in

Hieroglyphic or Hieratic. These texts are considered as products of a scholastic, scribal milieu (Giannotti, 2007; Rutherford, 2010). The longer coherent texts in 'Old Coptic' encode religious expressions with individual focus (a prayer for justice, a horoscope, and a related manual, a manual of lot divination, parts of handbooks of magic, mummy labels) or are of purely private character (Quack, 2017). Early specimens of standard Coptic (annotations, glossaries, and parts of notebooks with school exercises) are also remnants of scholastic educational activities (Fournet, 2020). From the present vantage point, it appears legitimate to connect the emergence of Coptic with the religious domain broadly defined and with the scholarly and scholastic activities that unfolded inside and around the gates of Egyptian temples.

Conclusion

In this chapter, I tried to show that the realm of religion broadly defined, where Egyptian enjoyed a strong position, may offer a nuanced view of Egypt's bilingual culture and of the relation between the native language and Greek. It is, therefore, worth special attention and further research at the interface of Greek and Demotic papyrology. Sociohistorical, sociolinguistic, and material approaches to the papyrological and inscriptional evidence raise important questions and yield insights in the constant negotiations between language use, identity, and factors such as family connections, education, requirements by the authorities, and religious practices.

Loss and fragmentation of the source material mean that a complete picture of bilingual settings and scenarios in the domain of religion in Greek and Roman Egypt is out of sight. We are, however, in a position to discern the crucial role of temple-trained scribes in the communication between the Egyptian-speaking majority and Greek authorities, as well as their contribution to the continuation of the native religious and legal traditions. While segments of the priesthood remained linguistically introvert for much of the Ptolemaic period, others were open to translation, cultural and linguistic. The incorporation of members of the Egyptian scribal families into Greek notary offices meant that bilingual notarial services were concentrated under the same roof, but the development ultimately undermined the economic power of the temples. The decisive push that the Romans gave to Greek by using it as a lingua franca propelled greater convergence. A manifestation of convergence is the development of Coptic, a result of graphic fusion of Egyptian and Greek. Its emergence, perhaps as a result of scholarly and scholastic activities in libraries and scribal schools attached to temples, confirms the significance of the domain of religion as an arena for bilingual encounters in Egypt and a field worth further investigation.

References

Adams, J.N. (2003) *Bilingualism and the Latin Language*. Cambridge: Cambridge University Press.

Adams, J.N., Janse, M. & S. Swain (eds.) (2002) *Bilingualism in ancient society: Language contact and the written text*. Oxford: Oxford University Press.

Arlt, C. (2008) The Egyptian notary offices in the Ptolemaic Fayum. In Lippert, S.L. & M. Schentuleit (eds.) *The Graeco-Roman Fayum. Texts and Archaeology*. Wiesbaden: Harrassowitz, pp. 15–26.

Bagnall, R. S. (1993) *Egypt in late antiquity*. Princeton: Princeton University Press.

(2021) *Roman Egypt: A history*. Cambridge: Cambridge University Press.

Bagnall, R. S. & P. Derow (2004) *The Hellenistic period: Historical sources in translation*. Malden, MA/Oxford: Blackwell.

Bentein, K. (2015) The Greek documentary papyri as a linguistically heterogeneous corpus: The case of the "*Katochoi* of the Sarapeion" archive. *Classical World*, 108, 461–484.

Botti, G. (1941) *Testi Demotici I* [Demotic texts I]. Firenze: Tipografia Enrico Ariani.

Bowman, A., Crowther, C., Hornblower, S., Mairs, R. & K. Savvopoulos (2021) *Corpus of Ptolemaic Inscriptions. Part I: Greek, Bilingual, and Trilingual Inscriptions from Egypt. Vol. 1: Alexandria and the Delta* (Nos. 1–206). Oxford: Oxford University Press.

Bresciani E., Bedini E., Paolini L. & F. Silvano (1978) Una rilettura dei Pap. Dem. Bologna 3173 e 3171 [A re-reading of Pap. Dem. Bologna 3173 and 3171]. *Egitto e Vicino Oriente*, 1, 95–104.

Bülow-Jacobsen, A. & V. McCarren (1985) P.Haun.14, P.Mich.679, and P.Haun.15: A re-edition. *Zeitschrift für Papyrologie und Epigraphik*, 58, 71–79.

Chaufray, M.-P. & W. Wegner (2016) Two early Ptolemaic documents from Pathyris. In Lippert, S.L., Schentuleit, M. & M. Stadler (eds.) *Sapientia Felicitas. Festschrift für Günter Vittmann*. Montpellier: Université Paul Valéry, pp. 23–49.

Clarysse, W. (1987) Greek loan-words in Demotic. In Vleeming, S. (ed.) *Aspects of Demotic lexicography. Acts of the Second International Conference for Demotic Studies (Leiden, 19–21 September 1984)*. Leuven: Peeters, pp. 9–33.

(1993) Egyptian scribes writing Greek. *Chronique d'Égypte*, 68, 186–201.

(2007) A bilingual archive from the Cynopolite Nome. In *Proceedings of the 24th International Congress of Papyrology, Helsinki 01–07.08.2004*. Helsinki: Finnish Society of Sciences and Letters, pp. 185–189.

(2010a) Egyptian temples and priests: Graeco-Roman. In Lloyd, A. (ed.) *A Companion to Ancient Egypt, Volume I*. Malden, MA/Oxford/Chichester: Blackwell, pp. 274–290.

(2010b) Bilingual papyrological archives. In Papaconstantinou, A. (ed.) *The multilingual experience in Egypt from the Ptolemies to the 'Abbāsids*. Farnham: Ashgate, pp. 47–72.

(2010c) Linguistic diversity in the archive of the engineers Kleon and Theodoros. In Evans, T. & D. Obbink (eds.) *The language of the papyri*. Oxford: Oxford University Press, pp. 35–50.

Coussement, S. (2016) *'Because I am Greek.' Polyonymy as an expression for ethnicity in Ptolemaic Egypt*. Leuven/Paris/Bristol CT: Peeters.

Cromwell, J. & E. Grossman (eds.) (2017) *Scribal repertories in Egypt from the New Kingdom to the early Islamic period*. Oxford: Oxford University Press.

Dahlgren, S. (2016) Towards a definition of an Egyptian Greek Variety. *Papers in Historical Phonology*, 1, 90–108.

Dahlgren, S. & M. Leiwo (2020) Confusion of mood or phoneme? The impact of L1 phonology on verb semantics. In Rafiyenko, D. & I. Seržant (eds.) *Postclassical Greek. Contemporary approaches to philology and linguistics*. Berlin/Boston: De Gruyter Mouton, pp. 283–301.

Depauw, M. (2006) *The Demotic letter. A study of epistolographic scribal traditions against their intra- and intercultural background*. Sommerhauzen: G. Zauzich.

(2012) Language use, literacy and bilingualism. In Riggs, C. (ed.) *The Oxford Handbook of Roman Egypt*. Oxford: Oxford University Press, pp. 671–689.

Evans, T. (2012) Complaints of the natives in a Greek dress: The Zenon archive and the problem of Egyptian interference. In Mullen, A. & P. James (eds.) *Multilingualism in the Graeco-Roman worlds*. Cambridge: Cambridge University Press, pp. 106–123.

Fournet, J.-L. (2009) The multilingual environment of late antique Egypt: Greek, Latin, Coptic, and Persian documentation. In Bagnall, R. (ed.) *The Oxford Handbook of Papyrology*. Oxford: Oxford University Press, pp. 418–451.

(2020) *The rise of Coptic. Egyptian versus Greek in late antiquity*. Princeton, NJ: Princeton University Press.

Giannotti, S. (2007) Istruzioni per un apprendista bibliotecario negli ostraka demotici e bilingui di Narmuthis [Instructions to an apprentice archivist in Demotic and bilingual ostraca from Narmouthis]. *Egitto e Vicino Oriente*, 30, 117–152.

Hickey, T. (2012) Writing histories from the papyri. In Bagnall, R. (ed.) *The Oxford Handbook of Papyrology*. Oxford: Oxford University Press, pp. 495–510.

Hoogendijk, F. & B. Feucht (2013) 'Satabous son of Herieus' (TM ArchID 151. Version 1). www.trismegistos.org/arch/archives/pdf/151.pdf

Grossman E., Dils P., Richter T. & W. Schenkel (eds.) (2017) *Greek influence on Egyptian-Coptic: Contact-induced change in an ancient African language*. Hamburg: Widmaier Verlag.

Jennes, G. (2019) Life portraits: People in worship. In Vandorpe, K. (ed.) *A companion to Greco-Roman and late antique Egypt*. Hoboken, NJ: John Wiley & Sons, pp. 473–481.

Kidd, S. (2011) Dreams in bilingual papyri from the Ptolemaic period. *Bulletin of the American Society of Papyrologists*, 48, 113–130.

(2013) Written Greek but drawn Egyptian: Script changes in a bilingual dream papyrus. In Piquette, K. & R. Whitehouse (eds.) *Writing as material practice: Substance, surface and medium*. London: Ubiquity Press, pp. 239–252.

Legras, B. (2011) *Les reclus grecs du Sarapieion de Memphis. Un enquête sur l'Hellénisme égyptien* [The Greek recluses of the Serapeum of Memphis. A Study of Egyptian Hellenism]. Leuven/Paris/Walpole: Peeters.

Leiwo, M. (2010) Imperatives and other directives in the letters from Mons Claudianus. In Evans, T. & D. Obbink (eds.) *The language of the papyri*. Oxford: Oxford University Press, pp. 97–119.

(2017) Confusion of moods in Greek private letters of Roman Egypt? In Bentein K., Janse M. & J. Soltic (eds.) *Variation and change in ancient Greek tense, aspect and modality*. Leiden/Boston: Brill, pp. 242–260.

Lewis, N. (1986) *Greeks in Ptolemaic Egypt: Case studies in the social history of the Hellenistic world*. Oxford: Oxford University Press.

(1993) The demise of the Demotic document: When and why. *Journal of Egyptian Archaeology*, 79, 276–281.

Love, E. (2016) *Code-switching with the Gods. The bilingual (Old Coptic-Greek) spells of PGM IV (P.Bibliothèque Nationale Supplément Grec. 574) and their linguistic, religious, and socio-cultural context in late Roman Egypt*. Berlin/Boston: De Gruyter.

Mairs, R. (2012) Bilingual 'tagging' of financial accounts in Demotic and Greek. *Zeitschrift für die Ägyptische Sprache*, 139, 38–45.

Mairs, R. & C. Martin (2008–2009) A bilingual 'sale' of liturgies from the archive of the Theban choachytes: P. Berlin 5507, P. Berlin 3098 and P. Leiden 413. *Enchoria*, 31, 22–67.

Messerer, C. (2017) *Corpus des papyrus grecs sur les relations administratives entre le clergé égyptien et les autorités romaines* [Corpus of Greek papyri concerning the administrative relations between the Egyptian priesthood and the Roman authorities], Vol. 1. Paderborn: Ferdinand Schöningh.

Moyer, I. (2016) Isidorus at the gates of the temple. In Rutherford, I. (ed.) *Greco-Egyptian interactions: Literature, translation, and culture, 500 BCE–300 CE*. Oxford: Oxford University Press, pp. 209–244.

Muhs, B. (2005) The grapheion and the disappearance of Demotic contracts in early Roman Tebtynis and Soknopaiou Nesos. In Lippert, S.L. & M. Schentuleit (eds.) *Tebtynis und Soknopaiu Nesos. Leben im römerzeitlichen Fajum* [Tebtynis and Soknopaiou Nesos. Life in Roman Fayum]. Wiesbaden: Harrassowitz, pp. 93–104.

(2014) Greek and Demotic in the Roman Fayyum. In Keenan, J., Manning, J. & U. Yiftach-Firanko (eds.) *Law and legal practice in Egypt from Alexander to the Arab conquest*. Cambridge: Cambridge University Press, pp. 110–118.

Mullen, A. & P. James (eds.) (2012) *Multilingualism in the Graeco-Roman worlds*. Cambridge/New York: Cambridge University Press.

Papaconstantinou, A. (ed.) (2010) *The multilingual experience in Egypt from the Ptolemies to the 'Abbāsids*. Farnham: Ashgate.

Peremans, W. (1964) Über die Zweisprachigkeit im ptolemäischen Ägypten [On Bilingualism in Ptolemaic Egypt]. In H. Braunert (ed.) *Studien zur Papyrologie und antiken Wirtschaftsgeschichte F. Oertel zum achtzigsten Geburtstag gewidmet* [Studies in Papyrology and Ancient Economic History offered to F. Oertel for his 80th Birthday]. Bonn: Rudolf Habelt, pp. 49–60.

Peremans, W. (1983) Le bilinguisme dans les relations gréco-égyptiennes sous les Lagides [Bilingualism in Greek–Egyptian relations under the Lagids]. In *Egypt and the Hellenistic World*. Louvain: Peeters, pp. 253–280.

Pestman, P. (1978) L'agoranomie: un avant-poste de l'administration grecque enlevé par les Égyptiens? [Agoranomia: An outpost of the Greek administration taken over by the Egyptians?] In Maehler, H. & V. Strocka (eds.) *Das ptolemäische Ägypten. Akten des internationalen Symposions 27–29 September 1976 in Berlin.* [Ptolemaic Egypt: Acts of the International Symposium at Berlin, 27th–29th September 1976]. Mainz: Philipp von Zabern, pp. 203–210.

(1985a) Registration of Demotic contracts in Egypt. P.Par. 65; 2nd cent. B.C. In Ankum, J., Spruit, J. & F. Wubbe (eds.) *Satura Roberto Feenstra, sexagesimum quintum annum aetatis complenti ab alumnis collegis amicis oblata*, 17–25. [A medley for Robert Feenstra, offered by pupils, colleagues and friends upon completion of his 65th year]. Fribourg: Editions universitaires.

(1985b) The competence of Greek and Egyptian tribunals according to the decree of 118 B.C. *Bulletin of the American Society of Papyrologists*, 22, 265–269.

Prada, L. (2013) Dreams, bilingualism, and oniromancy in Ptolemaic Egypt. Remarks on a recent study. *Zeitschrift für Papyrologie und Epigraphik*, 184, 85–101.

Quack, J. (2008) Demotische magische und divinatorische Texte [Demotic Texts of Magic and Divination]. In Krüger, A., Abusch, T., Borger, R. & O. Kaiser (eds.) *Texte aus der Umwelt des Alten Testaments (TUAT). Neue Folge. Band 4: Omina, Orakel, Rituale und Beschwörungen* [Texts from the Environment of the Old Testament (TUAT). New Series. Vol. 4: Omens, Oracles, Rituals and Execrations]. Gütersloh: Gütersloher Verlagshaus, pp. 331–385.

(2017) How the Coptic script came about. In Grossman, E., Dils, P., Richter, T. & W. Schenkel (eds.) *Greek Influence on Egyptian-Coptic: Contact-induced change in an ancient African language*. Hamburg: Widmaier Verlag, pp. 27–96.

Ray, J. (1976) *The archive of Ḥor*. London: Egypt Exploration Society.

Rémondon, R. (1964) Problèmes du bilinguisme dans l'Égypte Lagide [Issues of bilingualism in Egypt under the Lagids]. *Chronique d'Égypte*, 39, 126–146.

Renberg, G. (2017) *Where dreams may come: Incubation sanctuaries in the Greco-Roman world*. 2 vols. Leiden/Boston: Brill.

Renberg, G. & F. Naether (2010) 'I Celebrated a Fine Day': An overlooked Egyptian phrase in a bilingual letter preserving a dream narrative. *Zeitschrift für Papyrologie und Epigraphik*, 175, 49–71.

Ripat, P. (2006) The language of oracular inquiry in Roman Egypt. *Phoenix*, 60, 3–4, 304–328.

Rochette, B. (1995) La traduction de textes religieux dans l'Égypte gréco-romaine. [The translation of religious texts in Greco-Roman Egypt]. *Kernos*, 8, 151–166.

(1996) Sur le bilinguisme dans l'Égypte gréco-romaine [On bilingualism in Greco-Roman Egypt]. *Chronique d'Égypte*, 71, 153–168.

Rutherford, I. (2010) Bilingualism in Roman Egypt? Exploring the archive of Phatres of Narmuthis. In Evans, T. & D. Obbink (eds.) *The language of the papyri*. Oxford: Oxford University Press, pp. 198–207.

Ryholt, K. (2002) Nectanebo's dream or the prophecy of Petesis. In Blasius, A. & B. Schipper (eds.) *Apokalyptik und Ägypten. Eine kritische Analyse der relevante Texten aus dem griechisch-römischen Ägypten* [Apocalyptic literature and Egypt. A critical analysis of the relevant texts from Greco-Roman Egypt]. Leuven/Paris/Sterling, VA: Peeters, pp. 221–241.

Sicard, J. & K. de Bot (2013) Multilingual dreaming. *International Journal of Multilingualism*, 10, 3, 331–354.

Stadler, M. (2008) On the demise of Egyptian writing. Working with a problematic source basis. In Baines J., Bennet J. & S. Houston (eds.) *The disappearance of writing systems. Perspectives on literacy and communication*. London/Oakville CT: Equinox, pp. 157–181.

Stolk, J. (2017) Dative and genitive case interchange in Greek papyri from Roman-Byzantine Egypt. *Glotta*, 93, 182–212.

Tait, W. (1988) Rush and reed: The pens of Egyptian and Greek scribes. In Mandilaras, B. (ed.) *Proceedings of the XVIII International Congress of Papyrology*. Vol. 2. Athens: Greek Papyrological Society, pp. 477–481.

Thompson, D. (2009) The multilingual environment of Persian and Ptolemaic Egypt: Egyptian, Aramaic and Greek documentation. In Bagnall, R. (ed.) *The Oxford Handbook of Papyrology*. Oxford: Oxford University Press, pp. 395–417.

(2012) *Memphis under the Ptolemies*. Second ed. Princeton, NJ/Oxford: Princeton University Press.

Torallas Tovar, S. (2010a) Linguistic identity in Graeco-Roman Egypt. In Papaconstantinou, A. (ed.) *The multilingual experience in Egypt from the Ptolemies to the 'Abbāsids*. Farnham: Ashgate, pp. 17–43.

Torallas Tovar, S. (2010b) Greek in Egypt. In Bakker, E. (ed.) *A companion to the ancient Greek language*. Malden/Oxford: Blackwell, pp. 253–266.

Torallas Tovar, S. & M. Vierros (2019) Languages, scripts, literature, and bridges between cultures. In Vandorpe, K. (ed.) *A companion to Greco-Roman and late antique Egypt*. Hoboken, NJ: John Wiley and Sons, pp. 485–499.

Vandorpe, K. (2002) *The bilingual family archive of Dryton, his wife Apollonia and their daughter Senmouthis (P. Dryton)*. Brussel: Koninklijke Academie van België.

(2011) A successful, but fragile biculturalism. The Hellenization process in the Upper Egyptian town of Pathyris under Ptolemy VI and VII. In Jördens, A. & J. Quack (eds.) *Ägypten zwischen innerem Zwist und äußerem Druck: die Zeit Ptolemaios' VI. bis VIII.* [Egypt between internal discord and external pressure: The time from Ptolemy VI to Ptolemy VIII]. Wiesbaden: Harrassowitz, pp. 292–308.

(2014) Ethnic diversity in a wealthy household. In Keenan, J., Manning, J. & U. Yiftach-Firanko (eds.) *Law and legal practice in Egypt from Alexander to the Arab conquest*. Cambridge: Cambridge University Press, pp. 101–110.

Vandorpe, K. & W. Clarysse (2008) Egyptian bankers and bank receipts in Hellenistic and early Roman Egypt. In Verboven, K., Vandorpe, K. & V. Chankowski (eds.) *Pistoi Dia Ten Technen. Bankers, loans and archives in the ancient world. Studies in Honour of Raymond Bogaert*. Brussels: Peeters, pp. 153–168.

Vandorpe, K. & S. Vleeming (2017) *The Erbstreit papyri. A bilingual dossier from Pathyris of the second century BC*. Leuven: Peeters.

Vierros, M. (2008) Greek or Egyptian? The language choice in Ptolemaic documents from Pathyris. In Delattre, A. & P. Heilporn (eds.) *"Et maintenant ce ne sont plus que des villages…". Thèbes et sa région aux époques hellénistique, romaine et byzantine. Actes du colloque tenu à Bruxelles les 2 et 3 Decembre 2005.* ['And now it is just villages …' Thebes and its region in the Hellenistic, Roman and Byzantine period. Proceedings of a colloquium held at Brussels, 2–3 December 2005]. Brussels: Association égyptologique Reine Elisabeth, pp. 73–86.

(2012) *Bilingual notaries in Hellenistic Egypt: A study of Greek as a second language*. Brussels: Koninklijke Academie van België.

(2014) Bilingualism in Hellenistic Egypt. In Giannakis, G. (ed.) *Encyclopedia of ancient Greek language and linguistics*. Leiden: Brill, pp. 234–238.

(2021) Idiolect in focus: Two brothers in the Memphis Sarapieion (II BCE). In Bentein, K. & M. Janse (eds.) *Varieties of post-classical and Byzantine Greek*. Berlin/Boston: De Gruyter, pp. 39–74.

von Lieven, A. (2018) Some Observations on Multilingualism in Graeco-Roman Egypt. In Braarvig, J. & M. Geller (eds.) *Studies in multilingualism, lingua franca and lingua sacra*. Max Planck Institute for the History of Science, http://mprl-series.mpg.de/studies/10/

Wilcken, U. (1927) *Urkunden der Ptolemäerzeit (ältere Funde) I, Papyri aus Unterägypten.* [Documents of the Ptolemaic period (older finds) I, Papyri from Lower Egypt]. Berlin/Leipzig: De Gruyter.

Zauzich, K.-Th. (1968) *Die ägyptische Schreibertradition in Aufbau, Sprache und Schrift der demotischen Kaufverträge aus ptolemäischer Zeit.* [The Egyptian scribal tradition in light of the structure, language and script of the Demotic sales agreements from the Ptolemaic Period]. Wiesbaden: Harrassowitz.

3 Language Shift, Attitudes and Management in the Roman West

Alex Mullen

Travelers to western Europe would have encountered different soundscapes in the pre-Roman Iron Age and the end of the Roman period. In the western Roman provinces, a patchwork of local languages that existed in the Iron Age came under increasing pressure from Latin, and by the end of the imperial period the linguistic landscape had been reconfigured.[1] Meanwhile in the eastern provinces, Latin never developed a strong foothold: The mosaic of local languages, with regional link-languages such as Syriac, and Greek used as an imperial lingua franca, continued throughout the Roman period. Latin was regularly used in higher-level and highly 'Roman' contexts (Cotton et al., 2009; Millar, 1995) and in islands of Latinity, such as Berytus (Beirut), but it never became widely embedded as a vernacular of local communities as it did in the West.[2] Operationally, the Roman Empire functioned in both Latin and Greek (Adams, 2003a; Rochette, 1997).

To explain the spread of Latin in western provinces commentators have long sought evidence for a Roman language policy, deeming such reconfiguration unlikely without institutional support.[3] The general consensus is that there was

This output received funding from the European Research Council (ERC) under the European Union's Horizon 2020 research and innovation program under grant agreement No. 715626 (LatinNow). I am very grateful to James Clackson, Aneta Pavlenko, and Greg Woolf for their insightful comments on the previous versions of this chapter.

1 'West' and 'East' in this chapter refer to the two halves of the Roman world, the former composed of the western provinces stretching from Hadrian's Wall in Britain to the Balkans and including North Africa apart from Egypt, and the latter stretching from the Balkans, across Greece, to Syria and including Egypt. The conceptual line drawn by modern scholars, known as the Jireček Line (Jireček, 1911), is based on the boundary between Latin and Greek usage.

2 The timing of the change depends on the provinces in question. In parts of the Iberian Peninsula and southern Gaul, Latin spread as early as the second century BCE and had become the dominant language, at least in some contexts, during the first century CE. Elsewhere, for example in Britain, Latin only really began to spread widely in the first century CE and even by the end of Roman rule at the beginning of the fifth century CE, British Celtic was still being spoken, bilingually or monolingually, in some communities.

3 Early commentators compared modern imperial contexts and considered the Roman army central to the spread (e.g., Kahn, 1907). More recently scholars have devoted entire publications to the matter of Roman language policy (e.g., Dubuisson (1982) and Rochette (2011)). One issue plaguing this subject is a lack of clarity on what exactly language policy means.

none. Indeed, many Roman historians, particularly since the publication of Millar (1977), might wonder whether such a search may have been ill-conceived from the start, since policy-making does not seem to have been much deployed during significant periods of imperial history. Moreover, treating the Roman Empire as a single entity is unwise: It spanned several centuries, a vast geographical area, and numerous diverse communities. Language ideologies and practices in the Roman world were heterogeneous and shifting, as were methods of government and control. A better way to approach Latinization is to consider the differing perspectives and practices of various social groups. Scholars of cultural change have come to appreciate the importance of local languages (e.g., Millar, 1968) and commentators are now able to exploit a growing body of work on the so-called Palaeoeuropean languages and epigraphies.[4] Bi- and multilingualism, intertwined with the processes of language shift, maintenance, and death, created a variegated linguistic situation, with different levels of Latinization, local differences, and regional complexities over time and space. Thanks to developments in interdisciplinary methodologies and datasets, we are finally in a position to explore these differences and to consider their possible social contexts, including the role of language management.[5]

In what follows a crude, but important, distinction will be made between 'the elite' (differentiating between 'traditional' Roman and provincial elites) and the non-elite masses. 'The elite' is defined as a powerful group with access to higher-level education, positions of responsibility and often, but not always, wealth. This group expands and contracts to take in different professions and statuses, depending on the period, and membership can include anyone from emperors to penniless exiled poets. The term 'language policy' refers here to governmental-level decision-making and implementation of directives about language use. 'Language management,' a broader term, encompasses expression of language ideologies and lower-level policies/rules of often more limited reach. With this context in mind, I argue that, while the empire may not, at least until Diocletian, have had a wide-ranging language policy, there was an interest, at certain times and places, in language management.

3.1 Conceptions of Languages: The Discourse of the Elites

Elite Greeks and Romans discussed language throughout their literature. To do so, they relied on a range of terms, including Greek *dialektos, glossa*, and

4 See https:// ifc.dpz.es/ojs/index.php/palaeohispanica/issue/view/20 [last accessed 31.3.2021].

5 The ERC-funded project LatinNow is exploring differential Latinization, fates of local languages, bi- and multilingualism and literacy across the north-western provinces, using an interdisciplinary approach that combines sociolinguistics, epigraphy and archaeology. We have been able to take advantage of numerous large datasets (including 181,000 epigraphic records from the Europeana EAGLE project).

phone and Latin *lingua, sermo*, and *vox*. Often used interchangeably, these terms covered a wide semantic field comprising language, dialect, discourse, speech, rhetoric, and so on (for some usages, see Clackson, 2015a, pp. 13–16). At times, Greek and Roman writers approached these discussions from what we could term a 'sociolinguistic' perspective, but, as we shall see, their sociolinguistic interest was limited in focus and certainly, generally speaking, high-status Greeks and Romans display a relative lack of interest in languages other than Greek and Latin (Bozia & Mullen, 2021; Lejeune, 1949).

Romans had a complicated relationship with non-Latin languages. Their lengthy relationship with the Greek world began when Rome was but a collection of small settlements in the hills of Latium. They encountered Greek particularly in the Mediterranean trading sphere and in their contacts with nearby Greek colonies, including on the southern coast of Italy, known, together with Sicily, as *Magna Graecia*. As Rome grew, first within Italy and then beyond (Lomas, 2018), taking in numerous Latin and non-Latin speaking communities, it was with Greek language and culture that those with higher-level education were primarily obsessed. They wrestled with a complex: They simultaneously felt inferior to Greek cultural legacy and superior to the Greeks they had conquered in the second century BCE, viewed as decadent and effeminate (Clackson & Horrocks, 2007; Dubuisson,1981a). Their extensive cultural discussions are rarely narrowly about language; rather the Romans commentate on the broader cultural entanglements between themselves and the Greeks.

Bilingualism was commonplace among the Roman elite.[6] The eastern part of the Roman world used Greek as a lingua franca and few leading males at the heart of the Roman world would not have been bilingual, at least to an extent. Even those who challenged the stranglehold of the Greek legacy – such as politician Cato the Elder in the third–second century BCE and Fronto, Marcus Aurelius' Latin teacher, in the second century CE – did so from a standpoint of conversance with Greek language and culture. Close analysis of Greek code-switching in the Latin correspondence of the Roman elite shows that patterns of usage were dependent on the author, addressee, broader potential audience, topic, and the specifics of the cultural environment (Elder & Mullen, 2019). Every author had a subtly different sociolinguistic profile and a key conclusion of our studies of their complex repertoires is that the terminologies of bilingualism developed by Classicists do not necessarily capture this.

Despite bi- and multilingualism being commonplace, concepts akin to modern 'bilingualism' and 'multilingualism' do not seem to have been much in evidence in the Roman world, and modern ways of thinking about

[6] For studies of bi- and multi-lingualism in the Roman world, see Adams (2003a, 2003b, 2007), Adams et al. (2002), Biville (2018), Clackson (2015a), Cotton et al. (2009), Kaimio (1979), Millar (1968), Mullen & James (2012), Mullen (2013), and Rochette (1997, 2010).

bilingualism are not obviously in view. *Bilinguis* is used in Roman texts merely a handful of times and was often reserved to describe ambiguous, misleading speech rather than bilingualism as we understand it (Dubuisson, 1983; Poccetti, 1986). Elder (2019, p. 25) notes that, of the sixteen instances of the term in Latin literature up to 200 CE and late antique commentaries up to the early fifth century CE, nine express negative associations of untrustworthiness, two are physical descriptions of having two tongues, and only five have a sense of speaking two languages.[7] Another term, *utraque lingua*, 'both [our] languages,' indicates the notion of two linguistic parts of the same repertoire, expressing a strong cultural and literary content, rather than purely linguistic (Dubuisson, 1981b, p. 281). It seems that this term was used by Romans to refer to the entanglement of Greek and Latin culture,[8] whereas *bilinguis*, on the other hand, was usually reserved for 'foreigners' (Carthaginians, for example).

Elite Romans, who were not of provincial origins, were generally not especially interested in the myriad languages beyond 'their own' Latin and Greek, as far as we can tell from their extensive writings (Lejeune, 1949; Rochette, 1995). Mirroring Greek practice, highly educated Romans focused primarily on standardization of Latin, on linguistic purity and excellence (Clackson, 2015b) and the relationship in *utraque lingua*. They were clearly aware of the existence of other languages, referred to with terms such as *aliena lingua* and *alienus/externus/peregrinus sermo*, mentioned them in ethnographic discussions, remarked on the use of interpreters, and exhibited curiosity when it came to loanwords (Mairs, 2020; Wiotte-Franz, 2001). Yet compared to their obsession with Greek, these languages received little attention, perhaps with the exception of Etruscan (the Emperor Claudius apparently wrote a history of the Etruscans, which might have required mastery of the language (Cornell, 1976)) and Punic (Claudius also composed a history of the Punic-speaking Carthaginians; a treatise on agriculture by the Punic author, Mago, was translated into Latin; and there are several lines of Punic in Plautus' *Poenulus*). In an unusual testimony, the exiled poet Ovid bemoans being stuck among 'barbarians' who speak no Latin on the Black Sea and eventually claims to have learned Getan and Sarmatian (*Tristia*, 5.12.58). This is a rare instance of a well-educated Roman writing of his linguistic experience of a non-Latin speaking community, but we still get precious little information about the 'barbarian' languages themselves.

The 'local' provincial elites, particularly in non-Mediterranean provinces, had close links to non-Latin speaking communities and may have continued to

[7] Horace, *Satires*, 1.10.30; Curtius Rufus, 7.5.29; Ennius, *Annals*, 477; Lucilius, 1124; Porphyrion, *Commentary on Horace*, 1.10.30.

[8] For the occasional use of *utraque lingua/uterque sermo* beyond Latin-Greek bilingualism, see Biville (2018, p. 22).

speak local languages. But their voices are not commonly heard in the extant literature and when they are, the provincials, by virtue of their elite position, commonly felt the need to exhibit as much Romanness as possible. When terms such as *lingua Gallica* are used to describe provincial speech we are often unsure whether they refer to Gallic Latin (a contact-induced variety of Latin) or Gaulish (the Celtic language of Gaul) (Blom, 2009).[9] The African-born Emperor Septimius Severus (193–211 CE) was embarrassed by the fact that his sister *vix Latine loquens* 'scarcely spoke Latin' (*Historia Augusta*, 15.7), but whether she was speaking a Punic-influenced Latin or Punic is unclear.

3.2 Linguistic Attitudes and Practices in the Everyday Life of the Non-elites

It is, of course, even harder to reconstruct linguistic ideologies or attitudes for the masses of the provincial population who did not leave behind explicit commentaries on how they saw their relationship with languages, identities, and cultures. Most of them never engage directly in the written record given the very high levels of illiteracy among the provincial population.[10] Some provincials, however, contributed to the epigraphic record and we can scrutinize the remains for evidence of their language attitudes.

On the one hand, western provincials participating in the vast Roman documentary output would have had a clear view of what standard forms of Latin were, compared to any other languages they might have spoken. Formal military, administrative, and legal texts followed strict and widely adopted conventions about layout, linguistic and orthographic norms, formulae, and script (Mullen & Bowman, 2021; Willi, 2021). Financial and legal documents on stylus tablets, found in London and dated to the first century CE, demonstrate the wholesale adoption of Roman documentary practices even in the earliest phases of the new province Britannia (Cooley, forthcoming; Tomlin, 2016). In fact, it is hard to see how people engaged in formal documentary contexts across the Roman Empire, such as the writing of wills, military

[9] Rochette (1995, p. 12) claims that Latin grammarians do not refer to 'local' languages before the Byzantine period, with the exception of some etymological comments in Varro. This overlooks the work of the fourth-century grammarian Consentius (*De barbarismis et metaplasmis*) who discussed the barbarism of provincial speech, with the focus on regional varieties of Latin, and *barbarolexis*, words from foreign languages in Latin (Mari, 2021). Biville (2018) is right to temper the notion, inspired, in her view, by Lejeune (1949), that Romans were never interested in local languages, but her snippets of nonspecific evidence scattered over centuries hardly support her conclusion that Romans were interested in multilingualism.

[10] For the debates on levels of literacy (largely referring to Harris, 1989) and how we might more fruitfully approach it using a focus on *socio*-literacy, see Mullen (2021).

reports, and business contracts, would not have had a sense of linguistic norms and expectations.

On the other hand, the vast majority of provincials not directly involved in the Roman imperial documentary machinery were probably used to operating in a context of more flexible multilingualism, involving local languages (e.g., Celtic and Germanic varieties in the northern provinces) and regional varieties of Latin (Adams, 2007). These provincials, the majority of whom lived in rural settlements, did not have access to systematic education and, as far as we can tell, instructional materials for learning local languages in the West did not exist. The known glossaries, colloquia, grammars, lexica, and other learning aids were designed to teach Latin and/or Greek (Dickey, 2012), but the majority of provincials would never have come across one and, given the high levels of illiteracy, would not have been able to use it even if they had. Evidence for more rudimentary educational practices, for example, learning alphabets, can be found occasionally in the provinces and indicates usually ad hoc efforts to adopt literacy.

People engaged in production and trade, who often relied on internal administrative practices to organize their work, form one group that straddles the provincials participating in the formal Roman documentary output and the illiterate masses. Our evidence suggests that these participants, who may have learned Latin and literacy on the job, sometimes blended Roman documentary norms (layout, symbols, script, etc.) with a mix of Latin and local languages. Thus, La Graufesenque, a pottery production center in south-western Gaul, that functioned in the first and second centuries CE, produced firing lists in Gaulish, Latin, and a mixture of both (Mullen, in press). In a comparable situation, though one more embedded in Roman structures of power, at Bu Njem, a Roman fort in North Africa, the solider Aemilius Aemilianus sent letters in the third century CE to his Decurion recording the amount of grain provided by the local camel riders, that feature both Roman and local measurements and terms (Felice, 2019, pp. 244–257).

In the absence of a nation-state language ideology and widespread access to formal language instruction, languages may not have had a circumscribed meaning for many Roman provincials. Linguistic resources may have been carved up differently and attitudes to languages and identities may have been based on local concerns to which we now have no, or extremely limited, access (for instance, slightly different forms of Celtic used in neighboring villages or territories may have had salience). In this context, we might wonder whether provincials with what *we* would consider more than one language, might have seen themselves as having multiple languages or a single repertoire, and whether they might have thought of themselves as bi- or multi-lingual at all.

An alternative is to consider the possibility of *translingualism* (Mullen, 2022), a term deployed in modern sociolinguistics to describe multilingual contexts where flexible linguistic repertoires used in oral and/or written communication cannot be neatly divided into separate languages. This idea is relevant for thinking about the Roman world, in contexts where some individuals and communities may have had little awareness of their languages as strictly bounded and named entities. Written sources are not likely to reflect this complexity, since by their nature they tend to rely on standardized linguistic entities, but even these offer indications that at least some Roman provincials may have seen their repertoires as relatively fluid, perhaps not so readily splitting up languages into discrete units as we do.

The flexibility of linguistic resources is reflected in the texts on Roman spindle whorls from eastern Gaul (Dondin-Payre, 2005; Mullen, 2022). These small weights, which are on average 1.5 cm high × 2.5 cm in diameter, were placed at the end of the spindle to help regulate the speed of the spin (Fig. 3.1a). Imperial-period whorls do not appear to have been inscribed with the exception of this corpus of twenty-four. Half the known examples were found in Augustodunum (Autun, France); the rest are known from locations in France, Germany, and Switzerland (Fig. 3.1b). All but two are made from the same material, namely the bituminous schist, probably from the quarries of Autun. It seems very likely that the majority, if not all, of these whorls were made in Augustodunum and the most plausible date range for their production is 90–235 CE (Mullen, 2022).

The addressees seem to be female, and some texts have amatory or erotic content, for example MONI GNATHA GABI/BUÐÐVTON IMON, a Gaulish utterance, which can be translated as 'Come girl, take my little kiss/cock.' The texts are thought to have been composed by men (Meid, 1983), but there is no clear reason to assume a male author/commissioner in *all* the cases. If we think that at least some spinners were women working in groups in workshops, we might wonder whether some messages may have been created by female spinners for themselves and for other workers (e.g., SALVE SOROR 'hey sister). Coworkers in close quarters working on monotonous tasks often create distractions for themselves, such as in-group jokes or work songs, and a black schist whorl with white lettering would have delivered a striking visual effect, spinning until it became a blur and revealing the inscribed message when it slowed down.

The whorls relay direct speech or speak themselves: some in Latin, some in Gaulish (Lambert, 2018; Mullen & Darasse, 2020), and some in both. Unfortunately, the traditional terminology of bilingualism studies, namely code-switching, interference, and borrowing, transferred into Classics most effectively by Adams (2003a), does not help much with the analysis of some of these texts.

Take, for example, the following: NATA VIMPI / CVRMI DA 'pretty girl, give me beer' (Autun) and NATA VIMPI / VI(nu?)M POTA 'pretty girl, drink

(a) (b)

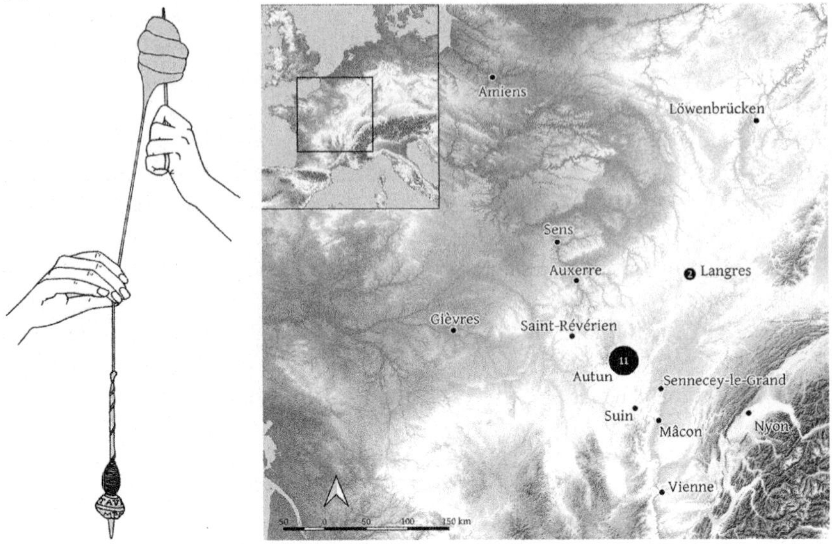

Fig. 3.1 (a) Spinning with a distaff, drop spindle, and whorl (drawing Jane Masséglia, LatinNow). (b) Distribution of inscribed Roman-period spindle whorls (map Pieter Houten, LatinNow).

?wine' (Auxerre) (Fig. 3.2). *(g)nata*, 'girl,' which also occurs as *gnatha* in other whorl texts, is a noun in Latin and Gaulish, a legacy of shared Indo-European ancestry. Adams (2007) tentatively suggests that "the similarity of *natus*, *-a* to Gaulish *gnatus*, *-a* gave it some currency in the Latin of Gaul alongside the more usual terms *filius* and *filia*, and by extension *puer* and *puella*, particularly in the feminine" (p. 303). We might consider this a neat choice of appellation if one wanted to communicate simultaneously to both Latin and Gaulish speakers. *vimpi*, here in the vocative, means 'pretty' in Gaulish, and is commonly attested on the spindle whorls and on other small objects such as brooches (e.g., AVE VIMPI 'greetings, lovely') (Feugère & Lambert, 2011). The origin of the word is unclear, but it is likely to be related to Welsh *gwymp* 'fair, pretty.' Given its widespread occurrence on portable Roman objects, it might also have been current in a regional form of Gallic Latin and may have worked bilingually.

The second half of the example from Autun follows the same pattern: the first word, *curmi* 'beer,' is Gaulish (it also occurs in the personal name Curmisagios 'beer seeker' and Old Irish *cuirm*, Welsh *cwrw* 'beer'), but is likely to have been borrowed into the Latin of the area. Terms for local beverages, such as beer, were commonly borrowed from local languages into regional varieties of Latin. At the turn of the fifth century CE, Marcellus of

Fig. 3.2 Replicas made by Potted History for LatinNow of spindle whorls with the texts NATA VIMPI/CVRMI DA; NATA VIMPI/VI(nu?)M POTA; MARCOSIOR MATERNIA (photo by Pieter Houten, LatinNow).

Bordeaux mentions *curmi* and another form referring to 'beer,' *cervesa*, as ingredients to put into cough mixture (XVI 33) (see also Nelson, 2003). The final word of the text, *da*, is the imperative of 'to give' and, due to shared Indo-European origins, exists in both Latin and Gaulish. Following this analysis, all four words could be understood as entirely Gaulish, entirely Gallic Latin, or both. The second half of the example from Auxerre is more difficult to interpret, due to the uncertainties over the interpretation of VIM (Mullen, 2022). The most likely interpretation, 'drink wine,' would take the first half as Latin/Gaulish/both and the second as Latin.

These texts do not fit neatly into the standard framework of bilingualism used in Classics and might be better understood as reflections of *translingualism*. This term is a useful addition to the conceptual toolkit for dealing with multilingual texts, such as those on the whorls and other texts in mixtures of language that cannot be neatly divided up into separate languages. It is a helpful reminder that the languages sectioned off, described and labeled by linguists, may not map onto the linguistic experiences of people who used them. This evidence on the ground suggests that local speech was not constrained by the socially and politically constructed notion of 'languages,' nor split into the distinct entities we are trained to recognize through the lens of Indo-European lexica and Latin grammars. The creators of spindle whorls in provincial Roman Gaul may not have seen 'language' in such black and white terms. Alternatively, they may have distinguished 'languages' but felt free to manipulate them without limitations imposed by the 'monolingual standard' norms. Through enigmatic evidence like this we can try to evoke the possible range of mindsets and contexts, however difficult that might be, of the ancient producers and consumers of language.

3.3 Evidence for Language Management in the Roman Empire

When we consider language management in the Roman Empire, we need to keep in mind these differing perspectives. In the past, modern nation-state ideologies inspired some scholars to turn to language policy to explain Latinization and language shift in the western provinces. For encouragement to seek out an imperial language policy one only had to "point to a linguistic map of modern Europe" (Kaimio, 1979, p. 327). Yet scholars have struggled to find evidence of a wide-ranging imperial language policy or directive determining the broad uptake of Latin across the western provinces. Of course, given the partial nature of what has been transmitted from the ancient world, we always have the issue of how to judge the absence of evidence. But the Roman world was a highly literate environment, and if there had been an imperial language policy, we might have expected to find direct trace. Given the apparent lack of imperial-wide policy-making prior to the third century CE, the lack of interest in local languages on the part of the elite, and the multilingual realities for the bulk of the empire's inhabitants, should we have expected an imperial language policy for the provinces? It seems likely that it would not have been a focus for the imperial administration and might have made little sense to the majority of those it would have targeted. Kaimio (1979) himself goes on to talk, relatively opaquely, about a "conscious language policy" but denies that there was ever *one* "systematized, far-reaching language policy" (*ibid.*) and argues that attitudes and tradition were the main drivers of language choice.

This is not to say that there was no hope or expectation among the elite that provincials would learn Latin. Roman elites appear to have considered language an important part of communal identity, as seen in the opening of Caesar's *Gallic Wars*, where the communities of Gaul are (crudely) divided according to *lingua, instituta, and leges* (language, customs, and laws). The ideology linking Latin to the empire and Romanness is expressed in Vergil's *Aeneid*, a politically charged epic, widely disseminated across the provinces as we see from writing exercises (see ink tablet 118 of the Vindolanda collection (Bowman & Thomas, 1994)). Vergil's Jupiter states that the sons of Italy will keep their ancestral customs and speech and the Trojans will be submerged: *faciamque omnis uno ore Latinos* 'I shall make all to be Latins of one language' (12.837). We also find anecdotes ascribed to emperors that suggest they sometimes made a show about language and Romanness, particularly concerning Roman citizenship and its association with the Latin language (Elder & Mullen, 2019; Rochette, forthcoming). The Emperor Tiberius once refused to let a solider respond in the Senate in Greek (Cassius Dio, 57.15, Suetonius, *Tiberius*, 71), and Claudius removed citizenship from a leading citizen of Greece because he did not know Latin, *Latini sermonis ignarum* (Suetonius, *Claudius*, 16.4). Roman authors also talk of 'nativization' of loanwords, which were imbued with Roman citizenship – a striking metaphor (for discussion, see Elder, 2019; Elder & Mullen, 2019). Still, these scattered testimonies do not amount to an official policy. Although we may be able to reconstruct elements of what we might call 'linguistic imperialism,' for most of the period we can uncover no official Latinization policy (Adams, 2003a,b; Dubuisson, 1982; Rochette, 2011). To use modern sociolinguistic terms, we can more easily recover aspects of language management.

Given the cultural context, it seems likely that language management took a targeted form, focusing on what the central powers needed to control. Evidence for language directives with narrower ambitions can perhaps be uncovered. One often cited piece of evidence comes from Valerius Maximus' collection of *Memorable Sayings and Doings*, written under Tiberius in the first century CE (Dubuisson, 1982, pp. 192–196). In this he describes magistrates of old (*magistratus prisci*) following the rule that they should always deliver *responsa* to Greeks in Latin and force Greeks to use a Latin interpreter not only in Rome but even in Greece and Asia (2.2.2). These comments seem to channel an idealized vision of the 'good old days,' no doubt intended to support Tiberius' ideological stance.[11] The precise remit of Valerius Maximus' statement is not specified, but if we take it to mean that leading Romans should communicate in Latin on Roman business with Greek-speakers, it is demonstrably not a reflection of universal practice in the Republican period (Greek was used by Aemilius Paulus to the Macedonian king in 168 BCE, by the consul Licinius Crassus in Asia in 131 BCE, and by Cicero in the Senate in Syracuse in 70 BCE). There is also no detail as to what form, if any, these rules for magistrates might have taken. It may have essentially been a cultural norm whose breach could attract reproach, if not specific punishment. Cicero underscores the absence of specific regulations when he takes umbrage at being accused of committing an *indignum facinus* 'shameful misdeed' by speaking to the Greeks in Greek in Greece (*In Verrem*, 2.4.147), implying that he felt he had stayed on the right side of a delicate, but

[11] Emperor Tiberius' linguistic strategies in the Senate, that most Roman of places, included apologizing for a Greek loanword in Latin (*monopolium*) and asking that the Greek word (ἔμβλημα) be replaced by a Latin word or phrase (Suetonius, *Tiberius*, 71.1, also Cassius Dio, 57.15.1–3) (Dubuisson, 1986), thus underscoring "his own linguistic sensitivity and desire to retain strict Latinity" (Elder & Mullen, 2019, p. 224).

unregulated, balancing act. Nevertheless, Valerius Maximus' words indicate that some Romans attributed great importance to the use of Latin in the work of representatives of Rome.

Provincial elites of local ancestry form a group generally thought to have been important in the representation of Rome and the Latinization process across the Roman West (Beltrán, 2015). Romans used a carrot and stick approach to promote loyalty among local leaders (Ando, 2000), since these would be crucial in serving as role models for the Roman way of life and encouraging peaceful submission of their communities. The question whether language management might have targeted them specifically is hard to answer. We might look to the testimonies of Plutarch and Tacitus who describe how leading Romans, Sertorius in the Iberian Peninsula (*Sertorius*, 14.2–3) and Agricola in Britannia (*Agricola* 21.2), chose to educate the sons of the local elites (Wolff, forthcoming). Their contexts are quite different – the former a Roman general leading a rebellion against the Roman Senate in the first century BCE and the latter a governor attempting the smooth integration of the new province in the first century CE – but both had the aim of making their respective populations more compliant by attempting to immerse them in Roman culture and its opportunities. However, these two testimonies stand out as rather unusual and the differential uptake of Latin and Roman culture among the local elites in the two provinces supports the suggestion that Romans had no uniform policy to promote Latin and to demote other languages.

We know that the local elite in the provinces did not take up Latin at the same pace or even unanimously. In some provinces, such as Britannia, the locals' lack of engagement with Latin epigraphy and the mere fact that Agricola deemed it necessary to teach Latin to the sons of the elite at the end of the first century CE suggest that they were not already immersed in it. Even in the early-to-be-incorporated province of Gallia Narbonensis, a leading local Roman citizen, Gaius Valerius Troucillus, still spoke Gaulish and was used as an interpreter in the mid-first century BCE by Caesar during the Gallic wars (see also Mairs, this volume). In the same area lapidary epigraphy in Gaulish flourished under Roman rule in the second and first centuries BCE, at least some of which can be associated with local elites.[12] The Roman state did not desire or need to control the use of local languages as long as they posed no

[12] Beyond the Mediterranean provinces, the second century CE villa at Meikirch (Switzerland) was clearly inhabited by affluent provincials, if not necessarily by local leaders, and has (to us incomprehensible) texts on its frescoes in what appears to be, at least in part, Gaulish. Lapidary Gallo-Latin is traditionally dated to up to the Caesarean period but largely on the incautious assumption that after that point locals with the means to put up lapidary texts were using Latin. Since much of the non-lapidary Gallo-Latin corpus can be dated to the imperial period it is not unlikely that some of the lapidary texts should be dated to the same era (Mullen & Darasse, 2020, p. 776).

threat: Romans provided the incentives for Latinization and, when they bothered to notice, enough of the relevant provincials seemed to have made the 'right' choice.

Control was clearly exercised over documents, however, as seen through the consistency found in military, administrative, and legal texts. We also have evidence for the rules themselves, for example, a series of testimonies relevant for the redaction of wills (Nowak, 2015). The jurists Gaius (second century CE) and Ulpian (third century CE) make it clear that wills written in Greek are not valid under Roman law (Gaius, 2.281; Ulpian, 32.11.pr.), though exemptions are made for the *fideicommissa* (directions in wills for an heir or legatee to transfer property to someone else) which could be written, according to Ulpian, "in any language," specifying Punic and *Gallicana* (Gaulish?), as well as the obvious Latin and Greek.[13]

The *Gnomon of the Idios Logos*, a papyrus handbook, dating to the mid-second century CE and listing rules governing the operations of a provincial treasury department, also contains the directive that Roman citizens cannot have wills composed in Greek, with exceptions for veteran soldiers (*BGU*, 5.1210). Following the extension of the citizenship to all free-born in the empire in 212 CE, significant numbers of newly enfranchised provincials who would have had their wills in Greek were subjected to this rule. This situation appears to have been rationalized by a ruling of Severus Alexander (222–235 CE) authorizing the production of wills in Greek. We do not have the original text of the pronouncement, but it is referred to explicitly in a will from Herakleopolites dated to 235 CE (*SB*, I 5294) (Rochette, 2000).[14]

There is even evidence from the fourth century CE of directives concerning the choice of script types for documentary sources. The use of the so-called New Roman Cursive for Latin (described as *litterae communes*) in provincial chanceries appears to have been enforced by an imperial edict of co-Emperors Valentinian I and Valens in 367/8 CE:

> Emperors Valentinian and Valens Augustuses to Festus, Proconsul of Africa. Our Serenity has observed that the practice of imitating Our **celestial imperial letters** (*litterae caelestes*) has arisen from the fact that the office of Your Gravity, in composing references of cases to the Emperor and reports to Him, uses the same kind of script as that which the bureaus of Our Eternity use. Wherefore, by the authority of this sanction, We command that hereafter this custom, a teacher of forgery, shall be abolished and that everything which must be written either from a province or by a judge shall be entrusted to **commonly used letters** (*litterae communes*), so that no person shall have the right to appropriate a copy of this style, either privately or publicly. (19.19.3, translated by Pharr, 1952, p. 241)

[13] Ulpian's text is transmitted to us via the much later Justinianic *Digest*, 32.1.11.
[14] For the law as practiced in the provinces, see Czajkowski et al. (2020).

Some have argued that the *litterae caelestes* being earmarked here for the very highest levels of bureaucracy describe a late form of the 'official' Old Roman Cursive script for Latin that developed in the early centuries of imperial rule. If correct, the restrictions against the use of that script had been so successful that from the later third century CE it almost vanishes from our evidence, employed only in high-level, formal contexts (Mullen & Bowman, 2021). The fact that we have direct evidence for interference in the type of script used for writing Latin suggests that focused directives controlling aspects of documentary output, such as the choice of language, were likely to have been active throughout the imperial period, even if we have only rare instances of the rules themselves.

Evidence of a more systematic imperial policy may appear under Diocletian (284–305 CE).[15] Rochette (1997, pp. 116–126) and others have claimed that there was a new and more aggressive language policy that aimed to bolster the role of Latin in provincial administration in the East. Numerous arguments have been made to counter this. Turner (1961) argues that the imposition of Latin occurred in very restricted contexts and that perhaps Diocletian "desisted from frontal attack" (p. 168). Adamík (2010) contends that there was a striking change in the language of the eastern imperial administration but that it had nothing to do with a language policy; rather it was the natural result of broader bureaucratic and governmental transformations. Adams (2003a, pp. 635–637) suggests that the evidence itself needs to be reconsidered, since there is no radical change in the use of Latin but the continuation of patterns of language choice that can be traced as early as the Republican period. Faced with such differing perspectives, an empirically based and wide-ranging survey of the linguistic choices in the eastern empire may be the only way to escape the impasse.

3.4 An Empire of Three Hearts

Influenced by modern nation-state ideologies and policies, scholars have searched for the evidence of a policy mandating the use of Latin in the West to explain the attested language change. The consensus is that there was none, at least not until Diocletian, and this surprising absence has sometimes been explained through the lack of means of enforcement (Kaimio, 1979, p. 328). But given the empire's ability, at least over much of its history, to count and tax its subjects, to persecute specific religious groups, and to maintain a well-organized army, it arguably could have attempted to enforce such a policy. A better explanation might be that no such pro-Latin and anti-local language

[15] The other is Justinianic, for which see Adamík (2003).

policy for the provinces was necessary or, perhaps in a sense, conceivable. The Roman center was not greatly interested in policies involving all its subjects, at least before the third century CE, and elite Romans were disinterested in languages other than Latin and Greek and did not consider any practical issue with their use, as long as the empire's functioning remained intact. The focus of their linguistic commentary was instead on the nature of 'their languages,' the relationship between Latin and Greek and the smooth administration of the provinces. However, though there may not have been an empire-wide policy of Latinization, there were certainly language ideologies and multiple more narrowly focused facets of language management concerning the use of Latin and Greek in the running of the empire.

Scholarly discussions on the presence or absence of language policy have centered on the practices of the 'traditional' elites and the administration of the empire (Dubuisson, 1982). But the Roman Empire was full of diverse communities and, like the early Latin author Ennius (c. 239–169 BCE), had three hearts: Latin, Greek, and local.[16] In providing a vision of the nature of Latinization in the western provinces and the existence, or not, of language ideologies and management, we need to remember to see the picture from different angles. Sociolinguists and historians have traditionally considered the sociolinguistic attitudes of the masses to be unimportant and/or impossible to reconstruct in the absence of explicit commentary. This chapter has tried to broaden the perspective and has briefly demonstrated how epigraphic remains can allow us to investigate sociolinguistic attitudes and practices of 'ordinary' provincials. The reconstruction of attitudes at different levels of society, including possible translingualism for at least some groups, enables us to demonstrate why language policies may not have made much sense in their linguistic worlds.

References

Adamík, B. (2003) Zur Geschichte des offiziellen Gebrauchs der lateinischen Sprache: Justinians Reform [The history of the official use of Latin: Justinian's reforms]. *Acta Antiqua Academiae Scientiarum Hungaricae,* 43, 229–241.

(2010) Sprachpolitik im römischen Reich: zur Frage einer angenommenen sprachpolitischen Reform unter der Tetrarchie [Language policy in the Roman Empire: the question of the posited language policy under the Tetrarchy]. *Acta Antiqua Academiae Scientiarum Hungaricae*, 50, 17–29.

Adams, J. N. (2003a) *Bilingualism and the Latin language*. Cambridge: Cambridge University Press.

[16] This is a comment made by the second-century-CE author Aulus Gellius. Ennius apparently said he had *tria cordia*, 'three hearts' because he spoke Greek, Oscan, and Latin (for contextualization of this comment, see Wallace-Hadrill, 2008).

(2003b) "*Romanitas*" and the Latin Language. *Classical Quarterly*, 53, 1, 184–205.
(2007) *The regional diversification of Latin 200 BC–AD 600*. Cambridge: Cambridge University Press.
Adams, J. N., Janse, M., & S. Swain (2002) *Bilingualism in ancient society. Language contact and the written text*. Oxford: Oxford University Press.
Ando, C. (2000) *Imperial ideology and provincial loyalty in the Roman Empire*. Berkeley/Los Angeles/London: University of California Press.
Beltrán, F. (2015). The epigraphic habit in the Roman world. In C. Bruun & J. Edmondson (eds.) *The Oxford Handbook of Roman Epigraphy*. Oxford: Oxford University Press, pp. 131–148.
Biville, F. (2018) Multilingualism in the Roman world. In *Oxford Handbook Topics in Classical Studies*, Online ed. Oxford: Oxford Academic, pp. 1–33. https://doi.org/10.1093/oxfordhb/9780199935390.013.101, accessed July 27, 2022.
Blom, A. (2009) *Lingua gallica, lingua celtica*: Gaulish, Gallo-Latin, or Gallo-Romance? *Keltische Forschungen*, 4, 7–54.
Bowman, A. & J. D. Thomas (1994) *The Vindolanda Writing-Tablets (Tabulae Vindolandenses II)*. London: British Museum Press.
Bozia, E. & A. Mullen (2021) Literary translingualism in the Greek and Roman worlds. In Kellman, S. & N. Lvovich (eds.) *Handbook of Literary Translingualism*. New York/Abingdon: Routledge, pp. 45–59.
Clackson, J. (2015a) *Language and society in the Greek and Roman worlds*. Cambridge: Cambridge University Press.
(2015b) Latinitas, Ἑλληνισμός and standard languages. *Studi e Saggi Linguistici*, 53, 2, 309–330.
Clackson, J., & G. Horrocks (2007) *The Blackwell history of the Latin language*. Malden/Oxford/Victoria: Blackwell Publishing.
Cooley, A. (forthcoming) The role of the non-elite in spreading Latin in Roman Britain. In Mullen, A. (ed.) *Social Factors in the Latinization of the Roman West*. Oxford: Oxford University Press.
Cornell, T. (1976) Etruscan historiography. *Annali Della Scuola Normale Superiore Di Pisa. Classe Di Lettere e Filosofia*, 6, 2, 411–439.
Cotton, H., Hoyland, R., Price, J., & D. Wasserstein (2009). *From Hellenism to Islam. Cultural and linguistic change in the Roman Near East*. Cambridge: Cambridge University Press.
Czajkowski, K., Eckhardt, B. & M. Strothmann (eds.) (2020) *Law in the Roman provinces*. Oxford: Oxford University Press.
Dickey, E. (2012) *The colloquia of the Hermeneumata Pseudodositheana Volume 1 colloquia Monacensia-Einsidlensia, Leidense-Stephani, and Stephani*. Cambridge: Cambridge University Press.
Dondin-Payre, M. (2005) Épigraphie et acculturation: l'apport des fusaïoles écrites [Epigraphy and acculturation: the contribution of the inscribed spindle whorls]. In Desmulliez, J. & C. Hoët-Van Cauwenberghe (eds.) *Le monde romain à travers l'épigraphie: Méthodes et pratiques*. Lille: Université Charles-de-Gaulle, pp. 133–146.
Dubuisson, M. (1981a) Problèmes du bilinguisme romain [Problems of Roman bilingualism]. *Les Études Classiques*, 49, 1, 27–45.
(1981b) Utraque lingua. *L'Antiquité Classique*, 50, 274–286.

(1982) Y a-t-il une politique linguistique romaine? [Was there a Roman language policy?]. *Ktéma*, 7, 197–210.

(1983) Recherches sur la terminologie antique du bilinguisme [Studies on the ancient terminology of bilingualism]. *Revue de Philologie*, 57, 2, 203–225.

(1986) Purisme et politique: Suétone, Tibère et le grec au Sénat [Purism and politics: Suetonius, Tiberius and Greek in the Senate]. In Veremans, J., Decreus, F. & C. Deroux (eds.) *Hommages à Jozef Veremans*. Leuven: Peeters, pp. 109–117.

Elder, O. (2019) *Language and the politics of Roman identity*. PhD thesis, University of Cambridge.

Elder, O. & A. Mullen (2019) *The language of Roman letters: bilingual epistolography from Cicero to Fronto*. Cambridge: Cambridge University Press.

Felice, E. (2019) *Multilingualism and Language Choice in the Imperial Roman Army*. DPhil thesis, University of Oxford.

Feugère, M. & P.-Y. Lambert (2011) Une belle gauloise... A propos d'une fibule inscrite de Laon [A pretty Gaulish girl... On an inscribed fibula from Laon]. *Etudes Celtiques*, 37, 147–152.

Hahn, L. (1907) Zum Sprachenkampf im römischen Reich bis auf die Zeit Justinians [On linguistic conflict in the Roman Empire up to the time of Justinian]. *Philologus*, 10, 677–718.

Harris, W. (1989) *Ancient Literacy*. Cambridge, MA: Harvard University Press.

Jireček, K. (1911) *Geschichte der Serben* [History of the Serbs]. Gotha: F.A. Perthes.

Kaimio, J. (1979) *The Romans and the Greek language*. Helsinki: Societas scientiarum Fennica.

Lambert, P.-Y. (2018) *La langue gauloise* [Gaulish]. Third edition. Paris: Editions Errance.

Lejeune, M. (1949). La curiosité linguistique dans l'antiquité classique [Linguistic curiosity in classical antiquity]. *Conférences de l'Institut de Linguistique de l'Université de Paris*, 8, 45–61.

Lomas, K. (2018) *The rise of Rome. From the Iron Age to the Punic Wars*. Cambridge, MA: Harvard University Press.

Mairs, R. (2020) Interpretes, negotiatores and the Roman army: Mobile professionals and their languages. In Clackson, J., James, P., McDonald, K., Tagliapietra, L. & N. Zair (eds.) *Migration, mobility, and language contact in and around the ancient Mediterranean*. Cambridge: Cambridge University Press, pp. 203–229.

Mari, T. (2021) *Consentius' De barbarismis et metaplasmis: Critical edition, translation, and commentary*. Oxford: Oxford University Press.

Meid, W. (1983) Gallisch oder Lateinisch? Soziolinguistische und andere Bemerkungen zu populären gallo-lateinischen Inschriften [Gaulish or Latin? Sociolinguistic and other remarks on 'everyday' Gallo-Latin inscriptions]. *Aufstieg und Niedergang der römischen Welt*, II.29.2, 1019–1044.

Millar, F. (1968) Local cultures in the Roman Empire: Libyan, Punic and Latin in Roman Africa. *Journal of Roman Studies,* 58, 126–134.

(1977) *The emperor in the Roman world 31 B.C.–A.D. 337*. London: Duckworth.

(1995) Latin in the epigraphy of the Roman Near East. In Solin, H., Salomies, O. & U.-M. Lierz (eds.) *Acta colloquii epigraphici Latini Helsingiae 3.–6. Sept. 1991 habiti*. Helsinki: Societas Scientiarum Fennica, pp. 403–419.

Mullen, A. (2013) *Southern Gaul and the Mediterranean. Multilingualism and multiple identities in the Iron Age and Roman periods*. Cambridge: Cambridge University Press.

(2021) Socio-literacy: an interdisciplinary approach to understanding literacy in the Roman North-West. In Moncunill, N. & M. Ramírez-Sánchez (eds.) *Aprender la escritura, olvidar la escritura: Nuevas perspectivas sobre la historia de la escritura en el Occidente romano* [Learning scripts, forgetting scripts: New perspectives on the history of writing in the Roman West]. Victoria: Anejos de Veleia, pp. 349–372.

(2022) Materializing epigraphy: archaeological and sociolinguistic approaches to Roman inscribed spindle whorls. In Cousins, E. (ed.) *Dynamic Epigraphy: New Approaches to Inscriptions*. Oxford: Oxbow, pp. 39–64.

(in press) Transformations de la Gaule sous l'Empire romain: une culture de l'écrit au service de la production de masse [Transformations of Gaul under the Roman Empire: The development of literacy for mass production]. In M. Coltelloni-Trannoy & N. Moncunill (eds.) *La culture de l'écrit en Méditerranée occidentale à travers les pratiques épigraphiques (Gaule, Ibérie, Afrique du Nord)* [Cultures of writing in the western Mediterranean through epigraphic practices (Gaul, Iberian Peninsula and North Africa)]. Leuven: Peeters, pp. 131–162.

Mullen, A. & A. Bowman (2021) *Manual of Roman everyday writing. Volume 1 Scripts and Texts*. Nottingham: LatinNow ePubs.

Mullen, A. & C. Darasse (2020) Gaulish. *Palaeohispanica*, 20, 749–783.

Mullen, A. & P. James (2012) *Multilingualism in the Graeco-Roman worlds*. Cambridge: Cambridge University Press.

Nelson, M. (2003) On a beautiful girl and some good barley beer. *Etudes Celtiques*, 35, 257–259.

Nowak, M. (2015) *Wills in the Roman Empire: A documentary approach*. Warsaw: University of Warsaw.

Pharr, C. (ed.) (1952) *The Theodosian code and novels, and the Sirmondian constitutions*. Princeton: Princeton University Press.

Poccetti, P. (1986) Lat. *bilinguis. Annali Dell'Università Degli Studi Di Napoli "L'Orientale". Rivista Dipartimento Del Mondo Classico. Sezione Linguistica,* 8, 95–129.

Rochette, B. (1995) Grecs et Latins face aux langues étrangères. Contribution à l'étude de la diversité linguistique dans l'antiquité classique [Attitudes of Greeks and Romans towards foreign languages. A contribution to the study of linguistic diversity in classical antiquity]. *Revue Belge de Philologie et d'histoire*, 73, 1, 5–16.

(1997) *Le latin dans le monde grec: recherches sur la diffusion de la langue et des lettres latines dans les provinces hellénophones de l'Empire romain* [Latin in the Greek world: research on the spread of the Latin language and texts in the Greek-speaking provinces of the Roman Empire]. Brussels: Collection Latomus.

(2000) La langue des testaments dans l'Egypte du IIIe s. ap. J.-C. [The language of wills in Egypt in the 3rd century CE]. *Revue internationale des droits de l'Antiquité*, 47, 449–461.

(2010) Greek and Latin bilingualism. In Bakker, E. (ed.) *A companion to the Greek language*. Malden/Oxford/Chichester: Wiley Blackwell, pp. 281–293.

(2011) Language policies in the Roman Republic and Empire. In Clackson, J. (ed.) *A companion to the Latin language*. Malden/Oxford/Chichester: Wiley Blackwell, pp. 549–563.

(forthcoming) The attitude of the Roman emperors towards language practices. In Mullen, A. (ed.) *Social factors in the Latinization of the Roman West*. Oxford: Oxford University Press.

Tomlin, R. (2016) *Roman London's First Voices: Writing tablets from the Bloomberg excavations, 2010–14*. London: Museum of London Archaeology.

Turner, E. (1961) Latin versus Greek as a universal language: the attitude of Diocletian. In *Language and culture: essays presented to A.M. Jensen*. Copenhagen: Det Berlingske Bogtrykkeri, pp. 165–168.

Wallace-Hadrill, A. (2008) *Rome's cultural revolution*. Cambridge: Cambridge University Press.

Willi, A. (2021) *Manual of Roman Everyday Writing. Volume 2 Writing Equipment*. Nottingham: LatinNow ePubs.

Wiotte-Franz, C. (2001) *Hermeneus und Interpres, zum Dolmetscherwesen in der Antike* [*Hermeneus* and *Interpres*, on interpreting in Antiquity]. Saarbrücken: Druckerei und Verlag.

Wolff, C. (forthcoming) The role of education in the Latinization of the Roman West. In Mullen, A. (ed.) *Social factors in the Latinization of the Roman West*. Oxford: Oxford University Press.

4 Languages at War: Military Interpreters in Antiquity and the Modern World

Rachel Mairs

The armed conflicts of the early twenty-first century have given a new prominence to the role of interpreters in war. For the most part, however, this public profile relates not to their actual service – to their mediation between languages, often for foreign military forces in the interpreters' home country – but to their own society's attitudes to their interpreting, and the situation this places them in. International news outlets such as the BBC and Al Jazeera have reported on Iraqi and Afghan interpreters employed by the United States and United Kingdom occupying forces, who find their lives threatened in their home countries for their 'collaboration' yet are unable to gain the right to settle abroad in the countries whose forces once depended on them.

News stories also give us direct access to the interpreters' own perspective, through interviews and first-person accounts of their experiences. An Afghan interpreter named Jamil, for example, told Al Jazeera: "I have been through the same ordeal as a [member of the] US army has; I have the scars which will be with me forever; if this doesn't prove my faithful service, then I don't really know what will do" (Al Jazeera, 2021). While such articles concentrate on the injustice of interpreters 'abandoned' to a violent fate by the foreign armies that used them, there is sometimes incidental information of interest to linguists. In the same article, another Afghan interpreter, Ameen, recalls the casual recruitment process the US military in Afghanistan used for interpreters. "When I think back now [to 2004], it was the easiest of job interviews anyone would hope for. I was asked: 'Do you speak English?' When I replied 'yes,' I was told, 'OK, tomorrow is your first day'" (Al Jazeera, 2021).

A rich body of recent scholarship has drawn on the first-hand testimony of war interpreters to explore the roles of language in armed conflict. From the Bosnian war of the 1990s (Kelly & Baker, 2013) to the ongoing Afghan conflict (Ruiz Rosendo, 2020), linguists and practicing interpreters have been

I borrow my title from the AHRC-funded 'Languages at War' project, a collaboration between the University of Reading, University of Southampton and Imperial War Museum, which ran between 2009 and 2012 and resulted in a number of important publications (e.g., Footitt & Kelly, 2012a, b; Footitt & Tobia, 2013).

able to tell the story of how language mediation works on a practical level and reveal the experiences, often traumatic, of the linguistic mediators involved. Linguists have even been able to reflect critically on the methodologies used in interviewing interpreters and the advantages and pitfalls of various approaches (Baker, 2019). For historians of interpreting, on the other hand, first-hand testimony is seldom available. An historian may come to their material with the same questions about interpreters as a modern linguist or sociologist – How were they recruited and trained? How did they learn their languages? How were they perceived by their employers and interlocutors? What translation strategies did they use? – but their ability to answer them must depend on the vagaries of historical evidence, which cannot be interrogated in the same way as a living person. My question in this article is a rather broad one: Can we identify commonalities in the activities and treatment of military interpreters across widely separated historical contexts?

My interest in this question derives from a pressing methodological and interpretative dilemma I have faced in my research on interpreters in the Graeco-Roman world (broadly understood) of the late first millennium BCE and early first millennium CE (see, most recently, Mairs, 2020a) and in the Middle East in the period between the Expédition d'Égypte of 1798–1801 and World War II (Mairs, forthcoming). My tendency is to recognize similarities in the treatment of interpreters in the different case studies with which I have worked. For example, if we might borrow a concept from translation studies into interpreting studies, the notion of the interpreter's 'invisibility' (Venuti, 2008) – the unrealistic perception of their role, by clients, as being the seamless and transparent transmission of language, without exercising personal agency – recurs time and again in different contexts. I shall explore some of these similarities further below.

At the same time, I find uncompelling attempts to construct grand, sweeping narratives of 'interpreting through the ages,' which are insensitive to the nature of the evidence and to specifics of time and place. It is commonplace, for example, for works on the history of interpreting to mention interpreting in ancient Egypt, usually with a reference that ultimately goes back in some way to Hermann's (1956) article *Dolmetschen im Altertum* [Interpreting in Ancient Times] (English translation in Pöchhacker & Shlesinger, 2002). Modern interpreters and historians of interpreting cannot very well be expected to follow up the references to the original hieroglyphic Egyptian texts cited by Hermann and others but, if they did, they would find that identifying ancient Egyptian interpreters is a much more problematic task. The words translated by some into English as 'interpreter' or the more old-fashioned (and Orientalist) 'dragoman' are in fact much more ambiguous, and would often better be translated as 'foreigner' or 'speaker of a foreign language' (see, e.g., Bell, 1973, 1976). There doubtless were interpreters in ancient Egypt, but the evidence for them is not clear-cut. Words translated as 'interpreter' in Greek (*hermēneus*) and Latin (*interpres*) are likewise ambiguous in their meaning (Mairs, 2020a). The challenge is therefore to adopt a diachronic approach to the study of interpreters that both recognizes continuities in their role and treatment and avoids the pitfalls of overgeneralization.

My aim in what follows is to present some of the methodological challenges and pleasures of working with historical source material in reconstructing the lives and careers of interpreters. I have chosen to focus specifically on military interpreters both because the source material is more copious and because the search for structural similarities stands a better chance of success within a particular occupational niche. Interpreters working in situations of armed conflict interact with one of history's great creators of paperwork – armies – and often alongside the kinds of elite literate individuals who leave their own written record. After surveying some of this evidence, I shall identify some common features that recur in the historical evidence on interpreters' lives and roles.

4.1 Locating Military Interpreters in the Historical Record

4.1.1 Military Records: Reading against the Grain

Researching the history of interpreters requires creative use of historical sources that usually do not 'want' to tell the stories we try to draw out of them. It requires reading against the grain of the archive. The first issue with which we are confronted is that military record-keeping is usually a monolingual enterprise, which obscures both linguistic diversity within an army itself and the different languages with which the army came into contact (an exception is the complex linguistic organization and hierarchies within and between units of the Habsburg army; see, e.g., Scheer, 2020; Stergar, 2019).

In the Roman army, for example, Latin was the sole language afforded any 'official' status. Roman military records on perishable materials have not survived for the most part (in the Roman Empire, writings of this sort are preserved only in dry climates, such as that of Egypt, or in isolated finds, such as the Vindolanda tablets from Britain). What we have instead are the vast numbers of inscriptions on stone generated by the army's operations, and by its soldiers acting in a private capacity. The army was one of the principal vectors of the 'epigraphic habit' – the tendency to mark important events with stone inscriptions – throughout the Roman provinces. Inscriptions generated by the Roman army systematically record the military rank of individuals mentioned, but they do not commonly record the position of interpreter, which was not a military rank like 'centurion' with an acknowledged place in the military hierarchy. This is despite the fact that the Roman army not only recruited speakers of many languages from across the empire but came into contact with still more languages as it campaigned beyond its borders. Individual multilingualism and the use of interpreters must have been a fact of life within the Roman army, but the Latin epigraphic record obscures this.

The few inscriptions that do mention interpreters are such a remarkable exception in an 'archive' which otherwise totally neglects their presence that we have to account for them. Why do these particular inscriptions go against the 'logic' of the archive? Take, for example, a list of discharged veterans from the Legio VII Claudia from Viminacium (now in eastern Serbia), dating to sometime after 195 CE, which names two soldiers, C. Valerius Valens and M. Ulpius Martialis, as interpreters (Fig. 4.1). The only other information we are given on the two men is that they are from Roman military colonies in Ratiaria (in modern northwestern Bulgaria) and Scupi (modern Skopje, in

Fig. 4.1 List of discharged veterans from Viminacium (CIL III 14507). Image in the public domain.

North Macedonia). Elsewhere, I have discussed this record alongside a cluster of roughly contemporary Latin funerary inscriptions of military interpreters from along the River Danube (Mairs, 2020b). I suggested that the reason why interpreters become visible precisely here is because legions were stationed in the same place for a long time and recruited the multilingual children of Roman soldiers and local women. Units in the Roman army could be deployed throughout the empire, but when they did settle in the same place for an extended period of time, the linguistic knowledge of ‘children of the regiment’ gained greater value. These were longer-term, ‘career interpreters’ of relatively high military rank, not ad hoc employees in a new posting, who were likely neither to leave a Latin inscription nor to be valued within military hierarchies. In this case, the way our epigraphic ‘archive’ is constructed allows us to use the mention or occlusion of interpreters to draw conclusions about their roles.

In themselves, however, documents such as the discharge record of C. Valerius Valens and M. Ulpius Martialis are reticent about many details, which is typical of military records. Unlike Roman ones, certain categories of British military record of the nineteenth and twentieth centuries do systematically record whether an individual was an interpreter, but again with little subsidiary information. Such is the case with the cards recording relatives’ claims for the pensions of British soldiers killed or injured in World War I, like the example illustrated here (Fig. 4.2). The pension of an interpreter named

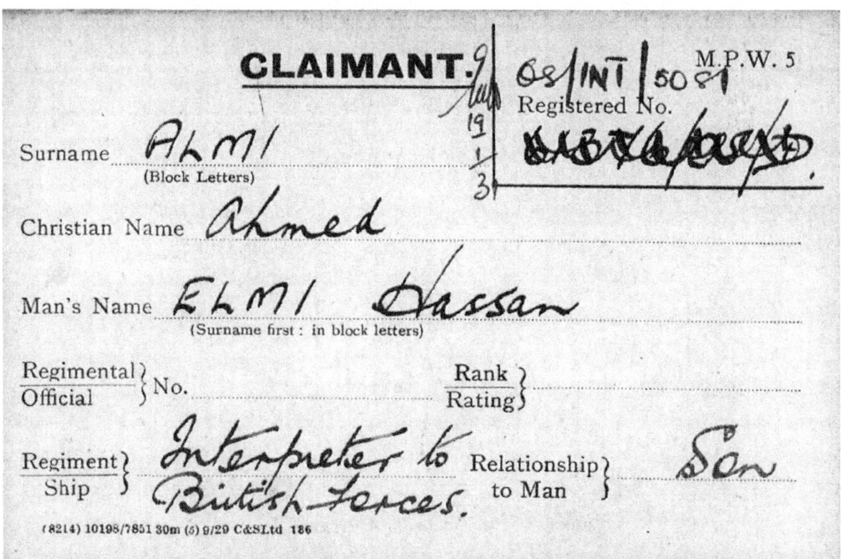

CLAIMANT. M.P.W. 5

08/INT/5081
Registered No.

Surname ALMI
(Block Letters)

Christian Name Ahmed

Man's Name ELMI Hassan
(Surname first : in block letters)

Regimental / Official No.
Rank / Rating

Regiment / Ship Interpreter to British Forces.
Relationship to Man Son

(8214) 10198/7851 30m (5) 9/20 C&SLtd 186

Fig. 4.2 Pension record card for Ahmed Almi. Image in the public domain.

Ahmed Almi is claimed by his son Hassan, who lived at an address in Cardiff (Western Front Association; London, England; *WWI Pension Record Cards and Ledgers*; Reference: *003/0007/ALL-AND*). We are given no other information about Almi – his ethnic origin, languages interpreted, or even age – just as we are not for C. Valerius Valens and M. Ulpius Martialis. From his name, we may assume that the language he interpreted for English speakers was Arabic, but there is no evidence for this. I have not been able to trace either Almi or his son in other records, which is a common problem when dealing with individuals with non-English names in British official sources, since they are frequently misspelled.

The conciseness or rarity of official records is not our only problem in researching military interpreters. There is also the issue that those who performed the role of interpreter will not always have done so in an official capacity. Individual armies may or may not keep the same careful records of civilian employees as they do of enlisted soldiers, which makes civilian interpreters especially difficult to locate in the archive. The individuals whom I shall discuss in the following section fall into this category, since they either acted as interpreter outside their official duties (Percy Long) or were never enlisted in the army (Procillus and/or Troucillus). One set of documents that records both enlisted and civilian interpreters can nevertheless act as a cautionary tale in assuming that the archivally visible interpreters were the only ones.

Records of campaign medals awarded to members of the British armed forces are available from 1793 to World War II. These lists can be searched and viewed using the commercial service Ancestry. For World War I, 'Medal index cards' also exist, which give a small amount of information on individuals awarded medals, often in abbreviated form.[1] These records cover all theaters of war, and they cover all those entitled to a medal for serving on a campaign, whether as an enlisted soldier or in a civilian role. They are therefore an excellent source of information on interpreters. They allow us to confirm where interpreters served and in what capacity, and sometimes even contain information that the individuals themselves sought to conceal. They are especially useful when used in combination with other sources. My own interest is primarily in materials relating to the Middle East, and I will illustrate my points by reference to two interpreters on whom I have conducted research: Solomon Negima and Getzel Selikovitch.

Solomon Negima was a Palestinian who worked as an interpreter for the British Army in the Sudan on the Nile Expedition of 1884–1885.[2] He appears

[1] See the UK National Archives research guide to these materials: www.nationalarchives.gov.uk/help-with-your-research/research-guides/british-military-campaign-and-service-medals/.

[2] 'Negima' is how he spelled his surname. It appears in the Medal Rolls as 'Negimae' and in several other spellings in different sources; the family today use a different spelling.

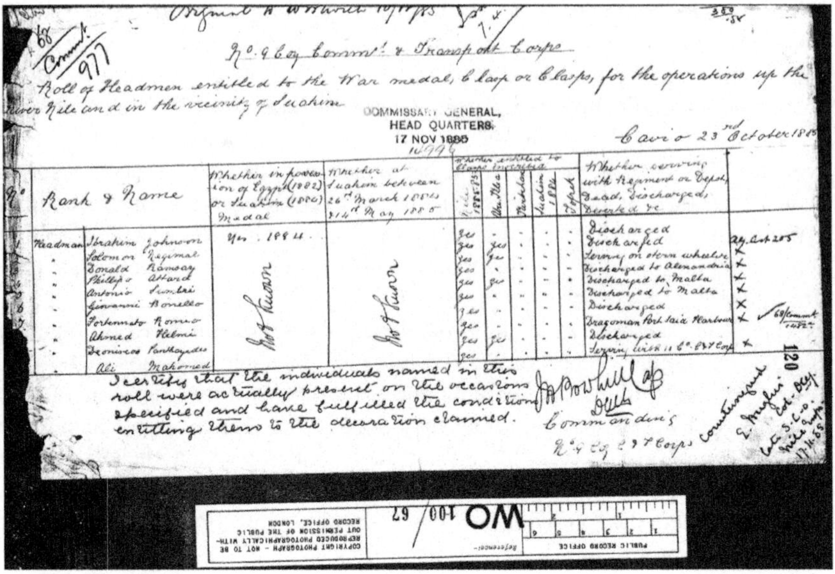
No. 9 Coy Commt. & Transport Corps

Roll of Headmen entitled to the War medal, Clasp or Clasps, for the operations up the River Nile and in the vicinity of Suakim

COMMISSARY GENERAL,
HEAD QUARTERS,
17 NOV 1885

Cairo 23rd October 1885

No. | Rank & Name | Whether in possession of Egypt (1882) or Suakim (1884) Medal | Whether at Suakim between 26th March 1885 & 14th May 1885 | Whether entitled to Clasps inscribed | Whether serving with Regiment or Depot, Dead, Discharged, Deserted &c.

Headman Ibrahim Johnson – Discharged
Solomon Negimah – Discharged
Donald Ramsay – Serving on stern wheeler
Phillipo Attard – Discharged to Alexandria
Antonio Sembri – Discharged to Malta
Giovanni Bonello – Discharged to Malta
Fortunato Romeo – Discharged
Ahmed Helmi – Dragoman Port Said Harbour
Leonidas Panthagedes – Discharged
Ali Mahomed – Serving with 1 C° C&T Corps

I certify that the individuals named in this roll were actually present on the occasions specified and have fulfilled the conditions entitling them to the decoration claimed.

Commanding No 9 Co C&T Corps

WO 100/67

PUBLIC RECORD OFFICE

COPYRIGHT PHOTOGRAPH – NOT TO BE REPRODUCED PHOTOGRAPHICALLY WITHOUT PERMISSION OF THE PUBLIC RECORD OFFICE, LONDON

Fig. 4.3 Medal Roll for Solomon Negima. Image in the public domain.

in the section of the Medal Rolls for 'Headmen' attached to the ninth company of the Commissariat and Transport Corps (WO [War Office] 100/67, Fig. 4.3). His main job was therefore in transportation logistics for the Royal Engineers. It is only from other sources, including the book of testimonials that he kept during his later career as a tourist guide and interpreter in Palestine, that we know that his work in the Sudan included interpreting at all. One of the British officers who wrote a recommendation letter for him recorded that Negima "was engaged as Headman but has really acted as Interpreter all through" (Captain H. P. Leach, 16 July 1885, in Mairs 2016, p. 16). Even in sources in which interpreters become 'visible,' we can still find their roles obscured. Negima seems to have moved into the role of interpreter once officers realized that he was multilingual (in Arabic, German, and English) and could read and write. Because he was not originally appointed as an interpreter, he does not pass into the archives as one. This should make us question the actual roles performed by his fellow 'headmen' in the Medal Rolls and consider whether they were linguistic as well as organizational: in particular Ahmed Helmi, who is recorded as 'Dragoman' at Port Said.

There are no surviving direct testimonies from interpreters who served on the Nile Expedition, but the Medal Rolls do allow us to reconstruct something of their experience. Solomon Negima, for example, is recorded as being present at the Battle of Abu Klea. This means that he was with the section of the expedition (the 'Desert Column') that proceeded overland, taking a short cut past a long bend in the Nile. From the (many) memoirs of British officers who were with this offshoot of the main force, we can then follow the route Negima took, the military actions in which he was involved, and the tasks undertaken by the Transport and Commissariat Corps (Mairs, 2016, pp. 23–33). This is despite the fact that these memoirs, in and of themselves, scarcely mention interpreters and have no record of Negima himself. In a sense, we are reading against the grain of the memoir, looking to reconstruct the life, not of the author but of another individual who followed the same path. Nevertheless, the specifically linguistic aspects of Negima's experience – how he used languages and with whom – are lost from the record.

In the same set of Medal Rolls, WO 100/67, we also find individuals who *are* recorded as interpreters. Getzel Selikovitch was not at Abu Klea, so he was with the 'River Column' that proceeded by boat along the Nile (Fig. 4.4). He is the only interpreter on this page of the records who does not have an Arab name; he was a Yiddish- and Russian-speaking Jew, born in the Russian Empire. Selikovitch's entry has been crossed out and annotated "this is the man who made false statements as to the death of Olivier Pain." The 'Olivier Pain Affair,' which erupted in the French and English press in the summer of 1885, concerned a French journalist covering the Nile Expedition who had died under mysterious circumstances. Selikovitch alleged that he had been

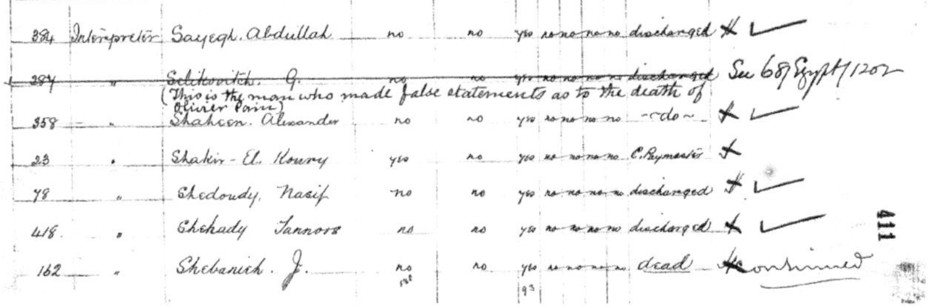
APPENDIX TO G.O. 97.

Regiment.

ROLL of Officers, Warrant Officers, Non-Commissioned Officers, and men entitled to the War Medal, Clasp, or Clasps for the operations up the river Nile, and in the vicinity of Suakin, 1884–5.

Station

Date

Regimental Number.	Rank.	Name.	Whether in possession of Egypt (1882), or Suakin (1884) Medal, and what clasps.	Whether at Suakin between 26th March, 1884, and 28th February, 1885.	Whether entitled to clasps inscribed. Nile, 1884–5.	Abu Klea.	Kirbekan.	Suakin, 1885.	Tofrek.	Whether serving with regiment or depot, dead, discharged, deserted, &c.	To be left blank.
At the time the decoration was earned.											
384	Interpreter	Sayegh. Abdullah	no	no	yes	no	no	no	no	discharged	✗ ✓
~~384~~	~~"~~	~~Selikovitch. G.~~ (This is the man who made false statements as to the death of Olivier Pain)	~~no~~	~~no~~	~~yes~~	~~no~~	~~no~~	~~no~~	~~no~~	~~discharged~~	See 68/Egypt/1202
358	"	Shaheen. Alexander	no	no	yes	no	no	no	no	– do –	✗ ✓
23	"	Shakir-El. Koury	yes	no	yes	no	no	no	no	C. Paymaster	✗
78	"	Shedoudy. Nasif	no	no	yes	no	no	no	no	discharged	✗ ✓
418	"	Shehady Tannors	no	no	yes	no	no	no	no	discharged	✗ ✓
162	"	Shebanich. J.	no	no	yes	no	no	no	no	dead	Continued

411

Fig. 4.4 Medal Roll for Getzel Selikovitch. Image in the public domain.

murdered by the British; the evidence in fact points to natural causes (Goldberg, 2004).

Selikovitch's commanding officer was Lieutenant-Colonel (later Field Marshal and Earl) Kitchener, who was interviewed for *Le Matin* during the scandal:

> 'What do you know of M. Selikovitch?'
> 'I rather dislike replying to that question, for it would be degrading to enter into a discussion with that personage, and to follow him in the abuse and bad temper which he has been for some reason led to indulge in. But not to be disagreeable to you, I may say that he was one of the interpreters whom I had under my orders. I have not spoken to him very frequently. At first, he had a very imperfect acquaintance with Arabic; but I had no occasion to expect any service from him in this respect, for I know Arabic much better than he does. The greatest fault I had to find with him was that I have caught him several times discussing politics with Egyptian soldiers, to whom he spoke in a way which was not in conformity with this duty, or with the place which he had accepted in my service.'
> 'They say you were rather severe with interpreters.'
> 'Well, I had an enormous responsibility. The army trusted me to protect it from an unexpected attack, and among the people I had to do with affability was somewhat out of place.'
> (*Le Matin*, 31 August 1885, 1. I give here the English translation that appeared in *The Times*, 1 September 1885, p. 3. It is unclear whether the original interview took place in French or English.)

Other sources confirm that Kitchener probably spoke better Arabic than Selikovitch did. Selikovitch later published an Arabic-Yiddish phrasebook for Jewish immigrants to Palestine (Selikovitch, 1918). Perhaps his most significant historical and linguistic legacy is one of which he was unaware. Eliezar Ben-Yehuda, architect of the revival of Hebrew as a spoken language, met Selikovitch in Paris in 1879 and heard from him for the first time "natural, simple conversation in Hebrew," which inspired him in his own linguistic ventures (Ben-Yehuda, 1993, pp. 33–34).

The August 1885 interview with Kitchener incidentally reveals something of the working conditions of interpreters on the Nile Expedition, who, as we shall see, are seldom mentioned in the memoirs of soldiers who served on it. Kitchener's euphemistic assertion that "affability was somewhat out of place" in his relations with interpreters indicates the very low priority they had in the eyes of soldiers and their commanders in the field. This attitude, as can be seen from the interviewer's line of questioning, extended to interpreters as a whole, not just to troublemakers like Selikovitch.

The Medal Rolls for the Nile Expedition do not just shed light on the careers of individual interpreters but can also be used to provide information on the corps as a whole. As noted above, Solomon Negima does not seem to have been the only 'Headman' who also functioned as an interpreter. Ahmed Helmi's position at Dragoman at Port Said, at the Mediterranean end of the Suez Canal, will also have involved language mediation. In 1892, the Indian scholar Shiblī Nuʿmānī even recorded finding speakers of Urdu among the officials at Port Said and Suez (Nuʿmānī, trans. Bruce, 2020, p. 23). Even if individuals cannot always be followed further in the archival record, their names can be revealing. Solomon Negima's fellow Headmen were Arab, British, Greek, Maltese, and Italian. The other interpreters on the same page of the Medal Rolls as Getzel Selikovitch were Arab, some with names indicative of Syrian or Palestinian Christians rather than Egyptians or Sudanese. Both records indicate the reach of the recruiting process for the Nile Expedition. In October 1884, as the expedition set out for the Sudan, one journalist in Cairo recalled that "the demand for interpreters by the military authorities was so urgent, and the price they offered were so high, as not only to drain but also to 'bull' the market" (Macdonald, 1887, p. 28).

4.1.2 Military Memoirs: Reading between the Lines

In contrast to the often impersonal details contained in the Medal Rolls, military memoirs are a copious source of information on the actual lived experience of war. The genre goes back to antiquity, although the past two hundred years or so have seen the publication of vast quantities of memoirs, especially for conflicts in Europe and North America. This literature can create the illusion that for some historical periods we know all about the lives of the combatants (and the noncombatants caught up in war), but the case of interpreters shows that first-person memoirs are as partial (in both senses of the word) a source of evidence as any other historical source. In the many examples I have surveyed, interpreting and language contact are seldom mentioned in more than passing. Details about the experiences of interpreters and the linguistic and social mechanisms of interpreting are frustratingly absent.

An early and influential example of the genre is the account written by Gaius Julius Caesar of the campaigns he led in Gaul in the 50s BCE, known today as the *Bellum Gallicum* or *Gallic War*. Caesar writes in the grammatical third person (referring to himself as 'Caesar'), but very much from a first-person perspective. The fact that interpreters were employed at all in relations between Romans and Gauls is only revealed through their absence in a particular case. This implies that they were present on other occasions described by Caesar, but not mentioned. Caesar states that he dismissed his *cotidiani interpretes* [usual interpreters] in a confidential meeting with a Gaulish chief and instead used his "close friend C. Valerius Troucillus, a leading citizen of the province of Gaul, in whom he had the greatest confidence in all matters" (*Gallic War* 1.19; discussed by Mairs, 2011, pp. 73–75; see also this discussion for the question of whether Troucillus and Procillus were in fact one and the same). In another incident, Caesar also used a Romanized Gaul, C. Valerius Procillus, as interpreter. Caesar's concern in each case was the loyalty and trustworthiness of interpreters, and, in each case, he made a similar choice of stand-in: men who were of Gaulish noble origin, but acculturated to Roman ways, as their tripartite Latin names reveal. Although Caesar emphasizes the bonds of aristocratic friendship that tied him to Procillus and Troucillus, this did not prevent him from treating them carelessly. Procillus was captured and nearly executed by the Germanic king Ariovistus while undertaking a commission for Caesar.

There is a direct line of continuity between first-person accounts of war in the ancient Graeco-Roman world and in more recent conflicts. As time has passed, the military memoir has become a more 'democratic' genre, in the sense that accounts by soldiers of all ranks have been written, published, and found an audience. In contrast, the nineteenth-century British military memoirs that I have examined in my research into Arabic learning in the colonial period Middle East were almost all written by officers: educated men of a relatively elevated socioeconomic class. British education of the day – however little of it men may have absorbed before joining the army – included the Greek and Roman 'Classics.' Caesar's *Gallic War*, which is written in fairly simple Latin prose and has thus long been a popular text for teaching the language, will have been familiar to them. It is not unusual to find direct Classical references in Victorian military memoirs (Caesar specifically, cf. Clarke & Horne, 2018, p. 10). Charles W. Wilson, who served on the Nile Expedition of 1884–1885, for example, compares a spear fight between an Arab and a British officer to scenes of gladiatorial combat from Pompeii (Wilson, 1886, p. 31). Caesar's *Gallic War*, which includes his campaigns in southern Britain, was particularly valued because – as a lecturer at the Ethnological Society in London in 1866 put it – it "throws the first ray of light on the forefathers of the people who, after many turns of fortune and much intermixture with other nations, eventually founded the British Empire and planted colonies in the New World and the antipodes" (Crawfurd, 1867, p. 202). There is therefore a measure of continuity and direct literary inspiration between ancient Greek and Roman military memoirs, and their successors in the British Empire in the nineteenth century. Among the many characteristics they share is ignorance, disregard, or erasure of the presence and work of interpreters.

Memoirs written by British soldiers in the Middle East in the colonial period tend to show very limited engagement with local languages, aside from including a few words of (usually rude) Arabic for 'local color.' An exception (and a welcome one after reading dozens of war memoirs on a very similar plan) is Percy Walter Long's *Other Ranks of Kut* (Long, 1938). Long served in the British Army in India and then in Mesopotamia during World War I as an ordinary enlisted soldier, not as an officer. He was eighteen at the start of the war, and census records reveal that he had left school by the age of fifteen and was working as a carpenter. He therefore had no university education and is unlikely to have had much exposure to ancient or modern languages in his secondary schooling. He had been in India before being deployed to Mesopotamia, and served as a driver. He was present at the British surrender at Kūt al-ʻAmāra in April 1916 and spent the following two and a half years in various Ottoman prisoner-of-war camps and jails, between extended periods on the run.

Long's account makes it clear that, for captured soldiers, knowing languages could literally mean the difference between life and death: "I undoubtedly owe my life to the fact that I was able to glean sufficient knowledge of the language of the various peoples among whom I stayed to serve me, for during the whole of my captivity it was this ability that enabled me to get food where others had starved – apart from other advantages" (Long, 1938, p. 70). Speaking and understanding Arabic (and later Turkish and Kurdish) allowed Long to barter for a better price in selling his army kit for food; to befriend fellow prisoners (reducing the risk of violence against him); to beg for food or clothing from locals; and to appeal to Ottoman officers and judicial authorities for better treatment. He had a good ear, and his other great advantages as a language learner were that he was young and that he was gregarious. It is difficult to assess how strong Long's command of any of these languages was, since he provides only occasional words and phrases (which are usually correct, but sometimes show an imperfect grasp of pronunciation). The important thing for Long was that he had enough to make himself understood.

Long's linguistic abilities were unusual among his fellow prisoners of war, which led to him being appointed 'terjiman' [interpreter] between the captured British and Indian soldiers and their Turkish and Arab captors. In his memoir, he uses the title with pride. On the march, his group is handed over from the command of one unit of Ottoman guards to another

> "and I was introduced to them as the Terjiman and Chaoush (Sergeant) of the party. Our Onbashi [Turkish officer] had apparently considered me worthy of promotion even if my late Commanding Officer had not! To the end of the journey I was considered to be in charge after this, and was referred to by our various guards and escort as Terjiman Chaoush" (Long, 1938, p. 57).

Long is frank about the advantages and disadvantages of his official role as interpreter. In one prisoner-of-war camp "as a *terjiman* I soon became regarded as an overseer, and, although I was not officially recognized as such, I assumed that status and played the role for all it was worth" (Long, 1938, p. 282). He sometimes received preferential treatment from his captors (greater mobility, the occasional cigarette) but also suspicion that he might be a spy.

Literary sources – especially memoirs and other forms of life writing – are therefore frustrating places to search for evidence of military interpreters. There is the very occasional gem, such as Percy Long's account of his period in Ottoman captivity as 'terjiman,' but for the most part the literary record at all periods consists of accounts by officers and commanders who used interpreters' services but did not consider them worthy of mention. The 'official' record both reveals and neglects interpreters in slightly different ways.

4.2 Common Trends

A comparative study of military interpreters from the ancient Roman world and from the nineteenth-century colonial Middle East reveals certain common themes. First, and most significantly, the surviving historical records generated by armies provide us with information on interpreters only to the extent to which this aligns with the priorities and logic of the archive itself. This is a fairly basic point, but it bears reiteration. Because armies have not generally accorded interpreters high status and official recognition (a theme I shall go on to discuss), 'finding' them means reading against the grain of the archive. Lessons learned from working on one historical context can productively be applied to others. Knowing that interpreters are only named as such in very specific geographical and social contexts in the Roman army, for example, can help us interpret other situations where, despite widespread multilingualism and language contact, interpreters are mentioned only rarely.

Connected with this, a diachronic perspective reminds us that, ironically, we cannot automatically expect to find historical evidence of interpreting in the same places where we find evidence of multilingualism. The Roman Empire was highly multilingual (for Latin in contact with other languages, see Adams, 2003), but this did not guarantee that interpreters and interpreting were accorded mentions in official records. Similarly, the Nile Expedition included speakers of many languages (notably Arabic and English, although West Africans and even Canadian Mohawks were also present, cf. Benn, 2009), but interpreters are scarcely mentioned in the memoirs of British officers. In both these contexts, individual multilingualism may have obviated to some extent the need for interpreting, but it remains clear that interpreters and their skills were not highly esteemed, and often distrusted.

Another common thread is that the recruitment and training of interpreters is seldom institutionalized. Such contexts do exist (for example, in diplomacy in Ottoman Istanbul, cf. Hitzel, 1997; Rothman, 2021; Testa & Gautier 2003), but they are historically quite rare. Armies, in particular, consistently display an ad hoc attitude to interpreter recruitment. Compare, for example, Caesar's abrupt conscription of two Gaulish nobles who were not practicing interpreters into service in this role, with the Afghan interpreter Ameen's "easiest of job interviews" for the United States Army. Solomon Negima, likewise, was recruited for one role on the Nile Expedition but given interpreting duties after it became known that he was literate and multilingual. Percy Long became an interpreter through necessity while a prisoner of war. This represents a persistent failure of armies to learn from past experience. While British soldiers in the nineteenth century might study Roman military tactics, they did not apparently seek to learn from Caesar's difficulties in recruiting trustworthy interpreters, still less in protecting them. Similarly, numerous past conflicts have demonstrated the vulnerability of interpreters to reprisals from their own communities, for perceived treachery in working with the enemy, and thus it might easily have been anticipated that Afghan and Iraqi interpreters working with foreign forces would find themselves at risk. (Here, the problem may be not so much a lack of an historical perspective as a lack of compassion.)

In a broader sense, the contexts I have considered here demonstrate a persistent reluctance by military authorities to treat linguistic knowledge as a 'hard' skill, on the same level as other specialist skills demanded by an army, and to invest in it accordingly. 'Interpreter' was not treated as a military rank in the Roman army and was not consistently recorded across the empire. Percy Long, who was not highly educated by British standards and did not come from a high socioeconomic class, repeatedly sets himself apart in his account from officers, who received better treatment as prisoners of war. His ability to pick up local languages (as he did with Hindustani during his first posting in India, then Arabic, Kurdish, and Turkish) did not translate into promotion within the ranks. Only as a Turkish prisoner of war was he accorded the official rank of 'interpreter,' because he was literate and multilingual: "Our Onbashi had apparently considered me worthy of promotion even if my late Commanding Officer had not!" (Long, 1938, p. 57). Although modern armies have specialist language training programs (such as the United States Defense Language Institute), they are still dependent to a great extent on civilian recruitment of interpreters for specific conflicts and peacekeeping missions (on Bosnia–Herzegovina, see Kelly & Baker, 2013). This neglect is doubtless in part due to cost and changing linguistic requirements, as well as ignorance on the part of monolinguals of the specialist skills involved in interpreting above and beyond language competence (cultural knowledge, diplomacy, memory). In my view, however, there is also a strong ideological aspect to the failure to treat interpreting as a 'hard' skill: the notion that the interpreter's role is to mediate 'transparently' and to make themselves in some way 'invisible' to the linguistic transaction.

There are, of course, areas of interpreters' lives and practice that the historical record does not allow us to explore. There are no recordings or transcripts of the conversations mediated by ancient Roman or nineteenth-century

British army interpreters, and we cannot look at the interpreters' use of language and linguistic decision-making processes. In many cases, we do not even know which languages they spoke. In situations such as this, a comparative approach is valuable – not because it allows us to 'fill in the blanks,' but because it opens up a repertoire of possibilities. In the absence of any other contemporary evidence, one might (naively) assume that the Roman army interpreters recorded along the Danube around the turn of the first to second centuries CE were the only ones. Exploration of other contexts, such as the copious records of the British Army, makes it very clear that absence in the official record does not have to mean absolute absence. Creative, comparative interrogation of taciturn sources – reading against their grain – can reconstruct something of the agency and presence of interpreters as individuals. This is as true of Roman epitaphs as it is of Victorian medal rolls. A diachronic historical perspective on interpreters can therefore go a long way toward helping us make interpreters historically 'visible.'

This approach therefore has much to offer historians, but does it have anything to offer practitioners? Armies are not lacking in historical perspective, but the ways in which they 'learn from history' are highly selective (Sangar, 2016). It has been argued, for example, that "nowhere is the value of historical knowledge demonstrated more than with Anglo-Afghan relations in the twenty-first century" (Campbell, 2015, p. 82). Indeed, discourse around British and US military difficulties in Afghanistan in the early 2000s frequently called upon historical comparisons, particularly with the Soviet Afghan War and the Anglo-Afghan Wars of the nineteenth century, but also with antiquity (on Alexander the Great in Afghanistan in contemporary perspective, see Holt, 2005). Comparative discussions of this sort naturally tend to focus on tactical and logistical considerations, from the army's perspective. It seems to me fairly obvious that armies could equally learn from history in their treatment and efficient employment of interpreters, yet this seems rarely to be a priority in operational planning.

References

Adams, J. N. (2003) *Bilingualism and the Latin Language*. Cambridge: Cambridge University Press.

Al Jazeera (2021) 'Betrayed': The Afghan interpreters abandoned by the US, Sayed Jalal Shajjan, June 13, 2021, Al Jazeera: www.aljazeera.com/features/2021/6/13/betrayed-the-afghan-interpreters-abandoned-by-the

Baker, C. (2019) Interviewing for research on languages and war. In Kelly, M., Footitt, H. & M. Salama-Carr (eds.) *The Palgrave Handbook of Languages and Conflict*. Cham: Springer, pp. 157–179.

Bell, L. (1973) Once more the *a.w*: 'Interpreters' or 'Foreigners'? *Newsletter of the American Research Center in Egypt*, 87, 33.

(1976) *Interpreters and Egyptianized Nubians in Ancient Egyptian Foreign Policy: Aspects of the History of Egypt and Nubia*. Unpublished thesis. University of Pennsylvania.

Ben-Yehuda, E. (1993) *A dream come true*, translated by George Mandel. Boulder, CO: Westview Press.

Benn, C. (2009) *Mohawks on the Nile: Natives among the Canadian Voyageurs in Egypt 1884–1885*. Toronto: Natural Heritage Books.

Campbell, H. (2015) Lessons to be Learnt? The Third Anglo-Afghan War. *The RUSI Journal* 160, 76–85.

Clarke, J. & J. Horne (2018) Introduction: Peripheral Visions – Militarized Cultural Encounters in the Long Nineteenth Century. In Clarke, J. & J. Joseph Horne (eds.) *Militarized Cultural Encounters in the Long Nineteenth Century*. Basingstoke: Palgrave Macmillan, pp. 1–21.

Crawfurd, J. (1867) On Caesar's Account of Britain and Its Inhabitants in Reference to Ethnology. *Transactions of the Ethnological Society of London*, 5, 202–215.

Footitt, H. & M. Kelly (eds.) (2012a) *Languages and the military: Alliances, occupation and peace building*. Basingstoke: Palgrave Macmillan.

(2012b) *Languages at war: Policies and practices of language contacts in conflict*. Basingstoke: Palgrave Macmillan.

Footitt, H. & S. Tobia (2013) *War talk: Foreign languages and the British war effort in Europe, 1940–47*. Basingstoke: Palgrave Macmillan.

Goldberg, Z. (2004) [Getzel Zelikowitz – The Journey to the Sudan, the Olivier Pain Affair and the confrontation with the anti-Semitic Drumont]
פן והעימות עם האנטישמי דרימון,” מעוף ומעשה גצל זליקוביץ – המסע לסודן, פרשת אוליביה
Ma'of u ma'aseh, 10, 179–205.

Hermann, A. (1956) Dolmetschen im Altertum [Interpreting in ancient times]. *Schriften des Auslands- und Dolmetscherinstituts der Universität in Mainz in Germersheim*, I, 25–29.

Hitzel, F. (ed.) (1997) *Istanbul et les langues orientales* [Istanbul and oriental languages]. Paris: L'Harmattan.

Holt, F. (2005) *Into the land of bones: Alexander the Great in Afghanistan*. Berkeley, CA: University of California Press.

Kelly, M. & C. Baker (eds.) (2013) *Interpreting the peace: Peace operations, conflict and language in Bosnia–Herzegovina*. Basingstoke: Palgrave Macmillan.

Long, P. (1938) *Other Ranks of Kut*. London: Williams and Norgate.

Macdonald, A. (1887) *Too late for Gordon and Khartoum: the testimony of an independent eye-witness of the heroic efforts for their rescue and relief*. London: J. Murray.

Mairs, R. (2011) Translator, Traditor: The Interpreter as Traitor in Classical Tradition. *Greece & Rome*, 58, 64–81.

(2016) *From Khartoum to Jerusalem: The dragoman Solomon Negima and his clients, 1885–1933*. London: Bloomsbury.

(2020a) Hermēneis in the Documentary Record from Hellenistic and Roman Egypt: Interpreters, Translators and Mediators in a Bilingual Society. *Journal of Ancient History*, 7, 2, 1–53.

(2020b) Interpretes, negotiatores and the Roman army: Mobile professionals and their languages. In Clackson, J., James, P., McDonald, K., Tagliapietra, L. &

N. Zair (eds.) *Migration, Mobility, and Language Contact in and around the Ancient Mediterranean*. Cambridge: Cambridge University Press, pp. 203–229.
(forthcoming) *Arabic Dialogues: Learning Colloquial Arabic through Phrasebooks 1798–1945.*

Nuʿmānī, S., translated by G. Maxwell Bruce (2020) *Turkey, Egypt, and Syria: A travelogue*. Syracuse, NY: Syracuse University Press.

Pöchhacker, F. & M. Shlesinger (2002) *The Interpreting Studies Reader*. London; New York: Routledge.

Rothman, N. (2021) *The Dragoman Renaissance: Diplomatic interpreters and the routes of orientalism*. Ithaca, NY: Cornell University Press.

Ruiz Rosendo, L. (2020) Interpreting for the Afghanistan Spanish Force. *War & Society*, 39, 42–57.

Sangar, E. (2016) The pitfalls of learning from historical experience: the British Army's debate on useful lessons for the war in Afghanistan. *Contemporary Security Policy*, 7, 223–245.

Scheer, T. (2020) *Language Diversity and Loyalty in the Habsburg Army, 1868–1918*. Unpublished Habilitationsschrift Thesis. Historisch-Kulturwissenschaftlichen Fakultät, Universität Wien.

Selikovitch, G. (1918) *Arabish–Idisher lehrer: yeg yayzer far di Idishe legyoneren in Tsiyon\ = Turjumān 'Arabi wa-Yahūdī* = אראביש-אידישער לעהרער: וועג וויזער פאר די אידישע ציון לעגיאנערען אין [Arabic–Yiddish Teacher: A Guide for Jewish Legionaries in Zion]. New York: Sh. Drukerman.

Simon, R. (2009) Teach Yourself Arabic - in Yiddish! *MELA Notes*, 1–15.

Stergar, R. (2019) The evolution of linguistic policies and practices of the Austro-Hungarian armed forces in the era of ethnic nationalisms: The case of Ljubljana-Laibach. In Prokopovych, M., Bethke, C. & T. Scheer (eds.) *Language Diversity in the Late Habsburg Empire*. Leiden: Brill, pp. 50–71.

Testa, M. & A. Gautier (2003) *Drogmans et diplomates européens auprès de la porte Ottomane* [Dragomans and European diplomats at the Ottoman porte]. Istanbul: Isis.

Venuti, L. (2008) *The Translator's Invisibility: A History of Translation*. Second Edition. London: Routledge.

Wilson, C. (1886) *From Korti to Khartum: A Journal of the Desert march from Korti to Gubat and of the Ascent of the Nile in General Gordon's Steamers*. Edinburgh; London: Blackwood.

5 How Multilingualism Came to Be Ignored in the History of Standard English

Laura Wright

Multilingualism has played an important role in the development of Standard English, but previous generations of scholars downplayed the multilingual element in its history to the extent of ignoring plentiful evidence of late medieval institutional code-switching altogether. In the late fourteenth and fifteenth centuries, code-switched record-keeping was the routine practice of the most prestigious institutions in the country, although no history of English mentions it and very little of it is published.

In this chapter, I firstly establish my claim that multilingualism led to Standard English by showing that Standard English is the descendant of coalesced supralocal Englishes which adopted the written conventions of Anglo-Norman and much of its word stock. I then track the 'monolingual origin' story, still repeated in textbooks today – namely, that Standard English supposedly developed mainly from the dialect of the 'East Midlands,' or 'Central Midlands,' or 'Chancery English,' or a mixture of the above, depending on the textbook. The 'monolingual origin' story goes back to the early 1870s, and in the third section I ponder why it was that the monolingual-source explanation has dominated for so long. I suggest contributing factors, implicating in particular the European tradition of seeing languages as discrete entities but ignoring code-switched varieties, and the dominance of three exceptionally eminent scholars who strayed off their main areas of expertise when making their East Midlands/Central Midlands/Chancery claims.

5.1 How Multilingualism Led to Standard English

On winning the Battle of Hastings in 1066, William Duke of Normandy brought his Anglo-Norman French-speaking administration to Britain, with the effect that Old English disappeared from the written record. The Norman custom was to speak Anglo-Norman French and write in Medieval Latin, but over the next three centuries, Anglo-Norman came to be a language of written record too.[1] It is

[1] A note on the label 'Anglo-Norman,' which sounds half-English, half-French, but was fully French. I keep the label, which signifies 'French as brought to Britain in 1066 and used there for

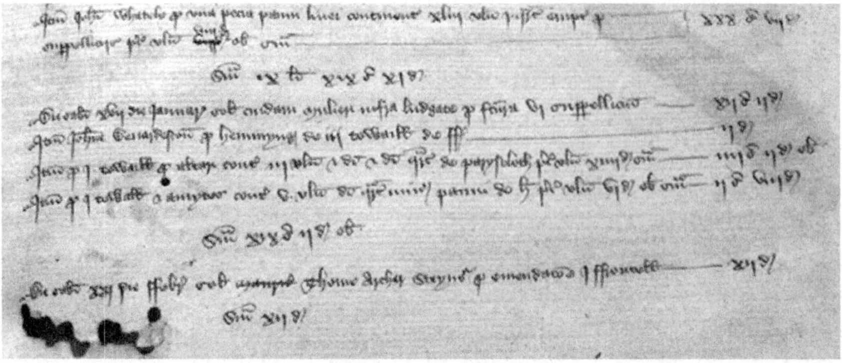

Fig. 5.1 Extract from London Metropolitan Archives CLA/007/FN/03/001, Bridge House Accounts Weekly Payments 1st series volume 1, fo 1. 1404–1405. Reproduced by permission from the London Metropolitan Archives.

often asserted that in medieval Britain, Medieval Latin and Anglo-Norman French were ‘high’ languages and English a ‘low’ language in terms of social prestige, but the language of money-management tells a different story. The nobility was of Anglo-Norman descent and the poorest sectors of English descent, but commerce and trade complicate that binary picture. Not all merchants, secretaries, or estate supervisors were noble, neither were all lawyers, yet trade and the law required knowledge of Medieval Latin and Anglo-Norman.

Written monolingual English reappeared at the end of the fourteenth century, but it is misleading to give this date as the start of the rise of English and the demise of Medieval Latin and Anglo-Norman without qualification, because the end of the fourteenth century was the beginning of the heyday of the mixed-language variety, where all three languages were routinely combined. Sustained monolingual English writing was not to become the norm until the sixteenth century. The mixed-language variety is not discussed in textbooks and has largely been ignored by linguists,

about 350 years’ in order to tie it to scholarship, particularly the *Anglo-Norman Dictionary*, as over this time-period the language developed in ways unlike its Continental French counterparts. Anglo-Norman would have been a mother tongue for the first generation after 1066, then maintained for three hundred years as a teaching medium for schoolchildren, only beginning to show the kinds of interference typical of second-language learning in adulthood in the 1370s, which was the last generation to acquire it and which retired in the 1430s (Ingham, 2009a, b, 2010, 2011, 2013).

probably because it was used for business rather than literature or religion and because nineteenth- and twentieth-century scholars judged it to be faulty Latin. In Wright (1997) I surveyed some historians' evaluations: 'degenerate Latin,' 'dog Latin,' 'ignorant copyists,' 'blunders in syntax,' and 'mistakes.' The mixed-language variety didn't have a label, and so scholars couldn't see it for what it was: a code-switched written linguistic system in its own right. Figure 5.1 demonstrates mixed-language business writing with seven short lines from the archive of London Bridge for the 1404 financial year.

Itm̄ Joh̄i Whatele ꝓ vna pecia panni linei continent' xliij vln̄ j q^{a}rt' empt' ꝓ suppellicijs p^{9}c^{9} vln̄ ~~vijjd~~ $^{viij.d'}$ ob̄ sm^{a} – xxxŝ vijd' Sm^{a} ix lī xixŝ xjd' Die sab̄i xvij die Januar̂ sol̄ cuidam mulieri infra ludgate ꝓ fcūra vj suppelliciū – xijŝ ijd' Itm̄ Joh̄ne Denardeston̄ ꝓ hemmyng de iij towaill̄ de fff̂ – ijd' Itm̄ ꝓ j towaill̄ ꝓ altari cont' iij vln̄ & dī & dī q^{a}rt' de paryscloth̄ p^{9}c^{9} vln̄ xiiijd' sm^{a} – iiijŝ ijd' ob̄ Itm̄ ꝓ j towall̄ & amytes cont' v. vln̄ dī q^{a}rt' min^{9} panni de h̄ p^{9}c^{9} vln̄ vjd' ob̄ sm^{a} – ijŝ viijd' Sm^{a} xixŝ ijd' ob̄ Die sabī xxj Die ffebr̂ sol̄ ~~maurie^{9}~~ Thome Archer Steyno^{a} ꝓ emendacōe j ffrontell̄ – xijd' Sm^{a} xijd'

[Item to John Whatele for one piece of linen cloth containing 43 ells 1 quarter bought for surplices price per ell ~~8d~~ 8½d sum 30s 7d Sum £9 19s 11d Saturday 17 day January paid to a certain woman within Ludgate for making 6 surplices 12s 2d Item to Joan Denardeston for hemming of 3 towels ('hand-cloths') of F(rontel, 'decorative hanging') 2d Item for 1 towel for the altar containing 3 ells and a half and half a quarter of pariscloth price per ell 14d sum 4s 2½d Item for 1 towel and amices ('scarves') containing 5 ells and half a quarter less cloth of h- price per ell 6½d sum 2s 8d Sum 19s 2½d Saturday 21 day February paid to ~~Maurice~~ Thomas Archer stainer for repairing 1 frontel 12d Sum 12d]

The grammatical matrix of this text is Medieval Latin (inflectional morphology, function words, and much of the content-word vocabulary); some of the word stock is from Anglo-Norman (*towaill̄, amytes, ffrontell̄, steyno^{a}*), some is from English (*cloth̄, ludgate, Whatele, Denardeston̄, Archer*), and some belonged to more than one language, either due to borrowing or being cognate, with morphological information expressed by abbreviation symbols (*Januar̂, ffebr̂, q^{a}rt', cont'*). There is a mixed-language prepositional phrase, *ꝓ hemmyng*, where *ꝓ* 'pro' is Latin and *hemmyng* is English, with word-final English morpheme *-ing* rather than a Latin one. Wright (2005, 2010, 2012, 2013, 2017, 2018, 2020b, c) discusses the rules and internal developments of mixed-language business writing, its nouns, verb stems, gender agreement, articles, word order, and *-ing* forms. Heavy use of abbreviation is typical of this text-type, having the effect of obscuring language-specific morphology. One reason for it is likely to be that it was cost-effective: a scribe who could abbreviate legibly and efficiently could write quicker. As a result, language boundaries cannot be easily drawn, and one generation's code-switched Anglo-Norman *towail* and *stainour* became the next generation's English *towel* and *stainer*.

Mixed-language business writing was used countrywide, and multilingual documents of numerous sorts were the norm. In compiling *A Corpus of Middle English Local Documents*, Stenroos (2020) and her team visited 82 English archives, identifying over 5,000 multilingual documents from 766 different locations written between 1399 and 1525. They found that local fifteenth-century administrative documents were predominantly written in Latin (Stenroos, 2020, p. 46). Schipor (2018) investigated 7,070 texts written between 1399 and 1525 held at the Hampshire Record Office. In this time, only 20 out of 7,049 texts (0.3 percent) were written in Anglo-Norman, this being the last generation to use written Anglo-Norman. The majority of municipal and manorial texts were multilingual, although episcopal writing remained monolingually Latin (as is to be expected of religious text-types). Manorial records contained most English, occurring in texts concerned with money-management, be it one-word switches, headings, rubrics, marginalia, or passages of continuous English. Stenroos (2020) and her team also found that "early texts in English are certainly found in much larger numbers in northern archives than in non-northern ones" (pp. 48–49); that is, the further away the scribe from the seat of established power and authority, the earlier the use of monolingual written English. This chimes with the distribution in London: The early monolingual English guild certificates of 1388/9 were written by guilds – the forerunners of workers' unions – pleading poverty (Barron & Wright, 1995; Wright, 1998), whereas by contrast the Bridge House Estate, the wealthy institution that maintained London Bridge, was still using mixed-language a century later. The implication is that power was invested in those who were educated in the Latin language via the medium of Anglo-Norman, and those who were not so educated and remained monolingually English were relatively powerless. As the powerless gained more power, they wrote in their native language.

The linguistic disruption of the 1370s and 1380s when passages of monolingual English first started to appear, and when Anglo-Norman began to show features of second-language learning in adulthood rather than childhood, was matched by a period of social upheaval. This social unrest had been brewing over the fourteenth century, and the reasons for it were complex. The lower ranks' increase in socioeconomic power had its roots in the Black Death of the first half of the fourteenth century, which decimated the population and relieved pressure on resources for those who survived and came after (Wright, 2020b). An attempt by the City of London to implement civic reforms to reduce the power of the Aldermen resulted in public book-burning, uprising, and brawls (Barron & Wright, 2021; Wright, 2018) and the Peasants' Revolt of 1381. Historian Caroline Barron views this as a cumulative process: "There were conflicting economic interests and, perhaps, class interests as masters fought to restrain the wages and opportunities of their workers and merchants who traded goods abroad came into conflict with artisans who made the goods," and "The more I have studied London in the late fourteenth century, the more convinced I have become that there is no single 'big issue' that caused the turbulence of London in Richard II's reign" (Barron & Wright, 2021, p. 3). The social classes who were unsatisfied with their lot and excluded from use of Medieval Latin and Anglo-Norman began to circumvent those who knew those languages by writing directly in English. By the 1430s the social change had extended so far that professional scribes also largely abandoned Anglo-Norman although not Medieval Latin, shifting their matrix language to English but proceeding conservatively and cautiously as bureaucrats and lawyers always do, retaining Romance lexis and orthographical conventions. Yet this description gives an unbalanced impression. Many archives show continuing vacillation between the three languages and mixed-language writing between 1370 and 1470, with one scribe switching into monolingual English and the next one back to monolingual Latin. Effectively, with regard to the languages of written record in the century between 1370 and 1470, social turbulence was mirrored by language turbulence.

The evidenced-based account is that Standard English followed a period of unstable written multilingualism – but it did not follow on directly. The monolingual English of the decades following the 1470s when mixed-language was finally abandoned was not yet standardized. It is known as *supralocal*, that is, containing sets of linguistic features that did not subsequently enter Standard English and emanated from influential centers. (This is not the same as regional dialect leveling, where idiosyncratic features of different dialects are smoothed out when speakers come into contact.) Supralocal clusters of morphemes, closed-class words, and spelling sequences fanned out far beyond their traditional regions. Supralocal Englishes have been identified in texts written in York and Swaledale (Fernández Cuesta, 2014), Cheshire, Shropshire and Staffordshire (Thengs, 2013), Cambridge (Bergstrøm, 2017), Bristol, Coventry and York (Gordon, 2017; Gordon et al., 2020), and London (Nevalainen, 2000; see also Nevalainen & Raumolin-Brunberg, 2016). By way of illustration, Nevalainen (2003, p. 128) reports London supralocal writing in a letter from King Henry VIII to Anne Boleyn dated 1528, where earlier *be* occurs rather than later Standard *are* in the indicative plural, *-th* rather than later Standard *-s* in the third-person singular present indicative, *which* instead of Standard *who* with human antecedents, and multiple negation instead of Standard single negation. This bundle of features also occurred in the early English writings of the London Bridge archive, a wealthy institution that was late in switching to monolingual English in the financial year 1479/1480:

The same wardeyns accompten for Ml̄ iiijxx viij lī ixd' ōb q^a of tharreragis of William Holte and Edward Grene last accomptauntꝭ here as it apperitħ in the fote of the same accompte

London Metropolitan Archives, CLA/007/FN/02/004, Bridgemasters' Annual Accounts and Rental, volume 4, fo 221v, 1501–1502
[the same wardens account for £1088 9d and three farthings of the arrears of William Holte and Edward Grene the last accountants here as it appears in the foot of the same account]

Supralocal English features are the Southern third-person plural present indicative *-en*, Southern third-person singular present indicative *-th*, cliticization of definite article *the* before a following word beginning with a vowel on the Anglo-Norman pattern, Anglo-Norman trigraph <*aun*> in the context of /a/ before a nasal consonant, and visible retention of Latin etymological *comptare* in the spelling of *accompt(-*. These features are all found in texts of the time many miles away from London, and none of them lasted into Standard English. Ignoring the English personal names, and ignoring the Roman numerals, out of the twenty-six words, sixteen are of English etymology (largely monosyllabic function words *the*, *same*, *for*, *of*, *of*, *and*, *last*, *here*, *as*, *it*, *in*, *the*, *fote*, *of*, *the*, *same*), six are of Anglo-Norman etymology (polysyllabic content words *wardeyns*, *accompten*, *arreragis*, *accomptauntꝭ*, *apperith̄*, *accompte*), and four are of Latin etymology (abbreviated currency and measurement terms *lī*, *d'*, *ōb*, *q*^{a}). So this is code-switching in the other direction, where the function words are English, the main lexical items are Anglo-Norman, and the currency terms are Medieval Latin. A simplified schema of the progression of business writing from the Norman Conquest of 1066 to 1500 is thus ML → [ML+AN] → [ML+AN+E] → [E + AN], where the brackets indicate code-switching and the first in a bracketed group is the matrix language. For example, one of the supralocal features that spread far and wide but did not standardize was the Anglo-Norman convention of expressing plurality in words ending in /l/ with <x>, such as *juelx* 'jewels' and *sealx* 'seals.' This convention was adopted in supralocal Englishes for words of English etymology too, such as *shamelx* 'shambles,' from Old English *sceamel* 'stall' (Stenroos, 2020, pp. 63–65; Wright, 2020b, p. 528; Thengs, 2020, p. 170). Supralocal plurals in *-lx* are found in texts written after 1480 from London to Lancashire, but they did not last.

Thus, the individual scribes who began to write in English over the course of the fifteenth century did not shift from monolingual Anglo-Norman and monolingual Medieval Latin to monolingual Standard English. Rather, they shifted from a Medieval Latin and Anglo-Norman matrix that contained much English to a supralocal English matrix that contained much Anglo-Norman. These supralocal Englishes then conventionalized over the course of the sixteenth and seventeenth centuries into Standard English. Durkin (2020, p. 348) reports that Standard English borrowed a 'huge spike' of French and Latin words in the late fourteenth century – the late fourteenth century being the point when Anglo-Norman as a monolingual language taught in childhood was abandoned. The route by which so much Romance vocabulary entered

English at this late date is now apparent via the shifting ratios from Romance matrix to English matrix. The definition of supralocal English is 'English matrix + Anglo-Norman words and spelling-sequences,' but because we now regard this simply as English, it is difficult to view it as code-switched.

5.2 Tracking the 'Monolingual Origin' Story

I now present a condensed version of an account expounded more fully in Wright (2020a), where I show that the long-lasting monolingual English explanations of – or rather, assumptions about – the origins of Standard English stem from *The Sources of Standard English* of 1873, written by Thomas Laurence Kington-Oliphant M.A. (Oxon) (1831–1902). Kington-Oliphant was a barrister, Justice of the Peace, a Fellow of the Society of Antiquaries, and a gentleman scholar. He was reacting against the work of John Earle (1824–1903), who was a priest and Professor of Old English at the University of Oxford. Under the subhead 'The King's English,' Earle (1871 [1879] § 9.67) had written:

> We have a phenomenon to account for. In the midst of this Babel of dialects there suddenly appeared a standard English language. It appeared at once in full vigour . . . Piers Plowman is in a dialect; even Wiclif's Bible Version may be said to be in a dialect; but Chaucer and Gower write in a speech which is thenceforward recognised as THE ENGLISH LANGUAGE, and which before their time is hardly found. This seems to admit of but one explanation. It must have been simply the language that had formed itself in the court about the person of the monarch. (p. 69)

Earle admired Chaucer (ca.1340s–1400) and regarded his writings as constituting "a standard English language," although nowadays it is not so regarded, being too early and too regional. Part of Earle's admiration was due to Chaucer's use of French-derived vocabulary, which he put down to Chaucer being a courtier, as he presumed that the French language was used at the royal court. (Actually, Chaucer was composing his verse during the turbulent social period when less powerful people were beginning to rebel and write in English, and his twelve-year post as Controller of Customs at the Port of London would have required him to write daily in mixed-language. His choice of using English for so much of his verse can be interpreted as socio-politically charged – seditious, even.) Kington-Oliphant did not buy Earle's royal-court explanation and venerated not Chaucer but another poet. He was aware that the Southern morphology of the sort used by Chaucer, that is, verb third-person plural present indicative *-en*, third-person singular present indicative *-th*, plural *be/ben*, had later become replaced in Standard English by third-person plural zero, third-person singular *-s*, plural *are*, first found in texts of more northerly provenance. (He overlooked, or may have been unaware of, the inconvenient fact that more southerly, non-London, morphology such as auxiliary *do* entered Standard English too.) Kington-Oliphant proffered the alternative explanation that the northerly features in Standard English stemmed from the dialect of the monk and chronicler Robert Manning of Bourne in Lincolnshire, who wrote the verse *Handlyng Synne* of 1303. Kington-Oliphant (1873) suggested that the works of Robert Manning had once been so highly influential as to cause other writers elsewhere to imitate its morphology, specifying five features on which he based his argument. The first and second were from the present-tense indicative verbal paradigm: "Southern ending in *en* was replaced by the Midland ending in *es*" and "the Present Plural *en* of the Midland verb replacing the older Plural in *eth*"; the third was from the pronoun paradigm: "the Midland *I*, *she*, *they*, and *beon* encroach upon the true Southern *ich*, *heo*, *hi*, and *beoth*"; the fourth was a preposition: "*mid* (cum) was making way for the Northern *with*" and the fifth was lexical: "his large proportion of French words and by his small proportion of those Teutonic words that were sooner or later to drop" (Kington-Oliphant, 1873, pp. 256–258). Kington-Oliphant (1873) introduced the East Midlands as the regional font of Standard English, by which location he meant the dialect area in which Bourne was situated: "The popularity of these works of the Lincolnshire bard must have spread the influence of the East Midland further and further" (pp. 256–257).

What Kington-Oliphant could not have known in 1873 was that subsequent processes of sixteenth-century supralocalization were to complicate what looked to him like a direct north–south progression. For example, Fernández Cuesta (2014, p. 345) surveyed twenty-five York clergy wills written in 1522–1550 and found a predominance of 56 percent *-th* over 44 percent *-s* in third-person singular contexts, and Bergstrøm (2017) also found high ratios of Southern verbal *-th* in documents produced in Cambridge in 1414–1546. "(I)n the North verbal *-th* is replaced by *-s* toward the end of the Old English period, but resurfaces again briefly in the Early Modern English period to be finally ousted by *-s* in the seventeenth century" (Fernández Cuesta, 2015, p. 106). This finding that verbal *-th* progressed northwards well after the composition of Manning's *Handlyng Synne* of 1303 is the opposite of what Kington-Oliphant had assumed had happened. Nor would modern scholarship claim a source for Standard English based on just five features, or from the writings of just one poet. Nevertheless, Kington-Oliphant's opinion was repeated throughout the earlier twentieth century as fact: Standard English came from the dialect of the East Midlands.

It is one thing to publish a hypothesis; it is another to get people to believe it. So how was it that the opinions of a barrister came to be passed on to posterity over those of an Oxford Professor of Old English? The answer lies with the influential reach of the *Encyclopaedia Britannica*. In 1878 Sir James Murray, Chief Editor of the *Oxford English Dictionary*, contributed an article on the 'English Language' to the ninth edition, which he revised together with his daughter Hilda for the 1910–1911 (eleventh) edition, presenting Kington-Oliphant's view: "An *East Midland* dialect, extending from south Lincolnshire to London, occupies the cradle-land of the standard English speech" (p. 598). Sir James was a *nonpareil* lexicographer and was no doubt familiar with such medieval English texts as had been transcribed and published (mostly by the Early English Text Society) by 1910, but his primary expertise lay neither in surveying medieval manuscripts nor in historical morphology, so he relied on Kington-Oliphant. He actually recast Kington-Oliphant's suggestion from 'the English as written in Bourne, Lincolnshire' to 'all the dialects between South Lincolnshire and London,' but this was neither noticed nor taken up.

By the mid-twentieth century it had been forgotten that either 'Bourne, Lincolnshire' or the land 'between South Lincolnshire and London' had been implicated. An East Midlands provenance for Standard English had become an orthodoxy, causing the great Swedish onomastician and philologist Eilert Ekwall to search for a mass fourteenth-century migration of Midlanders to London, on the (mistaken) assumption that London English equated to Standard English. Ekwall (1956) did this by means of examining locative placename surnames in early fourteenth-century London tax rolls. Not surprisingly he found no evidence for a Midlands migration, but his careful wording has been reported subsequently in textbooks as though he had: "Historians have identified a considerable migration of people from the East Midlands to London from the late thirteenth century to the mid-fourteenth century, some of whom must have become the 'dominant social class' whose language carried prestige and was imitated by others" (Freeborn, 1992, p. 95). Granted, Ekwall, unaware of the putative significance of Bourne, Lincolnshire, was seeking to find a homeland for Standard English in East Anglia, center of the medieval wool trade, and was hoping to find an exodus of wealthy East Anglian wool merchants taking up residence in London and so impressing the locals that they imitated East Anglian speech. He didn't find any evidence for this hypothesis and, scrupulous scholar that he was, was careful to say so. What he in fact found was spelling variation (a problem in need of explanation for Neogrammarians) and that most incomers hailed from London's hinterland.

In 1962 Michael Samuels, a medievalist, palaeographer, orthographer, and cocreator of the *Linguistic Atlas of Late Mediaeval English*, addressed a 'meeting of University Professors.' His script was lightly revised and published as Samuels (1963). He presented the professors with the further refinement that Standard English had evolved from the Central Midlands dialect as disseminated by Chancery clerks, which although he stressed was an interim finding, has subsequently been reported as fact. So how did Chancery come into the picture, and why the shift from East to Central Midlands?

In casting the office of Chancery in the role of mediator of standardization, Samuels was following German linguist Lorenz Morsbach (1850–1945), who in Morsbach (1888) had gathered together the earliest monolingual English passages that he could find, some of which had been printed in Furnivall (1882), and some of which would later be published in Chambers and Daunt (1931). Morsbach culled other English passages from the Latin-matrix *Rotuli Parliamentorum* and the Close Rolls, some extracts being from what he called the *Hof* or *Staatskanzlei*. The introduction of the role of the office of Chancery to the history of Standard English was thus a translation from German, although in Morsbach's original German text the *kanzlei* played no special role.

In 1962 Samuels was ten years into the thirty-four-year process of surveying texts for the *Linguistic Atlas of Late Mediaeval English*, which, however, did not include bureaucratic documents, let alone multilingual ones. (This omission has since been filled by Stenroos and colleagues' Corpus of Middle English Local Documents (MELD), which consists of transcriptions of more than two thousand local documents 1399–1525.) Samuels specified 'Chancery Standard' as "that flood of government documents that starts in the years following 1430. Its differences from the language of Chaucer are well known, and it is this type, not its predecessors in London English, that is the basis of modern written English" (Samuels, 1963 [1989], pp. 67–71). This sounds authoritative, but Dodd (2011a, b, 2012) has investigated proportions of Latin/French/English in documents issued by the Chancery office during the fifteenth century and reports that the comparatively few letters that were written in English were written to the office, not from it. Chancery cannot possibly have been influential in the rise of Standard English as its main language was Latin. And from the data presented, Samuels' claim is based on nothing other than spellings for word forms *again, any, but, each, gave, given, much, neither, not, old, saw, self, should, stead, such, their, these, they, though, through, while, will, world*, and the morpheme *-ande/ende/inde*.

Why then did he specify Chancery and a shift from East to Central Midlands? It is likely to have been because he could not locate Standard English spellings for his questionnaire of common words for the *Linguistic Atlas of Late Mediaeval English* in his survey of monolingual English East Midlands texts. As we now know, there was a period of code-switching and supralocalization between the abandonment of Medieval Latin and Anglo-Norman and the development of Standard English, but this was not yet apparent in 1962. The *Linguistic Atlas of Late Mediaeval English* had been envisaged as a tool for locating the origins of manuscripts by means of plotting their idiosyncratic spellings, a method not viable in the later fifteenth century due to supralocalization, whereby spelling sequences were used a long way away from their center of initiation. Samuels must have been expecting to see Standard English spellings, or something like them, coalescing in texts produced in the East Midlands, but could not find them in the predominantly literary and religious monolingual English texts he was analyzing. As bureaucratic documents were not included, he must have assumed that that was where the incipient spelling-standardization lay (Stenroos (2020) and her team have subsequently shown this to be a wrong assumption). He knew that Standard English does not contain the Southern morphology of Chaucer, so the Midlands in its generically central form was the closest place to London that might plausibly have donated features such as third-singular *-s* and plural *are* – features that modern scholarship ascribes to the phenomenon of supralocalization.

5.3 Why the Monolingual-Source Explanation Lasted So Long

Until recently, scholars missed the full picture in the development of Standard English by ignoring multilingual and, especially, mixed-language texts written for business purposes, and by not considering the preceding supralocal stage, which ported Anglo-Norman words and writing conventions into what appears from a modern perspective to be monolingual English, but which at the time was an English matrix containing code-switched Anglo-Norman. There are several reasons for this:

(1) None of these assertions, whether East Midlands, Central Midlands or Chancery, are easily verifiable without going into numerous archives, calling up numerous manuscripts, and utilizing the palaeographical skill necessary for analysis and synthesis. Instead, readers took these claims on trust. Kington-Oliphant, Morsbach, Murray, Ekwall, and Samuels were all significant – indeed, monumental – scholars in related areas. There was no reason to doubt them. And they were all partially correct. Kington-Oliphant identified a small amount of morphology of northerly origin in Standard English, now seen as the result of supralocalization. Morsbach extracted early passages of English from civic and bureaucratic Latin texts, although it is now known that they did not lead directly to a wholesale shift to monolingual English. Murray could see that Bourne could not be the font of Standard English and so widened the territory. Ekwall hypothesized about East Anglian English being influential but was careful to report that his results did not support this and what he found was variation. Samuels could see that neither East Anglia nor the East Midlands could be the homeland of Standard English. Their scholarship was not faulty; they presented evidence and arguments supporting their hypotheses. But they looked for the origins of Standard English in monolingual English texts of the sort published by the Early English Text Society – chronicles, verse, literary prose, saints' lives, and religious and literary writings of various sorts (Ekwall, with his interest in names, is an exception). They ignored business writing, and they did not look outside monolingual English.

(2) There are cultural reasons as to why historians of the English language overlooked the kinds of multilingual texts routinely surveyed by their contemporary economic historian colleagues. Multilingual texts produced by lawyers, merchants, and their related occupations were not the main focus of the Early English Text Society, who saw it as their business to get monolingual English literary culture into print, becoming the data on which philologists based their observations. Philologists studied historical phonology in order to appreciate metrical verse, and historical morphology and syntax in order to appreciate medieval prose. Philology had literary culture on its agenda, and in a context of courtly romance, trade was its social polar opposite. No chivalric knight wooing fair lady by *rondeau*, *virelai*, or *ballade* ever had a sideline in the import/export business.

(3) There was a long-standing tradition in Europe of regarding languages as discrete, seeing Latin as Latin, French as French and English as English, with no attention to code-switching. There is the matter of prestige, with Medieval Latin less prestigious than Classical Latin and Anglo-Norman less prestigious than Continental French, so that Medieval Latin and Anglo-Norman did not receive as much scholarly attention over the late nineteenth and twentieth centuries as their counterparts. In particular, the subsequent dominance of, and reverence for, Classical (Neo) Latin meant that the mixed-language variety was perceived by modern scholarship as faulty, erroneous, wrong. The medieval suspension and abbreviation system was edited out as irrelevant, merely a means of saving parchment, so that the porosity between the three languages was hidden from view by editors' guesses which, not being medieval themselves, were consistent and invariant – anachronistic, in other words. The 'discrete languages' perspective led to the common-sense assumption that when Medieval Latin and Anglo-Norman were abandoned, English replaced them, and that that English was early Standard English. That this is faulty has only been revealed by surveys of unpublished archival texts.

(4) Supralocalization and its adoption of Anglo-Norman vocabulary and writing conventions have only recently become apparent to scholars as a result of the accumulation of electronic corpora. Surveys of such corpora by Nevalainen and her colleagues at the University of Helsinki and Fernández Cuesta and her colleagues at the University of Seville allowed identification of supralocalized features, while Stenroos and her colleagues at the University of Stavanger revealed the extent of multilingualism. This would have been far harder to achieve in previous decades. Durkin (2014, 2020, p. 348) could only assess the date when the groundswell of Anglo-Norman lexis was

borrowed into Standard English when the contents of the *Oxford English Dictionary* became searchable electronically. He found that it largely happened in the fourteenth-century decades when Anglo-Norman was no longer learned in childhood, resulting in a shift in matrices from Latin to English: thereafter English contained the Anglo-Norman vocabulary that was previously contained by Latin-matrix mixed-language.

(5) Despite the enormous amount of it still extant, there is at present no corpus of medieval mixed-language business writing. Little of it is in print, and scholars who see the importance of it, and replicate its abbreviation and suspension symbols, are few. This is partly because there is so much mixed-language writing in archives, usually repetitious – year upon year of weekly payments, all saying much the same thing, replete with names of people and places, which linguists have always found hard to assimilate into the mainstream of their studies. A small monolingual English poem that a scholar can fit into a doctoral dissertation is by contrast a more manageable entity and does not require knowledge of Anglo-Norman and Medieval Latin grammar.

(6) Variation has only been theorized since the second half of the twentieth century. During Ekwall's working life, for example, variant letter-graphs constituted evidence of dialect interference. If the "wrong" letter-graph appeared in a spelling then it implied that someone from another dialect area had written it, leading to searches for migrations. This is the dominance of theory over data.

(7) Metaphors of competition between languages became common to the extent that they were normalized, such as those discussed by Sylvester (2020, p. 376), where English 'triumphed,' or 'dueled,' or 'won out.' These metaphors are still current even in code-switching literature; Sylvester finds competition between languages given as a motive in scholarly articles published as recently as 2018. A 'competing languages' perspective means that scholars effectively take sides, so that multilingual texts (which is what most medieval manuscripts written in Britain are) are filtered, or filetted, and only the language under consideration analyzed and reported.

(8) The profit-motive of the publishing industry has also been a factor, whereby publishing houses urge scholars to produce textbooks and related compendia in broad-brush strokes to be sold to the undergraduate market, with the concomitant result that explanations get repeated from textbook to textbook without fresh scrutiny.

The cumulative weight of all these reasons means that generations of students have repeated the words 'East Midlands' in their examinations, even while being uncertain as to where in England that might be: Huntingdon?

Peterborough? Grantham? Spalding? It is an inherently unlikely claim, and one which has baffled many.

References

Primary sources

London Metropolitan Archives, CLA/007/FN/02/004, Bridgemasters' Annual Account and Rental, volume 4, 1484–1509.

London Metropolitan Archives, CLA/007/FN/03/001, Bridge House Accounts, Weekly Payments: First series, volume 1, 1404–1412.

Secondary sources

Barron, C. & L. Wright (1995) The London Middle English Guild Certificates of 1388/89. *Nottingham Medieval Studies*, 39, 108–145.

(2021) *The London Jubilee Book, 1376–1387: an edition of Trinity College Cambridge, Ms O.3.11 folios 133–157.* London: London Record Society for 2020.

Bergstrøm, G. (2017) *"Yeuen at Cavmbrigg": a study of the medieval English documents of Cambridge*. PhD thesis, University of Stavanger.

Chambers, R. & M. Daunt (eds.) (1931) *A Book of London English 1384–1425.* Oxford: Clarendon Press.

Dodd, G. (2011a) The rise of English, the decline of French: Supplications to the English Crown, c. 1420–1450. *Speculum*, 86, 117–146.

(2011b) The spread of English in the records of central government, 1400–1430. In Salter, E. & H. Wicker (eds.) *Vernacularity in England and Wales, c. 1300–1550.* Turnhout: Brepols, pp. 225–266.

(2012) Trilingualism in the Medieval English Bureaucracy: The Use – and Disuse – of Languages in the Fifteenth-Century Privy Seal Office. *Journal of British Studies*, 51, 2, 253–283.

Durkin, P. (2014) *Borrowed Words: A History of Loanwords in English.* Oxford: Oxford University Press.

(2020) The relationship of borrowing from French and Latin in the Middle English period with the development of the lexicon of Standard English: Some observations and a lot of questions. In L. Wright (ed.) *The Multilingual Origins of Standard English.* Berlin: De Gruyter, pp. 343–364.

Earle, J. (1871 [1879]) *The Philology of the English Tongue*. Third Edition. Oxford: Clarendon Press.

Ekwall, E. (1956) *Studies on the population of medieval London.* Stockholm: Almqvist and Wiksell.

Fernández Cuesta, J. (2014) The voice of the dead: Analyzing sociolinguistic variation in Early Modern English wills and testaments. *Journal of English Linguistics*, 42, 4, 330–358.

(2015) The History of Present Indicative Morphosyntax from a Northern Perspective. In R. Hickey (ed.) *Researching Northern English*. Amsterdam/ Philadelphia: John Benjamins, pp. 99–130

Freeborn, D. (1992) *From Old English to Standard English.* Basingstoke: Macmillan.

Furnivall, F. (ed.) (1882) *Fifty Earliest English Wills in the Court of Probate, London: A. D. 1387–1439. Early English Text Society, Old Series, vol. 78*. London: Oxford University Press.

Gordon, M. (2017) *The Urban Vernacular of Late Medieval and Renaissance Bristol*. LOT 476. Netherlands Graduate School.

Gordon, M., Oudesluijs, T. & A. Auer (2020) Supralocalisation Processes in Early Modern English Urban Vernaculars: New Manuscript Evidence from Bristol, Coventry and York. In Esteban-Segura, L. & J. Calle-Martín (eds.) *Standardisation and Change in Early Modern English: Empirical Approaches. Special Issue of International Journal of English Studies*, 20, 2, 47–66.

Ingham, R. (2009a) Mixing languages on the manor. *Medium Ævum*, 78, 1, 80–97.

(2009b) The Persistence of Anglo-Norman 1230–1362: A Linguistic Perspective. In Wogan-Browne, J. (ed.) *Language and Culture: French of England 1100–1500*. Woodbridge: Boydell, pp. 44–54.

(2010) The Transmission of Anglo-Norman. In Ingham, R. (ed.) *The Anglo-Norman Language and Its Contexts*. Woodbridge: Boydell, pp. 164–182.

(2011) The decline of bilingual competence in French in medieval England: Evidence from the PROME database. In Langer, N., Davies, S. & W. Vandenbussche (eds.) *Language and History, Linguistics and Historiography – Interdisciplinary Problems and Opportunities*. Berne: Peter Lang, pp. 71–292.

(2013) Language-mixing in medieval Latin documents: Vernacular articles and nouns. In Jefferson, J. & A. Putter (eds.) *Multilingualism in Medieval Britain 1100–1500: Sources and Analysis*. Turnhout: Brepols, pp. 105–121.

Kington-Oliphant, T. (1873) *The Sources of Standard English*. Macmillan & Co.

MELD = A Corpus of Middle English Local Documents. Versions 2016.1 and 2017.1. Compiled by Merja Stenroos, Kjetil V. Thengs & Geir Bergstrøm. University of Stavanger. www.uis.no/meld

Morsbach, L. (1888) *Über den Ursprung der neuenglischen Schriftsprache*. Heilbronn: Henninger.

Murray, J. & H. M. R. Murray (1910–1911) English language. *Encyclopaedia Britannica. Eleventh Edition*, pp. 587–600.

Nevalainen, T. (2000) Processes of Supralocalisation and the Rise of Standard English in the Early Modern Period. In Bermúdez-Otero, R., Denison, D., Hogg, R. & C. McCully (eds.) *Generative Theory and Corpus Studies*. Berlin: De Gruyter, pp. 329–371.

(2003) *Sociolinguistic perspectives on Tudor English. SEDERI*, 13, 123–140.

Nevalainen, T. & H. Raumolin-Brunberg (2016) *Historical Sociolinguistics: Language Change in Tudor and Stuart England*. Second Edition. Abingdon: Routledge.

Samuels, M. (1963) Some Applications of Middle English Dialectology. *English Studies* 44, pp. 81–94. Reprinted in McIntosh, A., Samuels, M. & M. Laing (eds.) (1989) *Middle English Dialectology: essays on some principles and problems*. Aberdeen: Aberdeen University Press, pp. 64–80.

Schipor, D. (2018) *A Study of Multilingualism in the Late Medieval Material of the Hampshire Record Office*. PhD thesis, University of Stavanger.

Stenroos, M. (2020) The 'vernacularisation' and 'standardisation' of local administrative writing in late and post-medieval England. In Wright, L. (ed.) *The Multilingual Origins of Standard English*. Berlin: De Gruyter, pp. 39–86.

Sylvester, L. (2020) The role of multilingualism in the emergence of a technical register in the Middle English period. In Wright, L. (ed.) *The Multilingual Origins of Standard English*. Berlin: Walther de Gruyter, pp. 363–379.

Thengs, K. (2013) *English medieval documents of the Northwest Midlands: A study in the language of a real-space text corpus*. PhD thesis, University of Stavanger.

(2020) Knutsford and Nantwich: scribal variation in late medieval Cheshire. In Stenroos, M. & K. Thengs (eds.) *Records of real people: linguistic variation in Middle English local documents*. Amsterdam: John Benjamins, pp. 155–173.

Wright, L. (1997) The records of Hanseatic merchants: ignorant, sleepy or degenerate? *Multilingua*, 16, 4, 339–350.

(1998) Middle English variation: the London English Guild certificates of 1388/9. In Jahr, E. (ed.). *Language Change: Advances in Historical Sociolinguistics*. Berlin: Mouton de Gruyter, pp. 169–196.

(2005) Medieval mixed-language business texts and the rise of Standard English. In Skaffari, J., Peikola, M., Carroll, R., Hiltunen, R. & B. Wårvik (eds.) *Opening Windows on Texts and Discourses of the Past*. Amsterdam: John Benjamins, pp. 381–399.

(2010) A pilot study on the singular definite articles *le* and *la* in fifteenth-century London mixed-language business writing. In Ingham, R. (ed.) *The Anglo-Norman Language and Its Contexts*. York: York Medieval Press/Boydell Press, pp. 130–142.

(2012) On variation and change in London medieval mixed-language business documents. In Stenroos, M., Mäkinen, M. & I. Særheim (eds.) *Language Contact and Development around the North Sea*. Amsterdam/Philadelphia: John Benjamins, pp. 99–115.

(2013) Mixed-language accounts as sources for linguistic analysis. In Jefferson, J. & A. Putter (eds.) *Multilingualism in Medieval Britain (c. 1066–1520): Sources and Analysis*. Turnhout: Brepols, pp. 123–136.

(2015) On medieval wills and the rise of written monolingual English. In Calle Martín, J. & J. Conde-Silvestre (eds.) *Approaches to Middle English. Contact, Variation and Change*. Frankfurt am Main: Peter Lang, pp. 35–54.

(2017) On non-integrated vocabulary in the mixed-language accounts of St Paul's Cathedral, 1315–1405. In Ashdowne, R. & C. White (eds.) *Latin in Medieval Britain*. London: British Academy, pp. 272–298.

(2018) A multilingual approach to the history of Standard English. In Pahta, P., Skaffari, J. & L. Wright (eds.) *Multilingual Practices in Language History: English and Beyond*. Berlin: De Gruyter, pp. 339–358.

(2020a) A critical look at accounts of how English standardised. In Wright, L. (ed.) *The Multilingual Origins of Standard English*. Berlin: De Gruyter, pp. 17–38.

(2020b) Rising living standards, the demise of Anglo-Norman and mixed-language writing, and Standard English. In Wright, L. (ed.) *The Multilingual Origins of Standard English*. Berlin: De Gruyter, pp. 515–532.

(2020c) *The Multilingual Origins of Standard English*. Berlin: De Gruyter.

6 Multilingualism and the Attitude toward French in the Latin Kingdom of Jerusalem

Jonathan Rubin

The conquest of Jerusalem in the summer of 1099 marked the end of the First Crusade and the founding of a new Latin polity on the Eastern shores of the Mediterranean, known as the Kingdom of Jerusalem (Mayer, 2005; Richard, 1999). This kingdom, which would continue to exist, with changing borders, till 1291, was the home of a greatly varied population. Dominating this polity were Latins, that is people whose origins were in Central and Western Europe and who followed the Church of Rome. Some of these came on a series of military campaigns known as the Crusades,[1] others immigrated in order to resettle, for example, as peasants or merchants, and yet others were simply born there to Latin parents. This ruling sociocultural group, whose members are often referred to in the scholarship as Franks, seems to have remained a minority within the kingdom throughout the period. The majority consisted of Muslims, both sedentary and nomad; Eastern Christians, belonging to a variety of communities, such as the Melkite, Jacobite, and Armenian churches; and smaller Jewish and Samaritan communities. Furthermore, the kingdom continuously witnessed population movements as a result of which its composition remained dynamic. This had to do, firstly, with pilgrims and merchants, who were present in the kingdom temporarily but in significant numbers. As a consequence, they influenced the social environment they entered and were themselves affected by it. But the dynamic nature of the kingdom's population was not limited to the impact of commerce and pilgrimage: Latins, for instance, continued to immigrate to the Holy Land as Crusaders but also between the Crusades. Around the mid-thirteenth century, considerable Eastern Christian groups found refuge in the kingdom, having fled toward the Mediterranean coast in fear of the Mongol conquests; and, during the second part of the Crusader period, we see European Jews – using French as their day-to-day language – settling in the Holy Land (Rubin, 2018).

These basic conditions created a situation in which the users of a wide variety of languages found themselves sharing a quite restricted territory. At its

[1] In this paper I refer to Crusades only in the limited and partial sense of Latin military expeditions from the West to the Eastern Mediterranean between 1096 and 1291.

maximal dimensions, this kingdom included, in modern terms, all of the territories of Israel, the West Bank, Gaza, parts of western Jordan, and the southern part of Lebanon. The languages of the Latins included French, Occitan, Catalan, Italian, German, and English dialects. Muslims used Arabic, as did generally Eastern Christians, although, at least in some fields of activity, specific Christian groups used other languages, such as Greek, Syriac, and Armenian (Minervini, 2010). Such circumstances make the Kingdom of Jerusalem (and more generally the Latin East as a whole) a fascinating laboratory for the study of a wide range of questions related to multilingualism, such as what became the dominant language in this region? What evidence is there for the study of languages in the kingdom during the period of the Crusades? What impact did the above-mentioned conditions have on the languages that were in use in this region?

The present chapter is divided into two parts. Its first section provides some basic comments concerning the multilingualism that characterized the Kingdom of Jerusalem. The second part of this essay discusses one particular issue that, thanks to several surviving sources, can be explored quite closely: the development in the kingdom of an attitude toward the French vernacular that was, at the time, unusual and innovative in comparison to the perceptions that dominated western Christendom with regard to the relations between French and Latin. Before discussing these issues, it is necessary, however, to say something concerning the surviving source material from the Kingdom of Jerusalem and the challenges it presents.

Unfortunately, the limited extant material restricts our ability to provide complete answers to many questions related to multilingualism in this region. To begin with, as elsewhere, the medieval period has left us very little source material that sheds light on groups outside the upper echelons of society. In the Kingdom of Jerusalem, the historian is further challenged for two main reasons. Firstly, most of the archival material, which the kingdom would have transmitted to later generations, was destroyed with the violent capture and destruction of Latin cities and strongholds by the Mamluks in the second half of the thirteenth century. Secondly, very little source material survives from the kingdom that reflects the autochthonic point of view (Kedar, 1990). This limits, among other things, our ability to speak about the language practices of these groups during the period of the Crusades. In this short essay, I will try, nonetheless, to provide some insights reflecting what we do know about the use of languages in the kingdom.

6.1 The Kingdom of Jerusalem: Some Sociolinguistic Characteristics

The first important point that can now be made with regard to the sociolinguistic characteristics of the kingdom is that the dominant language, at least among the ruling milieus, was a unique French dialect that developed there and is often referred to as French of Outremer (Minervini, 2010, 2018). While we shall not attempt to provide an elaborate discussion of the characteristics of this dialect here, it is important to note that it reveals elements from several known French dialects, as well as Occitan and Italian influences (Aslanov, 2013; Minervini, 2018). A varied body of evidence reflects the significance of this dialect as a written language in the kingdom. Thus, for example, much of the juridical literature produced in the kingdom is in French, as are also some legal documents (Minervini, 2018). To these should be added literary works composed in French, such as the so-called continuations of William of Tyre's *Chronicon* (Rubin, 2018), a group of texts written as updates to the twelfth-century chronicle composed by this prominent archbishop of Tyre (died ca. 1186). Further evidence for the centrality of French in Outremer comes from its use by non-French westerners. An important example for this is the inclusion of a portion of the French translation of William of Tyre's *Chronicon* in a report written by Marsilio Zorzi, Venetian official representative, *bailo*, in Acre (Berggötz, 1990; Handyside, 2015; Jacoby, 1997, 2004; Rubin, 2018).

And yet, evidence that members of the kingdom's elite wrote, and read, in French may not be indicative with regard to the extent of its use in wider, non-elite circles. Such an evaluation is difficult to make, inter alia, because it is difficult to say what part of the Latin settlers originated in French-speaking regions. Several clues do suggest, however, that the dominance of the French of Outremer was not restricted to the kingdom's ruling elite. One notable, though quite late, piece of evidence in this regard comes from a sermon given in Acre by Thealdo Visconti, who had been elected pope (to be known as Gregory X) while he accompanied Prince Edward on the Ninth Crusade (1270–1272). Visconti is said to have presented this farewell sermon first in Latin, then in French (Mayer, 2005; Minervini, 2018; Paviot, 2008). An additional, quite remarkable, piece of evidence for the use of French across linguistic and social barriers comes from coinage. Among the coins minted in the kingdom during the late twelfth century, one included the legend PUGES DACCON, meaning 'a pougeoise [that is a quarter of a denier] of Acre' (Folda, 2005; Stahl, 2018).[2] French inscriptions from the kingdom point to the same direction (De Sandoli, 1974; Pringle, 2007).

Further evidence for the wide use of French in the kingdom comes from toponyms in that language, such as Blanchegarde or Casal Imbert (Minervini, 2010). While it is, of course, possible that toponyms would belong to a language that was not otherwise widely used, this seems unlikely in our case, since many of these sites would have had earlier Arabic names. Had French

[2] I am grateful to Dr. Robert Kool for introducing me to this fascinating find.

not been quite dominant, it is hard to see how such toponyms would have substituted the earlier Arabic ones. That the use of French place names was very common is supported by the fact that they appear not only in sources composed in that language, or by native French speakers, but also, for example, in the Latin pilgrimage accounts written by the German pilgrims Theoderich (ca. 1169) and Thietmar (1217–1218) (Huygens, 1994; Laurent, 1857), as well as in the Hebrew Book of Travels authored circa 1165 by Benjamin of Tudela (1907). Furthermore, some French toponyms survived among the Arabic speakers of the Holy Land well into the nineteenth and twentieth centuries. A site near Atlit (South of Haifa, Israel), which was referred to by the Franks of Outremer as Casel Destreiz or le Destroit, appears on the 1880 map of the Survey of Palestine as Kh[irbet] Dustrey, which must mean that Arabic speakers preserved the Frankish toponym for centuries (Pringle, 1997). A similar example is that of present Sinjil, to the north of Ramallah, which is based on the Frankish toponym Saint Gilles (Pringle, 1997). To this one may add that in some cases we find in Latin documents from the Kingdom of Jerusalem evidence for the oral use of French articles. Thus, for example, one of the villages mentioned in a grant dating to 1168 is referred to as Losserin. Since this village predates the Frankish period and is known in Arabic as Sirīn, one may safely assume that the Frankish form combines the Arabic toponym with a Frankish article (Tsafrir et al., 1994).

But French was not only widely used in the Kingdom of Jerusalem. It also seems to have played an important role in the development and preservation of a unique Frankish identity, which was clearly different from the local autochthonic one, but also distinct from that of French-speaking newcomers from the West. Being the language of the kingdom's aristocracy, it was also clearly prestigious. Indeed, Aslanov (2008, 2013) referred to it as a sociolect and Minervini (2018) argued that it was perceived as a medium of social integration. Its status might help to explain why, despite the fact that the kingdom's population varied so much in terms of linguistic background, Outremer French was widely used, and, to use Minervini's (2018) phrasing, became a vehicular language allowing communication between speakers of different native languages. The status of the French of Outremer probably also contributed to its early adoption as a written language, a theme to which we shall later return.

The circumstances described above raise a set of important questions concerning the learning of – and about – languages in the kingdom. But before we follow this line of inquiry it is important to note that gaining fluency in a foreign language is not the only manner of acquiring knowledge about it. In other words, one may imagine Muslims or Eastern Christians who did not have an opportunity to gain a high degree of knowledge in French, but who, through their continuous exchanges with French-speaking Latins, were able to pick up some basic words and phrases. The same holds true for the westerners: It is very likely that most of them were not capable of freely speaking Arabic, but they probably acquired some words and phrases (Minervini, 2018).

But what can we say, in a more concrete manner, about the engagement of the kingdom's inhabitants with foreign languages spoken by the neighboring populations? At the most basic level, it is noteworthy that at least some of the Latins were curious concerning the range of languages that were spoken and written in the world in which they now found themselves. A good example of this curiosity is found in the anonymous *Tractatus de locis et statu sancte terre*. A central part of this text is devoted to a survey of the various populations inhabiting the Holy Land. Significantly, as our author presents these groups, he comments on their scripts (Kedar, 1998). Thus, for example, he says that the Armenians have their own script (*littera*). But it is important to note that this author was not the only Latin to pay attention to this field of knowledge. In fact, in his *Historia orientalis*, Acre's famous bishop, Jacques de Vitry (d. 1240), elaborated the *Tractatus*' discussion of this matter. Thus with regard to the Armenians he wrote that they have their own language and letters, and that they pronounce the divine scripture in their everyday language, so that the clergy is understood by the laymen just as in the case of the Greeks (Jacques de Vitry, 2008; Rubin, 2018).

Another aspect of the exchange between the speakers of different languages in the kingdom is the lexical borrowing from one language into the other. Minervini (2012) has systematically studied Arabic and Greek loanwords in the French of Outremer, many of which involve commerce and warfare. In the absence of a study on the borrowing of Latin and French terms into Arabic, one may assume that the process in this direction was weaker than the other way around, but several examples for this phenomenon can be referred to. One interesting case is the use of what seems to be an Arabic version of the word *vassal* in an inscription from Farkha, a village not far from Nablus (Sharon, 2005). Additional cases come from the writings of Usāma Ibn Munqidh, the best-known member of the clan that held Shayzar between 1081 and 1157, and which played an important role in Syrian affairs in the eleventh and twelfth centuries. Usāma spent his life as a warrior and politician but was also a poet and a man of letters (Humphreys, 1960–2007). In his best-known work, the *Kitāb al-Iʿtibār* [Book of instruction by example], Usāma uses the form '*al-biskund*' for the word *viscount* (Old French [OF] *visconte*), refers to Frankish merchants as '*al-burjāsiyyah*' (OF *borgesie*), and employs the form '*sarjandi*' for *sergeant* (OF sergent) (Usamah Ibn Munqidh, 1987; see also Aslanov, 2006a).

Evidence for fluency in Arabic among the Latins of the Kingdom is quite limited but should not be overlooked. For example, in the negotiations that led to the surrender of the castle of Safed to Baibars (1266), we read that Lion, the Templar official in charge of the region's estates, "was very fluent in the

Saracen language" ("*savoit moult bien la lengue sarazineze*") (Minervini, 2000). Similarly, Philip Mainbeuf is described by the so-called Templar of Tyre as a knight who knew Arabic very well (Minervini, 2000) and Yves le Breton is referred to by Joinville as knowing Arabic (Jean de Joinville, 2010). These cases may be related to a significant body of evidence concerning Latin envoys/translators who are noted in the sources as competent in Arabic (Rubin, 2018). At the same time, however, the above-mentioned references to the possession of such skill as exceptional indicate that thorough knowledge of this language was unusual among the Latins of Outremer. A rare piece of evidence for the learning of written classical Arabic by Franks comes from a manuscript dating to 1196, which includes an Arabic medical text with Latin marginalia that were probably added in Acre during the thirteenth century. As certain characteristics of the manuscript suggest that it was intended for someone whose first language was not Arabic, it is likely that its owner was a Latin who was active in Acre and had learned Arabic there (Savage-Smith, 2006). Only one piece of evidence from the kingdom sheds light on an attempt to organize the teaching of Eastern languages. This occurred within the ranks of the Dominican order and provides the earliest piece of evidence for a program for the study of foreign languages within this organization (Rubin, 2018).

Evidence for Muslims and Eastern Christians who learned Latin or French is no easier to come by. It is, however, possible to present some evidence for such exchanges. Firstly, Muslim converts to Christianity are likely to have received at least some instruction in western languages. Additionally, an Old French-Arabic glossary, in which the French is transmitted in Coptic letters, suggests that Copts were instructed in French in thirteenth-century Acre (Aslanov, 2006b; Rubin, 2018). If this indeed was the case, it is possible that members of other groups received similar training. Further evidence, albeit indirect, for the study of French and/or Latin by members of Eastern Christian groups comes from their involvement in the Frankish bureaucracy (Ibn Jubayr, 2020; Kedar, 1990). Generally neglected evidence for the probable involvement of non-Latins in the military orders points to the same direction (Burgtorf, 2008; Minervini, 2000), as it would not have been possible without some knowledge of French.

Within the limited corpus of extant evidence, we also have some sources that reflect a degree of literary cooperation between speakers of Arabic and French but do not shed light on its precise nature, or on the knowledge held by the parties involved. One of these is an Arabic–French pharmaceutical glossary in which both languages are represented by Latin characters. This document, which has received relatively little scholarly attention, begins with a title in which its two authors are described: the first is Willame, described as a 'poulain,' that is a person of Frankish origin who was born in the East, and as a 'chevalier.' The other is Jacques, described as a 'new Christian' and as an apothecary. While there is no positive evidence with regard to the circumstances in which this text was written, its linguistic characteristics suggest that it was composed somewhere in Outremer around 1300 (Ineichen, 1971–1972; Minervini, 2012). An additional project was the translation of a collection of Marian legends from Latin or French into Arabic. This was a significant enterprise that included the translation of at least seventy-four stories and brought about their adoption by the Coptic and later Ethiopian churches. The available evidence suggests that these translations resulted from the cooperation of Dominican friars with members of the Coptic Church (Baraz, 1993, 1994; Rubin, 2018).

6.2 Innovativeness on the Periphery: The Attitude to French in the Kingdom of Jerusalem

Within these conditions, perhaps surprisingly, French was used by the Kingdom of Jerusalem's Frankish elite, in fields and ways in which it was not utilized at the time in western territories dominated by that language. In other words, it seems that there existed in the kingdom an ideology according to which French was able to convey complex ideas in fields that, at the time, were normally reserved to Latin (Minervini, 1995; Morreale & Paul, 2018).

One body of evidence in this regard is that of legal documents. As Morreale (2014) observed, while in the regions known today as France and Belgium "local vernacular dialects were employed as languages of legal record only sparingly in the mid-thirteenth century" (p. 440), in the Latin East French-medium legal documents were in circulation as early as the 1220s. Further evidence in this regard comes from translations from Latin into French. One can begin by noting that the earliest known French translation of Vegetius' *De re militari* was almost certainly produced in Acre, as a present from Eleanor of Castile to her husband, Prince Edward. Dating to the early 1270s, the surviving translation belongs to the very first stage of French translations of Latin works (Rubin, 2018). Furthermore, it seems that this translation was produced in a cultural context in which an older, now lost, French translation of *De re militari* was circulating (Rubin, 2018). An indication for the innovative nature of such projects is provided by Robert Lucas' survey of French translations of Latin classics to 1500: of the numerous translations that he mentions, only ten are dated to any time before the end of the thirteenth century (Lucas, 1970). In other words, one can confidently argue that among the Latins active in the kingdom, there was at least one translator who should be counted among the pioneers of the Latin-into-French translation movement.

Particularly noteworthy with regard to the attitudes that developed in the kingdom toward the use of French is a unique codex, now in Chantilly

(Musée Condé, fr. 433). This volume, which is probably the original codex presented by John of Antioch to his patron, William of Santo Stefano, includes four elements: an original introduction by John based on well-known Western traditions; French translations of Cicero's *De inventione* and the anonymous *Rhetorica ad Herennium* (referred to, by John, as one work titled *Rectorique de Marc Tulles Cyceron*); an original epilogue discussing the work of translators; and a short treatise on logic (Guadagnini, 2009). Like that of Vegetius' work, the original translations of the *Rectorique* were, at the time, an innovative undertaking. Monfrin (1963, 1964) mentions John's translation of the texts on rhetoric as one of the two, or perhaps three, earliest works that, on the one hand, are 'real translations' into French rather than adaptations, and, on the other, include texts that are not of a strictly technical character. Additionally, according to Minervini (1995), with the exception of some sections included in Brunetto Latini's *Trésor*, John was the first to translate a rhetorical work into French.

The novelty of John's project is also made evident by the inclusion of the treatise on logic in the codex he prepared. This short treatise, made with the explicit intention of introducing this field to those who could not learn it properly, consists mostly of excerpts from the two first books of Boethius' *De topicis differentiis*, translated into French with various editorial emendations. The degree of John's involvement in the development of this treatise is unclear at this stage, and he may have merely copied French excerpts that he happened to find somewhere else into the volume he was preparing. But Guadagnini makes a strong case for the argument that John found Boethius' text, perhaps already in the form of excerpts, in the Latin manuscript from which he translated the *Rectorique*, and then translated it into French (Guadagnini, 2013; Rubin, 2018). As Guadagnini (2013) writes, if John indeed translated these sections, we owe to him one of the earliest extant vernacular texts in logic. Be that as it may, as early as the 1280s, a vernacular treatise on logic circulated in Acre and in all likelihood was also produced in its cultural environment. The innovative nature of this project is indicated by the fact that it required the translator to create new French terms (Guadagnini, 2013).

One can thus conclude from his work that John was of the opinion that French could convey, in a precise manner, complex ideas in fields such as rhetoric and logic, which, at the time, were still normally reserved for Latin. But John actually presented his view of the vernacular quite clearly in the epilogue he attached to the *Rectorique*, where he argues that

> because the manner of speaking in Latin is not generally the same as that of French. Neither the properties of words nor the methods of arranging arguments and words in Latin are the same as those of French. And that is [so] generally in every language. Because every language has its own properties and its manner of speaking [*maniere de parler*] (for the French text, see Guadagnini, 2009).

John stresses here the difference, in terms of structure and vocabulary, between Latin and French, but he does so while arguing that the same kinds of differences exist between any two languages. In other words, the disparity between Latin and French is not a result of any deficiency on the part of the French language. Rather, all languages are unique and any two given languages differ from one another. This line of thinking, notes Lusignan (1987), leads to a conception, rare during the Middle Ages, that tends to view French and Latin as equal. Indeed, medieval thinkers often described the vernacular as incapable of transmitting complex ideas (Lusignan, 1987). John, on the other hand, reveals his belief in the capacity of the vernacular both in his practice as a translator and through his explicit – and unusual – discussion of the interrelation between Latin and the vernacular in the epilogue to his *Rectorique*.

At this stage one should clearly wonder how unique John's way of thinking about the vernacular may have been within the cultural climate of the Kingdom of Jerusalem. While it is difficult to provide clear answers to such questions, John was certainly not the only one in Acre to hold this view. We can be confident that William shared John's attitude toward the vernacular, not only because John's translations of the *Rectorique* were produced at William's request, but also as, some years later, William himself composed works in history and jurisprudence using French (Luttrell, 1998). It is also probable that others in their cultural circles held similar views on this issue: After all, a fancy codex, such as the Chantilly manuscript, was certainly meant to be shown. These findings support the hypothesis that there developed in the Kingdom of Jerusalem a comparatively advanced attitude toward the vernacular.

This can be further demonstrated through another aspect of John's work: his view of French grammar. Lusignan (1987) argued that the word *gramaire* was rare in the texts he surveyed, and that where it was found, it signified Latin. Furthermore, while during the thirteenth century some paradigms from Latin grammar were applied to French, it was only in the fourteenth century that French became the subject of grammatical reflection (Städtler, 1988). Against this background, the extent of John's innovation becomes evident. One place in John's translation of the *Rectorique* is particularly revealing in this regard. The original Latin text (Cicero, 1954) reads as follows:

Barbarismus est cum verbis aliquid vitiose effertur. Haec qua ratione vitare possimus in arte grammatica dilucide dicemus.
[A barbarism occurs if the verbal expression is incorrect. How to avoid these faults I shall clearly explain in my tract on Grammar.]

This is John's parallel text (for the full French version, see Guadagnini, 2009):

Barbarism si est quant aucune parole est trovee viciouse en soi meisme au prononcier ou en l'escrit: au prononcier si come qui diroit 'hospital' proloignant le . pi., en l'escrit si come qui escriveroit ou prononcieroit au devant dit mot .b. por .p. Par

quel raison nos puissons ces .ii. vices eschiver, l'art de gramaire nos enseigne bien clerement.
[Barbarism is when some word is found defective in itself in pronunciation or in writing; in pronunciation, as when someone would say 'hospital' protracting the 'pi'; in writing as when someone would write or pronounce in the said word 'b' for 'p.' By what method we can avoid these two defects, the art of grammar teaches us very clearly.]

John makes here a direct connection between the actual exercise of French in the kingdom and the term 'grammar.' In other words, he assumes that for his readers, the word 'grammar' is not restricted to Latin but rather naturally refers to the use of the vernacular. But this passage is also worthy of attention for another reason. As this text was composed for a major member of the order of Saint John, or the Hospitaller order, the decision to reflect on the word 'hospital' could hardly have been accidental. One should therefore also expect the error noted here to have been related to the everyday experiences of figures such as John of Antioch and William of Santo Stefano. And indeed, as an example of 'barbarism' John preferred to mention an error that may well reflect the influence of Arabic pronunciation on the vernacular: the pronunciation or writing of 'hosbital' instead of 'hospital.' This may well be related to a phenomenon we have referred to above: the use, at various levels of competence, of French by non-native speakers of this language.

John's innovative attitude to French grammar in the *Rectorique* is also reflected in his use of French grammatical terms. Generally speaking, French grammatical terms appeared during the twelfth and thirteenth centuries and were mostly used in vernacular discussions of Latin grammar (Städtler, 1999). Against this background, it is instructive that John inserted into his work the word for the past historic tense *preterit* (Eng. *preterite*) three times into places where the Latin original does not have the equivalent *praeteritum* (Rubin, 2018). The third of these seems to be the most instructive. It follows a more or less exact translation of a speech made by a general, presenting the dilemmas he faced in a certain situation. Following the general's comments, John adds "*Si faite subgection peut on torner autresi dou tout au preterit ou au futur*" [One can also turn a *subgection* thus made entirely into *preterit* or into *future*] (for the Latin text, see Cicero, 1954; for the French text, see Guadagnini, 2009).

What can we make of this insertion? Firstly, that the term *preterit* was familiar to John, who would have become acquainted with the *praeteritum* during his training in Latin. Furthermore, John was clearly confident that his audience was also acquainted with this term. Otherwise he would not have used it in a place in which his source text did not really require it. This conclusion can be supported by the two other aforementioned occurrences in which this term, along with two other terms denoting tenses, were added by

John to the text he translated in order to facilitate its reading (Rubin, 2018). But, more significantly, John's employment of the term here is clearly intended to suggest to his readers a certain manner of expression in French. This phrase thus reveals that John was capable of thinking about *preterit* in the context of French rhetoric and independently of Latin grammar, and that he expected his audience to be able to implement his advice in the vernacular. This is clearly different from the situation described earlier where French terms were used to describe Latin grammar. It thus seems that in Acre, at least in some quarters, an advanced attitude existed toward French grammar.

What were the reasons for the development of these pioneering attitudes toward the vernacular in a peripheral region, such as the Kingdom of Jerusalem? Might one not expect innovative ideas to develop more quickly in central locations, perhaps in or around the great study hubs of the medieval West? It is beyond the scope of this paper to present a thorough discussion of this problem, but I think that one hypothesis in this regard is worth mentioning. Perhaps it was precisely the distance from Europe's study centers that enabled this development: far from the great study centers of western Christendom, knowledge of Latin was possibly not as widespread as it was in France or Italy. This could have led to the use of the vernacular in fields in which this practice was unusual at the time elsewhere. This, in turn, would have increased the belief of contemporaries in the capability of French to transmit complex ideas in fields such as logic or rhetoric. Furthermore, the distance from the center also meant that there was no local dominant academic elite, committed to Latin as the language of learning, who would have opposed such developments (Rubin, 2018).

Conclusion

The Kingdom of Jerusalem can be seen as a fascinating laboratory for interactions between languages. Moreover, despite the fact that the corpus of extant sources from this lost culture is limited, it has enabled scholars to reach some significant conclusions. As we have seen, there is evidence for multidirectional lexical borrowing; for the use of toponyms that developed within one language by the speakers of other languages; for the curiosity of westerners with regard to Eastern languages; for the study, at a variety of levels, of 'neighbor languages'; and for the cooperative production of glossaries and translations. One particularly significant linguistic development that occurred within this cultural climate is the appearance of an innovative attitude toward French, which came to be employed in fields mostly reserved for Latin. Perhaps in this respect, the assumed peripherality of the Crusader States actually enabled linguistic developments that preceded similar trends in the West.

References

Primary Sources

Benjamin of Tudela (1907) *The itinerary of Benjamin of Tudela: Critical text, translation and commentary by Marcus Nathan Adler.* H. Frowde.

Berggötz, O. (1990) *Der Bericht des Marsilio Zorzi. Codex Querini-Stampalia IV3 (1064)* [The Report of Marsilio Zorzi. The Querini-Stampalia IV3 (1064) Manuscript], *Kieler Werkstücke, Reihe C: Beiträge zur europäischen Geschichte des frühen und hohen Mittelalters 2.* Lang.

Cicero (1954) *Ad C. Herennium de ratione dicendi* [To C. Herennius on Rhetoric], trans. H. Caplan. Cambridge, MA: Harvard University Press.

De Sandoli, S. (1974) *Corpus Inscriptionum Crucesignatorum Terrae Sanctae (1099–1291)* [A Corpus of the Crusader Inscriptions from the Holy Land (1099–1291)]. Jerusalem: Franciscan Printing Press.

Guadagnini, E. (2009) *La Rectorique de Cyceron tradotta da Jean d'Antioche: Edizione e glossario* [The rhetoric of Cicero translated by John of Antioch: Edition and glossary]. Pisa: Scuola Normale Superiore.

Huygens, R. (1994) *Peregrinationes tres: Saewulf, Iohannes Wirziburgensis, Theodericus* [Three Pilgrimages: Saewulf, John of Würzberg, and Theoderich]. CCCM 139. Turnhout, Belgium: Brepols.

Ibn Jubayr (2020) *The Travels of Ibn Jubayr,* trans. R. Broadhurst. London: Bloomsbury.

Jacques de Vitry (2008) *Histoire orientale* [Eastern History]. J. Donnadieu (ed. and trans.). Turnhout, Belgium: Brepols.

Jean de Joinville (2010) *Vie de Saint Louis* [Life of Saint Louis]. J. Monfrin (ed. and trans.). Paris: Éditions classiques Garnier.

Laurent, J. (1857) *Mag. Thietmari Peregrinatio* [Master Thietmar's Pilgrimage]. Hamburg: Nolte und Köhler.

Minervini, L. (2000) *Cronaca del Templare di Tiro: 1243–1314. La caduta degli Stati Crociati nel racconto di un testimone oculare* [The Chronicle of the Templar of Tyre: 1243–1314. The Fall of the Crusader States in the Account of an Eyewitness]. Naples, Italy: Liguori Editore.

Paviot, J. (2008). *Projets de croisade* [Crusade Projects]. Paris: Académie des inscriptions et belles-lettres.

Usāmah Ibn Munqidh (1987) *An Arab-Syrian Gentleman and Warrior.* trans. P. K. Hitti. Princeton, NJ: Princeton University Press.

Secondary References

Aslanov, C. (2006a) *Le français au Levant, jadis et naguère: à la recherche d'une langue perdue* [French in the Levant, past and present: In search of a lost language]. Paris: H. Champion.

(2006b) *Evidence of Francophony in Mediaeval Levant: Decipherment and Interpretation (MS. Paris BnF Copte 43).* Jerusalem: Hebrew University/Magnes Press.

(2008) L'ancien français, sociolecte d'une caste au pouvoir: Royaume de Jérusalem, Morée, Chypre [Old French, Sociolect of a Ruling Caste: The Kingdom of

Jerusalem, Morea, Cyprus]. In Fagard, B., Prévost, S., Combettes, B. & O. Bertrand (eds.) *Évolutions en français. Études de linguistique diachronique* [Developments in French. Studies in Diachronic Linguistics]. Berne: Peter Lang, pp. 3–19.

(2013) Crusaders' Old French. In Arteaga, D. L. (ed.), *Research on Old French. The State of the Art*. Dordrecht: Springer, pp. 207–220.

Baraz, D. (1993) Coptic-Arabic Collections of Western Marian Legends: The Reception of a Western Text in the East: A Case of Intercultural Relations in the Late Middle Ages. *Acts of the Fifth International Congress of Coptic Studies,* II, 23–32.

(1994) Bartolomeo da Trento's Book of Marian Miracles. *Orientalia Christiana Periodica*, 60, 69–85.

Burgtorf, J. (2008) *The Central convent of Hospitallers and Templars: History, organization, and personnel (1099/1120–1310)* (Vol. 50). Boston/Leiden: Brill.

Folda, J. (2005) *Crusader Art in the Holy Land: from the Third Crusade to the Fall of Acre, 1187–1291*. Cambridge: Cambridge University Press.

Guadagnini, E. (2013). Cicéron et Boèce en Orient: Quelques réflexions sur la Rectorique de Jean d'Antioche [Cicero and Boethius in the East: Some Reflections on John of Antioch's Rhetoric]. In Petrina, A. (ed.) *In principio fuit interpres* [In the Beginning there was the Translator]. Turnhout, Belgium: Brepols, pp. 37–46.

Handyside, P. (2015) *The Old French William of Tyre*. Leiden/Boston: Brill.

Humphreys, R. (1960–2007) Munḳidh, in Bearman, P., Bianquis, Th., Bosworth, C. E., van Donzel, E. & W. P. Heinrichs (eds.) *Encyclopaedia of Islam*, Second Edition. Brill. [Consulted online on November 30, 2021].

Ineichen, G. (1971–1972) Il glossario arabo-francese di messer Guglielmo e maestro Giacomo [The Arabic-French Glossary by Lord Guglielmo and Master Giacomo]. *Atti dell'Instituto Veneto di Scienze, Lettere ed Arti* [Acts of the Veneto Institute of Science, Letters and Arts], 130, 353–407.

Jacoby, D. (1997) The Venetian Privileges in the Latin Kingdom of Jerusalem: Twelfth- and Thirteenth-Century Interpretation and Implementation. In Kedar, B. Z., Riley-Smith, J. & R. Hiestand (eds.) *Montjoie: Studies in Crusade History in Honour of Hans Eberhard Mayer*. London: Variorum, pp. 155–175.

(2004) Society, culture, and the arts in Crusader Acre. In Weiss, D. & L. Mahoney (eds.) *France and the Holy Land*. Baltimore, MD: Johns Hopkins University Press, pp. 97–137.

Kedar, B. (1990) The subjected Muslims of the Frankish Levant. In Powell, J. (ed.) *Muslims under Latin Rule, 1100–1300*. Princeton, NJ: Princeton University Press, pp. 135–174.

(1998) The Tractatus de locis et statu sancte terre ierosolimitane. In France, J. & W. Zajac (eds.) *The Crusades and their sources: Essays presented to Bernard Hamilton*. Farnham: Ashgate, pp. 111–133.

Lucas, R. (1970) Mediaeval French translations of the Latin classics to 1500. *Speculum,* 45, 2, 225–253.

Lusignan, S. (1987) *Parler vulgairement: Les intellectuels et la langue française aux XIIIe et XIVe siècles* [To speak commonly: The intellectuals and the French language in the 13th and 14th centuries]. Paris: Vrin.

Luttrell, A. (1998) The Hospitallers' Early Written Records. In France, J. & W. Zajac (eds.) *The Crusades and their sources. Essays presented to Bernard Hamilton*. Farnham: Ashgate, pp. 135–154.

Mayer, H. (2005) *Geschichte der Kreuzzüge* [History of the Crusades]. Stuttgart: Verlag W. Kohlhammer.

Minervini, L. (1995) Tradizioni linguistiche e culturali negli Stati Latini d'Oriente [Linguistic and Cultural Traditions in the Latin States of the East]. In Pioletti, A. & F. Rizzo-Nervo (eds.) *Medioevo Romanzo e Orientale. Oralità, scrittura, modelli narrativi* [Romance and Oriental Middle Ages. Orality, writing, narrative models]. Soveria Mannelli: Rubbettino, pp. 155–172.

(2010) Le français dans l'Orient latin (XIIIe–XIVe siècles). Éléments pour la caractérisation d'une *scripta* du Levant [French in the Latin East (13th–14th centuries). Elements for the Characterization of a *scripta* of the Levant]. *Revue de Linguistique Romane* [Journal of Romance Linguistics], 74, 119–198.

(2012) Les emprunts Arabes et Grecs dans le lexique français d'Orient (XIIIe–XIVe Siècles) [Arabic and Greek Loanwords in the French Vocabulary of the East (13th–14th centuries)]. *Revue de Linguistique Romane* [Journal of Romance Linguistics], 76, 99–198.

(2018) What we know and don't yet know about Outremer French. In Morreale, L. & N. Paul (eds.) *The French of Outremer: Communities and Communications in the Crusading Mediterranean*. New York: Fordham University Press, pp. 15–29.

Monfrin, J. (1963) Humanisme et traductions au moyen âge [Humanism and Translations in the Middle Ages]. *Journal des savants* [Journal of the Learned] (Jan.–Mar.), 161–190.

(1964) Humanisme et traductions au moyen âge [Humanism and Translations in the Middle Ages]. In Fourrier, A. (ed.) *L'humanisme médiéval dans les littératures romanes du XIIe au XIVe siècle* [Medieval humanism in the Romance literatures of the 12th to 14th Centuries]. Klincksieck, pp. 217–246.

Morreale, L. (2014) French-language documents produced by the Hospitallers, 1231–1310. *Journal of Medieval History*, 40, 439–457.

Morreale, L. & N. Paul (2018) Introduction. In Morreale, L. & N. Paul (eds.) *The French of Outremer: Communities and Communications in the Crusading Mediterranean*. New York: Fordham University Press, pp. 1–13.

Pringle, D. (1997) *Secular buildings in the Crusader Kingdom of Jerusalem: An archaeological gazetteer*. Cambridge: Cambridge University Press.

(2007) Notes on Some Inscriptions from Crusader Acre. In Shagrir, I., Ellenblum, R. & J. Riley-Smith (eds.) *In laudem hierosolymitani: Studies in Crusades and Medieval Culture in Honour of Benjamin Z. Kedar*. London/New York: Routledge, pp. 191–209.

Richard, J. (1999) *The Crusades, c. 1071–c. 1291*, trans. J. Birrell. Cambridge: Cambridge University Press.

Rubin, J. (2018) *Learning in a crusader city: Intellectual activity and intercultural exchanges in Acre, 1191–1291*. Cambridge: Cambridge University Press.

Savage-Smith, E. (2006) New evidence for the Frankish study of Arabic medical texts in the Crusader period. *Crusades*, 5, 99–112.

Sharon, M. (2005) Vassal and Fasal: The Evidence of the Farkhah inscription from 608/1210. *Crusades*, 4, 117–130.

Städtler, T. (1988) *Zu den Anfängen der französischen Grammatiksprache* [To the beginnings of French grammatical language]. *Beihefte zur Zeitschrift für romanische Philologie* [Supplements to the Journal of Romance Philology] 223. Berlin: De Gruyter.

(1999) Témoins précoces de la terminologie grammaticale française [Early witnesses of French grammatical terminology]. *Travaux de linguistique et de philologie* [Studies in Linguistics and Philology], 37, 123–129.

Stahl, A. (2018) The *Denier* Outremer. In Morreale, L. & N. Paul (eds.) *The French of Outremer: Communities and communications in the Crusading Mediterranean*. New York: Fordham University Press, pp. 30–43.

Tsafrir, Y., Di Segni, L. & J. Green (1994) *Tabula Imperii Romani: Iudaea, Palaestina* [A Map of the Roman Empire: Iudaea, Palaestina]. Jerusalem: The Israel Academy of Sciences and Humanities.

7 Why Colonial Dutch Failed to Become a Global Lingua Franca

Roland Willemyns

In the wake of Columbus' expeditions, the sixteenth and seventeenth centuries witnessed a great many exploratory expeditions during which many lands were 'discovered,' that is, taken into possession by the countries that organized and/or sponsored those expeditions. It was the main superpowers of that time – England, Spain, Portugal, and France – that profited most from these expeditions and gained a lot of 'colonies' in the Americas, Asia, and Africa. They also managed to impose their languages on the colonies, turning them into global lingua francas. There was also another country that sent its fleets all over the world and conquered its share of the loot – the Netherlands. Dutch, however, never left its mark on the linguistic situation in Asia, the Americas, and Africa in a way comparable to English, French, Spanish, and Portuguese. To understand why that was the case, we will begin by asking 'What is Dutch?'

7.1 What Is Dutch?

It may seem strange that the language and the people of a country called the Netherlands or Holland should be called Dutch, a word many will recognize as being cognate with *Deutsch*, the German term for the German language. After all, even in Dutch the word *Duits* now means German. It is also intriguing that English uses two words to designate the language of the Low Countries, *Flemish* and *Dutch*, whereas French and German use three, respectively *Flamand*, *Hollandais*, *Néerlandais* and *Flämisch*, *Holländisch*, *Niederländisch*. Reassuringly, in Dutch only one term is now used – *Nederlands*. Based on the texts that have come down to us, the language of Holland was first called *Nederlands* in 1482. The term *Vlaemsch* [Flemish] has a longer history: it first occurred as an adjective in an English text in 1080 and from the thirteenth century onward appeared as a noun, gradually acquiring the meaning 'the language spoken in the County of Flanders' (Gysseling, 1971, 1975). In Holland, meanwhile, in the 1550s, another language name gained popularity – *Hollands* (Willemyns, 2013). From 1610, *Hollands* also turns up as a synonym for Dutch in general (Van der Sijs, 2004, 2006).

How confusing all of this really was can be deduced from the words of the famous Dutch linguist Lambert ten Kate who, in 1723, told his readers that the 'Belgian or Dutch' language (*Belgisch of Nederlandsch*), as it was used in the Dutch Republic – and two centuries before still went by the name of Flemish (*Vlaamsch*) – was then also called *Hollandsch*. This language, boasted ten Kate, was spoken to perfection only in Holland. Our Belgian language, he added, now proudly carries the name of *Hollandsch* (Willemyns, 2013, p. 6). It is only in the nineteenth century that the term *Nederlands* was resurrected and gained popularity in Holland, while *Vlaamsch* was increasingly used to refer to Belgian Dutch.

The intricate linguistic situation was further complicated by political realities: prior to the sixteenth century, there had never been a political entity called the Netherlands, nor had there ever been a political structure consisting exclusively of Dutch-speaking countries. It was the state-building policy of the House of Burgundy that gradually brought the Netherlands together. During the reign of Charles V (1519–1556), the entire Habsburg Netherlands were united in 1548 in the Burgundian Circle, which was linked very loosely to the rest of the Habsburg Empire. For the first time ever, the Netherlands, with some French-speaking parts, became more or less a political entity of its own.

At about the same time, Luther's and Calvin's ideas began to spread like wildfire in the Low Countries. The official persecution of the 'heretics' by the Inquisition, unpopular with the people and with the nobility, broadened the gap between the central government and local authorities. But it wasn't just the political and religious system that was creaking everywhere, the economy was in dire straits as well. On October 25, 1555, Charles V announced to the States General of the Netherlands his abdication in favor of his son Philip II. A fanatic, fundamentalist Catholic ruler, Philip II turned out to be a real 'Spanish' monarch, who reigned over his immense realm 'in which the sun never sets' out of Madrid. Philip II was not interested in his Netherlandic possessions as long as they stayed obedient and paid taxes and he stubbornly refused to grant his subjects religious freedom. The collective displeasure finally lit the fuse of the powder keg. The so-called 'iconoclastic fury' swept over southern Flanders in 1566, marking the beginning of the Eighty Years War (Willemyns, 2013). The Spanish opposition only made things worse. Eventually, the South was recaptured by Spain, while the rather passive North gained its independence. Dutch Protestantism was suppressed with the power of Spanish arms in Brabant and Flanders, where it was born and raised, but became the state religion of Holland that at first had been rather slow at taking sides.

Following the Fall of Antwerp in the summer of 1585, the split between the South and North became a fact. The Netherlands was divided into two separate parts, each with its specific political, cultural, religious, and social structures, corresponding roughly to present-day Belgium and the Netherlands. Southern Netherlanders in search of religious freedom and better living conditions began an exodus en masse to the North. Holland became the economic and cultural center of Europe, although, for a substantial part, the wealth and glory of Holland's so-called Golden Age was paid for by money coming from Flanders and Brabant and the intellectual input of the many refugees (Willemyns, 2003).

Yet long before the official end of the Eighty Years War in 1648, the commercial fleet of the young Northern Republic started cruising the world's oceans where it ran into the same enemy they were facing at home: the Spaniards. In their battle for colonies, the Dutch succeeded in getting their share, to the detriment of Spain and of their other seafaring rivals: the British, the French, and the Portuguese. In many colonies, therefore, one occupant chased the other until more or less stable conditions were established.

All of this accounts for the fact that the Netherlands appeared on the international scene of colonization as late as the seventeenth century, at a moment when the other colonizers had already taken possession of the best chunks. In most cases, the Dutch were not really 'discoverers': more often than not, they took possession, through military operations, of colonies already occupied or claimed by others. In many cases, as we will see, they also influenced the subsequent linguistic fate of those colonies. Therefore, before we turn to the main theme of this chapter, let us survey the most important overseas possessions the Dutch managed to conquer and the main linguistic consequences of this conquest.

7.2 The Territories that Once Spoke Dutch or a Dutch-Based Pidgin

In the seventeenth century, Holland's Golden Age, the East India Company (*Verenigde Oost-Indische Compagnie* or the VOC) and the West India Company (*Verenigde Westindische Compagnie* or the VWC) set sail to Asia, Africa, and the Americas and planted the flag of the young republic in 'new' lands and in the territories previously 'discovered' by others. In 1609, the Dutch arrived in North America, on board of *De Halve Maen*, steered by the English captain Henry Hudson. Fifteen years later, in 1624, New Netherland was recognized as a Dutch province with Dutch as its official language. A year later, the new conquerors settled in Manhattan, which became their capital, known as New Amsterdam (Van der Sijs, 2009). Yet the status quo did not hold. In 1664, Governor Peter Stuyvesant was forced to surrender the province to the English under the Treaty of Breda (1667), concluded after the Second Anglo-Dutch War. It was agreed that both countries would keep the possessions they had taken from one another. The Dutch possessions in what was to become the USA were transferred to the British, while the Dutch took possession of Suriname in South America, believing they made a better deal, in view of potential profits from the Suriname slave trade.

This wasn't their first foray to South America. In 1627 the Dutch merchant Abraham van Peere founded the colony of Berbice, in what is now the Republic of Guyana. As is often the case, the contact between different populations gave rise to a pidgin, known as Berbice-Dutch (Kouwenberg, 1991), developed as a mixture with three components: (a) Dutch, in the form of its Zeeland regional variety, van Peere's mother tongue; (b) the language of local Indians, and (c) the language enslaved Nigerians brought with them. Nowadays, the language is officially extinct: according to the international language databank Ethnologue, its last native speaker died in 2005. Another Dutch-based pidgin/Creole that used to exist in Guyana, Skepi, had died out even earlier (Robertson, 1989). Curiously, despite being Dutch-based, Berbice-Dutch and Skepi were not mutually intelligible (Van der Sijs & Willemyns, 2009). The so-called Negro Dutch, *Negerhollands*, spoken until the early twentieth century on the Danish Antilles (now US Virgin Islands) had met the same fate (Den Besten, 1986; Van der Voort, 2006).

Indonesia, formerly East Indies, stayed longer under Dutch rule than the New Netherland. The first Europeans to arrive there were the Portuguese (in 1512), but in 1602 the States General had awarded the VOC a monopoly on trade and colonial activities in the region. Their first permanent trading post was opened in 1603, and in 1619 the VOC conquered the Javanese city of Jakarta, which they named Batavia. In so doing they established a permanent foothold in Java, soon to become one of the richest colonial possessions in the world. Yet, despite the long tenure of the Dutch in the East Indies, their language never spread widely and was banned after Indonesia gained independence (a linguistic conundrum to which we will return in the next section).

In contrast, in Suriname (also discussed later) and in the six Caribbean islands with a Dutch past Dutch retains its official position. The islands are divided geographically into the (northern) Windward Islands – Saba, Sint Eustatius, and Sint Maarten – and the (southern) Leeward Islands – Aruba, Bonaire, and Curaçao (Mijts & Rutgers, 2010). The first settlement in Sint Eustatius was established in 1636, but afterwards the island changed hands twenty-two times between the Dutch, the Spanish, and the French. The Dutch were the first to colonize Sint Maarten in 1631, but within two years the Spanish invaded and evacuated the settlers. In 1817, the partition line was established between the Dutch and the French parts. The least populated island, Saba, was first sighted by Columbus but colonized by the Dutch in 1640. In the south, Aruba was colonized by Spain for over a century until it came under Dutch rule in 1636. In the same year the Dutch 'discovered' Curaçao, the largest and the most populous of the so-called ABC islands, and the neighboring island of Bonaire.

Dutch is the official language in all six islands, and all their citizens hold Dutch passports. Recently Papiamento and English also acquired the status of official languages. Papiamento, spoken on the ABC islands, is a Creole language that has evolved through the centuries and has been influenced by indigenous languages, as well as Spanish and Portuguese. Throughout colonial history, Dutch remained almost exclusively a language for administration and legal matters. Popular use of Dutch increased slightly toward the end of the nineteenth and in the early twentieth century, but it has never been the language of the people on the ABC islands. The northern islands, Sint Maarten, Saba, and Sint Eustatius, are polyglot societies with English as their habitual language of daily life. Dutch performs formal and official functions and is absent in all other domains, except for secondary schools, where it is the language of instruction.

On October 10, 2010, the political situation of five of the Caribbean islands changed dramatically. Curaçao and Sint Maarten both gained partial independence, with a status comparable to the *status aparte* Aruba has had since 1986. The smaller islands, Bonaire, Sint-Eustatius, and Saba, often called BES islands, are now 'special municipalities' within the Netherlands, that is they form part of the Dutch territory, stretching it to the Caribbean. Since all of them remain part of what is officially called the Kingdom of the Netherlands, the latter political construct now consists of four countries: the Netherlands proper with the three BES islands, Aruba, Curaçao, and Sint Maarten. According to Mijts and van Bogaert (2011), "the new structure of the Kingdom implies huge legislative and administrative transformations within the new 'states' and within the new municipalities of the Netherlands" (p. 297). Yet it should be kept in mind, as Mijts and Rutgers (2010) observe, that "as long as the Antillean youth continues to go to Holland for their university education, this intellectual elite will remain under Dutch influence" (p. 38).

Another linguistic permutation is observed in South Africa and Namibia, two countries where Dutch is no longer an official language but where Afrikaans, the only extant daughter language of Dutch, has been used up to the present. The genesis, history, and development of Afrikaans need a considerably larger amount of attention than would be possible in this chapter (for an in-depth discussion of the history and recent developments, see Ponelis, 1993; Stell, 2008). For our purposes it is important to note that in the twentieth century, the heyday of Afrikaans in South Africa coincided with the infamous policy of apartheid. After 1993 the future of Afrikaans has been compromised and nowadays a fight for its survival is taking place. The same applies to Afrikaans in Namibia, where English functions as an official language and Afrikaans as the lingua franca in large parts of the country (Donaldson, 1988).

To sum up, apart from the Caribbean islands and Suriname, where Dutch is the official language, and South Africa, where Afrikaans plays an important role, the remnants of Dutch in all the other colonies are less than impressive. The fact that the Dutch language almost never stayed in the colonies is partly attributable to the fact that leaders of the VOC and VWC never considered themselves responsible for the expansion of Dutch. Their language policy – and afterward that of the Dutch government – was, in Groeneboer's (1998) apt terms, "marked above all by pragmatism" (p. 1). It was a policy that hindered rather than promoted the spread of Dutch. If one wants to understand the reasons for this, the example of the East Indies, as present-day Indonesia used to be called, is very revealing, the more so since it was the largest Dutch colony and one where their tenure was the longest.

7.3 Dutch in Indonesia

From the beginning of their stay in Indonesia, the Dutch were torn between two ideas. On the one hand, they felt that (part of) the indigenous population could be bound to the motherland by means of the Dutch language. On the other, mastery of Dutch by the bulk of the population (the 'heathens,' as they were referred to) was considered a threat to the state (for an in-depth discussion based on archival materials, see Groeneboer, 1998). Yet even in times when the former consideration was preponderant, it was never the aim of the VOC to encourage mass competence in Dutch. Occasionally the knowledge of Dutch could bring certain privileges: in 1641 Governor-General Van Diemen ordered that only slaves with a fair command of Dutch could wear a hat (without which they could never be manumitted). Native women were allowed to marry a European only if they could communicate in Dutch. Still, these minor measures did not Dutchify the colony.

The strongest rival of Dutch in the early days was Portuguese, sprinkled with Malay words. After the Dutch ousted the Portuguese from the East Indies, their language remained omnipresent, as seen in the comments of Joan Maetsuyker, Governor-General of the East Indies, who complained in 1674 that "corrupted Portuguese is on the up and threatens to oust Dutch completely" (cited in Willemyns, 2013, p. 196). In many households in Batavia, Portuguese was the home language, and Dutch colonists themselves used Portuguese and Malay in certain communicative situations. Even the VOC used Portuguese to communicate with the Eurasians of mixed Portuguese and Asian descent. The churches of Batavia offered services in Dutch, Portuguese, and Malay. By the end of the eighteenth century Dutch had all but died out in the East Indies, whereas both Portuguese and Malay turned out to be the winners.

In the course of the nineteenth century, mainstream ideas about education changed drastically, both in Holland and among the colonial authorities in the East Indies. 'Education for all' was the new common ideal, and in 1818 the

East Indies authorities announced the creation of schools for the 'natives.' This, however, was easier said than done, since neither money nor qualified personnel were made available. As Van Reybrouck (2020) observes, the Dutch wanted to govern the huge Indonesia – stretching one eighth of the globe, three time zones, and more than 5,000 kilometers – with the number of civil servants smaller than the population of Utrecht in 1950. We can judge how scarce personnel was by the fact that the 12 million inhabitants of Java were governed by only 175 Dutch civil servants!

Since the first aim of Dutch language policies was to strengthen the position of Dutch among European settlers in the East Indies, the only schools effectively created were for them, an undertaking that had led to a broader diffusion of Dutch among the European community. Even so, it took more than fifty years to see the tide turning, since it took that long for the new educational system to reach its full effect. In 1870 no more than 20–30 percent of Europeans in the East Indies spoke Dutch, and by the turn of the century the proportion increased to 40 percent. Apart from the improved quality of education, the main factor securing this 'success' was the arrival of a larger number of Netherlanders.

Meanwhile, the Dutch authorities were not in agreement on which aims to pursue and – most importantly – how (or even whether) to finance the 'Dutchification' process. In the mid-nineteenth century there was a fierce debate in the Netherlands not so much on how, but more on whether, the Dutch language was to be promoted among the indigenous population. In contrast to British authorities in India, the Dutch did not favor a pronounced Western orientation in education. They felt that "an uncontrolled spread of Western knowledge by means of a European language would only endanger the existence of the colony" (Groeneboer, 1998, p. 297). In 1865 five indigenous languages were used as a medium of instruction in the islands, in 1900 thirteen, and by 1940 no less than thirty. A more convincing example of linguistic *divide et impera* carried to the extreme is hard to find. On the bright side, indigenous languages were studied closely to enable publication of schoolbooks, grammars, and dictionaries.

In 1864 the idea of promoting Dutch as the general medium of communication and of replacing Malay with Dutch as a lingua franca was abandoned for good. At the same time, the authorities agreed that promoting Dutch proficiency in a small indigenous elite could be advantageous for the administration of the colony and might strengthen the ties with the motherland. They also hoped that, in the long run, it would be cheaper to employ indigenous speakers of Dutch in a number of functions. This opening of 'the gateway to the West,' as it was called, resulted in yet another change of the educational system.

Rather abruptly Holland had become aware of the fact that it had a so-called 'debt of honor' to redeem vis-à-vis its Asian subjects. The 'native' was suddenly turned into a 'younger brother' to whom nothing should be denied of what had made 'the older brother,' Holland, so prosperous. From then on, Dutch was introduced as the language of instruction in all schools where native teachers and civil servants were trained. Moreover, schools that were supposed to be on a par with European schools were put at the disposal of native East Indians and Chinese. On top of that, a system of vocational schools was developed.

The main reason for this change in education policy wasn't Dutch generosity. Rather, the authorities hoped that training and employing a certain number of indigenous civil servants, teachers, lawyers, and physicians would help to keep a lid on the cost of the colonial administration. Nevertheless, in 1900 the estimated number of indigenous speakers of Dutch was no more than 6,000. In 1907, the Dutch-Indian school was introduced, followed in 1908 by the Dutch-Chinese school. In both systems, Dutch was the language of instruction and the schools were meant exclusively for a small native elite. Since a much larger number of locals was eager to learn Dutch, it is only fair to admit that Dutch officials, both in the colony and in the motherland, were unwilling to promote their tongue.

After World War I, the indigenous demand for Dutch language education grew more pressing. Debates among educational specialists, Dutch and East Indians alike, gave way to a consensus that Dutch should be the language of instruction, while at the same time the indigenous languages should be developed to better function as the languages of instruction. Still, the government not only considered it practically and financially impossible to meet the demand for more Dutch language education but also continued to believe it 'unwise' to do so. In 1931, the governmental Dutch-Indian Education Committee recommended to refrain from further expansion of the Dutch-Indian school system, contrary to the wishes of the indigenous people and recommendations by educational specialists. At the same time, drastic cutbacks in educational costs were implemented. The spread of Dutch schools stopped, and the number of enrolled students remained at the level of some 60,000 for the whole country. Consequently, the so-called 'wild schools' (a form of private instruction) became more numerous and popular, leading to an explosive increase of Dutch learners. At the same time, in 1928, the Indonesian nationalist movement had launched the slogan 'One country, one people, one language,' and declared the indigenous language Malay to be the symbol of national identity. Dutch, for Indonesian nationalists, was the symbol of colonialism.

On the eve of World War II, the government yet again devised a new bilingual educational policy to promote both Dutch and Malay but never had a chance to implement it. Although in 1942 the number of indigenous people with a knowledge of Dutch had increased to 860,000, it still represented no more than 1.2 percent of the Indonesian population. The Japanese occupation brought a ban on the Dutch language, and after the war there was no time left. In 1945 Indonesia declared independence, with Bahasa Indonesia, that is, Malay as spoken in Indonesia, as the national language. The Netherlands did not accept the declaration and tried to undo the independence with brutal force of arms (Van Reybrouck, 2020). Eventually, they were forced to recognize Indonesia's independence, and in 1949 sovereignty was transferred officially to Indonesians. Dutch was banned from both the administration and the educational system. Nevertheless, for decades to come the new leaders of the independent Republic of Indonesia were fluent in Dutch. In 1965 President Sukarno confessed in his memoirs: "Dutch is the language in which I do my thinking and even nowadays, when I am cursing, I am cursing in Dutch. When I pray to God, I pray in Dutch" (Sukarno, 1965, pp. 81–82).

The fact that proficiency in Dutch on the part of Indonesia's leading politicians was not matched among the people could be explained by the reluctance of the Dutch, both in the VOC times and afterwards, to make it possible for the people to learn the language they craved, since it was the only means to improve their socioeconomic position. Dutch language policy, often characterized as *kruidenierspolitiek*, a narrow-minded policy, has always been, as Salverda (1989) observed, too little and too late.

Malay remained the only working lingua franca of the Indonesian Archipelago because the Dutch authorities made sure that Dutch could never function as such. The difference between Bahasa Indonesia and Malay, as spoken in Singapore, Malaysia, and Brunei, is a large number of Dutch loanwords (Van der Sijs & Willemyns, 2009). Nevertheless, even today, in Indonesia the ability to read Dutch is indispensable in scientific research in many fields, since many of the necessary sources are in Dutch. Jurists and lawyers also need a thorough competence in Dutch. Even when all the legal codes have been translated into Indonesian (which may take a long time), they will need Dutch to consult historical jurisprudence. Consequently, Dutch is still taught in present-day Indonesia, and specific courses in Dutch are offered for the thousands of students who need to know the language (Salverda, 1989; Sunjayadi et al., 2011).

7.4 Dutch in Suriname

As mentioned earlier, Suriname officially became a Dutch colony in 1667 as part of the Treaty of Breda, in which New Amsterdam, the future New York, was ceded to the English. As soon as the Dutch took possession of the colony, Dutch had become its official language and has maintained this status ever since. Throughout its history, several other languages had been used alongside Dutch, above all Sranan (Tongo), an English-based Creole developed among the earliest slaves on the plantations (De Kleine, 2007). In the initial period of Dutch rule, the number of European settlers was very low, and the Dutch colonists were outnumbered by non-Dutch, including a significant Jewish population of Portuguese and German descent. In 1688, the colony's governor deemed it necessary to publish an ordinance stating that documents in languages other than *Nederduytsch* (Dutch) would no longer be accepted. After more than 300,000 enslaved Africans were brought to Suriname, the ratio of Europeans to non-Europeans went up to 1:12. Communication with and among the enslaved population was in Sranan, a custom that persisted into the eighteenth century.

Throughout the eighteenth century, the colony continued to have a highly international character. Dutch functioned as the official language of the government and, for the Dutch-born, as the language of education and religion. Sranan may have remained as the lingua franca, but school regulations of 1726 declared that it was forbidden for children to use Sranan in class. In 1760, the first school for non-white Surinamese opened its doors, presumably using Dutch as the medium of instruction. By 1830 free non-whites outnumbered the white population in Paramaribo, and since among Europeans less than a quarter was Dutch, the European community lacked linguistic and cultural coherence. A class of Surinamese intellectuals had emerged of mixed European and African ancestry, known as Creoles, most of whom received at least part of their education in Holland. Members of this elite group were proficient in Dutch and Sranan, held high social status, resided permanently in Suriname, and were able to develop a stable Dutch-speaking community that ultimately determined the fate of Dutch in the country.

Education played a decisive role in this process. Until the early nineteenth century, the quality of the schools and their teachers had left much to be desired. This situation changed after 1817 when the government began regulating elementary and secondary education, setting clear standards for teachers and subjects to be taught. The king of the United Kingdom of the Netherlands, the new country that emerged after the reunification of Holland and Belgium (1814–1830), was William I, a big believer in Dutch-medium education as a unifying factor in the kingdom and its colonial possessions. Both in Holland and in Flanders William I founded teacher training academies, in order to improve the quality of elementary teachers and schools. In Flanders, he succeeded in turning French-medium secondary schools, an inheritance of the Napoleonic occupation, into well-functioning Dutch-medium schools in the span of only six years. Similarly, in Suriname, the schools were directed to use Dutch as the medium of instruction. The enslaved population, on the other hand, was officially forbidden to receive any education until 1844. Afterward, the children of the enslaved were taught in Sranan, but the number of pupils remained very small.

This situation changed dramatically when, following the abolition of slavery and the manumission of more than thirty thousand enslaved persons in 1876, the Dutch government introduced compulsory education for every child aged seven to twelve. Simultaneously, it decided to pursue an active policy of assimilation, with the intention of transforming Suriname into a Dutch province. Dutch was made the sole medium of instruction in public and religious schools. As a consequence, the majority of the pupils entering the school system had to learn Dutch as a second language. This policy found strong support among the parents, aware that Dutch was the primary vehicle of social mobility.

In practical terms, the introduction of Dutch on a large scale throughout the educational system was delayed by the arrival of many Asian contract laborers. In a deliberate attempt to create a labor surplus and keep wages low after the abolition of slavery, the authorities recruited laborers from China and the East Indies. Between 1893 and 1917 more than thirty thousand workers were recruited in India. A similar number of Javanese arrived in Suriname between 1891 and 1938. At first, Asian immigrants mostly settled in the countryside. Although theoretically they were subject to the new laws regarding compulsory education in Dutch, an exception was made for them in 1890, as they were expected to reside in Suriname temporarily. As a compromise, 'coolie schools' were established, where education was provided by Indian teachers in Hindi and Urdu. As a result, British Indians and East Indians were largely unaffected by the Dutch assimilation policy, and the Dutch language did not penetrate into these immigrant communities until much later. It was mostly the population of African descent, the Creoles, who by the end of the nineteenth century were receiving instruction in Dutch.

Within the Creole population of Paramaribo, this group constituted the elite. As noted earlier, they were proficient in Dutch and Sranan, and their children acquired Dutch as a first language. Middle-class Creoles also favored Dutch language socialization, since they viewed Dutch as the vehicle for social advancement. Often children from upper- and middle-class families were forbidden to speak Sranan. In the first half of the twentieth century, the Creole and the European-born populations shrank to insignificance as compared to the descendants of the enslaved, who relocated to the city after the abolition of slavery and remained predominantly Sranan-speaking. These speakers of Sranan acquired Dutch as a second language in the classroom, which created a linguistic gap between the higher and the lower social classes. An even sharper distinction developed between the city and the countryside. Creoles lived predominantly in the city, while Asian immigrants remained in the countryside, where they had little exposure to Dutch. In the aftermath of World War II, the Asian population began to move to the city and, since they weren't proficient in Sranan, many adopted Dutch.

When Suriname gained independence in 1975, the Dutch presence came to an end but Dutch remained the sole official language of the country, used in public communication and in the media. If anything, the independence increased the exposure to European Dutch, as a result of the contact between Surinamers who emigrated to the Netherlands and those who remained at home. The lexicon, pronunciation, and some grammatical features of the Suriname variety of Dutch differ slightly from Dutch spoken in the Netherlands and Belgium (Gobardhan-Rambocus, 1993), and individual speakers may be situated along that continuum.

In the present-day multilingual Suriname, language use is partly shaped by ethnicity. Dutch is the language of the government, legislation, and jurisdiction, but many ethnic groups use their own languages in informal contexts and only Sranan and Dutch are spoken across ethnic boundaries (De Kleine, 2007). Sranan functions as the lingua franca in informal settings, while Dutch, the country's official language, is typically employed in more formal settings, including the media and education. The fact that Suriname has become a member of the *Nederlandse Taalunie* (Dutch Language Union), alongside Holland and Flanders, speaks for their determination to remain part of the Dutch language community (Van der Sijs & Willemyns 2009). This determination to have their 'Dutchness' recognized and accepted by all was made clear when Suriname forced UNASUR, the Union of South American Nations, to accept Dutch as one of its official languages, alongside English, Spanish, and Portuguese.

Conclusion

Now let me come back to the question in the title of this chapter. In 1940, French professor G.H. Bousquet, expressed his astonishment as to what he called "the bewildering apathy of the Dutch as far as their own language and culture are concerned.... The Dutch have striven and still strive, though vainly, to deprive their ward of contact with the outside world" (Bousquet, 1940, p. 89). Those familiar with colonial language policies could not help but share Bousquet's bewilderment. The VOC and, subsequently, the Dutch government did not promote the spread of Dutch in the East Indies – instead, they were content with the Portuguese-Malay Creole that served as a lingua franca in the region. Several reasons underlie this choice. The gigantic size of the country has to be taken into account, as well as the small number of civil servants sent to the East Indies and the avarice and pragmatism, first of the VOC and then of the government authorities who didn't really want to invest in a policy of 'Dutchification.' Moreover, unlike other colonial superpowers, the Dutch believed that educating 'the natives' and letting them learn Dutch would make them arrogant and threaten the power of their masters.

But even taking all this into consideration, the question remains of how other colonial powers in Asia, mainly the British and the French, succeeded in generating a completely different outcome. To begin with, both the French and the English were convinced that it was in their proper interest to impose their language and culture on their new subjects. In all their Asian colonies, they started by assimilating a small elite and training a middle class. In British India, the outcome of extensive discussions in the 1830s was a decision to introduce English language education. This policy, directed at the upper class, underwent no substantial changes up to independence in 1947. The French, for their part, were convinced that the teaching of French was *une mission civilisatrice* that would simultaneously strengthen the political role of France in the world. By spreading French over the whole of Indochina, they wanted to realize their ideal of *une France asiatique*. As a consequence, two or three times as much was spent on education in British India and French Indochina as in Dutch Indonesia. The Dutch, on the other hand, invested attention and money in codification and modernization of indigenous languages. Their policy of *divide et impera* was aimed at preserving the structures of colonial society.

The same attitude was attested in the Dutch colony of Suriname. The difference was that in South America the large number of Dutch-speaking Creoles and the smaller size of the overall population made the colonial language a more obvious choice as the national language. Yet there as well we encounter what Bousquet (1940) called "the bewildering apathy of the Dutch as far as their own language and culture are concerned" (p. 89). It was the determination of the Creoles that led to the adoption of Dutch as the habitual and official language of Suriname, an adoption achieved not thanks to, but in spite of, the Dutch. As counterintuitive as it sounds, the leading expert on Dutch language policy in Asia, Groeneboer (1998) had a point when he stated: "Of all the colonial European languages in Asia (Portuguese, Spanish, Dutch, English, and French) four now belong to the group of twelve great supranational languages of the world. Dutch colonial language policy helped to boost not Dutch but Malay into that group" (p. 2).

References

Bousquet, G.H. (1940) *A French view of the Netherlands Indies*. London/New York: Oxford University Press (Translation of Bousquet, G. H. (1939) *La politique musulmane et coloniale des Pays-Bas* [The Muslim and colonial policy of the Netherlands]. Paris: Hartmann.)

De Kleine, C. (2007) *A morphosyntactic analysis of Surinamese Dutch*. Munich: Lincom Europa.

Den Besten, H. (ed.) (1986) *Papers on Negerhollands, the Dutch Creole of the Virgin Islands*. Amsterdam: Publicaties van het Instituut voor Algemene Taalwetenschap nr. 51.

Donaldson, B. (1988) *The influence of English on Afrikaans*. Pretoria: Serva Publishers.
Gobardhan-Rambocus, L. (1993) Het Surinaams Nederlands [The Suriname Dutch]. In Gobardhan-Rambocus, L. & M. Hassankhan (eds.) *Immigratie en ontwikkeling. Emancipatie van contractanten* [Immigration and development: Emancipation of contractants]. Paramaribo: Anton de Kom Universiteit, 140–158.
Groeneboer, K. (1998) *Gateway to the West. The Dutch language in colonial Indonesia 1600–1950. A history of language policy*. Amsterdam: Amsterdam University Press.
Gysseling, M. (1971) De invoering van het Nederlands in ambtelijke bescheiden in de 13de eeuw [The introduction of Dutch in administrative documents in the 13th century]. *Verslagen en Mededelingen van de Koninklijke Vlaamse Academie voor Nederlandse Taal- en Letterkunde*, pp. 27–35.
(1975) Vlaanderen [Flanders]. In *Encyclopedie van de Vlaamse Beweging*, 2 vols. Tielt: Lannoo, pp. 1905–1912.
Kouwenberg, S. (1991) *Berbice Dutch Creole: Grammar, texts, and vocabulary*. Ph.D. dissertation, University of Amsterdam.
Mijts, E. & W. Rutgers (2010) Het bal ging niet door. De verzelfstandiging van de Nederlandse Antillen [The ball was cancelled: The emancipation of the Dutch Antilles]. *In Ons Erfdeel 53*, mei, 34–42.
Mijts, E. & V. van Bogaert (2011) Things fall apart. The new Kingdom of the Netherlands. *In the Low Countries*, 19, 296–297.
Ponelis, F. (1993) *The Development of Afrikaans*. Frankfurt: Peter Lang.
Robertson, I. (1989) Berbice and Skepi Dutch. *In Tijdschrift voor Nederlandse Taal- en Letterkunde*, 105–106, 3–21.
Salverda, R. (1989) Nederlands als wetenschappelijke bronnentaal voor Indonesische studiën in Indonesië [Dutch as the language of scientific documents for Indonesian studies in Indonesia]. In K. Groeneboer (ed.) *Studi Belanda di Indonesia – Nederlandse studiën in Indonesië*. Jakarta: Djambatan, pp. 401–409.
Stell, G. (2008) *Convergence towards and divergence from standard norms. The case of morphosyntactic variation and code-switching in informal spoken Afrikaans*. PhD dissertation, Vrije Universiteit Brussel.
Sukarno (1965) *Sukarno, an autobiography as told to Cindy Adams*. Indianapolis: Bobbs-Merrill.
Sunjayadi A., Suprihatin, C. & K. Groeneboer (eds.) (2011) *Veertig Jaar Studie Nederlands in Indonesië* [Forty years of study of Dutch in Indonesia]. Depok: Fakultas Ilmu Pengetahuan Budaya Universitas Indonesia.
Van der Sijs, N. (2004) *Taal als mensenwerk: het ontstaan van het ABN* [Language as a human construct: The origin of Standard Dutch]. The Hague: Sdu.
(2006) *Klein uitleenwoordenboek* [Concise dictionary of loanwords]. Den Haag: Sdu.
(2009) *Cookies, Coleslaw and Stoops. The Influence of Dutch on the North American Languages*. Amsterdam: Amsterdam University Press.
Van der Sijs, N. & R. Willemyns (2009) *Het verhaal van het Nederlands. Een geschiedenis van twaalf eeuwen* [The story of Dutch: A history of twelve centuries]. Amsterdam: Bert Bakker.
Van der Voort, H. (2006) Het Negerhollands. Een uitgestorven Creooltaal van de Maagdeneilanden [Negro Dutch: An extinct Creole language in the Virgin

Islands]. *In Tijdschrift voor Neerlandistiek in Scandinavië en Ommelanden*, Nov., 1–10.

Van Reybrouck, D. (2020) *Revolusi. Indonesië en het ontstaan van de moderne wereld* [Revolution. Indonesia and the genesis of the modern world]. Amsterdam: De Bezige Bij.

Willemyns, R. (2003) *Het verhaal van het Vlaams. De geschiedenis van het Nederlands in de Zuidelijke Nederlanden* [The story of Flemish. The history of Dutch in the Southern Netherlands]. Antwerpen: Standaard Uitgeverij & Utrecht: Spectrum.

(2013) *Dutch. Biography of a Language*. Oxford: Oxford University Press.

8 How Unique Was Russia's Multilingual Elite?

Gesine Argent

At a conference in Germany where I had given a paper on French in imperial Russia, an emeritus scholar shared a story of his German grandmother who spent some time in Russia in the early 1900s but did not speak any Russian. To get help in tricky situations in public, she approached any person wearing 'the right sort of clothes and behaving correctly' and addressed them in French. This strategy, she had found, usually produced the desired result. On a few occasions, she was advised – in French – to learn to speak Russian. By then, the role of French in Russia had significantly diminished compared to its heyday in the eighteenth and early nineteenth centuries; nevertheless the story illustrates some of the key points of this chapter. To begin with, languages in imperial Russia did not have straightforward trajectories with fixed beginnings and end points. Though French was no longer a key language for the Russian elite, it could still function as a lingua franca in the early twentieth century. The anecdote also illustrates the link between observable behavior, the image one presents to the world ('behaving correctly'), and language use. Most importantly, we see that the use of a foreign language can trigger negative reactions.

It has been frequently suggested that Russia's elite was unique in its long-term adoption of foreign languages in daily life. Romaine (1995), for instance, asserts that "in some countries it is expected that educated persons will have knowledge of another language. This is probably true for most of the European countries, and was even more dramatically so earlier in countries like pre-Revolution Russia, where French was the language of polite, cultured individuals" (p. 31). Thus, in one breath, she acknowledges that elite bilingualism is a feature of most European countries and singles out pre-revolutionary Russia as a particularly stark example. Hosking (1998) too subscribes to the idea of Russia's exceptionality: "In no other empire of modern Europe was the assimilation of a foreign culture as complete" (p. 159). The question of Russia's uniqueness has occupied thinkers and scholars in Russia and abroad. As Lieven (2002) puts it, "for very many Western historians of Russia, the country's uniqueness is a matter of faith. For many Russians it is the core of true religion itself" (p. ix). Language use is a key ingredient in deliberations on Russia's cultural borrowing (Marrese, 2010). The fact that other European countries had similar patterns of elite bilingualism raises an important question: Is multilingualism of Russia's eighteenth- and nineteenth-century elite really unique and, if so, in what ways?

In this chapter, I will draw on the findings of a major research project I participated in, "The History of the French Language in Russia,"[1] to discuss multilingualism of Russia's imperial elite and to consider its exceptionality in the European context in the timespan between the reign of Peter I 'the Great' (1682–1725) and the first two decades of the nineteenth century.

8.1 Researching Historical Multilingualism in Russia

The multilingual elite constituted a small percentage of the overall population of the Russian Empire. These families, however, were the *Kulturträger* who made important decisions and steered the destiny of the empire. Our knowledge of their language use stems from archival documents, data on language learning in schools, and multilingual private writing, which offer clues about which languages were used when. Like other historians of language, scholars of language use and attitudes in imperial Russia have to make use of what Labov (1972) calls "bad data" (p. 100) and Joseph (2012) tempers to "imperfect data" (p. 70), namely the remnants of historical documents that have survived fires, wars, moves, and changes of regime. These materials are fragile, frequently incomplete, and their cataloging and maintenance suffer greatly from the lack of funding for librarians and archivists, particularly evident after the collapse of the USSR. Databases like the Russian National Corpus (https://ruscorpora.ru), which contains over 300 million words, are of limited use to scholars of multilingualism, as material in foreign languages is limited and only encountered by chance.

In the course of my work, I have consulted a variety of archival materials: diaries and albums of noblewomen, personal correspondence, and lists and notebooks. Some collections have not been preserved well or survive only in part. At times, just when a document becomes interesting, a water stain obscures a whole page; in other cases, the handwriting is illegible. Frequently, the descriptions of archival holdings do not match the contents. For example, in a file entitled "collection of poems and prose works by F.N. Glinka [the poet Fyodor Glinka, 1786–1880]," we find a letter, written by someone else, to Pierre de Poletica, a diplomat in London (GATO f.103 op.1

[1] The project, directed by Derek Offord, was based at the University of Bristol from 2011 to 2015 and was funded by the Arts and Humanities Research Council UK. I was a postdoctoral research fellow on this project.

nr. 976).[2] It is impossible to trace how this document ended up in the folder. In a file titled "catalogue de livres de Médecine et de chirurgie," I found a loose sheet with a list of clothes, furniture, and jewelry in French with switches into Russian (II RAN f. 97 o. 1 d. 329). In the album of Avdotia Pavlovna Golenishcheva-Kutuzova, album entries give way to a few pages of diary entries, dated a decade later than the album (GATO f. 103 o.1 d.1115).

The fragmented nature of the data makes finding specific topics or types of documents challenging, and it is even harder to analyze speakers' attitudes toward different languages and their use. Frequently, comments on language matters appear as throwaway remarks in pieces of writing on completely different topics, making a systematic search for such side comments very difficult. In the sources I accessed, there is in fact not much language commentary. Obvious meta-discursive statements on such questions are often absent because mastery of a lingua franca was so normal as to merit no mention at all (Braunmüller & Ferraresi, 2003). Many nobles seem not to have given much thought to their multilingualism, and we hear only the loudest, most opinionated voices in the language debates.

8.2 The Rise of Elite Multilingualism

Until the reign of Peter I, Russia had been relatively isolated from other states. While it did house foreign communities, contact with non-Orthodox Christians was discouraged and travel outside of Russia was all but impossible. As a consequence, there was little incentive to master foreign languages. Accounts of diplomatic relations note that communication was hampered by this lack of knowledge. To give but one example, the imperial ambassador sent to Paris by Tsar Alexis (reigned 1645–1676) had to communicate with French speakers via two interpreters, one who interpreted from Russian into German and another who interpreted from German into French (Schaub, 2010, quoted in Offord et al., 2018, p. 374ff.).

Peter the Great wrought significant changes to the Russian Empire. Focused on progress and tighter links with those who possessed knowledge, skills, and expertise Russia could benefit from, the young tsar traveled to the west in 1697–1698 to learn about various fields and then invited foreign experts to settle in Russia. Peter introduced compulsory, western-style *assemblées* at the palace and began the move toward a culture of sociability and politeness. He

[2] The names of archives are listed in the Archives section. Abbreviations used in archival references are f. (*fond*, collection), r. (*razriad*, collection), op. (*opis'*, inventory), and d. (*delo*, file).

put particular emphasis on foreign language mastery crucial to reading learned books and instructions, and communicating with experts in a variety of fields, ranging from architecture to mining. The languages in high demand were those spoken by the people Peter took as inspiration for innovation: Danes, Swedes, Dutch, Germans, French, and English (Dahmen, 2015; Offord, 2014). Development and modernization of the empire required mastery of foreign languages, and in 1701, the Chancellery of Foreign Affairs (*posol'skii prikaz*) sent six clerks abroad to learn languages to be able to translate (Rjéoutski, 2013b). A cultural change was underway.

The recognition of the importance of foreign languages was connected to a drive for changes in education. In the seventeenth century, Russian schooling was not formalized and consisted of a tutor teaching his pupils what he knew. By the mid-eighteenth century, Russia had a number of educational institutions with formalized instruction. The Academy of Sciences, founded in 1724, had a university and a school with Latin as the medium of instruction, and German, French, and Greek as subjects. German and French were seen as particularly useful for society and communication (Rjéoutski, 2013b).

One of the first institutions for young nobles was the Noble Land Cadet Corps, founded in 1731. In 1736, it was decreed that all sons of nobility, aged seven to twenty, had to be schooled before entering military service. A follow-up edict specified what subjects they were to learn, including foreign languages of the parents' choice. Those who could afford to do so hired private tutors for this purpose, others sent their sons to the Cadet Corps (Rjéoutski, 2005, 2013b). By the end of the reign of Elizabeth in the 1760s, a new educational landscape had taken shape: there was the Noble Land Cadet Corps, the Naval Cadet Corps, the school and university attached to the Academy of Sciences in St. Petersburg, Moscow University, the Smolny Institute for Noble Maidens established in 1764, private schools founded by foreigners, plus private education at home with foreign tutors (Rjéoutski, 2005). As time went by, the motivation for learning foreign languages shifted from practical needs to demands of civilized and courtly life (Rjéoutski, 2013a). Letters from the nobleman Mikhail Shcherbatov to his son Dmitrii, written in 1775, highlight the importance of language learning for Russia's elite:

> Vous sçavez mon fils combien la langue allemande est necessaire en Russie; plusieurs provinces qui font partie de nôtre vaste empire parlent cette langue; nôtre proximité aux pays allemands; les diverses relations, que nous avons avec cette nation celte vous font cette obligation; vous etes dans une ville, ou la langue commune est l'allemande, tachez donc par votre application a vous instruire au plutôt.
>
> [You know, my son, how necessary the German language is in Russia; several provinces of our vast empire speak this language; our closeness to German lands; the various relations we have with this nation give you this obligation; You are in a city

where the communal language is German, so try to apply yourself to learning it.] (RGADA, f. 1289, op. 1, d. 517, fols 12–13; reprinted in Kalinina, 2011, pp. 352–354.)[3]

Another letter from 1775 emphasizes the importance of French:

Mon cher fils ! Je reçu votre Lettre en datte du 2/13 du mai, dont je vous remercie, quoi que je ne suis guere contant ni de votre stile, ni de votre orthographe françoise. C'est pour cella que je vous conseille en ami et en père de vous appliquer a lire les bons auteurs françois, et a tacher de former votre stile sur ces bons modeles;. . .; cinq années mon fils que vous avez passé en etude continuel de la langue françoise, devoient vous donner un peu plus de connoissance de cette Langue, qui est a present si rependus en Europe et par consequent necessaire tant pour la conversation, que pour l'instruction a cause du grand nombre de bons auteurs qui ont écrit en cette langue.
[My dear son! I have received your letter from 2/13 May for which thanks, although I am not at all content with your French style and orthography. That is why, as a friend and a father, I advise you to read good French authors and form your style according to good models ... the five years, my son, which you have spent continually studying the French language should have given you a bit more knowledge of this language which is at the moment so widespread in Europe and, consequently, necessary as much for conversation as for instruction because of the great number of good authors who have written in this language.] (RGADA, f. 1289, op. 1, d. 517, fols 33–34; reprinted in Kalinina, 2011, pp. 357–361.)

Shcherbatov wanted his son to be proficient in German and French because these languages were politically significant, useful for acquisition of knowledge, and needed for social reasons. At the same time, Shcherbatov had mixed feelings about the use of foreign languages and their influence on Russian noble families (Offord & Rjéoutski, 2013a).

French has frequently been described as the dominant language of the Russian nobility over a long period of time, as seen in Charques (1956, p. 102), Seton-Watson (1967, p. 67), and Evtuhov and Stites (2004, p. 7) (all quoted in Offord et al., 2018, pp. 35, 37). These accounts are problematic, firstly, because the Russian elite was a varied stratum ranging from the extremely rich and influential, who were close to the tsar and the court, to penniless nobles living in the provinces with no means of learning foreign languages or participating in the noble society of Moscow and St. Petersburg. It is also inaccurate to state that the nobles hardly spoke Russian. It was a common trope of Russian noble memoirs of the nineteenth century to complain that one's family and acquaintances spoke poor Russian and that instruction in Russian was not good enough (Marrese, 2010, p. 719), but such pronouncements may have expressed unease about cultural and political developments rather than offer an accurate description of language use. After

[3] Historical examples preserve the original spelling.

all, the evidence from documents of the time reveals that Russians wrote in Russian, and nobles needed to be able to communicate in Russian with the people living and working on their estates or the soldiers they commanded in military contexts (Offord et al., 2018).

Moreover, French was not the only language of importance in the Russian Empire. Dahmen (2015) offers an in-depth discussion of the significant role of German in education, administration, science, industry, and commerce. Shcherbatov's exhortations to his son above also show that in the eighteenth century it was important to know German. Following Peter I's manifesto inviting foreigners, many Germans settled in Russia. Furthermore, in the Great Northern War the Russian Empire acquired Baltic lands that were ruled by Baltic Germans. At the court of Empress Anne (1730–1740), the most influential courtiers were German, including many nobles from the Baltic governorates. German, however, did not reach the status of a language of sociability. English was popular at the court in the nineteenth century but overall was not used as much as French (Cross, 2015).

Toward the end of Peter's reign and beyond, French gained more prominence in Russia. At the time, it was the language of European diplomacy, of science, learning, and literature, and of the noble societies across Europe (Burke, 2014; Rjéoutski et al., 2014). The timing, however, differed across settings: in Italy, for instance, the rise of French began in the mid-seventeenth century, later than in England and the Netherlands (Minerva, 2014, p. 113).

Empress Elizabeth (reigned 1741–1762), a Francophile, introduced routine use of French at her court. The royal stamp of approval contributed to the cachet of French. What is more, better diplomatic relations between Russia and France at the start of the Seven Years War (1756–1763) meant that Russia had more French-speaking visitors. French was used in salons and Masonic lodges, at balls and card games, in the theater, and in fashion, writing, and architecture. Nobles, emancipated from compulsory service to the state by Peter III in 1762, had more leisure time to travel and needed French to communicate with their counterparts across Europe, who spoke French both in the social sphere and as a private family language (Argent et al., 2014, 2015).

French was also used to communicate with other nations, both directly and as a medium for propagandistic messages that promoted the image of Russia as a fully-fledged nation equal to Western nations, rather than a backwater at best and a tyrannical, barbarous place at worst (which is how an Englishman Giles Fletcher (1966 [1591]) described sixteenth-century Russia). Yet the negative reputation was difficult to shake off – in 1768, Sir George Macartney stated that Russians' "ridiculous imitation of foreign manners divest[ed] them of all national character" (cited in Cross, 1971, pp. 203–204).

Catherine the Great (reigned 1762–1796) mounted a publicity campaign aimed at portraying Russia as equal to the West. A German princess, who learned French before Russian, Catherine wrote plays in French, corresponded with the great figures of the Enlightenment, Voltaire and Diderot, and promoted foreign language teaching and closer links to the West. When the Frenchman Chappe d'Auteroche, an astronomer and geographer who had visited Russia to witness Venus passing across the sun in 1761, gave a very unflattering portrayal of the country in his travelogue *Voyage en Sibérie* in 1768, Catherine wrote a retort in French (or significantly contributed to it, see Levitt, 1998, for analysis). Catherine's pioneering *Instruction* (1767), a guide for the Legislative Commission that was to consider internal reforms and a new legal code, was published in French, German, Latin, and Russian, to ensure wide readership (Offord et al., 2018). The aim of the empress was to present Russia as a 'European power,' as she wrote in the *Instruction* (1767, p. 43). Of course, the use of French for international propaganda was not limited to Russia but was common across Europe (Argent et al., 2014).

Catherine also promoted Russian. In her correspondence with Voltaire, the empress praised Russian as a rich and strong language. To show that Russia was no backwater or mere imitation of the West, she made efforts to develop Russian language and literature – a literature in one's own language was a mark of a civilized nation (Offord et al., 2018). At the same time, Catherine was careful not to detract from the usage of foreign languages, lest she and her empire be considered quaint and un-European (Bruce, 2015). In 1787, the empress strengthened the role of Russian by signing a rescript that ordered Russian diplomats to write their reports to the sovereign in Russian (AVPRI f.32 d.702 fol. 10; quoted in Offord et al., 2018, p. 294).

Similar developments were underway elsewhere. In 1780, Frederick II of Prussia wrote (in French) that the German language, *une langue à demi barbare*, was in need of urgent development due to its lack of clarity, and so were German science and literature (cited by Böhm, 2014, pp. 180–181). Codification of Russian also made progress in the Catherinian age. In 1755, the famous polymath Mikhail Lomonosov wrote the first descriptive grammar of Russian, soon followed by others (e.g., Barsov, 1771; Kurganov, 1769). In 1783, Catherine made Princess Ekaterina Dashkova (1743–1810) the first president of the Imperial Russian Academy. In this role, Dashkova presided over the creation of a new dictionary of Russian, whose six volumes, published between 1789 and 1794, contained more than 43,000 words.

The founding of the Academy and the commissioning of the dictionary occurred at a time when there was a growing official concern about the high number of foreign teachers, who taught all kinds of subjects in foreign languages rather than in Russian (Offord et al., 2018). From the middle of the eighteenth century, writers started discussing Russia's cultural relationship with its western neighbors. The topos of pride in the Russian language started gaining currency, under the influence of French thought (Offord et al., 2018).

Dashkova's work on the dictionary was also informed by language pride. In the preface to the first volume, she stated that without a lexicon it would be impossible to prove the beauty, importance, and strength of a language (Dashkova, 1789, p. v). The idea of the dictionary, said Dashkova to the empress, was "to do away with the absurdity of using foreign words and terms while having our own" (Dashkova, 1958, p. 217). There were also other signs that despite the popularity of French, not everyone was satisfied with the reliance on a foreign language and the dependency that it seemed to bring. The writer Denis Fonvizin (1959 [1777–1778], p. 472) glumly remarked in the 1770s that a Parisian considered Burgundy a nearby province and Russia a distant one. Unease about the spread of the French culture and language in Catherine's age was not a uniquely Russian phenomenon – it drew on thinking that came from the West and was part of a wider European wariness of modernity and urbanity (Argent et al., 2014). One expression of this unease is the eighteenth-century European comic drama that portrayed linguistic gallophobia (Offord et al., 2018).

Endeavors to codify Russian and expressions of frustration at the use of foreign languages notwithstanding, the archival evidence points at an overwhelmingly "unproblematic cultural bilingualism" (Marrese, 2010, p. 705). For a significant part of the nobility, the use of foreign languages was not tantamount to an identity crisis. Multilingualism did not mean lack of loyalty or a wish to align oneself with a different country. On the contrary, in an empire that tried to orient itself toward Europe, multilingualism was an accomplishment, with language skills conferring cultural capital, authority, and power, in Bourdieu's (1986) terms (Offord et al., 2018). Most letter writers did not comment on their choice of language at all and seem to have found nothing remarkable in switching languages within letters or writing one letter in French and the next one in Russian. Nevertheless, in the early nineteenth century the unease mentioned above triggered debates about what was acceptable in terms of foreign language borrowing and use.

8.3 Debates on Language Use at the Turn of the Nineteenth Century

One significant language debate took place in the early nineteenth century between the famous writer and historian Nikolai Karamzin (1766–1826) and essayist and statesman Aleksandr Shishkov (1754–1841). This was what Blommaert (1999, p. 10) calls a formative debate, one that furnished stock arguments and tropes that persist to the present day. The conflict formed part of the drive to refine the Russian language (Offord et al., 2018), but the two figures disagreed on how this refinement was to be achieved. Karamzin (1964 [1802], 1982 [1802]) was in favor of linguistic borrowing and foreign models, mostly French, and reportedly used many borrowings himself in speech

(Kamenev, 1864). He also knew the value of French as the language of propaganda and wrote a piece in the journal *Spectateur du Nord* (1797) extolling the virtues of Russian literature to a European public. In an earlier text, Karamzin (2003 [1791]) opposed what he considered "parroting" and "aping" foreigners:

> Everyone here who can say as little as: "Comment vous portez-vous?", mangles the French language without any need, in order to speak with Russians not in Russian ... How can you not have national self-respect? Why be parrots and apes at once?

In 1818 he expressed the hope that Russian would soon take its rightful place among European languages (for an extended discussion, see Argent, 2015). Shishkov took a different view on how to perfect Russian. A firm believer that languages are cultural organisms, specific to nations (Cooper, 2008), he wanted modern Russian to be based on Church Slavonic and cleansed of foreign elements. In his 'Discourse on the ancient and modern style of the Russian language,' Shishkov (1813 [1803]) attacked "our slavish copying of the French" (p. 12) and writing in the Karamzinian style and complained that "without knowing our own language, we will copy them exactly like parrots copy people" (p. 8).

The two camps ridiculed and insulted one another (Argent, 2015), and are often written about as if their views were diametrically opposed, not least because they were later given the labels of 'archaists' and 'innovators' (Tynianov, 1967 [1929]). Overall, they were both conservative and concerned with how the Russian language should be developed into a fully fledged literary language that could serve all purposes. However, the Karamzinists distinguished between good French language and culture and 'bad' French revolutionaries and warmongers, while archaists believed that they could not be separated (Martin, 1997).

The early nineteenth century brought the Napoleonic wars, culminating in the French invasion of Russia and ultimate defeat in 1812. We might assume that warring with France meant that enthusiasm for the French language diminished or disappeared. In reality, some pledged to stop speaking French, but overall the reliance on French was not reduced by the war. The high nobility saw itself as part of a European corporation and had no problem separating French culture from political enmity with the French state. Already in the eighteenth century, most Russians who were concerned with such questions detached their view of the French language from their opinions of the French nation (Berelowitch, 2015). Nevertheless, the nineteenth century gave more traction to the idea that using foreign languages when Russian was perfectly serviceable was frivolous. Writer Aleksandr Bestuzhev (1797–1837), for example, expressed great anger that Russians, as he saw it, returned from the Napoleonic Wars "with laurels on their brow but French phrases on their lips" (Offord et al., 2018, p. 502). The statesman and governor of Moscow during the Napoleonic invasion, Fyodor Rostopchin (1763–1826), wrote many gallophobic texts. Despite his mastery of French and conventions of salon sociability (Offord & Rjéoutski, 2013b), Rostopchin turned against francophonie (Offord et al., 2018, p. 386). In 1807, he published a collection of pamphlets entitled 'Ox, французы [Oh, the French].' Interestingly, on the title page of the manuscript, Rostopchin added in French: "cela sera mieux mettre ox, иноземцы [it would be better to put 'oh, the foreigners']" (Ovchinnikov in Rostopchin, 1992, p. 325). To Rostopchin the problem was not specifically French influence but *any* influence from abroad, linguistic and otherwise. Such backlash as there was about elite language use was not confined to French.

French at the start of the nineteenth century still served as an emblem of a certain way of life and belonging to the urban elite. Alexander Bakunin (1768–1854), father of the revolutionary anarchist Mikhail Bakunin, sent letters in French from the provincial town of Tver' to his brother in Moscow, with some code-switching into Russian. In one letter, written in 1805, Alexander is trying to persuade his brother's family to visit and touts the charms of Tver':

> "Venez mes Chers amis, nous rejoindre et nous trouverons les moyens de ne pas nous ennuyer . . . Nous celebrerons les jours de nom et de naissance. Viendra me direz vous, le triste hyver, mais est-il bien plus gaÿ en ville? Je vous assure pas de beaucoup" (GATO f.103 op.1 d.1395, fol. 23obv).

> [Come join us, my dear friends. We will find the means to not get bored . . . We will celebrate name days and birthdays. You will say, "the sad winter", but is it really much jollier in the city? Not very much, I assure you.]

Some nobles, though, were using Russian more. For example, in 1816–1817, a member of the Panaev family kept an album completely in Russian (IRLI r.1 op. 42 nr. 21), while other contemporary albums, like that of Avdotia Golenishcheva-Kutuzova mentioned earlier, still feature many languages. Just as in Catherine's age, French was used to convey important messages to a wider public. In the 1820s, Ivan Vadkovskii (1790–1849), a commander in the Semionovskii regiment, wrote a French memoir, addressed to his sister and shared with the tsar and a wider audience, presenting his version of the 1820 uprising in his regiment (RNB Fr. 0.IV. d. 54). French was also adopted to sing praises to Russia. The short text "le retour dans la patrie" [the return to the motherland] (IRLI f. 196 op.1 d.104) from the 1820s praises foreign lands but concludes that Russia is better because it is the homeland. Writing in French did not automatically denote a lack of patriotism or love for Russia.

As the nineteenth century progressed, French was still used for all kinds of functions. Liubov Bakunina writing in Moscow to her parents in Tver' may have used it as a secret language:

15 январь 1831
Любезный Папинька и любезная Маминька.
Благодарю вас за письмо от 3го и обещение прислать. А то **ici on fait des projets sur cela**. Мы все здоровые и здесь совершенно благополучно. . . . я думаю на [illegible, 2 words] теперь из альбома стихи, [illegible, 2 words] Глинка. **Je n'ecris pas d'avantage parce que la lettre a étant** [f.133obv] **pas cachetée il peut s'y trouver des curieux**. [illegible, in Russian] целую ручки ваши и прошу благословения
[illegible, 2 lines] Любов

[15 January 1831
Dear Papinka and dear Maminka.
Thank you for the letter from the 3rd and the promise to send. So, **we will do some projects with that here**. We are all healthy and everything is completely fine here. . . . I think in [illegible, 2 words] now verses from the album, [illegible, 2 words] Glinka. **I am not writing too much because as the letter is not sealed, there might be curious eyes**. [illegible, in Russian] I kiss your hands and ask for your blessing
[illegible, 2 lines]
Liubov (GATO f.103 op.1 d.1395 [fol.133])]

Notably, Liubov switches to French to talk of projects, and later suggests that she is about to quote some album verses by Glinka (it is unclear which member of this family she means, possibly Fyodor), when in fact she is writing in French that she cannot write more because the letter may be read by those for whom the content is not meant.

In the mid-nineteenth century, ego-writing and correspondence still feature multiple languages. One example is from the diary of a member of the Bünting family (most probably Georg Wilhelm, 1826–1875) from 1856 (GATO f.103 op.1 nr. 3135a). While of German origin, the author wrote predominantly in French, with some German entries and Russian names and phrases. A loyal servant to the Russian Empire, who served in the Caucasus, he frequently writes about his relations with Russians, expressing the desire to impress them and work with them. Competent in three languages, Bünting uses them freely and without commenting on his choices throughout the diary, as seen in this entry that mixes German, **French** and *Russian*:

Mittwoch Okt 17.
Spät morgens ist M. *Кузнецов* wieder abgegangen, wie es schien, sehr erfreut von unserer Bekanntschaft **et nous invitent instamment de regarder sa maison à** *Каширское* **comme la nôtre**.

[Wednesday October 17.

Late in the morning, M. *Kuznetsov* left again, he seemed to be very glad to have made our acquaintance **and invites us immediately to consider ourselves at home at his house at** *Kashirskoe*.]

The slow decline of elite multilingualism in the latter part of the nineteenth century was not caused by a sense that Russian was finally ready to be deployed in all domains and genres. Toward the second half of the nineteenth century, the political and cultural hegemony of France was challenged by Britain and Germany, which contributed to the decline of French as the language of prestige (Offord et al., 2018). What's more, the new layer of society that gained influence did not have the same language skills as high nobility. The intelligentsia, as this group is known, consisted of educated people of limited financial means who were unable to educate their children in different languages. The increased activity of these individuals in the intellectual sphere meant that much of the communication at the higher echelons of society was now taking place routinely in Russian. Before the spread of nationalist ideologies, the use of French for social and cultural purposes did not mean disloyalty to the motherland, but with the rise of nationalism and questioning of the legitimacy of the autocratic state, the use of foreign languages and multilingualism began to seem suspect. Slavophiles, who came to the fore in the mid-nineteenth century, emphasized the difference between the multilingual elite and authentic Russia untouched by cultural westernization (Offord et al., 2018).

Conclusion

One of the distinguishing features of the Russian Empire is a wide chasm between the highest layers of society who were living 'European' lives and the large mass of people who spoke their 'native' languages (Lotman, 1985 [1977]). At the same time, as Marrese (2010) has argued compellingly, the thesis about the uniquely divided self of Russian nobles – torn between their true Russian selves and false performative Western identities – is not supported by the evidence. Recent studies show that in the eighteenth and nineteenth centuries many European countries had multilingual elites (Marrese, 2010; Rjéoutski et al., 2014). Cultural borrowing, as Marrese (2010) reminds us, "was not a Russian peculiarity but a means of defining social status throughout much of Europe into the nineteenth century" (pp. 738–739).

Another image that recurs time and again in writing about Russian multilingualism are parrots and apes, blindly imitating others. This image illustrates the root cause of anxiety about foreign language use: the fear that multilingual speakers are just talented imitators, deprived of creativity and a unique identity (Offord et al., 2018). In Sweden, for instance, followers of Gothicism argued that ancient Goths were superior to other peoples and there was "no reason to admire and imitate foreigners, particularly the French, or to use other languages instead of the mother tongue" (Östman, 2014, pp. 302–303). German philosopher Christian Thomasius also railed against 'imitation of the French' in the German-speaking world (1894 [1687], quoted by Burke, 2014, p. 45). In Russia, the topos was particularly widespread, not least because foreigners like Macartney, cited above, had been leveling the accusation of mimicry at the Russian elite.

The anxiety about Russia not having its own tradition was strongly expressed by the philosopher Piotr Chaadaev, who wrote (in French) in 1829: "nous n'avons jamais marché avec les autres peuples ... nous ne sommes ni de l'Occident ni de l'Orient, et nous n'avons les traditions ni de l'un ni de l'autre." [We have never marched in step with other nations ... we are neither of the West nor of the East, and we possess the traditions of neither.] (Chaadaev, 1991 [1829], p. 89). These anxieties and the diminishing advantages of foreign language mastery brought elite multilingualism to an end in a process of slow waning, rather than a sudden shift. The definitive break with multilingualism happened in the early twentieth century, after my colleague's German grandmother visited Russia and was able to determine by someone's appearance whether they spoke French. To sum up, ideas of what it means to be a learned and progressive nation, integrated into Europe as a fully fledged partner, first led to the rise of a multilingual Russian elite, and then to its gradual retreat.

Archives

AVPRI (*Arkhiv vneshnei politiki Rossiiskoi imperii* [Archive of the Foreign Policy of the Russian Empire]) f.32, op. 1, d. 702 – letter-book of rescripts to the Ambassador in Vienna, D.M. Golitsyn (1787)

GATO (*Gosudarstvennyi arkhiv Tverskoi oblasti* [Tver' Province State Archive]) f. 103, op. 1, d. 976 – collection of poems and prose works by F.N. Glinka (no date)

GATO f. 103, op. 1, d. 1115 – album belonging to Kutuzova (no date)

GATO f. 103, op. 1, d. 1395 – [correspondence of the Bakunin family] (1740–1861)

GATO f. 103, op. 1, d. 3135a – diary of one of the members of the Bünting family (1855–1859)

IRLI (*Institut russkoi literatury (Pushkinskii Dom) Rossiiskoi akademii nauk* [Institute of Russian Literature (Pushkin House) of the Russian Academy of Sciences]) r.1, op. 42, nr. 21 – the album of V. Panaeva (1816–1817)

IRLI f. 196, op. 1, d. 104 – The return to the motherland (1820)

RGADA (*Rossiiskii gosudarstvennyi arkhiv drevnikh aktov* [Russian State Archive of Ancient Documents]) f. 1289, op. 1, d. 517 – exercise book with letters from Prince Mikhail Mikhailovich

Shcherbatov to his son Dmitrii Mikhailovich Shcherbatov and his wife with an appended list of M. M. Shcherbatov's writings (1725–1789)

RNB (*Rossiiskaia natsional'naia biblioteka* [Russian National Library]) Fr. 0.IV. d. 54 – no title [explanation by Vadkovskii about the Semionovsky regiment uprising] (no date)

References

Argent, G. (2015) The linguistic debate between Karamzin and Shishkov: Evaluating Russian-French language contact. In Offord, D., Ryazanova-Clarke, L, Rjéoutski, V. & G. Argent (eds.) *French and Russian in imperial Russia*. 2 vols. Edinburgh: Edinburgh University Press, vol. 2, pp. 100–118.

Argent, G., Offord, D., & V. Rjéoutski (2014) Conclusion. In Rjéoutski, V., Argent, G. & D. Offord (eds.) *European francophonie: The social, political and cultural history of an international prestige language*. Oxford: Peter Lang, pp. 435–449.

(2015) The functions and value of foreign languages in eighteenth-century Russia. *The Russian Review*, 74, 1, 1–19.

Barsov, A. (1771) *Kratkie pravila rossiiskoi grammatiki* [Short rules of Russian grammar]. No publisher.

Berelowitch, V. (2015) Francophonie in Russia under Catherine II: General reflections and individual cases. *The Russian Review*, 74, 1, 41–56.

Blommaert, J. (1999) *Language ideological debates*. Berlin/New York: Mouton de Gruyter.

Böhm, M. (2014) The domains of francophonie and language ideology in eighteenth- and nineteenth-century Prussia. In Rjéoutski, V., Argent, G. & D. Offord (eds.) *European francophonie: The social, political and cultural history of an international prestige language*. Oxford: Peter Lang, pp. 175–208.

Bourdieu, P. (1986) The forms of capital. In Richardson, J. (ed.) *Handbook of theory and research for the sociology of education*. Westport, CT: Greenwood, pp. 241–258.

Braunmüller, K. & G. Ferraresi (2003) *Aspects of multilingualism in European language history*. Amsterdam/Philadelphia: John Benjamins.

Bruce, S. (2015) The pan-European justification of a multilingual Russian society in the late eighteenth century. In Offord, D., Ryazanova-Clarke, L., Rjéoutski, V. & G. Argent (eds.) *French and Russian in imperial Russia*, vol. 2. Edinburgh: Edinburgh University Press, pp. 16–30.

Burke, P. (2014) Diglossia in early modern Europe. In Rjéoutski, V., Argent, G. & D. Offord (eds.) *European francophonie: The social, political and cultural history of an international prestige language*. Oxford: Peter Lang, pp. 33–50.

[Catherine II] [1767] *Nakaz Komissii o sostavlenii proekta novogo ulozheniia* [Instruction to the commission for composing a new code of law]. [Moscow:] Pechat' pri Senate.

Chaadaev, P. (1991 [1829]) Lettres philosophiques addressées à une dame. Lettre première [Philosophical letters addressed to a lady. First letter]. In *Polnoe sobranie sochinenii i izbrannye pis'ma* [Complete works and selected letters], vol. 1. Moscow: Nauka, pp. 86–103.

Charques, R. (1956) *A short history of Russia*. London: Phoenix House Ltd.
Cooper, D. (2008) 'Narodnost' avant la lettre? Andrei Turgenev, Aleksei Merzliakov, and the national turn in Russian criticism. *Slavic and East European Journal*, 52, 3, 351–369.
Cross, A. (1971) *Russia under western eyes, 1617–1825*. London: Elek Books.
(2015) English – a serious challenge to French in the reign of Alexander I? *The Russian Review*, 74, 1, 57–68.
Dahmen, K. (2015) The use, functions, and spread of German in eighteenth-century Russia. *The Russian Review*, 74, 1, 20–40.
Dashkova, E. (1789) Predislovie [Foreword]. In *Slovar' Akademii Rossiiskoi* [Dictionary of the Russian academy], vol 1. [St Petersburg:] Pri Imperatorskoi Akademii nauk.
(1958) *The memoirs of Princess Dashkova: Russia in the time of Catherine the Great*. Fitzlyon, K. (Trans and ed.). London: John Calder.
Evtuhov, C. & R. Stites (2004) *A history of Russia: Peoples, legends, events, forces, since 1800*. Boston, MA: Houghton Mifflin.
Fletcher, G. (1966 [1591]) *Of the Rus commonwealth*. Ithaca, NY: Cornell University Press.
Fonvizin, D. (1959 [1777–1778]) Pis'ma iz vtorogo zagranichnogo puteshestviia [Letters from the second journey abroad] (1777–1778). In Makogonenko, G. P. (ed.) *Sobranie Sochinenii* [Collected works], vol 2. Moscow: Gosudarstvennoe izdatel'stvo khudozhestvennoi literatury.
Hosking, G. (1998) *Russia: People and empire 1552–1917*. London: Fontana Press.
Joseph, B. (2012) Historical linguistics and sociolinguistics: Strange bedfellows or natural friends? In Langer, N., Davies, S. & W. Vandenbussche (eds.) *Language and history, linguistics and historiography: Interdisciplinary approaches*. Oxford: Peter Lang, pp. 67–88.
Kalinina, S. (ed.) (2011) *Perepiska kniazia M. M. Shcherbatova. Publikatsiia so vvedeniem, komentariiami i imennym ukazatelem* [The correspondence of Prince M. M. Shcherbatov. Published with an introduction, comments and an index of names]. Moscow: Drevlekhranilishche.
Kamenev, G. (1864) Pis'ma [Letters]. In Galakhov, A. (ed.) *Istoricheskaia khristomatiia novogo perioda russkoi slovesnosti* [Historical chrestomathy of the new period of Russian literature], vol 2. St. Petersburg: Tipografiia morskogo ministerstva, pp. 77–79.
Karamzin, N. (1797) Lettre au Spectateur du Nord [Letter to the *Spectateur du Nord*]. *Le Spectateur du Nord, Journal politique, littéraire et morale*, 4, 53–71.
(1964 [1802]) O bogatstve iazyka [On the richness of language]. In Berkov, P. & G. Makogonenko (eds.) *Izbrannye sochineniia v dvukh tomakh* [Selected works in two volumes], vol. 2. Leningrad: Khudozhestvennaia literatura, pp. 280–287.
(1982 [1802]) Otchego v Rossii malo avtorskikh talantov? [Why is there so little writing talent in Russia?] In *Izbrannye stat'i i pis'ma* [Selected essays and letters]. Moscow: Sovremennik, pp. 101–104.
(2003 [1791]) *Nikolai Karamzin: 'Letters of a Russian traveller', 1789–1790,* trans. and ed. by A. Kahn. Oxford: Voltaire Foundation.
Kurganov, N. (1769) *Rossiiskaia universal'naia grammatika* [Russian universal grammar]. St Petersburg: Tipografiia Morskogo kadetskogo korpusa.

Labov, W. (1972) Some principles in linguistic methodology. *Language in Society*, 1, 1, 97–120.
Levitt, M. (1998) An antidote to nervous juice: Catherine the Great's debate with Chappe d'Auteroche over Russian culture. *Eighteenth-Century Studies*, 32, 1, 49–63.
Lieven, D. (2002) *Empire: The Russian empire and its rivals*. New Haven, CT: Yale University Press.
Lomonosov, M. (1950–1957 [1755]) Rossiiskaia grammatika [Russian grammar]. In *Polnoe Sobranie Sochinenii* [Complete works] (vols. 1–10). Vol. 7. Moscow: Izdatel'stvo akademii nauk SSSR, pp. 391–578.
Lotman, Iu. M. (1985 [1977]) The poetics of everyday behavior in eighteenth-century Russian culture. In Nakhimovsky, A.D. & A. S. Nakhimovsky (eds.) *The semiotics of Russian cultural history*. Ithaca, NY: Cornell University Press, pp. 67–94.
Marrese, M. (2010) "The poetics of everyday behavior" revisited: Lotman, gender, and the evolution of Russian noble identity. *Kritika: Explorations in Russian and Eurasian History*, 11, 4, 701–739.
Martin, A. (1997) *Romantics, reformers, reactionaries: Russian conservative thought and politics in the reign of Alexander I*. DeKalb, IL: Northern Illinois University Press.
Minerva, N. (2014) The two Latin sisters: representations of the French and the French language in Italy. In Rjéoutski, V., Argent, G. & D. Offord (eds.) *European francophonie: The social, political and cultural history of an international prestige language*. Oxford: Peter Lang, pp. 113–144.
Offord, D. (2014) Francophonie in imperial Russia. In Rjéoutski, V., Argent, G. & D. Offord (eds.) *European francophonie: The social, political and cultural history of an international prestige language*. Oxford: Peter Lang, pp. 371–404.
Offord, D. & Rjéoutski, V. (2013a) French in the education of the nobility: Mikhail Shcherbatov's letters to his son Dmitrii. *French in Russia*. https://doi.org/10.5523/bris.3nmuogz0xzmpx21l2u1m5f3bjp
(2013b) French in the nineteenth-century Russian salon: Fiodor Rostopchin's 'memoirs'. *French in Russia*. https://doi.org/10.5523/bris.3nmuogz0xzmpx21l2u1m5f3bjp
Offord, D., Rjéoutski, V., & G. Argent (2018) *The French language in Russia: A social, political, cultural, and literary history*. Amsterdam: Amsterdam University Press.
Östman, M. (2014) French in Sweden in the seventeenth, eighteenth and nineteenth centuries. In Rjéoutski, V., Argent, G. & D. Offord (eds.) *European francophonie: The social, political and cultural history of an international prestige language*. Oxford: Peter Lang, pp. 273–306.
Rjéoutski, V. (2005) Les écoles étrangères dans la société russe à l'époque des Lumières [Foreigner-run schools in Russian society during the age of Enlightenment]. *Cahiers du Monde russe*, 46, 3, 473–527.
(2013a) Apprendre la 'langue de l'Europe': le français parmi d'autres langues dans l'éducation en Russie au siècle des Lumières [Learning the 'language of Europe': French among other languages in education in Russia during the age of Enlightenment]. *Vivliofika: E-journal of Eighteenth-Century Russian Studies*, 1, 5–19.
(2013b) Le français et d'autres langues dans l'éducation en Russie au XVIIIe siècle [French and other languages in education in Russia in the eighteenth century]. *Vivliofika: E-journal of Eighteenth-Century Russian Studies*, 1, 20–47.

Rjéoutski, V., Offord, D., & G. Argent (eds.) (2014) *European francophonie: The social, political and cultural history of an international prestige language*. Oxford: Peter Lang.
Romaine, S. (1995) *Bilingualism*. Oxford: Basil Blackwell.
Rostopchin (1992 [1807]) Mysli vslukh na Krasnom kryl'tse rossiiskogo dvorianina Sila Andreevicha Bogatyreva [The Russian nobleman Sila Andreevich Bogatyrev thinks out loud on the staircase of honour]. In G. D. Ovchinnikov (ed.) *Okh, frantsuzy!* [Oh, the French] Moscow: Russkaia kniga ("Sovetskaia Rossiia"), pp. 148–152.
Schaub, M.-K. (2010) Avoir l'oreille du roi: l'ambassade de Pierre Potemkine et Siméon Roumiantsev en France en 1668 [Having the ear of the king: the embassy of Pierre Potemkin and Simeon Rumiantsev in France in 1668]. In Andretta, S. (ed.) *Paroles des négociateurs. Entretien dans la pratique diplomatique de la fin du Moyen Age à la fin du XIXe siècle* [Words of negotiators. A discussion of diplomatic practice from the end of the Middle Ages to the end of the nineteenth century]. Rome: École française de Rome, pp. 213–228.
Seton-Watson, H. (1967) *The Russian Empire, 1801–1917*. Oxford: Clarendon Press.
Shishkov, A. (1813 [1803]) *Rassuzhdenie o starom i novom sloge rossiiskogo iazyka* [Discourse on the ancient and modern style of the Russian language]. St Petersburg: V meditsinskoi tipografii.
Slovar' Akademii Rossiiskoi [Dictionary of the Russian academy]. (1789–1794) (vols. 1–6). St Petersburg: Pri Imperatorskoi Akademii nauk.
Thomasius, C. (1894 [1687]) *Von Nachahmung der Franzosen* [On the imitation of the French]. Leipzig: Göschen.
Tynianov, I. N. (1967 [1929]) *Arkhaisty i novatory* [The archaists and the innovators]. Munich: Wilhelm Fink Verlag.

9 Language Ideology and Observation: Nineteenth-Century Scholars in Northwestern Siberia

Susan Gal

It is a truism that the assumptions with which scholars approach their subject matter have deep effects on what they take to be evidence and how they handle it. Comparative study of linguistic practices through the reports of historical observers requires attention to the ideas of those observers. Scholars studying linguistic descriptions from the overseas colonial and missionary projects of Europeans in the sixteenth to the nineteenth centuries have shown that the accompanying language specialists held presuppositions that shaped their understandings of the practices they observed (Errington, 2008; Harries, 1988; Irvine, 1993). What we read in their reports reflects some combination of the practices the linguists witnessed and the ideas with which they approached those practices. More generally, scholars of the knowledge produced in the colonial encounter – including linguistic knowledge – have urged us to attend as much to the ideologies of the observers as to what they claim to have observed (Cohn, 1996). This approach is equally relevant to linguistic knowledge produced through the exploration of Europe's land empires, as earlier studies have argued (Friedman, 2011; Gal, 2015; Graber & Murray, 2015; Irvine & Gal, 2000). In this chapter, I analyze writings by several linguist-ethnographers, historians, and a traveler from the late eighteenth to mid-nineteenth century who all wrote about speakers in one part of northwestern Siberia. My focus is on the ideological work of these observers, who partly shared a perspective but also had distinct viewpoints on the linguistic practices they separately witnessed in that single region and time.[1]

The first goal of this chapter is to demonstrate the effects on these scholars of European ideological presumptions about language. Ideologies of language are understandings about the structure and use of linguistic forms in a social world (Woolard, 2018). Sometimes as discourses, sometimes tacitly, all speakers in all societies hold such views, which link linguistic practices to identities, institutions, and values (Gal & Irvine, 2019). Although such ideas differ widely across social groups, the scholars I discuss in this chapter shared

[1] My sources are English-, Hungarian-, and German-language writings, through which I have accessed Russian ethnographies. Translations are mine unless otherwise indicated.

a single image: Languages were deemed natural objects with firm boundaries, separate from the empirical world for which the language merely provides words; each language was supposedly spoken by a territorially distinct social group; and the language unified that group into a people by carrying its historical 'spirit' or essence. Phenomena that violated this image were ignored. In short, like all ideologies, this one involves 'erasure': elision, neglect, or denial of whatever does not fit the preferred or expected pattern. There is a presumption of monolingualism in this ideological formation: one linguistic code, for one people, with one essence, each such unit arrayed alongside the others across the map of the world. Multilingualism in this view means an individual speaking two or more of these bounded codes, with translation between them.

Language ideologies, like all ideologies, are contestable and open to change. This one has been problematized repeatedly in debates and conflicts with other perspectives. Moreover, the image it presents was not uniformly characteristic of actual practices in any of the European states in which these scholars lived and worked. Only later did it become commonplace as practice, in some parts of the continent.[2] Yet, this Europe-based ideology, in modified form, has become widely institutionalized, naturalized, and dominant for many speakers all over the world. It is therefore important to emphasize that in other ideological frameworks, practices that might equally be called 'multilingualism' take quite different forms. Linguistic and social categories can be put in relation to each other in multifarious ways, as ideals and as practice. For instance, in some ideologies it is the porousness of linguistic codes that is highly valued, not boundedness. In some, multiple languages are in daily use, distinguished according to the different social functions they serve; none is deemed adequate for all uses; none is seen to indicate speakers' identity; none is felt to be one's 'own.' Contrariwise, in other frameworks, people identify as their 'own' languages they do not actually speak or know (see Lüpke, 2015; Singer & Vaughan, 2018).[3] Since everyone has language ideologies, the intertwining of observers' ideologies with the practices and ideologies of those they observe produces the reports we examine in historical investigations.

The reports from nineteenth-century northwestern Siberia are, in many ways, products of the European ideology of the time. However, within a

[2] French was spread in France over the course of the nineteenth century (Weber, 1976). Etkind (2011) describes the many languages even in single cities across the Russian Empire. Geographically between these two, there were struggles for and against multilingualism in the Habsburg lands (Gal, 2011). As the latter work notes, censuses are deceptive, giving only a state's-eye-view of language use.

[3] Such patterns occur mostly in nonstandardized language communities, though not necessarily small ones or indigenous ones; this chapter does not take up the added ideological complexity of standardization projects.

shared field of ideas, these reports differ among themselves, neglecting different phenomena. Therefore, the second goal of this chapter is to give an accounting of how the more specific practical and intellectual interests, political agendas, and social positionalities of observers shaped their reports, as did the relationship some of them assumed to exist between themselves and the speakers they described.

The first section adumbrates strands of the dominant European ideology of language among professional observers and literate elites in the late eighteenth to nineteenth centuries. The second provides examples showing that many scholars, in keeping with that ideological framing, produced grammars that they understood to pertain to individual languages. In contrast, the writing of an amateur observer of social life, the physicist and geographer Adolph Erman (1806–1877), makes evident many practices the professionals elided, including what might well be called multilingualism. A final section argues that certain qualities were also differentially projected onto speakers in accord with the presumptions of the observers.

9.1 Strands of European Language Ideologies

The ideas taken for granted by European students of language, as they developed a comparative 'science of language' around the turn of the nineteenth century, were later shared by many other literate Europeans. Arguments about them have been described in recent decades by cultural and intellectual historians. The idea that language merely names the social world and is otherwise autonomous from it is traced by Aarsleff (1982, pp. 42–83) to Locke's writings, as taken up in later centuries. Indeed, the academic discipline of linguistics defined its object as an 'organism' to be discovered, not a human practice (Morpurgo Davies, 1992, pp. 83–97; Turner, 2014, pp. 125–146). This is clear in the work of August Schleicher (1821–1868), whose evolutionary claims were shared by many contemporaries, yet most agreed that language cannot be influenced by human will and is, in this way, autonomous from speakers and society. Late in the century, the Neogrammarians extended this idea by sketching mechanisms of language change without interest in social or psychological factors. They also contributed to the assumption of boundedness. We know the importance of this through an influential Neogrammarian claim that there are no 'mixed languages,' which was countered by their contemporary Hugo Schuchardt (1971 [1884]), who declared that all languages are mixed and that language is porous, not firmly bounded.

A third presumption, pursued by descendants of Locke's Enlightenment views, put a further twist on the supposed separation of language from social life, namely that a people's essence is evident in language, especially in poetic forms, which could provide evidence of the posited deep history of those who spoke the languages (Bauman & Briggs, 2003). Tracking relationships among speakers of different languages, metaphorized as 'kinship,' were the subject matter and goal of comparative and historical grammar. In the influential view of Johann Gottfried Herder (1744–1803) and later of Wilhelm von Humboldt (1767–1835), languages express a social group's – a people's – unique sensibilities. Herder's was by no means the first or only such claim; rather, his "argument reinforced, and was reinforced by, a venerable idea that languages corresponded to 'nations' in the special sense of peoples bound together by physical inheritance" (Turner, 2014, p. 127). As historians have amply documented, this idea has since had many (re)interpreters in Europe (see Almási & Šubarić, 2015; Burke, 2004).

A further aspect of this ideological matrix was the ranking of languages and language families on a 'civilizational' dimension, placing Indo-European above Semitic (Olender, 1991), with even more drastic hierarchy posited in overseas colonial projects (Errington, 2008). A final strand was the presumption that language is tied to territory. This provided a foundation for professional dialectology, for following the posited migrations of peoples, and for mapping languages as a way of accounting for them (Gal & Irvine, 2019; Irvine & Gal, 2000).

It makes sense to characterize these ideologies as European, since they contrasted with linguistic theories developed elsewhere (see Pollock, 2006). Also, they were not limited to linguists but widely held. As an implied ideal, the implied monolingualism had political implications. If linguistic differences were not man-made, and if a population's spirit was encased in a language, then the language could be an independent warrant for the unity of that population. These ideas were recruited to legitimate political projects. For instance, as early as 1808, the philosopher Johann Gottlieb Fichte (1845–1846) roused Berliners' sentiment against Napoleonic rule by famously declaring: "Wherever a separate language can be found, there is also a separate nation which has the right to manage its affairs and rule itself" (p. 453).

The examples in the next section show some of the ways that new methodological conventions of language scholars were inspired by and contributed to sustaining these presumptions. Yet, there were also differences among scholars on the basis of their training or professional interests, differences that become apparent by juxtaposing their reports.

9.2 Erasures in Describing the Unwritten Languages of Northwestern Siberia

Some of the earliest descriptions of Siberia's languages were made in conjunction with surveys of natural resources, settlement patterns, and geographical features. They were done by observers who arrived from various German lands in the eighteenth century, invited by Russian monarchs. As Vermeulen (2015) shows, for the monarchs, the goals of the great expeditions across Siberia were to plan administrative control, to identify exploitable resources, and to search for specimens for sumptuous display, as in the courtly Kunstkamera, Peter I's collection of curiosities. By contrast, the scholars' interest in Siberia came from what has been called 'the Göttingen paradigm,' after the university where it emerged (Békés, 2018). This approach dispensed with the biblical account of language origins, and turned instead to a naturalist, empirical interest in language and social groupings. It was part of the intellectual currents associated with Herder, indeed the Enlightenment ideas that later characterized many German-speaking universities. The scholars engaged in the surveys would come to be called the Russian 'German school' of ethnography and history. For instance, August Ludwig Schlözer (1735–1809), an influential participant in the Siberian research and occasional intellectual sparring partner of Herder, was a Göttingen student, stayed in touch with other Göttingen thinkers, and later returned there as professor, and was also affiliated with the Imperial Academy of Sciences in Russia. He was inspired by the earlier influential writings of Leibniz to attempt a mapping of all the peoples of the world – hence also of Siberia – by documenting their languages.

Scholars who came from one or another of the German states insisted that what they identified as language difference in Siberia marked ethnic or what some called tribal difference. For instance, the German scholar Gerhardt Friedrich Müller (1705–1783), Schlözer's teacher and patron, studied at the University of Leipzig, where his work gained the attention of Peter the Great, who invited him to take up residence at the Academy of Sciences that Peter had just established. Müller was sufficiently respected and accepted as a Russian scholar that he later took a leading part in the Great Northern Expedition to Kamchatka. About the documentation of Siberia, he wrote: "[N]ot mores and customs, not food and economic pursuits, and not religion, for all these may be the same in peoples of different tribes and different in peoples of the same tribe. The only foolproof standard is language: where languages are similar, there are no differences among peoples," (translated in Slezkine, 1994, p. 55). The results were to be comparable around the world and ranked according to a single 'natural' hierarchy. In surveying the dauntingly large territory of Siberia, Müller compiled exhaustive lists of information to be gathered in the expeditions. One of his lists was over nine hundred pages long. Yet the priorities were clear. The first two categories to be requested from local elders, or government officials who served as informants, were "grouping of peoples" and "languages" (Vermeulen, 2015, pp. 168–170).

Although some of these scholars were natural scientists, most were trained as historians, philosophers, and philologists, that is, as students of written texts. Yet, the disciplinary methods of nineteenth-century philology – the study of ancient writings in libraries and archives – were notably ill-suited for investigating unwritten languages in rough-and-ready field situations such as the Siberian expeditions.[4] Methods for collection of linguistic materials had to be (re)imagined. How to make spoken language into a stable form, analyzable after it was 'collected,' and presented in such a way as to gain credence of scholarly audiences, without the aid of sound recordings? The methods developed were guided by the language ideologies that scholars presumed. Word lists were the first kind of evidence gathered; mappings of languages onto territories became an important presentational form.

The *Vocabularium Sibiricum*, organized by Johann Eberhard Fischer (1697–1771) around 1760, was one of the early lists. It contained 2,432 words from 40 languages, with commentary in Russian and German. That list was later taken to the University of Göttingen as a database for further linguistic study of the world's languages by others. It was already possible, in that period, to classify Siberian languages by 'family' and these lists were organized accordingly (Vermeulen, 2015, pp. 131–218). In 1823, as collecting continued, Klaproth's famous *Asia Polyglotta* was even larger and came with a color-coded map outlining the supposed territory of each group of languages. In these maps, borders were clearly defined, though what the borders and territories actually represented was less obvious: the legend identified 'language families' (*Indo-Germanen*, *Semiten*, *Tungusen*). The presumption seems to have been that by naming language families, one would identify groups of speakers, who would necessarily be living in the territory outlined on the map. Accordingly, Klaproth's map assigned a spatial location for each language group, with no overlaps, in keeping with European assumptions.

But words alone could not provide the material for writing grammars and discovering historical relationships among languages. By the mid-nineteenth century, scholars of Siberian languages were eager to engage in these much more complex projects. Yet, the problem of gathering data remained formidable. Matthias Alexander Castrén (1813–1852), the great Finnish-Swedish scholar of Siberian languages and cultures, complained in mid-century that he needed "more abundant and reliable material than the ones [then] available in written forms and for this [he was] . . . compelled to carry out expeditions in different parts of Europe and Asia" (Castrén, 1853, p. 3). On fieldwork trips, Castrén searched for "songs, proverbs, tales, traditions about origins" (Lukin, 2017) that, when transcribed, would create a kind of library. Such frozen genres would stand in for the philologists' evidence: a literature for unwritten languages. Who would supply such evidence? The expeditions advised that inquiries be posed to "experienced" old people (Vermeulen, 2015, p. 175). But

[4] Some evidence on methods first appeared in Gal and Irvine (2019). My thanks to Judith T. Irvine and Victor Friedman for discussions and comparisons.

problems remained. Castrén (1853, p. 213) complained about the difficulty of finding "language masters" who had patience and knowledge enough to recite in the repetitive way needed for longhand transcription. Another important early explorer of Siberia, the Hungarian linguist and ethnographer Anton Reguly (1819–1858), wrote in frustration from Siberia to his colleagues in Budapest that he had finally found a shaman who agreed to sing the traditional songs, but the shaman had trouble remembering what some of the words meant (cited in Munkácsi, 1892).

These informal comments in letters and on the margins reveal the field-linguists' efforts to constitute the evidence they needed and display their attention to particular kinds of oral materials: easily decontextualized ones that speakers can repeat accurately (i.e. not improvised). They also hint at their practice of relying on single informants and their corresponding working assumption that one person would suffice to provide material for describing a language. Although these methods were ingenious and provided data, they also involved erasures. Different ways of speaking on different occasions or purposes would not be captured, nor variations between types of speakers, nor possible multilingualism of informants, nor – among other questions – what kinds of speakers were likely to be bilingual, if that is what other speakers considered them to be, and in which other codes.

The demands of presenting the data also created constraints. By the 1860s, maps and lists were augmented with grammatical sketches in a conventional format that was also shaped by the same ideological presumptions. Monographs or long articles were always about single languages, they usually included a grammar and short dictionary. Texts of brief genres were sometimes appended as examples. Occasionally these texts were translations of biblical passages or Christian prayers, without mentioning who had done the translation (a missionary? a local speaker? the linguist?). Recent work on Reguly's methods, for instance, reveals the identity of his major informant-translator, details of their collaboration, and much ethnographic information (Severényi & Varnai, 2021). But these were not part of the usual nineteenth-century reports. This genre of presentation was very widespread for languages in all parts of the world (Blommaert, 2008). In such grammatical sketches, it was an idealized image of 'the language' that was represented. The cramped hand and frustrated ear of the fieldworker were erased, as was the necessary selection among speech genres and informants.

The work of Pál Hunfalvy (1810–1891) provides a good example of the monograph genre. He was perhaps the premier Hungarian linguist of his time, a man from a German-speaking family, a leader at the Academy of Sciences in Budapest, who was well aware of the intellectual currents at Göttingen and other German universities (Gal, 2015). Like other academic linguists, he described northwestern Siberian languages as spread over a landscape, not as the knowledge of a single person, although a single person was invariably the source. For instance, he began each such monograph with a careful geographical description of the language's supposed physical 'boundaries' – rivers, hills – and presumed 'ethnic' limits, that is, borders with groups supposedly speaking other languages (e.g. Hunfalvy, 1875). What later might turn out to be topographical names were often treated as names of ethnolinguistic groups. In this mode, Reguly also produced valuable maps for his funders in St. Petersburg, ones that marked not only natural resources but also the posited limits of languages and peoples. Mapping conventions were conducive to imagining languages as bounded wholes, geographically separated. This contributed to the impression, already presupposed ideologically, that northwestern Siberia was a land of single-language speakers, some rare few of whom might learn two of these bounded languages.

Yet, there are reasons to doubt this picture. We get a far different view, if much less linguistically detailed, from one traveler's account, that of the distinguished German natural scientist – physicist, meteorologist, and geographer – Adolph Erman (1806–1877). His casual yet astute social observations offer a valuable check on the social context of the more technical linguistic accounts. Born and trained in Berlin, Erman was awarded a medal by London's Royal Geographical Society for his work as an explorer. The juxtaposition of his descriptions with those of the linguist-historians allows the conclusion that, as far as variation and multiple languages are concerned, the ideological work of erasure by the linguists produced a simplification of the sociolinguistic field that fit with their reigning presumptions.

Erman visited Siberia starting in 1827, as part of a Norwegian expedition, and succeeded in verifying the existence of the Siberian magnetic pole and the depth of permafrost at Yakutsk. But he also saw much else. His two-volume *Travels in Siberia* (1850) describes visits to the settlements of Obdorsk (now Salekhard) and Beresov (now Beryozovo), which, as it happens, were centers of field linguistics and ethnographic research for many decades, having been visited by Müller in the 1740s, noted on Klaproth's map of 1823, and visited by Castrén and Reguly as well in the subsequent decades.

Obdorsk was founded in the late sixteenth century, on the site of a Khanty (Ostyak)[5] settlement at the bend of the Ob River, before it empties into the Kara Sea and the Arctic Ocean. Such colonies were the result of extended violent conflict between Russian colonial entrepreneurs and indigenous people. It was a frontier market town, the kind that had parallels in many other countries, such as the settler colonial regime of the nineteenth-century

[5] I use the current official names of these groups/languages, putting in parentheses their former names, some of which have become pejorative. Most nineteenth-century sources use the former names.

western USA, although it was in quite a different administrative milieu (Bassin, 1991; Etkind, 2011). Erman mentions many categories of people gathered there for the annual market festival: Russian state servitors and peasants, also Russian bakers, traders, and metalworkers as well as Russian Orthodox missionaries. There were Cossack guides who translated for Erman when he needed to engage with other populations present in numbers: Khanty, Mansi (Vogul), Nenets (Samoyed), Polish craftsmen, Tatar, Udmurt (Votyak), and Komi (Zyrian) traders.

Hundreds of people came to Obdorsk's annual market, from December to February. Erman reports that they rendered at that time the required tribute (*yasak*) paid in fur: bear, wolf, ermine, and other pelts. The market, he noted, was one at which pelts were also exchanged for alcohol, metal equipment, and ornaments. With their reindeer, tents, and huts, these groups – hunters and herders – camped on the hills around the core Russian settlement during the festival, and spoke a wide range of languages. The Russian Orthodox Christian missionaries in Obdorsk and Beresov – the latter a larger settlement further south up the Ob River – won some converts, but those only slightly Christianized or not at all celebrated bear ceremonies and shamanic rites that Erman describes with evident interest.

Like other observers at the time, Erman assumed that in this region subsistence mode would match language, territory, group, and name: Nenets were reindeer herders in the mountains; Khanty and Mansi were hunters and fishers along rivers; settled farmers were supposedly Russian peasants; Cossacks were drivers. Yet he writes about meeting people he classifies as Russian fishermen, Khanty reindeer herders, and all sorts who traded or had settled and become townspeople. As per European ideology, he expected each named ethnic category to speak its 'own' language. Yet, he was often surprised: children with Russian fathers were fluent in Russian and in their mothers' Khanty; post-drivers – usually Cossacks – knew Khanty; people of various ethnic categories spoke Russian, making it remarkable that a Khanty elder spoke only 'poor Russian.'

In one notable observation, Erman relates that it was Cossacks from further south who served as his interpreters in Obdorsk for "intercourse with the Khanty":

> [but later] we were obliged to take with us [on our trip] one of the inhabitants of Obdorsk, because these people [Khanty] alone are familiar with the jargon which has sprung up from the intercourse of the Nisovian Khanty with the Nenets of the coast and mountains [and] in which their traffic is carried on (Erman, 1850, II, pp. 58–63).

On that trip he remarks that "of the four younger [Khanty] men in our party, two only seemed to give a preference to the Khanty language, and to use it between themselves; the other two had adopted the Nenets tongue and clothing, either because they were descended from, or had their chief traffic with, that people" (Erman, 1850, II, p. 63). Similarly, he observes "natives adopting Russian customs" of food and clothing and Khanty adopting Nenets customs of clothing and herding and knowing the Nenets language "better than their own" (Erman, 1850, I, p. 23). As Erman notes, the fair

> brought the permanently settled Russians into immediate contact with the nomad tribes. . . enticed by Russian wares, these travel-loving men begin to draw near about the end of December, but it is not till February that the barter is carried on in liveliest manner . . . All these various nations and tribes can make themselves understood to one another, and also to the traders of this place who make use of the Khanty exclusively, as the commercial language; . . . a few Cossacks understand the Nenets language also. (Erman, 1850, II, pp. 33–34)

Such comments, sprinkled throughout Erman's account, document a great deal of sociolinguistic variation: marriage across linguistic lines; communication across social categories; even change of allegiance and adoption of others' codes. Some people seem to have specialized in translation; both Khanty and Russian were trade languages, and he notes the development of a specialized 'jargon' for communication between specific interlocutor-types. The question of genre also opens up, as Erman recounts his experiences among Khanty in Obdorsk:

> Music, poetry and a very well-developed kind of pantomimic art, are here inseparably united . . . the traditional preservation of a poem seems to be rare among the Khanty and their songs are for the most part improvisations, which they produce at the spur of the occasion, and always accompany with pantomimic action. It sometimes happens that the same incident continues to be the favorite theme for years together, being treated however in various ways according to the individual taste of the singer. (Erman, 1850, II, p. 42)

These diverse practices and improvised genres were omitted by most professional linguists. Yet none was new at the time of Erman's observations. Slezkine's (1994) deep history of Siberia finds descriptions of similar encounters in the seventeenth century, along with a shift away from some of these languages and to various other regional languages.

Erman shows repeatedly that Russian was a 'strangers' language' used with him by speakers in Obdorsk. Furthermore, although he surmises that most people in Obdorsk knew Khanty, it is clear from his observations that many did not control the whole range of Khanty ways of speaking, that is, its register forms. Only some would be able to use Khanty for raising children, spontaneous creation of epic songs, or participation in a bear ceremony. Yet, many others – Nenets speakers, Komi speakers, Russian-speaking farmers, merchants, and officials – knew enough Khanty to use it as what Erman calls a 'commercial language.' Conversely, some Khanty-speaking drivers used

Russian in talking to their horses but perhaps not for much else (Erman, 1850, I, p. 331).

Thus it is evident that the kinds of variation that sociolinguists and linguistic anthropologists would now expect in a town like Obdorsk – a meeting and trading place of many groups – were indeed present. There were special ways of speaking at ceremonies and in storytelling. There were spatial and register differences, and notable surprises for Erman that today would be called 'multilingualism.' The linguists who visited Obdorsk doubtless witnessed similar diversity. And indeed, Russian ethnographers who visited at the very end of the nineteenth century remarked: "[M]any of the indigenous people spoke more than one language, to varying degrees of fluency, and the question of which language was their 'first' or 'native' language did not seem relevant to them" (summarized and translated in Grenoble, 2003, p. 165).[6]

In sum, the monographs from European fieldwork at Obdorsk in the late eighteenth and early nineteenth centuries that presented single languages, territorially defined, based on single speakers were ignoring other patterns that other observers noted. Without some sample of improvised speech events, even some grammatical features in everyday use might be missing. Nevertheless, the descriptions satisfied linguists' chief intellectual agenda of producing monolingual grammars and comparative classifications.

9.3 Qualities of Languages and Speakers

Erasures are one aspect of ideological work; another is what Gal and Irvine (2019) have called *rhematization*: listeners project onto speech the images they hold of the speakers, or conversely, impose on speakers the images they hold about the speech they hear. In either case, the qualities ascribed to the speakers are 'heard' in the speech and vice versa, thereby confirming preexisting stereotypes of people, whether positive or negative. In turn, observers' agendas and interests, as well as their social positionalities, shaped the images or stereotypes with which they encountered the people and languages of northwestern Siberia. When administrative goals included stereotyped images of the people to be governed, then that could constrain the qualities perceived. When nationality and posited 'kinship' of a European nation to Siberian groups were a priority, observers' national commitments (however acquired) shaped perceptions. The physicist-meteorologist, with his ethnographic curiosity projected different qualities than linguists with their focus on grammar. The point is a familiar one: observation and recognition are perspectival. Added here is the specificity of qualities projected onto speech and speakers.

6 The conclusions presented here about language ideologies seem to hold for an area further east in Siberia in the 1900–1930s, as recently reconstructed by Khanina (2021).

Until the end of the nineteenth century, Russian elites saw Siberia largely as an administrative problem and source of extractable wealth. Russia had conquered it in the seventeenth century, and the indigenous populations of the frigid northwest – hunters, nomads, herders – were long categorized as 'aliens' (Slocum, 1998) defeated in border wars and colonized, their territory occupied, not part of national space, instead remote and unpleasant, fit for prisoners and other undesirable exiles. The Russian administrative reform of 1822 attempted to reframe governance by specifying three ranked subsistence categories of people: settled, nomads, wanderers. The indigenous populations of the Siberian northwest were mostly of the lowest categories, nomads and wanderers. On the presumed developmental scale, they were seen as in 'childhood.' They had no writing and were therefore imagined to have no poetry or verbal art; their languages were imagined to show "relative simplicity and limited vocabulary" (Slezkine, 1994, p. 134). Among the many people of Siberia, they were widely perceived as the extreme in backwardness, totally 'lacking culture,' dirty, wild, primitive. They were prey to exploitation in trade and to Russian colonists' arbitrary treatment of them.

Late in the nineteenth century, Russian researchers' attention turned to Siberia, and excellent ethnographic accounts were produced (summarized in Shimkin, 1990). Nevertheless, there was a long-standing belief on the part of Russian officials that the Northern languages were 'simple' – like the peoples – and could be learned easily. Grenoble (2003) reports that early Soviet officials in Obdorsk complained about the failure of Russian workers to learn Nenets, "although it has only '600 to 700 everyday words,'" a comment that "reflects a complete misunderstanding of the morphosyntactic complexities of the language" (p. 166). It is also a striking example of projecting onto linguistic forms the perceived simplicity of a people-category, itself based on a hierarchy of subsistence stereotypes.

In contrast to the Russian administrators, the eighteenth-century scholars from Germany were fascinated by Siberia's location in the world of languages. They placed groups of speakers in specifically linguistic categories to create a grid for *universal* – not only imperial or geographic – ranking of languages, and posited deep historical relations among languages (and hence, by ideological connection, peoples). They implicitly presumed their own role to be high status experts, detached observers of such a grid.

Unlike Russian administrative concerns and the 'German school's' universalizing, the interests of a Hungarian and a Finnish-Swedish observer were avid and focused on specific languages of northwestern Siberia, because they were seen as clues to the researchers' national pasts. This interest had a long history. In the late eighteenth century, Leibniz had noted that Finnish, Saami (Lapp), and Hungarian (i.e. Magyar) languages resembled each other; the Siberian word lists suggested this too. Two Hungarians – Sajnovics in

1770 and Gyarmathi in 1799 – had found 'affinities' among languages classified today as Finno-Ugric, within the more general category of Uralic. Gyarmati was probably inspired by Schlözer to do this work (Vermeulen, 2015). The two Hungarians pointed to lexical parallels, distinctive grammatical features in declension, comparison, and conjugation, and in ways of using suffixes and affixes (Wickman, 1988).

As the contributions to Indo-European studies in the eighteenth and nineteenth centuries vastly extended the pasts of much of Europe, elites seeing themselves as Hungarian or Finnish and aspiring to national consciousness searched for similar deep pasts. But, unlike German and English scholars, they lacked ancient written sources. This took them, by the 1840s, to Siberia, in search of linguistic 'kin' whose language forms and genres were expected to provide evidence to extend their own national histories. The Finnish-Swedish scholar, M. A. Castrén, mentioned earlier, was the first to describe many of what are now considered the Finnic and Permian groupings of Uralic languages, as well as other languages of Siberia. He also did much ethnographic and folkloric research. Recent commemoration of the Hungarian researcher, Antal Reguly, has clarified his contributions (Severényi & Varnai, 2021). He returned from Siberia with material objects, ethnographic, folkloric, and linguistic materials, much of which went to Russian collections. His particular interest was in the heroic epic songs and rituals of the Khanty and Mansi, whose languages are now counted, with Hungarian, as the Ugric group of Uralic. Reguly was supported financially by academic circles in St. Petersburg at a time when interest in Siberian peoples was overshadowed, in Russia, by scholarly interest in Russians. Because he died young, he did not analyze his own collections; Hunfalvy and József Budenz started that work. Decades later, Bernát Munkácsi (1860–1937), a member of the Hungarian Academy of Sciences, continued the task.

Reguly and Castrén found qualities other than 'simplicity' in the speakers and languages of northwestern Siberia. In Obdorsk, Castrén projected the town's relative location onto the languages there, calling them 'pure,' because they were supposedly isolated. Comparing language forms near Obdorsk with those further south, he equated spatial with temporal difference, arguing that by comparing more northerly (pure) with southerly forms he could distinguish what "is original and what was added later" (Stammler-Gossmann, 2009, p. 200). Even more telling for our purposes are the narratives Castrén and Reguly wrote, connecting their own preferred national (stereotypic) qualities to the presumed qualities of selected Siberian peoples. Recall that the linguistic 'affinities' among Uralic languages, as located by eighteenth-century scholars, were matters of grammar, not of qualities. And it was on the basis of grammatical features that they established relations of 'kinship' among languages. Yet, in their linguistic and even in their broader ethnographic work in Siberia,

Castrén and Reguly, when analyzing myths and epics, connected their own national stereotypes and qualities with Siberian peoples. Such projections are a regular aspect of linguistic ideologies. It is nevertheless important to note that scholars are not immune to the process, and to note the characteristics they attributed to the people they studied.

For example, traveling in 1845 among Udmurt speakers, Castrén found qualitative similarities that, he wrote, were not just "philological correspondences" between European and this Siberian people and landscape, they were equivalences:

They [Finns and Udmurt] correspond to each other in having a quiet civilized, and work-filled life, far removed from what one sees in other countries. . .. That is how I find the Udmurt – devout, simple and innocent, like our Finnish peasants. . . [and like] the genius of Spring [here in Udmurtia] with its mild air, soft breezes and gentle butterflies. (cited in Hirnsperger, 2013, pp. 98–99)

The qualities of Udmurt people – mildness, softness – match those of 'our' Finnish peasants not only as linguistic facts (philological correspondences) but also as sensory experiences. Both match the gentle and calm qualities of the Udmurt landscape. Elsewhere, Castrén specified that these Siberians are just like Finns of an earlier time, casting them as contemporary ancestors. Castrén might well have idealized other Siberian peoples as well, and his research certainly enabled him to make wide-ranging comparisons among Siberian peoples. Here, his insights serve as an example of an ideological process.

Reguly's vision turned out to be similarly analogical but quite different in the qualities he picked out. Reguly left Hungary in search of 'the origin of the Hungarians' in 1839. That was a reform period, one of increasing patriotic sentiment, attention to expanding the language, and much creative, intellectual work as well as the establishing of the Academy of Sciences. His chosen research field identified him as committed to a Hungarian [Magyar] national cause. Like his contemporaries, he took the Mansi to be the closest linguistic kin of Hungarians and described, in an 1844 letter from the Obdorsk region, the theme of Mansi epic song:

They [the Mansi] recount with enthusiasm war-like acts of their past heroes and champions, some of whom are gods, fighting external enemies – the Komi and Nenets – others are princes who struggle with their brothers and neighbors to rule over territories. Their songs tell of military victories and mournful defeats. (cited in Munkácsi, 1892, pp. viii–ix)

Evidently aware of other contemporary researchers, Reguly himself made explicit the contrast between this description and Castrén's, and in doing so he created a useful analogy. The Mansi people's aggressive spirit of sociality, Reguly wrote, directly contrasts with the spirit of other Finno-Ugric peoples whose poetry tells of the inner, individual life. Reguly drew a comparison *within* the Finno-Ugric language family by contrasting Mansis and Udmurts in the putative past, as fiery and warlike vs. calm and civilized. The implication must have been clear to his colleagues, that this was similar to a qualitative distinction evident between their supposed descendants, the nineteenth-century Hungarians and Finns.

The identification of Hungarians with Mansi's "war-like acts" was probably not coincidental. Reguly's image of the Mansi matched the self-stereotypes of Hungarian elites at the time he left the country, especially those who were on the cusp of an armed revolution (1848) against Habsburg rule. This was a matter strikingly parallel with the Mansi interest in "struggle with neighbors to rule over territories." Arguably, we see here one example of how ideological processes played out in qualitative descriptions of Siberian people's folklore and language. This too is a form of politics, where the sociopolitical concerns of the observers – contrasts relevant in their own countries and contexts – are projected onto the groups they observe. This gives a glimpse of one way to understand both the motivations and the results of the ideological work of scholars writing about early nineteenth-century northwestern Siberia.

Conclusion

The presumptions about language that have been crucial in European intellectual developments, especially since the early nineteenth century, are hardly the only possible ones, although they have been heavily institutionalized and naturalized. The sociolinguistic literature is replete with examples where other assumptions prevail. My goal in this chapter has been to draw attention to the way language ideologies – along with specific agendas, positions, and interests – shape the observational practices and evidential conventions of scholars. Because we know from comparative evidence that 'multilingualism' is not a single and self-evident conceptual unit but rather a sociopolitically fraught cover term for many different configurations of linguistic practice, it is indispensable in any study of linguistic practices to consider the mediating and framing role of language ideologies – that is, metadiscourses about language – among the speakers observed and characterized as well as among those who observe and describe them. Linguists are no less influenced by language ideologies than other scholars and other speakers.

References

Aarsleff, H. (1982) *From Locke to Saussure: Essays on the study of language and intellectual history.* Minneapolis: University of Minnesota Press.

Almási, G. & L. Šubarić (eds.) (2015) *Latin at the crossroads of identity: The evolution of linguistic nationalism in the Kingdom of Hungary.* Leiden/Boston: Brill.

Bassin, M. (1991) Inventing Siberia: Visions of the Russian East in the early 19th century. *American Historical Review*, 96, 3, 763–794.

Bauman, R. & C. Briggs (2003) *Voices of Modernity*. New York: Cambridge.

Békés, V. (2018) A "nyelvrokonság" terminus fogalomtörténeti fordulatai [Conceptual changes in the term "linguistic kinship"]. In Bakró-Nagy, M. (ed.) *Okok és okozat: A magyar nyelv eredetéről történeti, szociálpszichológiai és filozófiai megközelítésben* [Causes and consequences: On the origins of the Hungarian language]. Budapest: Gondolat Kiadó, pp. 29–60.

Blommaert, J. (2008) Artefactual ideologies and textual production of African languages. *Language & Communication*, 28, 291–307.

Burke, P. (2004) *Languages and communities in early modern Europe*. New York: Cambridge University Press.

Castrén, M. A. (1853) *Reiseerrinerungen aus den Jahren 1838–1844* [Memories of travels from the years 1838–1844]. Edited by A. Schiefner. St Petersburg: Buchdrückerei der Kaiserlichen Akademie der Wissenschaft.

Cohn, B. (1996) The command of language and the language of command. In Cohn, B. *Colonialism and its forms of knowledge: The British in India*. Princeton: Princeton University Press, pp. 16–56.

Erman, A. (1850) *Travels in Siberia: Down the Obi to the Polar Circle*. Vols. 1–2. Translated by W.D. Cooley. Philadelphia: Lea and Blanchard.

Errington, J. (2008) *Linguistics in a colonial world*. New York: Blackwell.

Etkind, A. (2011) *Internal colonization: Russia's imperial experience*. London: Polity Press.

Fichte, J. (1845–1846) Reden an die deutsche Nation [Addresses to the German nation]. In Fichte, I. (ed.) *Sämmtliche Werke*, vol. 7. Berlin: Veit, pp. 264–499.

Friedman, V. (2011) Balkan languages and linguistics. *Annual Review of Anthropology*, 40, 275–291.

Gal, S. (2011) Polyglot nationalism. *Langage et Société*, 136, 1, 31–54.

(2015) Imperial linguistics and polyglot nationalism. *Balkanistica*, 28, 1, 151–174.

Gal, S. & J. Irvine (2019) *Signs of difference: Language and ideology in social life*. New York: Cambridge University Press.

Graber, K. & J. Murray (2015) The local history of an imperial category: Language and religion in Russia's eastern borderlands 1860–1930. *Slavic Review*, 74, 1, 127–152.

Grenoble, L. (2003) *Language policy in the Soviet Union*. Dordrecht: Kluwer.

Harries, P. (1988) The roots of ethnicity: Discourse and the politics of language construction in South-East Africa. *African Affairs*, 87, 346, 25–52.

Hirnsperger, M. (2013) Finno-ugrische Ethnologie und Nationalismus im 19. Jahrhundert: Sjögren, Castrén und Ahlqvist in Spannungsfeld nationaler Ideen. [Finno-Ugric ethnology and nationalism in the 19th century: Sjögren, Castrén and Ahlqvist in the tense field of the national idea.] In Donecker, S. et al. (eds.) *Wege zum Norden: Wiener Forschungen zu Arktis and Subarktis* [Roads to the North: Vienna research on the Arctic and Subarctic]. Vienna: Lit Verlag, 87–106.

Hunfalvy, P. (1875) *Az északi osztják nyelv* [The northern Khanty language]. Budapest: Akadémiai Kiadó.

Irvine, J. (1993) Mastering African languages: The politics of linguistics in 19th century Senegal. *Social Analysis*, 33, 27–45.

Irvine, J. & S. Gal (2000) Language ideology and linguistic differentiation. In Kroskrity, P. (ed.) *Regimes of Language*. Santa Fe, NM: School of American Research, pp. 35–83.

Khanina, O. (2021) Languages and ideologies at Lower Yenisei (Siberia): Reconstructing past multilingualism. *International Journal of Bilingualism*, 25, 4, 1059–1080.

Lukin, K. (2017) Matthias Alexander Castrén's notes on Nenets folklore. *Journal de la Société Finno-Ougrienne*, 96, 169–211.

Lüpke, F. (2015) Ideologies and typologies of language endangerment in Africa. In Essegby, J. et al. (eds.) *Language documentation and endangerment in Africa*. Amsterdam: John Benjamins, pp. 60–99.

Morpurgo Davies, A. (1992) *History of linguistics. Volume IV Nineteenth century linguistics*. New York: Routledge.

Munkácsi, B. (1892) A vogul-osztják népköltés irodalma [The literature of Khanty-Mansi folk poetry]. In *Regék és énekek a világ teremtéséről, vogul szövegek és fordításaik* [Tales and songs about the creation of the world: Vogul texts and translations]. Budapest: Magyar Tudományos Akadémia.

Olender, M. (1991) *Languages of paradise: Race, religion and philology in the 19th century*. Cambridge: Harvard University Press.

Pollock, S. (2006) *The language of the gods in the world of men: Sanskrit, culture and power in premodern India*. Berkeley: University of California Press.

Schuchardt, H. (1971 [1884]) *Slawo-deutsches und Slawo-italienisches: Mit Schuchardts übrigen Arbeiten zur Slavistik und mit neuen Registern* [Slavic-German and Slavic-Italian]. Edited by D. Gerhadt. Munich: Wilhelm Fink Verlag.

Severényi, S. & Z. Varnai (eds.) (2021) Tematikus összeállítás: Reguly 200. Reguly Antal tudományos munkássága két évszázad távlatából [Special section: Reguly at 200. Reguly Antal's scholarly work in a 200-year perspective]. *Magyar Tudomány*, 182, 1, 1–44.

Shimkin, D. (1990) Siberian ethnography: Historical sketch and evaluation. *Arctic Anthropology*, 27, 1, 36–51.

Singer, R. & J. Vaughan (eds.) (2018) Special Issue: Indigenous multilingualisms. *Language and Communication*, 62B, 83–196.

Slezkine, Y. (1994) *Arctic Mirrors: Russia and the small peoples of the North*. Ithaca: Cornell University Press.

Slocum, J. (1998) Who, and when, were the inorodtsy? The evolution of the category of 'aliens' in imperial Russia. *The Russian Review*, 57, 2, 173–190.

Stammler-Gossmann, A. (2009) A life for an ideal: Matthias Alexander Castrén. *Polar Record*, 45, 234, 193–206.

Turner, J. (2014) *Philology: The forgotten origins of the modern humanities*. Princeton: Princeton University Press.

Vermeulen, H. (2015) *Before Boas: The genesis of ethnography and ethology in the German Enlightenment*. Lincoln, NE: University of Nebraska Press.

Weber, E. (1976) *Peasants into Frenchmen*. Stanford: Stanford University Press.

Wickman, B. (1988) The history of Uralic linguistics. In D. Sinor (ed.) *The Uralic languages: Description, history, and foreign influences*. New York: Brill, pp. 792–818.

Woolard, K. (2018) Language ideologies. In Stanlaw, J. (ed.) *International encyclopedia of linguistic anthropology*. New York: Wiley-Blackwell.

10 Studying Historical Multilingualism in Everyday Life: The Case of the Habsburg Monarchy in the Nineteenth Century

Jan Fellerer

A Frenchman speaks French, naturally (cf. Weber, 1976). It almost seems a truism. In fact, however, it required wide-ranging political and social engineering to turn peasants into, say, Frenchmen who speak French. National projects, at least in their European manifestation, typically aimed at monolingual societies and individuals as the dominant pattern. We may deplore modern nationalism, and the brutalities it led to since its arrival on the political scene in the nineteenth century, but the movement had a progressive agenda as well. The rise of modern life required efficient communication across large populations and areas without recourse to an elitist lingua franca. It also needed new symbols for supra-regional forms of collective identity. One of the era's most successful tools toward these ends was to select and validate preexisting monoglot communities, and to extend their reach. At the same time, this engendered a tunnel vision of linguistic identity in the service of the extralinguistic cause of national exclusivity. As Evans (2004) put it, "linguistic self-ascriptions quickly became subsumed in national ones, to which they continued to add a cutting edge" (p. 14).

The Habsburg Monarchy has long been identified as a prime example for the study of the rise of ethnolinguistic nationalism (cf. Kann, 1950; Wandruszka & Urbanitsch, 1980, to refer to just two influential surveys). On the eve of its demise, the empire stretched from the Carpathian Mountains in the east to Lake Constance in the west, and from the Central Bohemian Uplands in the north to Dalmatia in the south. These vast Central European lands were home to a highly linguistically diverse population. In speech, there were Hungarian and German varieties, Yiddish, the better part of all existing Slavonic languages and dialects, Italian, Romanian, and further Romance dialects, to name just the larger linguistic groups. In the constitutional era, heralded shortly after the revolution of 1848, and then gradually reintroduced on a firmer footing following the monarchy's defeat in Upper Italy in 1859, the imperial authorities funneled this diversity into a fixed selection of officially recognized languages. To refer to Evans (2006) again, "once the choices were made, linguistic practice hardened, [and] national cultural edifices came under rapid construction" (p. 111).

A crucial ingredient was the politicization of the Romantic notion that a nation is defined by its language. As Josef Jungmann (2007 [1806], p. 107), one of the leading figures of the Czech National Revival, put it, "one could not imagine ... a nation without its own language" (for the Czech original, see Vodička, 1948, p. 34). Intense language planning was necessary to elevate a particular dialect, or blend of dialects, to a literary, standard, and, ultimately, national language. It was aimed at creating "a form of decontextualised, neutral, widely accessible and learnable language," which often also meant that "the users of standard national languages were intended to be (or become) monolingual" (Costa et al., 2017, pp. 5, 12). These normative aspirations posed challenges to the linguistic reality in the late Habsburg Monarchy. In many areas people were not monolingual. They switched between languages and mixed dialects. The reasons for this varied. It could be a necessity or a deliberate choice. It could be due to indifference or poor literacy. At any rate, in the late monarchy and the successor states, there was an ever-increasing pressure on people to subscribe to one language and, by extension, to the eponymous nation (Judson, 2006; Moritsch, 1991; Stourzh, 1994). Those who did not, or could not, came to be called names, like 'amphibians' (Zahra, 2008).

Still, hybrid and multilingual practices remained an important aspect of everyday life in many areas. They pose a great methodological challenge because, unlike contemporary settings, they cannot be subject to direct observation and elicitation techniques. To meet this challenge, we must find the right sources and analyze them in a way that is adequate in sociolinguistic and in historical terms. The purpose of the present chapter is to address this task. The first section discusses sources that allow us to reconstruct multilingualism at the societal level. These are the late monarchy's well-known census data, ethnographic maps, and language laws. The second section then turns to the arguably more interesting question of how multilingualism worked in daily life. It proposes less obvious sources that may grant privileged glimpses into what happened on the ground, when people had direct dealings with each other, at their workplace, in commercial transactions, during leisure activities, within their private circles. The conclusion then summarizes what we can and what we cannot learn from the two types of sources under consideration about multilingualism in parts of late-imperial Central Europe.

10.1 Ethnographic Maps, Census Data, and Language Laws

This section critically assesses the sources that may offer insights into the workings of societal multilingualism in the Habsburg Monarchy in the nineteenth century. They allow us to reconstruct the large-scale distribution of the empire's languages in different geographical areas and their populations, and in the key public domains of the modern state, notably in education, administration, the judiciary, military, and in religious affairs. We will see the two main caveats that pertain to these sources. One is that they offer a bird's eye view only, without elucidating what actually happened on the ground, in the streets, inns, houses, flats, workshops, fields, offices, regiments, and stores of the many multilingual communities. The other, arguably more serious one, is that they impose the ideological framework of the time. As has been frequently observed before (e.g., Stergar & Scheer, 2018), they privilege a picture of increasingly strict linguistic compartmentalization aimed at managing national aspirations, rather than reflecting actual linguistic practice in daily life.

Vested interest in the regional and social organization of multilingualism in the Habsburg dominions was not a novelty of the nineteenth century. It had started to preoccupy the monarchy's elites much earlier (cf. Fischer, 2001, on Slovene, German, and Latin in early modern Carniola, southern Carinthia, and Styria). However, there was a noticeable shift since the Josephinian decade of 1780 to 1790 in particular. It heralded the era of a centralizing state that described, measured, catalogued, and registered all corners of the realm, its populations, and languages. The six-volume *Geographical Handbook of the Austrian State* of 1790–1792 by the lawyer and geographer Ignaz de Luca is a pertinent example. Josephinism also gave rise to the beginnings of some of the monarchy's modern national movements, such as the Czech National Revival. In their infancy, they may have held the potential of complementing the modernization of Habsburg statecraft through vernacular democratization (Evans, 1990), as long as this did not impede implementation of German as the main official language. However, this prospect soon faded, and the national movements imbued linguistic categorization with new and powerful symbolism.

Unitary glossonyms, such as 'German,' 'Slovene,' 'Czech,' became key descriptive as well as normative terms. A highlight of their comprehensive application to the Habsburg Monarchy was Czoernig's *Ethnographic Map of the Austrian Monarchy* of 1855/56. In the first volume, Czoernig (1857, vol. 1, pp. 23–74) reported in detail on the languages that were spoken in particular localities. Despite the various shortcomings of Czoernig's collection method (cf. Deák, 2001; Labbé, 2010), his comprehensive account still allows us to identify the monarchy's bi- and multilingual areas in a way that no earlier source does. However, it does so on the taxonomic terms of the times. For example, Czoernig (1857, vol. 1, p. 32) has the western part of Austrian Silesia divided by a 'German-(Upper) Moravian border,' with 'Czech' as a synonym for '(Upper) Moravian.' He also makes allowance for 'mixed' areas. Even though all this was predominantly based on linguistic observations, it was meant to map ethnicities, rather than languages. As a consequence, the mapping remained oblivious to two crucial facts: many individuals were bilingual in one form or another and the linguistic varieties they used in speech were not actually 'German' and 'Czech.' They were, rather, the Middle German dialect of the eastern Sudetes with strong Slavonic influence and a Lach or Silesian-Moravian dialect of Czech with some transitional features reminiscent of Polish. Neither of them would have been readily intelligible to a notional 'German' or 'Czech' speaker elsewhere.

Czoernig's ethnographic approach was soon superseded by demographic statistics as a strictly quantitative discipline (cf. Brix, 1982). From 1880, the Central Commission for Statistics conducted decennial censuses in the Austrian half of the monarchy. Each individual was asked to declare their 'everyday language' (*Umgangssprache*) from a closed list of nine options: 'German,' 'Czech-Moravian-Slovak,' 'Hungarian,' 'Italian-Ladin,' 'Polish,' 'Romanian,' 'Ruthenian' (i.e. Ukrainian), 'Serbian-Croatian,' or 'Slovene.' This will have put many intent on providing a genuine answer in a difficult position. For instance, for the western part of Austrian Silesia, the census of 1890 recorded 239,841 respondents opting for 'German,' 55,917 for 'Czech-Moravian-Slovak' (mainly in the provincial capital Opava (Troppau) and the surrounding district), 696 for 'Polish,' and 13 for other languages (K. K. Statistische Central-Commission, 1892, p. 162). However, the alleged 'German' speakers were, in actuality, predominantly Catholic Austrian subjects and citizens who were native in a distinct Silesian dialect. In a similar vein, many of the alleged 'Czech-Moravian-Slovak' speakers still saw themselves as speaking *po našemu* [in our way] – a term common in Teschen Silesia (Holub, 2011, p. 225) – rather than in 'Moravian,' let alone 'Czech.' At the time, a pejorative variant of the term 'Moravian' – *Moravci* – typically referred to the Lach speakers across the border in Prussia. In fact, 'Moravian' was altogether ill-suited for the Lach speakers of the historically non-Moravian Principality of Opava.

The difficulties of choosing from a closed list of nine languages in the Austrian censuses did not stop there. The Yiddish-speaking Jews of Austrian Silesia and elsewhere did not find their everyday language listed at all. Worst of all perhaps, if, in one form or another, one conversed in both 'Czech' and 'German' in everyday life, what should have been one's 'everyday language'? The reason for these shortcomings was that the census rubric effectively became a proxy for nationality, that is, an ethnolinguistic attribution that had to be classificatory and exclusive. This is why the Austrian statistical bureau had initially sought to avoid language as a census rubric altogether, until internal pressure and international standards made this stance untenable (Brix, 1982). We will see in the next section that, interestingly, imperial authorities, such as the courts, continued to ignore the language issue and did not classify people in that way.

The corresponding decennial censuses in Hungary had respondents declare their 'mother tongue,' and whether they spoke any other language of the country, which encompassed Hungary, Fiume, and Croatia-Slavonia. In practice, the languages that were registered for each country were 'Hungarian,' 'German,' 'Romanian,' 'Slovak,' 'Ruthenian,' 'Croatian,' 'Serbian,' and 'others.' As far as speaking any other language of the country was concerned, what this actually meant was knowledge of Hungarian as a second language (cf., e.g., Országos magyar kir. statisztikai hivatal, 1895, pp. 32–37). From the point of view of Hungary's statistical bureau, this was an attempt to track the assimilation of the non-Magyar population, or, at least, the success of implementing Hungarian as the language of the state and its citizens (Gal, 2011). Bilingualism was considered a necessary, transitional evil at best. Otherwise, the discourse of ethnolinguistic nationalism in late nineteenth-century Hungary and elsewhere had it as a potentially corrupting force that jeopardized a clear sense of national belonging. The census respondents themselves, however, may have had entirely different ideas about this. As Gal (2011) argues, the practice of child exchanges between Hungarian-, German-, and Slovak-speaking families well into the twentieth century is a potent example of how many of them deliberately raised their children as polyglots with a multilayered linguistic and national identity. Child exchange was equally well established among Czech- and German-speaking families in Bohemia (Zahra, 2008), even though, as mentioned, the Austrian censuses did not allow for individuals to declare themselves bi- or multilingual.

In short, the linguistic data gathered in the Austrian and Hungarian censuses from 1880 to 1910 were biased in various ways. Still, they offer a useful tool to identify in considerable detail which areas were bi- or multilingual, and to what extent. The societal bi- and multilingualism that the monarchy's statistics agencies recorded became subject to an ever-increasing number of language laws. These laws stipulated which language should be used on what occasion in public domains, notably in administration, education, the judiciary, and the military. They are an eloquent testimony to the underlying language ideologies of the time. An important shift occurred in the constitutional aftermath to the revolution of 1848–1849. For the first time, a law included a complete and fixed list of the languages officially considered customary in the lands of the monarchy. This was in the context of the introduction of a general 'Imperial Law and Ordinance Gazette.' The regulation stipulated that the gazette should be published in the German original and in translations into 'Italian,' 'Magyar,' 'Bohemian (with Moravian and Slovak),' 'Polish,' 'Ruthenian,' 'Slovene' (with Windish and Carniolan), 'Serbian-Illyrian' (in civic Cyrillic script), 'Serbian-Illyrian' (with Croatian in Latin script), and 'Romanian' (with Moldavian-Wallachian) (Fischel, 1910). These are effectively the same standard and national languages in waiting that we already encountered as a rubric in the censuses of 1880–1910.

Once the monarchy's multilingualism was configured in these terms, public domains could be readily portioned into subdomains in which one or another of the officially sanctioned languages should be used by law. For instance, the administrative apparatus was divided into imperial, provincial, and autonomous local authorities. Each of them operated in three distinct areas of activity. Internal administrative processes were set apart from dealings between authorities, and these, in turn, were separate from dealings with members of the public (Mischler & Ulbrich, 1906). These subdomains allow us to reconstruct how the state agencies valued and hierarchized the languages that they proscribed for them.

What's more, these subdomains provide a dimension, key to any meaningful sociolinguistic study: a set of extralinguistic parameters with which linguistic variation is said to correlate. The compartmentalized world of official communication in the late monarchy readily translates into Fishman's (1965) notion of domains of language behavior. For each of them, we can investigate and quantify the actual linguistic choices made, that is, how often one or another language was used in particular domains and subdomains. Empirical studies of this kind can draw on the large paper trail that the late monarchy's public agencies left behind in archives across Central Europe (cf. Rindler Schjerve, 2003, on district offices, courts, and school authorities; Scheer, 2014, on the military) and elucidate the workings of bi- and multilingualism in public life at the time.

They also allow us to check language policies against actual linguistic practices. The comparison can be telling. For instance, the legislation concerning the above-mentioned Imperial Law Gazette changed frequently between 1849 and 1869. In one form or another, it stipulated that there should be translations from German. In practice, however, it was at the provincial level, rather than at the central ministry of justice in Vienna where these translations were mostly made in the 1850s and 1860s (Fellerer, 2005). This shows that multilingualism, by then legally sanctioned by Vienna, was still relegated in practice to a provincial matter. In the Austrian half of the monarchy, this didn't change until 1869 when all the translations of the Imperial Law Gazette were in fact prepared at the center of power in the imperial capital itself.

Albeit revealing in certain respects, the study of language policies and actual linguistic practices in public domains has an important limitation too. In historical sociolinguistics, it remains wedded to the written medium, and a monolithic understanding of languages in terms of glossonyms, such as 'German,' 'Slovene,' 'Slovak.' Yet, everyday life in multilingual communities is first and foremost based on oral communication. It tends to involve more complex forms of linguistic competence and practices, notably different degrees of individual bilingualism, code-switching, and code-mixing. To take account of this, and to gain a better understanding of what happened on the ground in the late monarchy's bi- and multilingual villages, towns, and cities, we must look toward entirely different sources, as I shall outline in the next section.

10.2 Memoirs, Satirical Magazines, and Criminal Court Records

This section critically assesses sources that take us closer to the multilingual reality of the late monarchy on the ground, in everyday life, when people had direct dealings with each other in the streets, marketplaces, houses, workshops, and inns of their locality. They are texts that, in one way or another, recreate past daily life in a bi- or multilingual setting. The example that comes to mind most readily is the many memoirs that have come down to us from the late monarchy. They may include passages in which the author recounts experiences of a bi- or multilingual neighborhood, family, upbringing, or career, such as the life of Václav Holek, a German-Czech worker, teacher, and social democrat from northern Bohemia (1909, with a Czech translation in 2011). Holek was not at all interested in linguistic matters. His main focus was poverty and politics. Still, the narrative regularly features instructive passages on the author's daily life as a Czech and German speaker in various areas of northern Bohemia, before he left for Dresden in search of work. His son, Heinrich, who became a successful writer, also left a memoir that recounts his childhood between German and Czech (Holek, 1927, see also Zahra, 2008).

Memoirs aside, there are other, less expected textual sources. The following discussion will first focus on the burgeoning satirical press of late nineteenth-century Austria. It will then turn to criminal court records as another gateway into understanding multilingualism in past daily life. Humorous magazines often had a distinctly local focus and employed stereotypes to identify particular social groups, and to cast judgment on their alleged behavior or views. A prime device to that end was linguistic characterization, in particular nonstandard forms of usage, notably dialect, 'non-fluent' bilingualism, code-switching, and code-mixing. It is not possible here to expand on these widely discussed concepts describing types of nonnormative linguistic performance by speakers in situations of societal bi- and multilingualism (for a brief introduction to the particularly problematic term 'non-fluent' bilingualism, see Edwards, 1994, pp. 55–60). Whichever their precise linguistic manifestation, the satirical press frequently featured them in the form of stylizations that deliberately deviated from the officially sanctioned standard languages.

Take, for instance, the satirical magazine *Strachopud* [Scarecrow] from Lviv, the capital of the crown land Galicia in the northeast of the Austrian half of the late monarchy. The magazine was a relatively stable fixture of the city's satirical press from the 1870s. In ideological terms, it was close to Galicia's so-called Russo- or Moscophiles, Ukrainian activists and intellectuals who thought of themselves as part of the Russian nation. They counted on association with it as a potential means of political and cultural emancipation from Habsburg-backed Polish dominance over the province and its capital city (Wendland, 2001). In its own voice, *Strachopud* employed a form of Russian that incorporated numerous western Ukrainian linguistic features. The peculiar amalgam did not exist in speech, but it built upon a long history of mixed written forms of expression among Galicia's Ukrainians. At the same time, the magazine employed further linguistic stylizations to pinpoint specific constituencies of the city's population. For example, toward the end of its existence, in the year 1912, it featured a column titled *Kocja* (*Strachopud*, 1912, nos. 3, 7, 11, 18–19). This was the name of a fictitious female correspondent who sent in hostile letters to the magazine to hurl abuse at its Russophile orientation from the point of view of a fervent, yet still generally Habsburg-loyal, Polish nationalist from Lviv. Fictitious readers' letters were a popular genre in the satirical press of the time in general. They provided a format to mount a clichéd caricature of the writer as a representative of a particular social group, with the aim of denouncing their alleged views and behavior. Linguistic characterization was central to that end.

The following illustration shows the caricature accompanying the column. It is addressed at a fictitious *Maszercio*, presumably a hypocoristic modeled on French *Ma chère.* As was customary, this was published anonymously to avoid the hand of the censor.

Here is a passage from the column in which our fictitious *Kocja* expresses her delight at an anti-Russian gathering of Poles in central Lviv:

Ach jag to miło beło popaczeć na tylo tysięczny tłum protestantuf, protestujących przeciw narodowyj krzywdzie, zrżądzonyj nam przez moskala! Powiadam ci, - że z radości pierś mi wezbrała jak Czarny potok w Kołomyi po dyszczu i aż mi oddech zaparło, a sercy to mi tak tiochkało jak motor fatalnego samochodu p. Richtmana, co to nidawno pszyjechał u wy Lwowi przez jakoś kobito.
[Oh how lovely it was to see a crowd of so many thousands of protesters protesting against the harm that was done to our nation by the Muscovite! I'm telling you that my breast filled with joy like the Black Brook in Kolomyja after rain, and it took my breath away, and my heart was beating like the engine of the fatal car of Mr Richtman that recently ran over some woman in Lviv.]

The column is composed in a stylized form of the local urban Polish dialect of late-Habsburg Lviv. This was a variant of so-called southeastern 'borderland' Polish. It had developed under strong influence of the surrounding southwestern Ukrainian vernacular. Some of the various Ukrainian-inspired

Fig. 10.1 *Kocja* column in *Strachopud* 11 (1912), pp. 3–4. Public domain.

dialectalisms reflected in the passage are the raised articulation of unstressed vowel phonemes, such as [i] for /ɛ/, as in *nidawno* for *niedawno*; and the lowered articulation of the phoneme /ɨ/ close to [ɛ] in stressed syllables, as in *beło* for *było* [was] (Seiffert-Nauka, 1992). At the same time, some Ukrainianizing traits of the passage transcend the usual range. What is not normally attested in Lviv Polish is, for example, the verb *tiochkać* [to beat strongly] (with regard to the heart), the reduplication of the local preposition in the form *u wy Lwowi* [lit. in in Lviv], and the adjectival fem. dat. sg. ending –*yj*, as in *narodowyj* [national], instead of the usual dialectal ending –*y* for Standard Polish –*ej* (Seiffert-Nauka, 1992). These were synchronous Ukrainianisms, modeled on Ukrainian *t'ochkaty*, a Ukrainian reduplication attested in *u-vi-jty,* [lit. in-in-go, that is 'to enter'], and the consistent retention of word-final –*j* in southwestern Ukrainian (even though, admittedly, fem. dat.

sg. *–yj* might also be under the influence of Standard Polish). The author must have chosen these linguistic markers to betray our fictitious correspondent as someone with a Ukrainian linguistic background, even though she had fully adopted the local Polish vernacular in a bid to emulate the city's dominant language and culture. In the same vein, her name itself appears to be the polonized form of the Ukrainian nickname *Kotja*, lit. 'kitten.' How accurate stylized texts of this kind were in structural-linguistic terms is a question I cannot pursue further here (for more detail, see Fellerer, 2020). However, they must have undoubtedly served the purpose of signposting nonstandard usage typical of a particular social group; in our case, that of Lviv commoners of Ukrainian extraction who had, as it were, traded up to the city's local, Polish-based vernacular. Otherwise, the intended satirical effect would have been lost on the contemporary reader.

The corollary for the purpose at hand here is that these texts reveal some of the actual linguistic complexities hidden behind the monolithic glossonyms of the national era. These had historical Lviv as a 'Polish-Ukrainian' speaking city, without acknowledging Yiddish, and without recognizing that the city's multilingualism first and foremost involved nonstandard usage in the form of dialect, code-mixing, code-switching, and 'non-fluent' bilingualism.

The same point can be made if we move to another capital city of the late monarchy. In Prague, we find that the city's Czech satirical press was not just in Czech. It played, to some extent, on the city's more complex linguistic landscape that also included German and Yiddish, albeit the latter decreasing fast in the nineteenth century. Take, for example, a fictitious conversation between two coachmen in an issue of the satirical magazine *Nový Paleček* [Tom Thumb] of 1894. The illustration in Fig. 10.2 shows the accompanying caricature and the beginning of the text titled *Na štaflu* [At the carriage stand].

Here is a passage further into the conversation between the two coachmen. They talk about their business woes at a time of political turmoil around the so-called *Omladina* trials.

A vostatně já sem spokojenej. Kšefty se dělaj. Když bouchnou někde dvéře vod sklepu, tak hned je tu mladej pán, samej cvikr, samej krabatl – to je jako z novin – ten tam jede, kde to bouchlo, za chvíli tam inej pán v cylindru, proč to bouchlo. Jeden to spisuje a druhý to hned maluje a tak jezdím furt. Teď, co to vybouchlo u tý „Voršuskasy", tak nejezdím na štafl, objedu Prahu a ritů houf!

[But lately I'm calmer. There is business. When the doors of a shop bang somewhere, then, immediately, there's a young gent, all pince-nez and tie – like from the papers. He goes where it banged, and a moment later there's another gent in a top hat; why it banged. One writes it down and another paints it straightaway, but I drive on anyway. Now, something exploded there at that Advance Payment Bank, and so I don't go to the carriage stand. I'll drive around Prague, and there are rides galore!]

Fig. 10.2 *Na štaflu* in *Nový Paleček* 11 (1894), p. 88. Public domain.

The text is written in the colloquial form of Central (Prague) 'Common Czech' with numerous loans from (Austrian) German. Some typical colloquialisms represented in the stylized text are [ej] for /iː/, e.g., masc. nom. sg. *mladej* for Standard Czech *mladý* [young]; [iː] for /ɛː/, e.g., fem. gen. sg. *tý* for *té* [that]; and 3rd pl. *dělaj* for *dělají* [do] (Townsend, 1990). The Germanisms of the passage are *cvikr* [pince-nez], *krabatl* [tie], *furt* [constantly], *štafl* [stand], *rit* [ride], and *houf* [a lot]. Some less, some more established, they testify to the significance of language contact in the linguistic landscape of historical Prague.

Such contact-induced nonstandard vernaculars were usually the most characteristic variants used in speech in the late monarchy's bi- and multilingual localities. One can identify them with the help of the satirical press, provided that one submits the texts to careful source criticism. That is, one must read them with close reference to the historical context and events to which the texts refer, and mindful of the ideological direction and prejudices of the press organ where they appeared. In particular, it is important to keep in mind that the linguistic stylizations were clichéd, sometimes maliciously so. They were meant to signify, but not to document, actual linguistic practices.

To understand when the contact-induced nonstandard vernaculars were used in actual practice, I propose to look at another source – criminal court records. The charges brought by the prosecutor, witness testimonies, other pieces of written evidence, and the courts' judgments contain a wealth of information about the individuals involved in each case, their contacts, and daily routines. These texts thus effectively recreate the social networks of ordinary people whose life and activities rarely went on record anywhere else. The notion of social networks is an important tool in variationist sociolinguistics (Milroy, 2002). When applied to past bi- or multilingual communities, it helps reveal the communicative situations in which speakers of different languages came into direct contact with each other. The varieties they typically used on these occasions can be reconstructed from what the court records tell us about their social and linguistic background, in conjunction with our knowledge of what nonstandard lects were in use at the time.

In short, criminal court records can be a window into the workings of bi- and multilingualism in daily life in past societies. To be sure, the texts rarely provide any direct linguistic evidence. They are composed in the official 'internal' administrative language of the province or district, and they show little or no traces of the nonstandard vernaculars many defendants and witnesses will have undoubtedly used. However, the information they contain about them allows us to make inferences about their actual linguistic conduct. For an illustration, we will now return to Lviv, the capital city of the late-Habsburg province of Galicia. The court responsible for criminal and serious civil matters in the city and the Lviv court district was the Imperial-Royal Provincial Court. Its rich records are held in fonds 152 of the Central State Historical Archive of Ukraine in Lviv.

Let us turn to one particular case study. It concerns the housemaids Eudokia *vulgo* Ewa Zacharko and Józefa Tomasiewicz (sub-fonds 2, file 20491). Accused of a theft that occurred on October 3, 1900, the defendants were tried by jury, found guilty, and sentenced on February 9, 1901. The entire act is in Standard Polish, even though this was undoubtedly not the language of the main defendant, Ewa Zacharko. Zacharko was twenty-eight years old and a member of the Greek Catholic Church. She hailed from the village of Machnówek north of Lviv, close to the border with the Russian Empire. Approximately two thirds of its population spoke 'Ruthenian,' that is, south-western Ukrainian, according to the Austrian census of 1900 (K. K. statistische Zentralkommission, 1907, p. 620). There can be little doubt that Zacharko as a Greek Catholic was one of them, even though the records are typically silent on the language or languages individuals spoke. The courts did not consider language a significant attribute. What was important was that officialdom had done its duty and compiled all the relevant documents in the courts' official language, Polish. If a witness or defendant gave their testimony in

Ukrainian – as was their right – the official would have still taken this down in Polish. Rather than language, the emphasis was on other attributes, most importantly religion, but also place of birth, parents, age, and education. In the case of Zacharko, the records explicitly mention that she had 'no education' and could not read or write, a frequent occurrence in Galicia even as late as 1900 (e.g., Baczkowski, 2006). Given compulsory elementary school attendance and the availability of a parish school in her village (Chlebowski et al., 1884, p. 874), this probably means that Zacharko left school early and that she migrated to Lviv in search of work at an early age.

The court records refer to various engagements as a domestic worker before she entered the services of the Mościskers, a middle-class Jewish family at 8 Staszic Street in the relatively affluent southern district of the city (now Tomašivs'koho Street). Józefa Tomasiewicz, a twenty-two-year-old Roman Catholic of Łęki Dolne, an exclusively Polish-speaking village in western Galicia (K. K. statistische Zentralkommission, 1907, p. 460), was Zacharko's immediate colleague in the Mościskers' household. The witness testimonies show that Zacharko also had regular interaction with the Polish-speaking maids of other households at 8 Staszic Street, such as that of Aniela Wiszniewska and her sister Klara Migocka, the victim of the theft. Zacharko, in the presence of Tomasiewicz, had gained access to their attic and taken money and various valuable household items. She gave one of them, a piece of linen, to her fiancé, Antoni Tyśnicki, with the request that his sister should use it to sew a shirt for her. Tyśnicki, a carpenter and, at the time, a recruit at the thirtieth infantry regiment with Polish as its official language of command, was a Roman Catholic from suburban Lviv. It is highly likely that he was a speaker of the local south-eastern 'borderland' dialect of Polish.

The picture that emerges is that Zacharko's main means of communication in her social network of peers, employers, and fiancé must have been a variant of the local Polish dialect with strong contact-induced Ukrainian features. This was the dominant vernacular in late-Habsburg Lviv. It reflected the fact that, since the late 1860s, political control over the city and the province was largely in the hands of the Habsburg-loyal Polish estates. Their language, however, was certainly not Zacharko's or Tyśnicki's dialect. It was Standard Polish, and, until earlier in the nineteenth century, Latin in writing. Zacharko had adopted the local dialect not out of choice but to adapt to the diglossic reality in the city at the time. The fact that she went by the Polish first name 'Ewa,' rather than her actual Christian name 'Eudokia,' suggests that she had done so with considerable consistency. As soon as the court received a copy of the birth certificate from Zacharko's Greek Catholic parish, it added '*recte* Eudokia' to any mention of the name 'Ewa' in the documents. That is, it clarified that her actual Christian name was not Ewa, but Eudokia, which clearly identified her as a Greek Catholic. As mentioned, the authorities continued to give precedence to confessional and religious divides over linguistic distinctions. Zacharko's main linguistic persona in Lviv appears to be similar to what the stylization of the *Kocja* columns in *Strachopud* took aim at: a lower-class female resident of Lviv with a Ukrainian linguistic background but assimilated to the local Polish dialect. At the same time, it must not be overlooked that Zacharko's social network also included fellow Ukrainian dialect speakers. The court case reveals that she had taken most of the stolen items, concealed in a large parcel, to the place of Teodor and Anastazya Wołczak, or Wawczuk in some of the documents. They are the only individuals in the file referred to as Zacharko's friends. They were Greek Catholics and residents – in the case of Teodor native – of the suburban, almost exclusively 'Ruthenian'-speaking village Humieniec/Humenec' south of Lviv (K. K. statistische Zentralkommission, 1907, p. 342). We do not know how Zacharko and the Wawczuks knew each other, but it is highly likely that they were fellow speakers of southwestern Ukrainian dialects who would have used their vernacular when they met.

The 'Ukrainian' maid in 'Polish' Lviv is a well-worn stereotype. Even though compelling in its simplicity, this description obscures the actual, more nuanced manifestation of bi- and multilingualism in everyday urban life. For example, Zacharko's bilingualism must have developed gradually. Illiterate in both Polish and Ukrainian, her adopted southeastern 'borderland' Polish dialect could readily accommodate a variable amount of grammatical and lexical influence from her native southwestern Ukrainian dialect. Zacharko must have had a high degree of linguistic integration into her Polish-dialect speaking social network at work, in her lodgings, and her private life. Yet, the latter also provided occasions when she spoke her native Ukrainian dialect. The court file on the criminal case for which Zacharko went on record allows for this more nuanced reconstruction of her linguistic conduct in multilingual Lviv. One must add that it is also a sad illustration of the socioeconomic hardship that someone like Ewa Zacharko suffered.

As the term 'reconstruction' suggests, and as mentioned before, the criminal court records rarely offer direct evidence of who used what lect, especially nonstandard ones, in everyday life in bi- and multilingual localities of the late monarchy. They contain a range of information about the individuals involved, their origin, religion, education, trajectory in life, occupation, residence, their social circles, and, occasionally, their knowledge of written languages. It is this information, in conjunction with our knowledge of the local linguistic landscape, that allows us to make inferences about their lingustic choices in particular communicative situations. The outcome are likelihoods, but not certainties. For example, it is likely that Zacharko and Tyśnicki conversed in their respective variants of south-eastern 'borderland' Polish when they met. At the same time, it is not entirely inconceivable that Zacharko spoke in her southwestern Ukrainian dialect if, exceptionally, Tyśnicki perceived it as sufficiently intelligible to guarantee successful communication. Thus, we are dealing with likelihoods, rather than certainties. This is the main limitation of criminal court records as a source to study historical multilingualism in everyday life. We can mitigate against this by way of looking at a number of cases to see whether they converge on likely patterns of who used a particular lect and on what occasion. In the absence of direct documentation, the results remain inferential, rather than proven.

Conclusion

The multilingual world of the late Habsburg Monarchy has come down to us in a variety of sources. There are maps, census data, language policies, and choices in the domains of public life. They allow us to reconstruct the geographical and large-scale societal distribution of languages. However, they do so on their own terms, wedded to the primacy of written national languages, and silent on all forms of nonstandard usage and language mixing. I argued that a completely different range of sources was needed to overcome these constraints. Memoirs, the satirical press, and criminal court records afford glimpses into the actual linguistic practices of the time. Yet, they come with their own limitations. They invite an inductive approach, and with it, its pitfalls. An individual biography, a stylized satire of local society, or a chunk of past everyday life around some alleged wrongdoing – these pieces of evidence suggest probable patterns of people's actual linguistic conduct. However, they do not provide certainties. If we could travel in time and observe firsthand, we might well find that some conclusions were wrong. To mitigate against this, we must triangulate the sources. The geographical and societal macro-view puts a check on what was possible on the ground. The linguistic stereotypes recurrent in satire whittle down the linguistic continuum to some salient nonstandard, mixed, and switched varieties. For the selection to stack up, the social networks that emerge from the criminal court records must reveal plausible interactional sites where these varieties were in use. In short, this chapter encourages an approach to historical multilingualism that will be discouraged in other fields of study: eclecticism of sources and data.

Bibliography

Baczkowski, M. (2006) Analfabetyzm w Galicji w dobie konstytucyjnej [Illiteracy in Galicia in the constitutional era]. In Patek, A. & W. Rojek (eds.) *Naród – Państwo. Europa Środkowa w XIX i XX wieku. Studia ofiarowane Michałowi Pułaskiemu w 50-lecie pracy naukowej* [Nation – state. Central Europe in the 19th and 20th centuries. Studies dedicated to Michał Pułaski upon 50 years of scholarly work]. Kraków: Uniwersytet Jagielloński, pp. 97–113.

Brix, E. (1982) *Die Umgangssprachen in Altösterreich zwischen Agitation und Assimilation. Die Sprachenstatistik in den zisleithanischen Volkszählungen 1880 bis 1910* [Everyday languages in Old Austria between activism and assimilation. The language statistics of the Austrian population censuses 1880–1910]. Wien; Köln; Graz: Böhlau.

Chlebowski, B., Walewski, W., & F. Sulimierski (eds.) (1884) *Słownik geograficzny Królestwa Polskiego i innych krajów słowiańskich* [Geographical dictionary of the Kingdom of Poland and other Slavonic countries], vol. 5. Warszawa: Władysław Walewski.

Costa, J., De Korne, H., & P. Lane (2017) Standardizing Minority Languages. Reinventing Peripheral Languages in the 21st Century. In Lane, P., Costa, J., & H. De Korne (eds.) *Standardizing Minority Languages. Competing Ideologies of Authority and Authenticity in the Global Periphery*. New York: Routledge, pp. 1–23.

Czoernig, C, von (1857) *Ethnographie der oesterreichischen Monarchie* [Ethnography of the Austrian Monarchy], vols. 1–3. Wien: Staatsdruckerei.

Deák, Á. (2001) Volkszählung in Ungarn in den Jahren 1850–1851 [Population census in Hungary in the years 1850–1851]. *Chronica, History Department of the University of Szeged,* 1, 113–127 [http://acta.bibl.u-szeged.hu/5725/1/chronica_001_113-127.pdf, last accessed January 2021].

Edwards, J. (1994) *Multilingualism*. London/New York: Routledge.

Evans, R. (1990) Joseph II and Nationality in the Habsburg Lands. In Scott, H. (ed.) *Enlightened Absolutism. Reform and Reformers in Later Eighteenth-Century Europe*. Basingstoke: Macmillan, pp. 209–219.

(2004) Language and State Building. The Case of the Habsburg Monarchy. *Austrian History Yearbook*, 35, 1–24.

(2006) Nationality in East-Central Europe. Perception and Definition before 1848. In Evans, R. (ed.) *Austria, Hungary, and the Habsburgs. Essays on Central Europe 1683–1867*. Oxford: University Press, pp. 101–113.

Fellerer, J. (2005) *Mehrsprachigkeit im galizischen Verwaltungswesen (1772–1914). Eine historisch-soziolinguistische Studie zum Polnischen und Ruthenischen (Ukrainischen)* [Multilingualism in the Galician administration (1772–1914). A historical-sociolinguistic study of Polish and Ruthenian (Ukrainian)]. Köln: Böhlau.

(2020) *Urban multilingualism in East-Central Europe. The Polish Dialect of Late-Habsburg Lviv*. Lanham: Lexington Books.

Fischel, A., von (1910) *Das Österreichische Sprachenrecht. Eine Quellensammlung* [Austrian language laws. A collection of sources]. Brünn: Irrgang.

Fischer, W. (2001) Diglossie und Zweisprachigkeit im südlichen Innerösterreich, 1500–1700 [Diglossia and bilingualism in southern Inner Austria, 1500–1700]. *Frühneuzeit-Info*, 12, 1, 70–85.

Fishman, J. (1965) Who speaks what language to whom and when? *La Linguistique*, 1–2, 67–88.

Gal, S. (2011) Polyglot nationalism: Alternative perspectives on language in 19th century Hungary. *Langage et société*, 136, 31–54.

Holek, H. (1927) *Unterwegs. Eine Selbstbiographie* [On the way. An autobiography]. Wien: Bugra.

Holek, W. (1909) *Lebensgang eines deutsch-tschechischen Handarbeiters* [Biography of a German-Czech manual labourer]. Jena: Eugen Diederichs.

Holub, Z. (2011) Šlonzáci, Vasrpoláci, Laši, Gorali, Moravci, Prajzáci a lidé Ponašymu [Lachs, Gorals, Prajzáks and People speaking 'our way']. In: Pospíšil, I. & A. Zelenková (eds.) *Literární historiografie a česko-slovenské vztahy* [Literary historiography and Czech-Slovak relations]. Brno: Tribun EU, pp. 211–227 [https://digilib.phil.muni.cz/handle/11222.digilib/134246, last accessed January 2021].

Judson, P. (2006) *Guardians of the nation. Activists on the language frontiers of imperial Austria.* Cambridge, MA: Harvard University Press.

Jungmann, J. (2007) Second conversation concerning the Czech language. In Trencsényi, B. & M. Kopeček (eds.) *Discourses of collective identity in Central and Southeast Europe (1770–1945), vol. 2: National romanticism. The formation of national movements.* Budapest/New York: CEU Press, pp. 103–111.

Kann, R. (1950) *The multinational empire: Nationalism and national reform in the Habsburg Monarchy, vols. 1–2.* New York: Columbia University Press.

K. K. Statistische Central-Commission (ed.) (1892) *Die Ergebnisse der Volkszählung vom 31. December 1890 in den im Reichsrathe vertretenen Königreichen und Ländern. 1. Heft: Die summarischen Ergebnisse der Volkszählung* [The results of the population census of 31 December 1890 of the Kingdoms and Lands represented in the Imperial Council. 1st issue: Summary of the results of the population census]. Wien: K. K. Hof- und Staatsdruckerei.

K. K. statistische Zentralkommission (ed.) (1907) *Gemeindelexikon der im Reichsrate vertretenen Königreiche und Länder. Bearbeitet aufgrund der Ergebnisse der Volkszählung vom 31. Dezember 1900* [Municipality gazetteer of the Kingdoms and Lands represented in the Imperial Council. Based on the results of the population census of 31 December 1900], vol. XII. Wien: K. K. Hof- und Staatsdruckerei.

Labbé, M. (2010) Die „Ethnographische Karte der Oesterreichischen Monarchie". Ein Abbild der Monarchie [The 'Ethnographic Map' of the Austrian Monarchy. A representation of the Monarchy]. *Jahrbuch der Österreichischen Gesellschaft zur Erforschung des 18. Jahrhunderts*, 25, 149–163.

Milroy, L. (2002) Social Networks. In Chambers, J., Trudgill, P. & N. Schilling-Estes (eds.) *The Handbook of Language Variation and Change.* Malden/MA: Blackwell, pp. 549–572.

Mischler, E., & J. Ulbrich (1906) *Österreichisches Staatswörterbuch. Handbuch des gesamten österreichischen Rechts* [Austrian State Dictionary. Complete handbook of Austrian law], vol. 2. Wien: Hölder.

Moritsch, A. (1991) *Vom Ethnos zur Nationalität. Der nationale Differenzierungsprozeß am Beispiel ausgewählter Orte in Kärnten und im Burgenland* [From ethnic group to nation. The rise of national distinctions through the example of select communities in Carinthia and Burgenland]. Wien/München: Verlag für Geschichte und Politik, Oldenbourg Verlag.

Országos magyar kir. statisztikai hivatal [National Hungarian Royal Statistical Office] (1895) *Magyar statisztikai évkönyv. Új folyam.* [Hungarian statistical yearbook. New series], vol. 2. Budapest: Athenaeum.

Rindler Schjerve, R. (ed.) (2003) *Diglossia and power. Language policies and practice in the 19th century Habsburg empire.* Berlin/New York: De Gruyter.

Scheer, T. (2014) Die k.u.k. Regimentssprachen. Eine Institutionalisierung der Sprachenvielfalt in der Habsburgermonarchie (1867/8–1914) [The languages of the Royal and Imperial regiments. The institutionalization of linguistic diversity in the Habsburg Monarchy (1867/8–1914)]. In Ehlers, K. et al. (eds.) *Sprache, Gesellschaft und Nation in Ostmitteleuropa. Institutionalisierung und Alltagspraxis* [Language, society and nation in East-Central Europe. Institutionalization and everyday practice]. Göttingen: Vandenhoeck & Ruprecht, pp. 75–92.

Seiffert-Nauka, I. (1992) *Dawny dialekt miejski Lwowa. Część 1: Gramatyka* [The old urban dialect of Lviv, part 1: Grammar]. Wrocław: Wydawnictwo UW.

Stergar, R. & T. Scheer (2018) Ethnic boxes: The unintended consequences of Habsburg bureaucratic classification. *Nationalities Papers*, 46, 4, 575–591.

Stourzh, G. (1994) Ethnic Attribution in Late Imperial Austria. Good Intentions, Evil Consequences. In Robertson, R. & E. Timms (eds.) *The Habsburg Legacy. National Identity in Historical Perspective*. Edinburgh: University Press, pp. 67–83.

Townsend, C. (1990) *A description of spoken Prague Czech*. Columbus/Ohio: Slavica.

Vodička, F. (ed.) (1948) *Boj o obrození národa. Výbor z díla Josefa Jungmanna* [The struggle for national awakening. Select writings of Josef Jungmann]. Praha: F. Kosek, pp. 31–50.

Wandruszka, A. & P. Urbanitsch (eds.) (1980) *Die Habsburgermonarchie 1848–1918, vol. 3: Die Völker des Reiches* [The Habsburg Monarchy 1848–1918, vol 3: Ethnic groups of the empire]. Wien: Akademie der Wissenschaften.

Weber, Eugen (1976) *Peasants into Frenchmen. The Modernization of Rural France (1870–1914).* Stanford: Stanford University Press.

Wendland, A. (2001) *Die Russophilen in Galizien. Ukrainische Konservative zwischen Österreich und Russland, 1848–1915* [The Russophiles of Galicia. Ukrainian conservatives between Austria and Russia, 1848–1915]. Wien: Akademie der Wissenschaften.

Zahra, T. (2008) *Kidnapped souls. National indifference and the battle for children in the Bohemian lands, 1900–1948*. Ithaca: Cornell University.

11 Multilingualism and the End of the Ottoman Empire: Language, Script, and the Quest for the 'Modern'

Benjamin C. Fortna

In considering the intricate linguistic situation of the late Ottoman Empire, it is useful to think of layers of language. The empire's many linguistic strata, like its variably polyglot population, frequently overlapped – to the point of piling up many times in multilingual individuals and communities – or remained relatively thin in the case of monolingual majority. Even then, as we shall see, speakers of one language were inherently engaged in a kind of multilingualism, given the extent to which the supposedly discrete tongues were influenced by neighboring vocabulary and even grammar. The situation was even more complex when we consider that Ottoman Turkish contained several linguistic registers, ranging from 'high' or literary Turkish to 'low' or the rough vernacular of everyday life. Yet, broadly speaking, in the late imperial period of the nineteenth and early twentieth centuries and then much more emphatically in the post-Ottoman era, the trend was in the direction of monolingualism. This was the result of a number of interrelated factors, including technological change, rising literacy rates, and state policies aimed at imposing national unity. Together they militated for linguistic simplification, alphabetic reform, and the reduction of other perceived barriers to popularization. The layers of language that had been the hallmark of imperial culture would soon become thinner and less overlapping, but they would never disappear.

In the opening chapter of his recent book on late Ottoman port cities, Fuhrmann (2020) offers an arresting anecdote that reveals the ways in which individual linguistic layers were formed in the imperial era and then submerged in the period of its national successor states. A Greek colleague described the way her grandfather's dementia had revealed the linguistic strata of his past as his condition worsened. The disease, "a gradual erosion of an individual's personality as it has evolved throughout his or her life," caused the elderly man to lose his memory in stages. The first to go were the most recent memories. It was as if he were traveling back in time to his childhood in the late Ottoman Empire. Two important linguistic ruptures, Fuhrmann notes, "managed to particularly startle his relatives. At some point the man stopped speaking Greek and would only talk in Turkish anymore. But in a later stage, his use of Turkish came to be replaced by the singing of French Christian and children's songs" (p. 7).

This man's dementia, it seems, managed to reveal the linguistic phases of his life. As a member of the Karamanlı community of Turkish-speaking 'Greeks' (called "Rum" in the Ottoman context) of Anatolia, he had probably attended a French missionary school. When his family was forced to move across the Aegean Sea to mainland Greece in the population exchanges of 1923, organized on the principle of religious and not ethnolinguistic belonging, he would have had to learn modern Greek, perhaps as a beginner. His illness, in effect, revealed the linguistic layers of his life, laying bare but in reverse order the linguistic sedimentation that was laid down in the late Ottoman and nation-state eras. Subsequent nationalist policy on language would attempt to impose rather simplistic but sometimes brutally effective alterations to this accumulated linguistic stratigraphy.

In this chapter I attempt to provide some background on the multilingual situation in the late Ottoman Empire, analyze the ways in which language was increasingly but problematically expected to align with ethno-national identity, and discuss the various attempts to engineer a 'solution' to the 'problem' of linguistic diversity in the late- and post-Ottoman eras. A central theme will be the ways in which technological change, which manifested in the form of such vehicles as the telegraph and movable type, served as an impetus for attempts to 'modernize' language, both its script and its syntax. Stepping back from the mechanics of language and the attempts to change it, we will see that despite the teleology of national historiography, the move from multi- to monolingualism in the late Ottoman Empire and after was an unnatural and messy affair. As an examination of the late Ottoman era from a linguistic perspective reveals, the Ottoman case does not lend itself easily to the nationalist trajectories into which it was made to fit by the dominant political and cultural narratives that became almost sacred in the empire's successor states.[1] By focusing on both the ideological and technological propellants of the period, this chapter attempts to disentangle the main features of the move from predominant multilingualism to an aggressively pursued monolingualism of the nation-state era.

11.1 The Linguistic Situation in the Late Ottoman Empire

The late Ottoman Empire was remarkably polyglot. Even though the borders of the empire had shrunk from their greatest extent, reached in the sixteenth

[1] For an excellent overview of the Ottoman multilingual scene, see Strauss (2011); for a comparative look at the Ottoman to post-Ottoman transition in the Balkans, Anatolia, and the Arab lands, see Anscombe (2014).

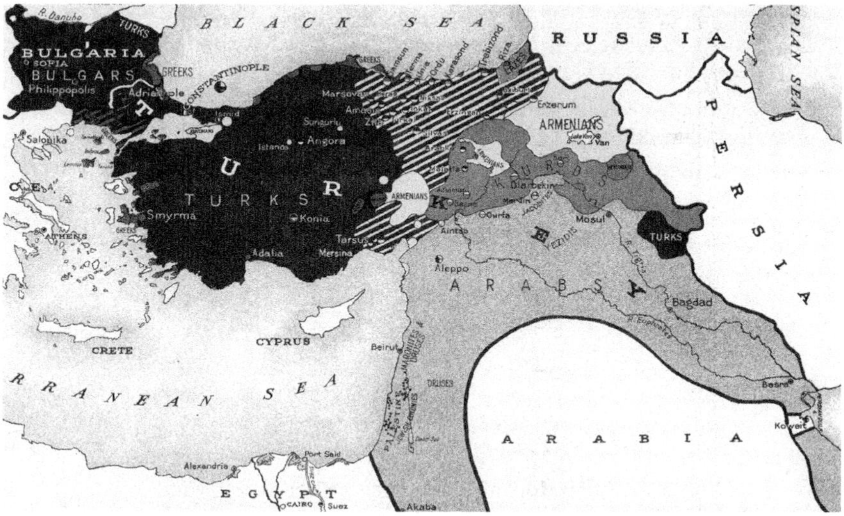

Fig. 11.1 Subject nationalities of the German alliance (detail), 1917. Cornell Library Digital Collections, public domain.

and seventeenth centuries when it ranged from Central Europe in the West to the Iranian plateau in the East and from the Caucasus in the North to Sudan in the South, the languages spoken remained extraordinarily diverse in the nineteenth and early twentieth centuries, reflecting the varied origins of its many ethnolinguistic subjects (Fig. 11.1).

Even as the empire contracted, the number of languages spoken tended to rise due to the mixed origins of the refugees flooding into its diminishing territory as a result of the upheavals in the surrounding regions, including ethnic cleansing and other forms of demographic engineering. Attempts at counting the languages spoken in the Ottoman lands, volatile and frequently contested under any circumstances (cf. Duchêne & Humbert, 2018; Duchêne et al., 2018), were particularly difficult; even more challenging was the aim of mapping those tongues onto space.

Although such linguistic diversity might have been seen as a source of the multiethnic empire's sociocultural strength, it was increasingly considered to be a political weakness. In an era of increasingly strident nationalist fervor, which frequently bore the signs of social Darwinism, such linguistic richness was seen as a sign of vulnerability. While some Ottoman intellectuals encouraged a decentralized approach that would allow for regional differences, others emphasized centralization. The latter tendency ultimately prevailed, since at every key juncture it was the centralizers who triumphed, first under the reform-minded *Tanzimat* [Reorganizations] era (1839–1876) when political power was transferred from the palace to the newly established ministries of the central bureaucracy, then under Sultan Abdülhamid II (reigned 1876–1909) who reclaimed dynastic control, and subsequently under the rule of the Committee of Union and Progress (1908–1918), a group of revolutionary centralizers who ruled from behind the scenes until just before World War I. Each era had its own desiderata, but centralization was a common objective among all the major rulers of the empire's final decades. When the Turkish Republic was established in 1923, it continued and, in many respects, intensified the drive toward centralization. A unified language policy was, as we shall see, a key component of the new nation-state's approach.

It was hardly surprising that these very different Ottoman rulers, concerned as they were with the notion of unity and the assumed geopolitical weakness that the lack of such unity would entail, aimed to forge an imperial whole out of its varied peoples. The concept of the 'union of the elements' was a frequently hailed aspiration, even if it now looks stunningly impractical in retrospect. To gain a sense of the size of the task at hand – and, indeed, of the irony inherent in such an approach – consider a publication from 1911 urging all Ottoman peoples to form a united front, namely, *İttihad-ı Anâsır-ı Osmaniye* [the union of all Ottoman elements]. Its authors on the Union of All Ottoman Elements Committee considered it necessary to publish their appeal in no less than nine languages and in multiple scripts. Even so, they ignored some of the empire's important tongues, including Albanian, Kurdish, and Rumanian, not to mention the numerous languages of the Caucasus.[2] As Hanioğlu (2008) aptly notes, this publication "gives some idea of the multilingualism of the empire" (p. 33). The elusive search for political unity perforce ran through – and across – the question of linguistic diversity.

The main language of the empire, namely, Ottoman Turkish, was in important respects itself multilingual. While its grammatical frame was Turkish, its vocabulary drew heavily from Arabic and Persian reservoirs (to say nothing of the borrowings from many other languages, a subject to which we return below) and it even borrowed grammatical and syntactical elements from Arabic and Persian as well. The recourse to what was effectively three languages (the term *elsine-i selâse* referred to the three languages whose mastery was required for proper Ottoman literary production)[3] made Ottoman Turkish "one of the richest and most complex languages in the

[2] The authors of the pamphlet do not indicate the reasons for omitting these tongues, but one can guess that the fact that Albanian and Kurdish are deeply divided by dialect was an important factor. Additionally, Kurdish did not yet have a standard literary form in this period. Rumanian had ceased to be as important for the empire after Romania achieved independence following the 1877–1878 Russo-Ottoman War.

[3] This term illustrates one way in which Ottoman Turkish incorporates Arabic and Persian vocabulary and grammatical structures. Here, two words of Arabic origin, *elsine* [languages]

Fig. 11.2 Baker standing in front of the "American Bakery" that displays signs in Armenian, Ladino (in Hebrew characters), English, Ottoman Turkish, Greek, and Russian with samples of bread attached to the mullions, Ortaköy, Istanbul, Turkey, 1922. Library of Congress Prints and Photographs Division, Public domain.

world" (Hanioğlu, 2008, p. 35). There was also a wide gap between the learned and popular registers of Ottoman Turkish, to the degree that it has been considered in retrospect to have constituted a case of diglossia (Strauss, 1995b, p. 233). When we consider that besides Turkish, Arabic, and Persian, the empire's important languages included Greek, Armenian, Albanian, Kurdish, Bulgarian, and Serbian, we can see that the linguistic scene was very rich indeed. In different parts of the empire, certain individual languages were dominant, for example, Arabic in, say, Baghdad, Turkish in the urban areas of central Anatolia, or Greek in several of the coastal cities, such as Izmir/Smyrna (Strauss, 2011, p. 129). In the numerous areas with a high degree of ethnic mixing, numerous tongues were seen (Fig. 11.2) or heard.

and *selase* [three] are connected with the Persian particle *-i* known as the *izafet*, a common feature of Ottoman Turkish.

Compounding the situation even further was the fact that certain groups in the empire crossed the presumptive boundaries separating the population by religion, language, and script. For example, there were the aforementioned Karamanlıs, Greek Orthodox Christians who spoke Turkish, as well as Turkish-speaking Armenian Christians and Muslims who spoke Slavic tongues. As Strauss (2003, p. 39) has noted, because these groups did not fit nationalist expectations, they were often excluded from consideration in nationalist historiography.

Then there are the exogenous languages to consider. In the classical period of the empire the *lingua franca* of the Mediterranean, a linguistic medley that included a large number of Italian and Greek terms, served to grease the wheels of commerce, especially the seaborne variety (Kahane et al., 1958). Russian played an important role, especially in the empire's eastern provinces, and left its mark in distinctive loan words that remain extant to this day in modern Turkish, such as *şapka* [hat] and *palto* [overcoat], to name only two (conversely, Russian has a considerable list of Turkish loanwords) (Pelekani, 2014).

The dominant European language of the late Ottoman era was French. Fuhrmann (2020) describes command of French as "the ultimate prerequisite to enter the semi-elitist space within Ottoman urban society" (p. 226). By the nineteenth century advancement in the growing ranks of the imperial bureaucracy, itself modeled in large part on French administration, required a solid command of French. Indeed, the exemplar of the Ottoman state secondary school was the Galatasaray Lycée (*Galatasaray Mekteb-i Sultanisi* or, more commonly, *Galatasaray Lisesi*), an Istanbul institution founded on a French model, whose first directors were French, and in which French and Ottoman Turkish were the joint languages of instruction. Satirical accounts abound in late Ottoman fictional literature of the deracinated Ottoman subject whose speech is so interlaced with French vocabulary that he or she (but usually he) cannot be understood by his fellow Ottoman subjects (Mardin, 1974). (The modern Turkish legacy of this approach can be seen in President Recep Tayyip Erdoğan's populist mocking of political opponents and state officials by invoking the term 'monşer,' derived from French *mon cher* [my darling].)

In other words, in its last decades the empire's linguistic scene was rich and getting even richer. Apart from the fact that a Western European language such as French became *de rigueur* for the advancement of state officials, reflecting the growing importance of Western influence even if it never culminated in full-on colonization, the empire's political and territorial retrenchment, far from reducing its linguistic complexity, added to it. As the balance of power shifted from the Ottoman Empire to its rivals in the West, chiefly Austro-Hungary and Russia, it was forced to give up the lands it had conquered in its fifteenth- and sixteenth-century expansions.

To take only two milestones on the route of Ottoman territorial retreat, we can cite the treaty of Küçük Kaynarca of 1774, by which the Ottomans ceded control of the Crimea. Russian occupation of the northern shores of the Black Sea, once an 'Ottoman lake,' followed fairly swiftly. Just over a hundred years later the Ottoman army suffered a disastrous defeat in yet another war with Russia, the Russo-Ottoman War of 1877–1878. The Berlin Congress of 1878 made official the scale of the empire's losses; from Iran to Montenegro the Ottoman borders shrank, ceding, for example, Bosnia-Herzegovina to Austro-Hungary, Thessaly to Greece, Kars and Batum to Russia, and Cyprus to Britain, while creating an autonomous Bulgaria and Crete. In short, the Ottomans lost approximately 230,000 square kilometers of territory and between 5 and 6 million subjects (Fortna, 2008, p. 47).

As the empire's territory contracted as a result of these and other wars lost and treaties signed, the number of languages being spoken inside them increased due to the influx of refugees who sought safety in Muslim territory, as mentioned earlier. Particularly prominent was the mass immigration of peoples from the Caucasus during the last third of the nineteenth century, the result of Russian expulsions and other forms of ethnic cleansing (Strauss, 2016, p. 115). Given the long-standing relations between the largely Muslim population of the Caucasus and the Ottoman Empire, the lands across the Black Sea formed their natural refuge. They brought with them a host of languages that most Ottomans struggled to recognize. As a result, the new arrivals and their language were referred to collectively but inaccurately as 'Circassian' (Çerkes). Conversely, when the empire lost territory, the languages spoken by its inhabitants did not disappear.

But perhaps the strongest, if generally unremarked – perhaps due to the tendency to focus on change and the impact of the new – influence on late Ottoman language was the collective weight and inertia of the Ottoman classical literary tradition. The sheer volume and cumulative heft of the legacy of poetry, the chief genre of the Ottoman and, indeed, of the broader Islamicate literary tradition, was formidable. The range of formal genres and meters, not to mention stylistic conventions, were high barriers to the mastery that was traditionally associated with membership in the Ottoman cultural elite. In an age of growing populism, expanding education, and rising literacy rates, the required fluency of expression in literary Turkish, Arabic, and Persian – and therefore the remove from the everyday language of the street – began to seem oppressive to many, especially those who favored a more popular form of literary expression.

The emerging expectations of the late Ottoman period provoked Ottoman observers to reassess the condition of the Ottoman language in the empire's final decades. Tentative at first, this reevaluation culminated in radical change in the Turkish Republic and its 'Language Revolution' (*dil devrimi*). Two

Fig. 11.3 Greek chiropodist in Salonica (Thessaloniki) advertises his services in Ottoman Turkish, Greek, French, Armenian, and Ladino in 1920, three years after the city ceased to be part of the Ottoman Empire. Library of Congress Prints and Photographs Division, Public domain.

broad but interrelated areas of concern appeared in discussions concerning Ottoman Turkish in the late imperial era: linguistic complexity and the 'problems' associated with the script in which it was written. Suffice it to say that these newly identified issues were symptomatic of the pressures on and changes to late Ottoman society effected by the strains of the modern era. Apprehensions concerning, first and foremost, the empire's ability to survive in a rapidly modernizing and increasingly competitive era were compounded by two other distinct but interrelated factors, namely, technological change and nascent populist nationalism.

11.2 Linguistic Complexity

As mentioned above, the cumulative weight of the classical Ottoman literary tradition was heavy. In the late nineteenth century, one symptom of the clash of outlooks between traditionalists and modernizers that was further complicated by the influence of Western literary trends took the form of the 'Decadents controversy' (*dekadanlar tartışması*) in Ottoman letters. This was sparked by an 1897 article critiquing the current trends in literature in which, the conservative author Ahmet Midhat Efendi (1844–1912) opined, linguistic artificiality made it impossible to understand what was actually being said.[4] At a time when the Ottoman press was expanding dramatically, this controversy produced "a moment of collective anxiety about the written register of the Turkish language, now disseminated more widely than before" (Seviner, 2020, pp. 19–20). Ahmet Midhat took particular aim at the "unnecessarily ornate and opaque" nature of the language concocted by some of the younger generation of writers who, in his view, were less than fully versed in classical Ottoman literature but still played with some of its themes and tropes, thereby producing an unsettled – and unsettling – effect. He advised the fictional friend who has been frustrated in trying to read these tortured works that he will have to "read in Ottoman Turkish but think in French" in order to decode the offending prose. As Seviner (2020, pp. 19–20) points out, Ahmet Midhat used the term Decadents to imply both a move toward the immorality of French literature and toward a decontextualized mishmash that borrowed tropes from classical Ottoman literature in nonsensical ways. He was thus engaging in both a form of "verbal hygiene" (Cameron, 2014 (1995)) and policing of literary and sociocultural norms.

The issue of language, both indigenous and exogenous, and the inevitable questions of translation produced by the increasingly complicated linguistic state of the empire were foregrounded in late Ottoman literary production. Translation questions, both textual and cultural, are central to several of the

[4] The term 'artificiality' is used by Seviner (2020, pp. 19–20) in her analysis of Ahmet Midhat's critique of what he considered to be the vogue for incomprehensible language employed in the literary production of the 1890s. Interestingly for our purposes, Ahmet Midhat Efendi was able to read Turkish in the Armenian script. He is on record as championing the use of the Armenian script as a superior vehicle for rendering Turkish (Cankara, 2015, pp. 6–7). It is likely that Ahmet Midhat mined Armenian literature for use in his prolific writings.

most important late Ottoman novels, which often played on the perceived cultural divide between *alaturka* [Turkish] and *alafranga* [Frankish, i.e. Western] habits, attitudes, appearances, and, of course, utterances. Late Ottoman authors focused on language to highlight the fault lines of the period. The figure of the overly Westernized dandy was a common feature of late Ottoman novels and short stories. He and sometimes she provided the opportunity to critique deracination and cultural loss. A penchant for slavishly aping Western sartorial fashion provided an obvious and visually satisfying target to both writers and cartoonists alike (Brummett, 2000; Şeni, 1995). But a linguistic critique was frequently more cutting. Characters were skewered for overelaborate phrasing, extended sentences, circumlocutions and, in general, the artificial nature of their language. Reflecting the impact on late Ottoman society of a number of important changes, ranging from the foreign economic and political pressures to changes in thought, taste, and consumption (Levi, 2020), many late Ottoman fictional characters struggled to resolve the challenges of arriving at the appropriate modes of thought, action, and appearance. Cultural anxiety about who the Ottomans were and where their society was headed permeated the literature of the period and was frequently indexed in linguistic and scriptural terms.

11.3 Script 'Problems' and Solutions

In the late Ottoman period, the main script in which Ottoman Turkish was written came to be seen as overly complex and therefore problematic. The language had developed over several centuries into "an admixture of Turkish with Persian and Arabic vocabulary, written in a script combining Arabic and Persian letter forms" (Ertürk, 2011, p. 6). This had worked well for centuries, perhaps mainly because only a relatively small percentage of the population could read and write. Over the course of the nineteenth century, educational offerings in the empire expanded at an unprecedented rate as schools were founded by foreign missionaries, local communities, and the Ottoman state. In these 'new-style' schools, printed materials, textbooks in particular, played an increasingly important role. A secondary effect of the new educational dispensation that replaced erasable slates with individually owned books and increasingly journals and magazines aimed at young readers was the creation of a new market of young readers (Fortna, 2011). In an era of rising literacy, the Ottoman Turkish language and its dominant script increasingly faced calls for reform; what had 'worked' for centuries was now thought to be overly complicated and therefore in need of simplification.

The fact that Ottoman Turkish was at the same time communicated via other scripts, in particular the Greek and Armenian alphabets, reveals an important aspect of the transition from a premodern to a modern conception of the relationship between language and script. It was increasingly expected that there be a one-to-one correspondence between language and script. This new expectation was as crucial to nationalist fantasies about language as it was awkward in the Ottoman context. To take only one important example, the first 'Turkish novel' was actually written in the Armenian script. The author of *Akabi Hikayesi* [The Story of Akabi] was an Ottoman Armenian named Hovsep Vartanyan. Vartan Pasha, as he was known to the Ottoman establishment, also wrote a history of Napoleon published in both Arabic and Armenian scripts (Strauss, 1995a, p. 211). *Akabi Hikayesi*, published in Istanbul in 1851, is an ill-starred love story featuring the eponymous girl Akabi, from the Armenian Orthodox community, and Hagop, an Armenian Catholic. It is remembered less for its literary merit than for the fact that, uncomfortably for subsequent Turkish nationalists, it was written by an Armenian and in the Armenian alphabet.

The role of the several scripts used to render the Ottoman Turkish language in this period was not inconsequential. It should not be surprising that the first novel in Turkish appeared in a 'non-Muslim' script, such was the propensity for the mixing and matching of languages and alphabets. There was also considerable literary production of Turkish in Greek and Hebrew letters, for example. Ottoman Armenians and Greeks and other non-Muslims were influential in the adaptation of typography, an increasingly crucial factor in the linguistic situation in the empire. Unlike the Arabo-Persian script, the non-Muslim languages all used separate letters, that is, without ligatures connecting the individual letters, a feature that greatly facilitated their adaptation to print. Put another way, the modified Arabic and Persian script used to render Ottoman Turkish was written in a cursive mode that did not allow for the separation of individual letters of the alphabet. For centuries this had not been problematic as scribal and literary culture all depended upon handwritten texts. The advent of printed texts, movable type, and the telegraph placed new and increasingly uncomfortable demands on the Ottoman script.

Script was the operative word; each of the letters deployed in Ottoman Turkish, and Arabic and Persian, for that matter, had multiple forms, depending on its position in a given word, initial, medial, or lateral. Each letter also had its stand-alone version. To make the situation even more challenging for typesetters, various type styles preserved aspects of the calligraphic legacy of handwritten texts. Thus, for example, some favored combining letters vertically as well as horizontally, so that the typesetter needed far more 'sorts' to present the word on the page using the accustomed combination of glyphs and ligatures. By one estimate, Ottoman-language typesetters required at least 500 and in some cases as many as 1,600 to 2,000 signs in their type cases, whereas those working in more simple scripts such as Latin, Greek, or Armenian used less than 100 (Kuzuoğlu, 2020, p. 416). There was thus a practical impetus that combined with the ideological basis for the reform to militate for a change to the Ottoman script.

Other 'problems' were of longer standing but began to be voiced in the new environment that increasingly sought to spur Ottoman linguistic reform. One set of difficulties centered on the lack of correlation between the vowels of Ottoman Turkish and the letters available for representing them in the Arabic script. Another focused on other 'deficiencies' of the Arabic alphabet (Lewis, 1999, p. 28). For example, the Arabic letter for 'k' (kaf) performs multiple duties in Ottoman Turkish and produces correspondingly different sounds. Another issue raised by would-be reformers of the Arabo-Persian script was the visual similarity that existed between and among consonants, including, for example, the letters 'b,' 'p,' 't,' 'th,' (or 'se') and 'n.' All were designated by placing one or more dots above or below a similar-looking basic letter sign which, the reformers argued, were "susceptible to optical confusion" (Kuzuoğlu, 2020, p. 416). Cumulatively, emphasizing the practical problems newly associated with the existing script resulted in pressure to change it.

11.4 Toward a New Alphabet

Animated by a desire to eliminate such problems with a view to ensuring scientific and literary progress in the Muslim world, literary and bureaucratic figures in the Ottoman and neighboring lands began to call for modifying the existing script from the 1850s onward. As Kuzuoğlu's (2020) recent research has shown, the impact of non-Muslim advocates for change and the role played by non-Muslims in adapting their alphabets to the new technologies of the day provided important stimuli to rethinking the Arabo-Persian script (p. 416). Münif Pasha (1830–1910), founder of the Ottoman Scientific Society and chief interpreter at the Sublime Porte, suggested two solutions in 1862. One was to add diacritical marks to distinguish between the letters by adopting the three diacritical marks used in Arabic as well as five newly created signs to represent the full phonology of Turkish. The other, more radical, recourse was to separate the letters from each other and render them unconnected to each other, with the relevant diacritical marks to appear on the line as opposed to above or below it. The following year brought a proposal from the Azerbaijani playwright and interpreter to the Russian viceroy in the Caucasus Mirza Fatali Akhundzade (1812–1878), who had traveled to Istanbul to present similar ideas. Both reformers were driven in part by technological, that is to say, typographical, concerns. By reforming the Ottoman alphabet, these 'typographic Muslims' aimed to build on the work of their non-Muslim counterparts to reduce the barriers to printing and communication that they deemed to be hindering progress in the Islamic world (Kuzuoğlu, 2020, p. 415).

The passage of time and the spread of technological change, including the telegraph and the insistence it placed on separating letters for rapid communication via Morse code,[5] increased pressure for alphabetic reform in the Islamic world. In the Ottoman lands, the reign of conservative Sultan Abdülhamid II (r. 1876–1909) halted the reformist cause for a time, but the work recommenced after he was deposed. With the heavy-handed censorship of the Hamidian era lifted, there was an explosion of publications in the Ottoman Empire, which seems to have resuscitated the work of rethinking the alphabet. A Society for Alphabet Reform (*ıslah–ı huruf cemiyeti*) was formed in 1911 and soon produced a stand-alone alphabet. This caught the attention of Enver Pasha (1881–1922), the rising figure in the Ottoman military. Enver ordered the use of alphabet with separate letters across the Ottoman military in 1914. Although a number of key publications were produced in this script, it was soon abandoned owing to confusion and a lack of training with the alphabet. Still, the precedent had been set in the Ottoman lands, which would have important implications for the Turkish Republic.

Meanwhile neighboring states persevered with alphabetic change. A revised version of the Latin alphabet was published in Azerbaijan in 1919, and the New Turkish Alphabet was introduced into Muslim regions that fell under Soviet control in 1922. It was formally adopted as the official script of the Azerbaijan Soviet Socialist Republic in 1924 (Kuzuoğlu, 2020, pp. 428–429), a further sign that the Arabo-Persian alphabet and the religious-cultural world it represented were in retreat.

11.5 Toward Monolingualism

By this point, the Ottoman Empire had ceased to exist. The Turkish Republic had been created in 1923 out of what was left of the central Ottoman lands after the Arab provinces had been captured by the Allies toward the end of World War I. Comprised of Eastern Thrace, Istanbul, and Anatolia, the new Republic was territorially and demographically diminished. Further drastic demographic change was effected by the population exchanges organized by the League of Nations in 1923. This compulsory exchange was, as mentioned above, arranged on the basis of religion and not language or ethnicity. Perhaps four hundred thousand Muslims departed Greece for Turkey while as many as 1.6 million Greek Orthodox traveled across the Aegean in the other direction. Many of them, like the boy who would later revert to his earlier language mentioned by Fuhrmann, spoke the language of the region they were departing but not of their new countries. The net effect was cultural alienation on the

[5] For an excellent overview of the impact of the telegraph, see Carey (1983).

individual level and a collective blow to the multilingual nature of the old regime.

The new Turkish Republic heartily embraced the cause of monolingualism as it tried to impose a culture of homogeneity on what was still a remarkably diverse population. The linguistic situation in Anatolia had been radically altered by the Great War and its immediate aftermath. Its Armenian population had been deported or massacred during the war and the subsequent population exchanges removed most of the Greek-speaking population, along with the Turkish-speaking 'Greeks,' as already mentioned. Nevertheless, the territory of the republic included substantial numbers of non-Turkish speakers, including most prominently Kurds but also a fair number of Greeks, Armenians, Laz, and a number of Muslim refugees from the Balkans and the Caucasus. Faced with this reduced but still palpable multilingual terrain, the Republic led by Mustafa Kemal Atatürk aggressively pursued efforts aimed at monolingualism, epitomized by the "Citizen, Speak Turkish" campaign. Kurdish was suppressed in public, only achieving limited legality in the 1990s. Meanwhile the 'Alphabet Revolution' (*harf devrimi*), imposed in 1928 (Lewis, 1999, p. 27 ff.), revealed the heavy hand of state involvement in linguistic engineering. Whereas, as noted above, late Ottoman efforts at script reform were influenced by the alphabets at work in the empire (many of which were used to convey Turkish), the Republican effort relied on adaptation of a writing system used in one or more other languages, albeit from Western and Central Europe rather than from other former members of the Ottoman imperial linguistic stable. From 1928 onward, with only a period of one year to adapt, only the modified Latin alphabet called the New Turkish Alphabet would be legal in the country. Not content to leave it at that, the Kemalist state set about radically altering the Turkish that it was imploring its new citizens to speak. The Language Revolution (*dil devrimi*), which began in 1932, usually translated by the less radical 'Language Reform,' proceeded to purge Turkish of its 'foreign' vocabulary. This meant eliminating the countless words of Arabic, Persian, and other origin that the language had depended on for centuries and replacing them with 'ancient' Turkish words, many of which were actually neologisms concocted by members of various commissions and societies established with this end in mind.

The enormity of this task was not lost on Western journalists in Turkey. Groping for similes that would allow their readers to grasp the scope and radical nature of the change, American correspondents painted a picture of what a similar overhaul would mean for the English language. Readers of the *Hartford Courant* in September 1932 learned that

> [a] language conference will be held the end of September under his [i.e., Atatürk's] leadership, to purify the Turkish vocabulary. Ancient Turkish words, unused for

centuries, will be resurrected to replace the Persian and Arabic words which form a large part of the current Turkish speech. The effect will be comparable to the replacing of Latin and Greek derivatives used in English, with the vocabulary of Beowulf, the early Anglo-Saxon epic poem (N.A., 1932).[6]

Two years later the *New York Times* correspondent remarked that

> [a]s great as have been the changes, such as the abolition of the fez and the substitution of Latin for Arabic characters, the purification of the language will affect the Turkish people even more deeply, for they must now forget all except about a tenth of the words they have been accustomed to use in everyday speech and must learn an almost entirely new language. It is as if English-speaking peoples decided to banish from their speech all Norman and Latin words, confining themselves entirely to words of Saxon origin (Kernick, 1934).

Comparing the attempt to strip away the multilingual aspects of Turkish to a similar purging of English was fairly apt. Although the reforms only partly succeeded – many neologisms 'stuck' while others disappeared and much Persian and Arabic vocabulary remains in Turkish today – inevitably the language was greatly diminished, certainly in a quantitative sense but also qualitatively since the ability to draw on a larger vocabulary was reduced. One simple gauge of this is to compare the size of an Ottoman Turkish lexicon with its much more slender modern equivalent.

The impact on Turkish society reached far beyond the realms of lexicography. The "catastrophic success,"to use Lewis' (1999) term for the language reform, was widespread. In the decades that followed, for example, the Arabic vocabulary in Turkish-language newspapers declined from 51 percent in 1931 to 26 percent in 1965 (Lewis, 1999, pp. 158–161). The surname law of 1934 stipulated that all citizens must adopt a surname, not a hitherto common practice, and that the names they chose be of Turkish origin. Place names were similarly Turkified. In Eastern Anatolia the preponderance of Kurdish, Armenian, Arab, and Syriac names was drastically eliminated in favor of Turkish toponyms. In one province in Eastern Anatolia, namely, Mardin, roughly nine out of ten place names were changed (Öktem, 2008, paras. 44–45).[7] The replacements were often unimaginative or generic but served the Republican regime's purpose of marking the territory as part of its drive toward monolingualism.

Conclusion

The monolingual direction pursued by the Turkish Republic has been replicated in many of the other Ottoman successor states. Family and place names

[6] Thanks to Nicole Crisp for this source.

[7] Interestingly, some names have reverted to their original versions, such as the Dersim where in 2019 the municipal council voted to restore that name in place of Tunceli, which had been imposed after Ankara's brutal military conquest in 1938.

have been changed, and not only in Turkey, but many words and surnames retain vital clues to the multilingual past. Numerous Greek, Armenian, and even Arab surnames contain Turkish elements. Examples include the honorific *Hatzi* or Chatzi of countless Greek names that preserves the Turkish *Hacı*, itself derived from Arabic *hajji* [pilgrim], and the patronymic *-oglou* (Turkish -oğlu). Armenian names frequently preserve Turkish elements, such as trades or other attributes, as in Kuyumciyan (from Turkish *kuyumcu*, son of the jeweler or goldsmith). George Deukmejian (1928–2018), the former Governor of the US state of California, owed his surname to the Turkish term for 'founder' or 'metal worker' (*dökmeci, dökümcü*) and his wife Gloria's maiden name was Saatjian, derived from the Turkish 'watchmaker' (*saatçi*). The outrageously murdered Saudi Arabian journalist and dissident Jamal Khashoggi's family name is an Arabized version of the Turkish term *kaşıkçı*, meaning 'spoon maker' or 'spoon seller.'

Such onomastic evidence of intercultural relations is so widespread as to be generally overlooked, but from time to time the repressed multilingual clues jarringly reappear. In 2007 a controversy developed when a journalist published evidence that the iconic presidential residence of Çankaya in Ankara had been Armenian property before it had become Atatürk's official home (Kezer, 2012, p. 169 ff.). In the face of outrage and vehement denial, the Armenian script adorning a fountain on the property mutely testified to the surname of the original Armenian owners and thus raised the awkward question of how the property had changed hands during World War I. Like the elderly Greek man whose dementia revealed the linguistic history and displacement of his youth, the fixed marble fountain silently evoked a repressed past, one when the empire's multilingualism was both unremarkable and relatively uncontroversial.

References

N.A. (1932) "Turkey Must Drop Present Language Is Kemal's Order" *The Hartford Courant*. September 20.

Anscombe, F. (2014) *State, Faith, and Nation in Ottoman and Post-Ottoman Lands*. Cambridge: Cambridge University Press.

Brummett, P. (2000) *Image & Imperialism in the Ottoman Revolutionary Press, 1908–1911*. Albany: SUNY Press.

Cameron, D. (2014 (1995)) *Verbal Hygiene*. London: Routledge.

Cankara, M. (2015) Rethinking Ottoman Cross-Cultural Encounters: Turks and the Armenian Alphabet. *Middle Eastern Studies*, 15, 1, 1–16.

Carey, J. (1983) Technology and Ideology: The Case of the Telegraph. *Prospects*, *8*, 303–325.

Duchêne, A. & P. Humbert. (2018) Surveying Languages: The Art of Governing Speakers with Numbers. *International Journal of the Sociology of Language*, 252, 1–20.

Duchêne, A., Humbert, P., & R. Coray (2018) How to Ask Questions on Language? Ideological Struggles in the Making of State Survey. *International Journal of the Sociology of Language*, 252, 45–72.
Ertürk, N. (2011) *Grammatology and Literary Modernity in Turkey*. Oxford: Oxford University Press.
Fortna, B. (2008) The Reign of Abdülhamid II. In Kasaba, R. (ed.) *The Cambridge History of Turkey: Vol. 4: Turkey in the Modern World.* Cambridge: Cambridge University Press, pp. 38–61.
(2011) *Learning to Read in the Late Ottoman Empire and the Early Turkish Republic*. London: Palgrave Macmillan.
Fuhrmann, M. (2020) *Port Cities in the Eastern Mediterranean: Urban Culture in the Late Ottoman Empire*. Cambridge: Cambridge University Press.
Hanioğlu, S. (2008) *A Brief History of the Late Ottoman Empire*. Princeton: Princeton University Press.
Kahane, H., Tietze, R. & A. Tietze (1958). *The Lingua Franca in the Levant: Turkish Nautical terms of Italian and Greek origin.* Urbana: University of Illinois Press.
Kernick, J. (1934). Turks are Hunting for Family Names. *New York Times*, December 2.
Kezer, Z. (2012) Of Forgotten People and Forgotten Places: Nation-Building and the Dismantling of Ankara's Non-Muslim Landscapes. In D. Fairchild Ruggles (ed.) *On Location: Heritage Cities and Sites*. New York: Springer, pp. 169–191.
Kuzuoğlu, U. (2020) Telegraphy, Typography, and the Alphabet: The Origins of Alphabet Revolutions in the Russo-Ottoman Space. *International Journal of Middle East Studies*, 52, 413–431.
Levi, M. (2020) How not to Translate: Cultural Authenticity and Translatability. In Recaizade Mahmut Ekrem's *Araba Sevdası* and Ahmet Midhat Efrendi's *Felatun Bey ile Rakım Efendi*. In Ringer, M. & E. Charrière (eds.) *Ottoman Culture and the Project of Modernity: Reform and Translation in the Tanzimat Novel.* London: I B Tauris, pp. 37–52.
Lewis, G. (1999) *The Turkish Language Reform: A Catastrophic Success*. Oxford: Oxford University Press.
Mardin, Ş. (1974) Super Westernization in Urban Life in the Ottoman Empire in the Last Quarter of the Nineteenth Century. In Benedict, P., Tümertekin, E., & F. Mansur (eds.) *Turkey: Geographical and Social Perspectives*. Leiden: Brill, pp. 403–442.
Öktem, K. (2008) The Nation's Imprint: Demographic Engineering and the Change of Toponymes in Republican Turkey. *European Journal of Turkish Studies*, 7.
Pelekani, C. (2014) Turkish Loanwords in Russian Language. *Tehlikede Diller Dergisi/ Journal of Endangered Languages*, Winter https://dergipark.org.tr/en/download/article-file/305218
Şeni, N. (1995) Fashion and Women's Clothing. In Tekeli, S. (ed.) *Women in Modern Turkish Society: A Reader*. London: Zed Books, pp. 25–45.
Seviner, Z. (2020) Thinking in French, Writing in Persian: Aesthetics, Intelligibility and the Literary Turkish of the 1890s. In Ringer, M. & E. Charrière (eds.) *Ottoman Culture and the Project of Modernity: Reform and Translation in the Tanzimat Novel*. London: I B Tauris, pp. 19–36.
Strauss, J. (1995a) The Millets and the Ottoman Language: The Contribution of Ottoman Greeks to Ottoman Letters (19th–20th Centuries). *Die Welt des Islams*, 35, 2, 189–249.

(1995b) Diglossie dans le domaine ottoman. Évolution et péripéties d'une situation linguistique [Diglossia in the Ottoman realms. The evolution and vicissitudes of a linguistic situation]. *Revue du Monde Musulman et de la Méditerranée*, 75–76, 221–255.

(2003) Who Read What in the Ottoman Empire (19th–20th Centuries)? *Middle Eastern Literatures*, 6, 1, 39–76.

(2011) Linguistic Diversity and Everyday Life in the Ottoman Cities of the Eastern Mediterranean and the Balkans Late 19th–early 20th Century. *The History of the Family*, 16, 126–141.

(2016) Language and Power in the Late Ottoman Empire. In Murphey, R. (ed.) *Imperial Lineages in the Eastern Mediterranean: Recording the Imprint of Roman, Byzantine and Ottoman Rule*. London: Routledge, pp. 115–142.

Vartan Pasha (1991 (1851)) *Akabi Hikayesi: İlk Türkçe Roman* [The Story of Akabi: The First Turkish Novel]. Istanbul: Eren Yayıncılık.

12 "Multilingualism Is Now a Must": Discourses on Languages and International Cooperation at the Council of Europe

Zorana Sokolovska

The purpose of this chapter is to examine the discourses of multilingualism in the Council of Europe, one of several institutions that have gained visibility in the 1990s as a platform for *inter*-national cooperation (Muehlmann & Duchêne, 2007). In and of itself, the topic isn't new – the geopolitics of languages in Europe has been a major subject of debates at international conferences and multistate institutions since World War I (Duchêne, 2008; Meillet, 1918; Moret, 2011). And when the Council of Europe was established in 1949 to advance (western) European unity and to promote democracy, the rule of law and human rights, language learning, teaching, and use have been regularly debated by its main bodies, the Committee of Ministers and the Parliamentary Assembly (Sokolovska, 2021).

In the 1990s, as geopolitical conditions had changed and more countries joined in, the Council of Europe engaged in a new set of language debates that led to the development of influential guidelines, recommendations, and reference frameworks for language testing, education, and policy.[1] To put it in other words, argues Pujolar (2007a), "international law is gradually incorporating language policy issues in ways that introduce limitations to state sovereignty" (p. 77). This is not to say that inequalities between language groups are finally being solved. "It just means," continues Pujolar (2007a), "that it is increasingly difficult for nation-states and for national elites to draw on the old discourses on language to maintain their legitimacy, and that this forces them to develop new ideological frameworks, strategies and tactics to maintain their dominant position" (pp. 77–78). Among these developments are a redefinition of the functions and values assigned to languages and the production of "new

I would like to thank Aneta Pavlenko, Pia Lane, and Alexandre Duchêne, the anonymous peer-reviewers, and Felix Meyenhofer for their feedback on the previous versions of this chapter. Many thanks to Mary Carozza for editing this chapter.

[1] This particularly pertains to the *Common European Framework of Reference for Languages: Learning, Teaching, Assessment*, the *European Charter for Regional or Minority Languages*, and the 1998 recommendation of the Committee of Ministers concerning modern languages. For other documents, see https://www.coe.int/en/web/language-policy/home (accessed October 5, 2021).

legitimizing discourses that make sense in the context of globalisation" (Duchêne & Heller, 2007, p. 10), including a discursive shift from the emphasis on monolingualism toward celebrations of linguistic diversity. The purpose of this chapter is to analyze language discourses mobilized by nation-states in a debate that took place in the Parliamentary Assembly of the Council of Europe in 2001, during the celebration of the European Year of Languages, which, more than ever, put languages at the center of the Council's political agenda.

I will begin by introducing the Council of Europe as a platform for international cooperation, where languages are viewed as an essential aspect of partnerships and collaboration. Then, I will examine how language categories are used by representatives of the Council's member states to form *language power blocs*, that is, alliances of nation-states that pursue their linguistic and cultural agendas on the international political scene (Pujolar, 2007a). I will conclude with a critical reflection on the novelty of 'multilingualism' as an acceptable and desired discourse and practice, mobilized in the name of international cooperation, and at the same time deeply anchored in the ideologies of the nation-state.

12.1 The Council of Europe: A Platform for International Cooperation

Located in Strasbourg, France, the Council of Europe is a European institution that was founded in the aftermath of World War II, the time period that saw the establishment of other intergovernmental institutions whose missions were primarily oriented toward military partnerships (e.g., NATO or the North Atlantic Alliance) and economic cooperation (e.g., the European Coal and Steel Community, the predecessor of the European Union). In this institutional landscape, the Council of Europe distinguished itself by focusing on improving international cooperation on the basis of shared humanist values and principles. Article 1 of the Statute of the Council of Europe states:

a) The aim of the Council of Europe is to achieve a greater unity between its members for the purpose of safeguarding and realising the ideals and principles which are their common heritage and facilitating their economic and social progress.
b) This aim shall be pursued through the organs of the Council by discussion of questions of common concern and by agreements and common action in economic, social, cultural, scientific, legal and administrative matters and in the maintenance and further realisation of human rights and fundamental freedoms.[2]

[2] Council of Europe. *Statute of the Council of Europe*, May 5, 1949. https://www.coe.int/en/web/conventions/full-list/-/conventions/rms/0900001680935bd0?module=treaty-detail&treatynum=001 (accessed July 20, 2021).

The Council of Europe was founded on May 5, 1949, and is composed of the Committee of Ministers, a decision-making organ, and the Parliamentary Assembly, a consultative and deliberative body. The Parliamentary Assembly of the Council of Europe consists of individual representatives from each member state. The number of these representatives and consequently of votes is determined by the size of the country. The Parliamentary Assembly formulates recommendations that form the basis for decisions taken by the Committee of Ministers and transmitted to member states in the form of recommendations or conventions. The outcome of the Parliamentary Assembly's discussions thus paves the way for the elaboration of the Council of Europe's official discourse on languages.

Until 1989, the geographical range of the Council was limited to twenty-three Western European countries. After the fall of the Iron Curtain, between 1989 and 2007, twenty-four Central and Eastern European nations joined the Council, doubling the number of member states. At the time, it was generally believed that the Council of Europe was the most suitable European organization to welcome the Central and Eastern European states, working on transformation into Western-style democracies under precarious economic conditions that prevented them from quickly joining the European Union (Bitsch, 2001). In this context, the Council of Europe positioned itself as a "school of democracy" (Wassenberg, 2012, p. 222) and gained new visibility, popularity, and legitimacy as a platform for pan-European political cooperation. Language teaching and learning, in this context, acquired new importance as a means to international communication and successful collaboration.

12.2 Improving Cooperation through Language Teaching and Learning

Since the 1950s, language teaching has been the subject of Council debates, aimed at improving cooperation and creating stability by focusing not on *differences* between Western European member states but on what they have in common. In the spirit of this approach, languages were constructed as a shared European heritage and linguistic plurality conceived not as an obstacle to communication but as a common good to be promoted and protected.

By 2001, the Committee of Ministers and the Parliamentary Assembly had issued several recommendations on teaching and learning languages.[3] The Council also created two important international treaties for managing languages: the *European Cultural Convention* (1954) and the *European Charter for Regional or Minority Languages* (1992). Another major

[3] Council of Europe. *Language Policy – official texts*. https://www.coe.int/en/web/language-policy/official-texts (accessed July 10, 2021).

achievement was the *Common European Framework of Reference for Languages: Learning, Teaching, Assessment* (CEFRL), the final version of which was published in 2001. The document offered influential definitions of 'plurilingualism' and 'multilingualism' and provided a basis for developing language courses, curriculum guidelines, examinations and textbooks and determining levels of foreign language proficiency (from A1 to C2).

The publication of the CEFRL was one of the highlights of the European Year of Languages, organized jointly by the Council of Europe and the European Union in 2001. The "European Year" is the name of an annual international campaign aiming "to raise awareness of certain topics, encourage debate and change attitudes."[4] The Year of Languages was created to celebrate languages, promote linguistic diversity in Europe, and encourage people to learn several languages. The fact that 'European' modifies the 'year' and not 'languages' draws attention to the fact that celebrations include all languages spoken in Europe, not only the official languages of European nation-states (Sokolovska, 2016).

12.3 The 2001 Debate: A Discursive Space and a Multilingual Moment

The debate analyzed here was held during the European Year of Languages and took place on September 28, 2001, during the 32nd sitting of the Parliamentary Assembly.[5] At the heart of the debate was the six-page report of the Committee on Culture, Science and Education (Doc. 9194, September 10, 2001, n.p.), summarized as follows:

> European Year of Languages 2001 is based on the principle that each language is unique, that all languages are equally valid as modes of expression for those who use them, and that this rich worldwide linguistic heritage has to be preserved.
>
> Developing plurilingualism, which is necessary in order to respond to changes in Europe, is one of the Year's core objectives. Throughout life, each person can, or should be able to, acquire the ability to communicate in several languages, if not master them. In order to provide a valued record of this ability, the Council of Europe has devised a major instrument, the European Language Portfolio.
>
> The report also proposes that language policies be put in place, with the aim above all of encouraging cultural and linguistic diversity and promoting social and interethnic cohesion, by protecting minority languages, encouraging people to learn the languages of neighbours and neighbouring cultures and protecting cultural works in European languages in the context of globalisation.[6]

[4] European Union. European Years. https://europa.eu/european-union/about-eu/european-years_en (accessed July 10, 2021).

[5] Parliamentary Assembly, 2001, ordinary session official report, thirty-second sitting, September 28, 2001, pp. 1162–1170. The document is available in the Archives of the Council of Europe.

[6] Parliamentary Assembly, 2001. European Year of Languages – report. Doc. 9194. The report also contains a draft recommendation that, if needed, can be amended and voted on during the debate.

The report was presented by the Spanish parliamentarian, Lluís Maria de Puig, on behalf of the Committee on Culture, Science and Education. The presentation was followed by a debate, where ten parliamentarians spoke. Then, the draft recommendation contained in the report was adopted unanimously by the twenty-nine members present.[7]

The Parliamentary Assembly where the debate was held can be defined as a historically situated discursive space (Duchêne, 2008) where language ideologies – defined here as socially and culturally conditioned ideas and beliefs on languages, their functions, and values (Blommaert, 2005; Woolard & Schieffelin, 1994) – are discussed, negotiated, and appropriated by representatives of member states. Language ideologies are constructed and transmitted by means of discourse. Consequently, within a given debate, discourse becomes "a crucial symbolic resource onto which people project their interests, around which they can construct alliances, on and through which they exercise power" (Blommaert, 1999, p. 5). Discourse is also the locus of *categorization*, an ideological process constructed in and by discourse, the results of which are, in our case, language categories. Both language ideologies and language categories are resources used by the representatives of nation-states to mobilize in order to create language power blocs, understood here as tactical (re)positionings of nation-states by means of discourse, based on representatives' shared ideas and beliefs on languages, their value and purpose. At the same time, the representatives' discourses, and the debate's outcome (i.e. the adoption of the recommendation) shape the Parliamentary Assembly's official discourse on languages.

The debate also functions as a *multilingual moment*, that is, a moment in the social history in which a specific metalinguistic commentary on language ideas and practices is developed (Critten & Dutton, 2021, pp. 12–13). In line with this thinking, the 2001 debate is a multilingual moment in which the mobilization of languages as a resource for political cooperation attained particular salience in the post-1989 context (for other multilingual moments in the history of the Council of Europe, see Sokolovska, 2021). It is also worth mentioning that – contrary to the European Union practice of internal multilingualism, which member states view as a symbol of political equality (Gazzola, 2004) – the Council of Europe has designated two official languages, French and English, understood as an apolitical means of communication (Garrido Sardà & Sokolovska, 2022). The debate on languages is thus a locus for instrumentalizing and politicizing languages by the participating nation-states.

[7] Parliamentary Assembly, 2001. Recommendation 1539. https://pace.coe.int/en/files/16954/html (accessed July 20, 2021).

The discourse analysis in this chapter is based on a critical approach that emphasizes the connection between discourse and social structure and suggests that social, political, cultural, *and* historical circumstances that condition the discourse production need to be treated as context (Blommaert, 2005). More specifically, this analysis considers the "layers of historicity" (Blommaert, 2005, p. 130) in which a specific discourse is embedded and to which it refers. In what follows, I will take a critical look at the 2001 debate and conceptions of languages and multilingualism constructed and instrumentalized within it. Without claiming to be exhaustive, I will focus on three intertwined layers of context in which these discourses were embedded: the social history of Europe, the institutional history of the Council of Europe, and the history of language debates at the Council of Europe.

12.4 The 2001 Debate: Language Power Blocs and Hierarchies

12.4.1 Discourses Constructing Languages as Unique and Equally Valid

As mentioned earlier, the 2001 debate took place during the European Year of Languages. Conceived as a celebration of languages, the event laid the groundwork for the general discourse on the importance of languages conducted by the ten parliamentarians who took the floor. To strengthen their arguments, some of the parliamentarians aligned their statements with ideologies of language equality and language uniqueness:

(1) Lluís Maria DE PUIG (Spain) (interpreted from French by the Council interpreters[8]): …The report seeks to make one even more aware of the importance of languages. That is why it states from the outset that each language is of unique value. Language is, of course, above all a means of communication, but it is also a very important part of culture…

Language is also an element of our identities, and we are all attached to our own languages. As a classical author wrote, "my home country is my language." Language is our link with reality, with society, with a land and with a culture. (PA Official report, September 28, 2001, p. 1162)

(2) Josef JAŘAB (Czech Republic): Indeed, the need to recognise the importance of all languages as a means of communication, manifestations of

[8] The official report was published in the Council's official languages, French and English. Each linguistic version counts as an official one. In this chapter, I analyzed the English version of the official report. The addresses that were not made in English were interpreted either from French (official simultaneous interpretation) or from another language (interpretation arranged by the speaker in one of the official languages, then simultaneously interpreted into the other official language).

peoples' cultural identities and differences, authentic proofs and reservoirs of cultural diversity and wealth, not just in Europe but on the whole planet, has been emphasised. That is healthy, especially in view of the strong globalising forces that are active in the world today. (PA Official report, September 28, 2001, p. 1164)

(3) Rory KIELY (Ireland): . . . Languages open doors. The European Year of Languages 2001 is based on the principle that each language is unique and equally valid as a mode of expression. Developing plurilingualism is a necessity if we are to respond to change in Europe. (PA Official report, September 28, 2001, p. 1166)

(4) Anatoliy RAKHANSKY (Ukraine) (interpreted from a language other than French): Every language was important and politicians should not use languages for political ends. The recent film festival in Yalta, where hundreds of films were shown in many languages, had illustrated the need to respect languages from all countries, no matter what their size. (PA Official report, September 28, 2001, p. 1169)

The four parliamentarians cited here refer to the principle found in the report summary and in the report itself, namely "that each language is unique, that all languages are equally valid as modes of expression for those who use them, and that this rich worldwide linguistic heritage has to be preserved" (Doc. 9194, September 10, 2001, n.p.). Several observations can be made regarding the principle that organizes their discourse on languages. Comparing and declaring languages as (un)equal implies that languages are considered as countable objects, and thus nameable, internally homogenous and distinguishable from each other (Gal, 2006). This set of features, as Gal (2006, p. 14) points out, does not refer to "language" as the capacity to speak, but as a "European invention" whose roots date back to the Enlightenment and the Romantic era that followed. Languages, therefore, are understood as the authentic expression of the distinct spirit of a particular group, such as a nation, but also as universal, anonymous voices "that can be used equally by everyone precisely because they belong to no-one-in-particular. They are positioned as universally open and available to all in a society" (Woolard, 2008, p. 306).

This understanding of languages also has a political aspect, related to an imagined homogeneity in a nation, state, language, and culture, a paradigm that played a central role in the construction of modern national identities (Pujolar 2007a). It appears, therefore, that ideologies of language equality and language uniqueness draw on essentialist conceptions of language, and function as a proxy for nation-states in international debates. In other words, alluding to the equality and uniqueness among languages is a way of indicating the (desired) political equality among member states. It is also a means for the nation-states' strategical (re)positioning around shared beliefs on the (equal and unique) value and role of languages.

At the time of the debate, forty-three countries were members of the Council of Europe, half of which, as noted earlier, joined the organization in order to expedite their membership in the European Union. However, not all forty-three member states were equal in terms of size, demographics, economic development, and political influence, and this inequality could negatively affect the terms and prospects of European cooperation. The conception of languages as a proxy for nation-states is therefore mobilized to illustrate and even try to influence the language and power distribution among the member states, as seen in the address to the Assembly given by the Lithuanian representative:

(5) Sigita BURBIENE (Lithuania): It is said that language skills are a critical factor in one's personal career. Those skills are usually in English, French, German, Russian and Italian, the languages of big nations, but what about Bulgarian, Hungarian, Estonian or Lithuanian? Foreign investors working in Lithuania do not even try to learn Lithuanian. Why would they? They speak English.

Democratic Europe pays a great deal of attention to the problem of minority languages, and that is good. However, we must ask, what are the languages of minorities? When we look at nation-states, everything is clear, but if we take a closer look at smaller nations in united Europe, it is less so. Not many of us are given the opportunity to address this audience in our native language and, of course, that has an effect on our speeches, which are not as expressive as they should be. (PA Official report, September 28, 2001, p. 1165)

The Lithuanian representative clearly articulates the link between languages and political entities, which she refers to as "big nations" and "smaller nations" and draws attention to the unequal treatment of languages with respect to the size of the nations in question: the bigger the country, the greater the chance that its (official) language will be taught, learned, and thus used. Moreover, her term "big nations" refers not only to a country's geographical area but also to its political weight in Europe, even in the world. Her address, therefore, draws attention to the hierarchy where languages of the "big nations" supersede those of "smaller nations," thus undermining the presumed equality among languages of the member states.

We can also see her address as a strategy employed to influence, even strengthen, the status of the Lithuanian language on the international arena. Indeed, although in the post-Soviet period Lithuania was successful in implementing the shift toward the titular language and in spreading its use to all areas of public life, the rapid rise of English raised concerns about the threat to the development of national identity (Pavlenko, 2008). One can also argue that the representative positions herself as a spokeswoman for the "smaller nations" by using the first-person plural forms ("we," "us," "our") and therefore as a spokeswoman for nation-states that share the same concerns regarding the rising use of English in their respective countries, on the international and national job market, and even at the Council of Europe.

Interestingly, the Lithuanian representative situates the languages of 'smaller nations,' such as Lithuanian, among the 'languages of minorities,' thereby mobilizing a defined concept and language category in a specific way.

12.4.2 Language Categories and Ideologies

Although the category 'minority languages' was invoked in almost all of the parliamentarian addresses, the actual referent varied.[9] While Burbiene used it to denote languages of 'smaller nations,' like her own Lithuania, the Irish representative used it to refer to Irish, one of the official languages of the country he represents:

(6) Rory KIELY (Ireland): There are many minority languages. Everyone should have the right to speak their mother tongue and to learn languages of their choice... In the past in times of tyranny, there were countries where it was made almost impossible for the indigenous population who wanted to use or speak their mother tongue or minority language to do so. Despite that, owing to dedication and the utmost perseverance, those mother tongues and minority languages have survived. The mother tongue in my country is the Irish language or Gaelic. However, it is a minority language because English has become the spoken language. (PA Official report, September 28, 2001, p. 1167)

When referring to Irish in his address, Kiely places the term 'minority language' in close proximity to 'mother tongue,' thus constructing them as quasi-synonyms. Following Pennycook's (2002) argument that the notion of the mother tongue should be understood as a "strategically essentialist (and) a politically important argument" (p. 24) that reproduces fixed categories of languages and identities, we can say that the Irish representative uses the term 'mother tongue' in order to mark the difference in symbolic status between Irish (mother tongue but minority language) and, English (not-a-mother-tongue and majority language), and in doing so, to attest to the existence, even the vitality, of Irish. De Puig's use of the term 'minority language' goes in the same direction:

[9] *The European Charter for Regional or Minority Languages* (1992) created a new legal framework for defining and managing regional or minority languages in Europe. The category 'regional or minority languages' was not used as such in the 2001 debate.

(7) Lluís Maria DE PUIG (Spain) (interpreted from French by the Council interpreters): During our proceedings we have said a great deal about major languages. I would like to conclude with a few words in my mother tongue, a minority language. [*Speaking in Catalan*] Thank you. (PA Official report, September 28, 2001, p. 1168)

The Spanish representative employs the term 'minority language' in order to refer to Catalan, the latter being his mother tongue, as he indicates twice during the debate. Catalan is one of the four co-official languages of Spain, used in some regions of Spain, such as Catalonia, and is widely seen as a component of Catalan national identity, which gives rise to linguistic and political tensions (Pujolar, 2007b). The fact that the Irish, Spanish, and Lithuanian representatives use the category 'minority language' to denote the official – or one of the official – languages of a country whose status is inferior compared to official languages of more powerful nations opens the door for using the category to formulate shared concerns and demands regarding the recognition of their respective languages. Furthermore, it supports the argument that a group of nation-states can form a language power bloc against the domination of English (5, 6) or other "major language" (7), because this language domination is believed to threaten the future of other languages.

This positioning is strengthened through another conception of 'minority languages,' which some parliamentarians formulate as a subcategory of 'endangered languages':

(8) Lluís Maria DE PUIG (Spain) (interpreted from French by the Council interpreters): An effort must therefore be made to save this linguistic diversity and these languages, in particular those already regarded as endangered, which we refer to as minority, less-widespread or regional languages. (PA Official report, September 28, 2001, p. 1163)

(9) José CESÁRIO (Portugal) (interpreted from a language other than French): For many centuries, Portugal had asserted itself as a nation-state, and language had been an important part of this. There were many languages in the world and many were minority languages. They all deserved to have a future and to be passed on to future generations. (PA Official report, September 28, 2001, p. 1168)

In these two addresses, 'minority languages' is a category used to refer to a group of languages whose future is uncertain, as both they and, by extension, language diversity are endangered. Although the precise danger faced is not specified, it can be presumed to be the majority language on a given territory, whose superior status accords greater privileges to its speakers. Thus, in Ireland, English poses a threat to Irish and in Spain, Spanish poses a threat to Catalan.

The discourse on language endangerment also takes other shapes. For instance, the Armenian representative makes the case for protection of languages on a larger territorial scale, the Caucasus region, divided between Russia, Armenia, Georgia, and Azerbaijan:

(10) Ashot GALOYAN (Armenia): The Caucasus, the most complex region in the world, the cradle of civilisation, represents the southern flank of the European community. The multiplicity of languages and cultures in the region enables the states involved to demonstrate their political will, and to continue to implement cultural and language policies intended to protect all languages spoken in their territories from the risk of extinction. (PA Official report, September 28, 2001, p. 1167)

In turn, the Lithuanian representative situates the danger on the level of the 'big nations' that threaten the existence of languages, such as Bulgarian, Hungarian, Estonian, or Lithuanian, spoken by 'smaller nations.' She therefore seeks alliances with other representatives of such states:

(11) Sigita BURBIENE (Lithuania): As *you know*, Latin is also studied even though no one uses it in everyday life and it is a dead language. *None of you* wants your language to be studied in universities as Latin is now. [my emphasis] (PA Official report, September 28, 2001, p. 1165)

Although it is unlikely that languages of small nations will disappear as long as they are officially used in the territories of those nations, Burbiene uses the comparison to Latin in order to give a tangible argument and to raise alarm – without, however, taking into account the political and social history of Latin that led to its status as a 'dead language.'

Together, these arguments suggest that if a language is endangered or runs the risk of extinction, it is due to the existence of another language whose official status and prestige are more widely recognized. Hence, the issue is not purely linguistic in nature. In their study on discourses of endangerment, Duchêne and Heller (2007) argue that "discourses of language endangerment are discourses about some broader sense of endangerment, about some threat from outside (from some Other) to the social order" (p. 4). Drawing on this statement, as well as on the assumption that languages function as a proxy for nation-states, I suggest that protecting languages from extinction is a way of protecting the existing social and political order in Europe by lending greater visibility to smaller nations and to the new nation-states established after 1989. The category of 'endangered languages' and its underlying ideologies allow these nation-states to form a language power bloc around shared interests in obtaining linguistic and political recognition.

Another language category that united nation-states is 'languages of the neighbors.' Several parliamentarians voiced their support for teaching and learning the languages of neighboring countries:

(12) Ivan POPESCU (Ukraine) (interpreted from a language other than French): The majority should also be encouraged to speak minority languages. In north Tyrol the population spoke German although the region was in Italy. In south Tyrol the population should speak Italian. Speaking different languages enhanced mutual understanding. (PA Official report, September 28, 2001, p. 1163)

(13) Josef JAŘAB (Czech Republic): . . .we should fully grasp the potential of multilingualism and of languages, our own, our neighbours, or those of faraway countries, and use it in our endeavours towards mutual understanding, meaningful coexistence and mutual cultural, social and human enrichment. (PA Official report, September 28, 2001, p. 1164)

(14) Sigita BURBIENE (Lithuania): I have another proposal for colleagues. It echoes a point made by Mr Popescu. We have discussed many times various forms of transborder co-operation, so perhaps we should try to promote the languages of our neighbours in schools, at least in those close to our national borders, even if we have no minorities speaking those languages. Russians and Estonians could learn each other's language, as could the Danish and the Germans, the Armenians and the Azeris, and in my own case the Lithuanians and the Latvians. Such a practice could promote better understanding and neighbourliness between nations. (PA Official report, September 28, 2001, p. 1165)

The argument underlying the addresses given by Popescu and Burbiene is that promotion of the languages of neighboring countries is a linguistic trade-off: One country will promote a neighboring country's languages if the other country reciprocates. Enhancing 'neighborliness' through language teaching instrumentalizes languages as tools for transborder politics, especially as the neighboring countries can be either immediate allies or enemies in geopolitical conflicts.

12.4.3 'Multilingualism' as a Terrain for Staking Out Internationally Shared Interests

Despite acknowledging the real inequalities between languages, no parliamentarian took a stance against the teaching, learning, and use of *several* languages during the 2001 debate. On the contrary, some of the parliamentarians explicitly supported multilingual education:

(15) Lluís Maria DE PUIG (Spain) (interpreted from French by the Council interpreters): I would add that learning several languages is not very

difficult. Education specialists know that children have a great capacity for learning. It is not exceptional for an 18-year-old student to have a working knowledge of four or five languages. This is quite possible from an educational standpoint. (PA Official report, September 28, 2001, p. 1163)

(16) Ivan POPESCU (Ukraine) (interpreted from a language other than French): Encouragement of the study of several languages had the potential to be very significant in helping to avoid conflict. (PA Official report, September 28, 2001, p. 1163)

(17) Rory KIELY (Ireland): It is therefore essential that each person should acquire the ability to communicate in, if not to master, several languages. A focus on those aims should be a priority in school curricula, but older people should also aim to acquire the ability to speak several languages... I congratulate the Council of Europe and the European Union on organising the European Year of Languages 2001, which I trust will develop proper awareness and highlight the value of linguistic diversity and the importance of offering all citizens the opportunity to develop at least a degree of competence in several languages. (PA Official report, September 28, 2001, p. 1166)

Developing skills in several languages is encapsulated in the term 'plurilingualism,' defined in the report "as a certain ability to communicate in several languages, and not necessarily as perfect mastery of them" (Doc. 9194, September 10, 2001, n.p.). This definition draws on the Common European Framework of Reference for Languages,[10] which defines 'plurilingualism' as an individual competence and 'multilingualism' as a societal phenomenon. Despite the formal distinction, however, both terms are used interchangeably in the debate and are anchored in the discourse celebrating language diversity, characteristic for the European Year of Languages. Examples of this discourse in the debate include the statements that "multilingualism is now a must" as well as "a necessity and a source of advantages" (de Puig, Spain, pp. 1163, 1168); that "(d)eveloping plurilingualism is a necessity if we are to respond to change in Europe" (Kiely, Ireland, p. 1166); and that "we should fully grasp the potential of multilingualism and of languages, our own, our neighbours, or those of faraway countries, and use it in our endeavours towards mutual understanding, meaningful coexistence and mutual cultural, social and human enrichment" (Jařab, Czech Republic, p. 1164).

The general celebratory discourse on multilingualism, including the excerpts cited here, suggests that, within the debate, 'multilingualism/plurilingualism' is understood as a symbolic resource onto which nation-states

[10] Council of Europe. 2001. *CEFR*. https://rm.coe.int/1680459f97 (accessed July 27, 2021).

project their interests and around which they construct alliances. Here, it is useful to draw on Muehlmann's (2007) study of environmental and linguistic discourses, in which she discusses the notion of diversity as "a new terrain on which the representation of an apparently globalized, common interest is staked out," and argues that this is achieved "by erasing [the] contestations, contradictions, and negotiations that 'diversity' encompasses" (p. 23). Following this line of argument, I suggest that representatives in the Parliamentary Assembly view multilingualism as a win-win solution that permits all languages – regardless of their perceived status and place in the European language hierarchy (for instance, minority, endangered, less common) – to be taken into consideration in the Council's promotional campaign for language teaching and learning. The terms 'multilingualism' and 'plurilingualism' thus allow all languages to have, at least in theory, equal chances of being learned, taught, and used.

In addition, building on the assumption that languages function as a proxy for nation-states, multilingualism/plurilingualism can be seen as a strategy for all member states in the Council of Europe to be positioned, at least theoretically, as equal members and legitimate political voices on the international political scene. But because the discourse on multilingualism fails to address language hierarchy issues, it reproduces them under the illusion of equality. These hierarchies are then materialized in the recommendations produced by the Council of Europe and used in the development of national language policies.

Conclusion

In this chapter, I have examined language categories and ideologies mobilized in addresses made by nation-state representatives in the Council of Europe's Parliamentary Assembly. The results of the analysis suggest that negotiations involving the place of languages in the European curricula function as a proxy for negotiating the status and legitimacy of a nation-state on the international level. It also shows that language can serve as a resource for forming language power blocs and international alliances on the European political scene, which underwent a considerable period of expansion after 1989. Consequently, the language debate serves as a terrain for mediating and managing Europe as a political and a geographical entity.

The analysis of the 2001 debate also identifies a critical tension. While the purpose of the European Year of Languages is to celebrate linguistic plurality, the representatives consistently drew attention to the fact that not all European languages are equal, that is, not all languages are viewed and valorized in the same way on the job market, in school, and in the public sphere. The categories of 'minority language,' 'mother tongue,' 'endangered languages,' and 'languages of neighbours,' employed by the parliamentarians, point to the existence of a language, and by implication, nation-state hierarchy.

By exposing these tensions and inconsistencies, this chapter lays the foundation for further discussion of the role of multilingualism in post-1989 Europe. For over three decades now, the discourse on multilingualism of the Council of Europe has been widely touted as innovative and forward-looking, and the recommendations of the Council's Committee of Ministers and Parliamentary Assembly have had a considerable impact on the development of national language education policies. However, as several chapters in this volume show, multilingualism was not invented at the end of the twentieth century and bilingual education could be pushed back as far as the Old Babylonian scribal program in 2000–1600 BC (see Pavlenko's introduction to this volume). The history of language debates in the Council of Europe is only a brief episode in the millennia-long history of defining and managing multilingual practices, and it is marked by the transformation in geopolitical interests and creation of new institutional spaces for discussing language politics across Europe.

Moreover, within the Council of Europe, the promotion of plurilingual competence within the member states serves as a compromise that enables European nation-states, irrespective of size or political weight, to maintain an image of linguistic and political equality and to remain internationally visible. In this context, new values and meanings are assigned to old phenomena and practices, such as individual multilingualism, societal multilingualism, and the teaching and learning of multiple languages. Consequently, even within the context of the twenty-first-century internationalization and despite the Council's renewed emphasis on language teaching and learning, nationalist ideologies challenging and reproducing existing hierarchies remain the driving force in the language debates.

References

Bitsch, M-T. (2001) *Histoire de la construction européenne de 1945 à nos jours* [History of the construction of Europe from 1945 to the present day]. Brussels: Edition Complexe.

Blommaert, J. (1999) The debate is open. In Blommaert, J. (ed.) *Language ideological debates.* Berlin: Mouton de Gruyter, pp. 1–38.

(2005) *Discourse. A critical introduction.* New York/Cambridge: Cambridge University Press.

Critten, R. & E. Dutton (2021) Medieval English Multilingualisms. *Language Learning*, 71, 12–38.

Duchêne, A. (2008) *Ideologies across nations. The construction of linguistic minorities at the United Nations*. Berlin/New York: Mouton de Gruyter.

Duchêne, A. & M. Heller (2007) *Discourses of Endangerment: Ideology and Interest in the Defence of Languages*. London: Continuum.

Gal, S. (2006) Migration, minorities and multilingualism: Language ideologies in Europe. In Mar-Molinero, C. & P Stevenson (eds.) *Language Ideologies, Policies and Practices.* London: Palgrave Macmillan, pp. 13–27.

Garrido Sardà, M. & Z. Sokolovska (2022) Regard historique sur les régimes multilingues de deux organisations internationales: le Conseil de l'Europe et le Comité international de la Croix-Rouge [A historical perspective on the multilingual regimes of two international organisations: The Council of Europe and the International Committee of the Red Cross]. *Mots. Les langages du politique*, 128, 27–44.

Gazzola, M. (2004) *Language policy and linguistic justice in the European Union: The socio-economic effects of multilingualism. SSRN Scholarly Paper*. Rochester, NY: Social Science Research Network.

Meillet, A. (1918) *Les langues dans l'Europe nouvelle* [Languages in the new Europe]. Paris: Payot.

Moret, S. (2011) Antoine Meillet et le futur des empires après la Première guerre mondiale [Antoine Meillet and the future of empires after the First World War]. *Langages*, 182, 2, 11–24.

Muehlmann, S. (2007) Defending diversity: Staking out a common global interest? In Duchêne, A. & M. Heller (eds.) *Discourses of endangerment: ideology and interest in the defence of languages*. New York: Continuum, pp. 14–34.

Muehlmann, S. & A. Duchêne (2007) Beyond the nation-state: international agencies as new sites of discourses on bilingualism. In M. Heller (ed.) *Bilingualism: a social approach*. Basingstoke: Palgrave Macmillan, pp. 96–110.

Pavlenko, A. (2008) Multilingualism in post-Soviet countries: Language revival, language removal, and sociolinguistic theory. *International Journal of Bilingual Education and Bilingualism*, 11, 3–4, 275–314.

Pennycook, A. (2002) Mother tongues, governmentality, and protectionism. *International Journal of the Sociology of Language*, 154, 11–28.

Pujolar, J. (2007a) Bilingualism and the nation-state in the post-national era. In Heller, M. (ed.) *Bilingualism: a social approach*. Basingstoke: Palgrave Macmillan, pp. 71–95.

(2007b) The future of Catalan: language endangerment and nationalist discourses in Catalonia. In Duchêne, A. & M. Heller (eds.) *Discourses of endangerment: interest and ideology in the defense of languages*. London: Continuum, pp. 121–148.

Sokolovska, Z. (2016) *Année* et *Journée européenne des langues*: célébration du plurilinguisme et légitimation de l'Europe [*European Year and Day of languages*: celebration of plurilingualism and legitimation of Europe]. *Bulletin suisse de linguistique appliquée*, 104: 51–66.

(2021) *Les langues en débat dans une Europe en projet* [Debating languages in the making of Europe]. Lyon: ENS Éditions/Langages.

Wassenberg, B. (2012) *Histoire du Conseil de l'Europe (1949–2009)* [History of the Council of Europe (1949–2009)]. Brussels/Berlin/New York: P.I.E./Peter Lang.

Woolard, K. (2008) Language and identity choice in Catalonia: the interplay of contrasting ideologies of linguistic authority. In Süselbeck, K., Mühlschlegel, U. & P. Masson (eds.) *Lengua, nación e identidad: la regulación del plurilinguismo en España y América Latina* [Language, nation and identity: regulation of multilingualism in Spain and Latin America]. Frankfurt am Main/Madrid: Vervuert/Iberoamericana, pp. 303–323.

Woolard, K. & B. Schieffelin (1994) Language ideology. *Annual Review of Anthropology*, 23, 55–82.

13 The Role of the Past in Language Revitalization

Pia Lane

I remember the first time I spoke Kven. I was fourteen, and my grandfather had just passed away. One afternoon I answered the phone and a man asked if he could speak with my grandfather. I tried to explain what had happened in Norwegian, but it was obvious that he did not understand, so I said *Eilif on kuolu* – "Eilif is dead." I remember the shock of the person on the other end of the telephone line and my feeling of inadequacy as I was not able to soften the blow of such a harsh message. My grammar and pronunciation were perfect, but not having spoken Kven, I lacked the pragmatic resources to deliver bad news in a compassionate manner. This moment was also tainted by a feeling of shame: my grandfather had just passed away and I could not convey this message appropriately in his mother tongue.

I grew up in a multilingual region in Northern Norway in a family where Kven, Norwegian, and Sámi were spoken, but I only learned to speak Norwegian because the adults did not speak to us in Kven, their mother tongue, but in Norwegian, a language they learned when they started school. At the time, my parents were not alone in doing this, as Norway had implemented assimilation policies directed toward the minoritized peoples in the North, which in turn contributed to language shift. Norwegian was a second language of my parents, but they nevertheless spoke only Norwegian to the children, believing that this was best for us. I remember the evenings when I listened to the adults laughing, gossiping, telling stories, and joking, all in Kven, the rhythm of the language lulling me to sleep. Another wave of shame comes when I think of my grandfather who was so resourceful, eloquent, and funny in his own language but had to write messages to my monolingual Norwegian teachers in Norwegian, which erased his eloquence. My silence and my grandfather's silence intertwined.

I actually started speaking Kven thirteen years after my grandfather passed away. As a university student, I went to Finland to study Finnish, a language closely related to Kven. A few years later, I returned to my village to do

This work was partly supported by the Research Council of Norway through its Centers of Excellence funding scheme, project number 223265.

fieldwork for my MA thesis, and now I could talk to the people in our silenced language. But this was hard, too. I had learned to speak standard Finnish, and people refused to talk to me saying that I spoke *oikia soumia* [proper Finnish], whereas they did not. This posed problems for my fieldwork; now most of them only wanted to speak Norwegian with me or suggested that I rather speak to some of the people who had immigrated from Finland and spoke 'proper Finnish.' After a bit of a struggle, I realized that I had to adapt my vocabulary to the local Kven dialect and to explain to others that I (and the Research Council of Norway that funded my MA project) were interested in the language spoken in my village, not Finnish spoken in Finland. Another challenge was that I was hesitant and shy to speak Kven, feeling that I had not mastered the language properly, something I will return to in the analysis.

In this chapter, I will discuss how such experiences and feelings of insecurity may come about and affect language revitalization processes. I use the term *language revitalization* to refer to community and individual efforts to maintain an indigenous or minoritized language, though in this chapter I focus primarily on the experiences of individuals. The past is a key aspect of revitalization processes, present in at least two different ways. Firstly, even though the goal of language revitalization is to create speakers for the future, such processes have often been concerned with bringing back a language from the past. This has been pointed out by other scholars (cf. Costa, 2017), so in this chapter, my main focus is on the second way we encounter the past, namely through facing hurts of the past, which have been passed down through generations and have consequences today. The interconnectedness between our past and present is complicated. In his book *How societies remember*, Connerton (1989, p. 2) says that extracting our past from the present is difficult because present factors influence our recollections of the past and our experience of the present very largely depends upon our knowledge of the past. In the case of revitalization, our internalized language attitudes and views may be implicit, unacknowledged, or taken for granted, but they still affect our actions and social practices. I will return to a more in-depth discussion of the role of the past in language revitalization later in this chapter.

The purpose of this chapter is to come to terms with what it means to be simultaneously a researcher who studies language revitalization and a person who has a personal experience of language shift and revitalization, and to shine a light on the complexity of personal experience of the process, often portrayed positively and as contributing to healing (cf. Hinton et al., 2018). I will begin with an overview of Norwegian language policies that contributed to language shift. Then I will discuss tensions in revitalization processes with an emphasis on emotional experiences. I conclude with some reflections on why it is important to pay attention to individual experiences and to recognize the contradictory forces exerted on those who engage in language revitalization efforts.

13.1 Northern Norway: Norwegianization, Assimilation, and Language Shift

Norway is a relatively young nation-state, having gained independence from Sweden in 1905 but the idea of Norway as a nation emerged in the nineteenth century. Deeply influenced by romantic ideas, this nation was imagined as a group of people with common origin, culture, and language (Kjeldstadli, 2006), in short, homogenous and monolingual (Niemi, 2003). This was particularly striking in the Northern areas, a multilingual zone of contact between speakers of Finnic, Sámi, Russian, and Scandinavian languages divided between Finland, Sweden, and Norway (Pietikäinen et al., 2010). Since Kven speakers came from today's Northern Finland and Northern Sweden, Kven retained Swedish loanwords (later removed from Finnish) but did not have the new vocabulary adopted from southern dialects during the standardization of Finnish. Hence, the vocabulary of Kven is quite different from Finnish.

From the middle of the nineteenth century Norwegian authorities implemented a range of laws and regulations aimed at limiting the use of Kven and Sámi languages – these oppressive policies became known as *Norwegianization* (Niemi, 2003; Pietikäinen et al., 2010). The goal of the policies was to assimilate the northern populations, and they resulted in a devaluation of local culture and an abrupt language shift to Norwegian. In 1898 the Ministry of Church Affairs and Education issued a decree stating that in schools it was

> imperative that the Lappish and Kven languages are not used apart from when circumstances make it absolutely unavoidable. (Kirke- og undervisningsdepartementet, 1898, my translation)

Boarding schools for Kven and Sámi children promoted the use of Norwegian, and a regulation of the Land Sales Act (1902) stipulated that land in the northern areas could only be sold to people who spoke Norwegian:

> Sales may take place to Norwegian citizens only, and with a particular view to furthering the settlement of a population that is suitable for the district, for its cultivation and for its utilization in other ways, that can speak, read and write the Norwegian language and that use it for their everyday tongue. (my translation)

Controlling land sales and ownership was a means of regulating ethnicity and language in the northern border region (Bull, 2012). Combined with ongoing modernization and economic development, these stringent assimilation policies compelled Kven and Sámi to abandon their mother tongues and shift to Norwegian. *Language shift* takes place on the societal level when a group starts using a new language for in-group communication. The process may happen abruptly, but is often gradual as the national language or the language of colonizers replace the local language(s) in an increasing number of social domains:

> Language choices, cumulated over many individuals and many choice instances, become transformed into the processes of language maintenance or language shift. (Fishman, 1965, p. 73)

Studies of language shift and revitalization see intergenerational language transmission as essential for the future of a minoritized language (Fishman, 1991). When parents stop speaking the mother tongue to their children, the children are unlikely to acquire the language, though they may gain passive competence. Language shift is known from numerous contexts across the globe (Austin & Sallabank, 2011), and one of the earliest studies is Haugen's (1953) study of Norwegian in the USA where he pointed out that social pressures worked in one direction because of the difference in ascribed prestige and status between the speakers of Norwegian and English. In the Norwegian context, the official assimilatory policies not only enhanced the differences in status between Norwegian vs. Kven and Sámi but also directly limited the use of the two languages.

The disruption of intergenerational language transmission has long been seen as the key factor in the loss of a minoritized language, although King (2009) and Comajoan-Colome and Coronel-Molina (2021) argue that other domains also play a role. The disruption is a consequence of the choices speakers make, but rational explanations only partially account for language shift. Due to social pressure and seeing the national language as a means for prosperity and a better future, parents choose what they see as best for their children.

In my home village, this was Norwegian, a language that was not our parents' mother tongue. A recurring statement was that they did not wish to place the same burden on their children as the one they had to carry, and therefore chose not to speak their first language to us. When meeting national official institutions, such as the educational system, many Kven and Sámi experienced a position of double shame: their mother tongue was treated as worthless, and they could only try to replace it with Norwegian, a language they had not fully mastered (Lane, 2010). The experience of starting school 'without a language' had silenced many indigenous children, who later as adults passed the heritage of silence on to their children by using only the national language with them. For many, the feeling of shame became internalized to such an extent that people did not even question the hegemonic discourses of the inferiority of languages other than the national language (see Lane (2010) for an analysis). Even though this was the dominant, unquestioned, common-sense world view, our parents' choices were embedded in a context where languages other than Norwegian were seen as inferior and not worth keeping and passing on, attitudes described by Dorian (1987) as an ideology of contempt. Sicoli (2011, p. 162) reminds us that rational explanations of shift and maintenance that focus too much on individual agency make larger social structures that shape possibilities for agency invisible. Agency, our capacity to act, is not located only in individual action, but contingent and constrained by the social systems we are part of, particularly in situations of language shift (Sicoli, 2011). Therefore, our parents' language choices were conditioned by deep social, cultural, and political historical processes, and a chain of individual choices led to a collective outcome, namely that the entire village during a short period changed the language of interaction with children.

The Finnic varieties spoken in Norway and Sweden today have been recognized as languages, named Kven and Meänkieli. Norway ratified the European Charter for Regional or Minority Languages (1992) under the auspices of the Council of Europe, whose aim is to promote and support democracy, human rights, and the rule of law. The Charter entered into force in Norway in 1998, and Kven was recognized as a language, and not a dialect of Finnish, in 2005. Today Kven is the official name of the language in Norway. In my data, and particularly in the earlier interviews, people generally refer to the language as Finnish, but frequently modify it as 'old Finnish,' 'Bugøynes Finnish,' or 'our Finnish' (Lane, 2010, 2017). In the examples in this chapter, their use of the term *Finnish* should be understood as equivalent to *Kven*, unless otherwise specified.

In the remainder of this chapter I will discuss some of the paradoxes and tensions in revitalization, based on my own experiences, observations during repeated field research visits to my home area (1996–present), an interview in the Kven newspaper *Ruijan Kaiku*, published data from studies of revitalization of Sámi, and sociolinguistic interviews conducted by field assistants in conjunction with two research projects under my direction (Lane, 2010, 2017). I have translated into English excerpts from the latter interviews, and the original interviews are included in the Ruija corpus, a speech corpus from multilingual areas in Troms and Finnmark counties.

13.2 Revitalization of Kven: Looking Back in Time

In many contexts around the globe speakers of indigenous minority languages strive to reverse language shift and revive languages that are no longer spoken as first languages (Hinton et al., 2018). Language revitalization is a complex, many-faceted, and sometimes contradictory process. Sociolinguists note that the process presupposes that such a thing as a *language* exists and highlight the dangers of deciding which clusters of linguistic features count as a language (Duchêne & Heller, 2007; Moore, Pietikäinen, & Blommaert, 2010).

The term *revitalization* presupposes that something is in danger, weakened, or threatened – hence, it is often seen as a response to language endangerment. This is underscored by the prefix *re-*: speakers are revitalizing a language or bringing a language back to greater vitality. This conception can be problematic though because it indirectly situates the language as something of the past and a 'dead' object that needs to be resurrected. However, the aim of revitalization is to create speakers for today and for the future (Hornberger & King, 1996) and make room for the language in new domains (McCarty, 2008). A focus on the past, therefore, is a double-edged sword: it can bring about a sense of belonging, but the history might be seen as a liability by younger people whose focus often is on the present and future. Norwegian was associated with progress and modernity, as observed by Lindgren (2014), who conducted fieldwork in Räisa (a municipality in Northern Norway) in the 1960s and 1970s. Her interviewees explained that it was necessary to shift to Norwegian, because the village would remain old-fashioned and not partake in the new societal development if people did not stop speaking Finnish

Perceiving minoritized languages as 'old-fashioned' is not uncommon. In an interview with the Kven newspaper *Ruijan Kaiku*, one of the members of a young Kven band who wrote and performed the song *Megavoima* [Mega Power] in Kven and Norwegian explained that they wanted to make a modern rock song with cool lyrics: "I think it is about time that Kven becomes more modern, that it gets to the future and updates, not just remaining stuck in a time loop" (my translation). The song does not address the importance of Kven – instead it takes a playful stance, both through the seamless transitions between Norwegian and Kven and because the singers make fun of illegal snow-scooter driving. As such, it is situated in a local but decidedly contemporary context. The hybrid nature of the performance resonates more with contemporary music genres than 'traditional' Kven music. The same can be said about artists rapping in Sámi. When discussing the Sámi rap artist Amoc, Pietikäinen (2008) states that

> [i]ndigenous languages are good and vital enough to be used in new, contemporary contexts: native languages are also modern languages, not solely languages of grandparents, rituals and tradition. (p. 33)

A too strong focus on the past, as Romaine (2006) reminds us, is problematic because going back in time is not possible, neither for speakers nor for languages. Romaine (2006) cautions against adopting a view of modernism "that anchors societies to different historical points aligned on a single linear trajectory from a traditional past to a modern present according to the extent of their socioeconomic and political development" (p. 445). If a language like Kven is seen as a static and fixed object that can be retrieved from the past, it becomes a hindrance for modernity precisely because potential new learners associate it with the past only. However, if language revitalization is seen as rooted in history but shaped to and being shaped by our present and possible futures, reclaiming Kven may also be appealing to the next generation of speakers. In his discussion of language reclamation, Leonard (2017) emphasizes a community's right to set 'associated goals in response to community needs and perspectives,' a perspective that opens up for a stronger focus on individual experiences and also provides room for hybrid and fluid language practices, such as in the song *Megavoima*. In the context of this chapter, I understand *language reclamation* as the actions and process of taking back a language that was spoken in one's home, but a language one did not learn while growing up (for other definitions, see Leonard, 2017). *Revitalization* is a more abstract and generic term that privileges language; therefore I will use *reclamation* to refer to individual experiences of acquiring and using a minoritized language.

13.3 Revitalization: Shadows of the Past

The past is also present in a manner that has received considerably less attention in research on language revitalization. Language revitalization is often portrayed as positive and emancipatory because it allows speakers to find and develop their own voice, identity, and belonging, as underscored by Hinton et al. (2018): "[L]anguage revitalization movements are seen by the speech communities as paths to healing, justice, and empowerment" (p. xxii). While revitalization can contribute to healing from pain and stigma caused by oppressive policies in the past, it can also force us to face unacknowledged hurts still lingering in communities and lives of individuals. In the beginning of this chapter, I alluded to my own emotional struggles when I started speaking Kven as an adult. Fieldwork observations, conversations with friends and relatives, and reading blogs and social media posts made me realize that this experience is not at all uncommon in Kven and Sámi communities.

I started speaking Kven when I was in my mid-twenties, and while I expected this to be difficult because of the lexical and grammatical differences between Kven and the other languages I knew, I was not at all prepared for the emotional challenges I faced. I felt exposed and insecure and worried that the 'genuine' speakers would find my linguistic skills inadequate or even lacking. Such experiences are not uncommon when people set out to reclaim the language spoken by former generations, which they did not speak growing up. This sentiment is described as *språksperra*, and a Norwegian word is used perhaps because these matters are not often talked about in Kven or Sámi. The term *språksperra* could be translated into English as 'the language barrier' or 'language block'[1] – something that prevents us from talking and has to be overcome. The term is often characterized as a fear of speaking by those who have learned Kven and/or Sámi via the educational system and/or have acquired receptive competence at home. In other words, like me, they have sufficient knowledge to speak but find the transition to speaking the language difficult and emotionally challenging. In a similar context Todal (2007) described this as a barrier to speaking Sámi, even for those who had a good grasp of grammar, substantial vocabulary, and good pronunciation, quoting Ivar, who said:

> The barrier came in when one was little, the words one knew were not good enough, plus that one now is unsure of oneself when speaking with older [people] who know much more. (p. 205) (my translation from Norwegian)

Though Ivar does not offer any explanation for how this barrier came about, his statement situates its origin in his childhood. Part of the explanation might be that he, like my generation, was spoken to in Norwegian only, and changing language when a communication pattern is established is not easy (Rasmus & Lane, 2021). What I wish to focus on here, however, is something that resonates with my own experience and observations. Ivar says that the words he knew were not good enough and he felt unsure when talking with more proficient speakers. This illustrates that encountering the language barrier has both an *inner* and an *outer* dimension, an affective experience when we speak, attempt to speak, or talk about reclaiming a language.

The *outer* dimension is our fear of being judged as inferior by more proficient speakers. An orientation to the past may also lead to portraying a version of a language spoken (at some indeterminable point in the past) as authentic, better, or proper, which in turn positions some speakers as more authentic than others. Revitalization then may create new language hierarchies where those who have acquired a language at home and not via the educational system or as an adult are perceived as better speakers. Such 'traditional' speakers may, with the best of intentions, correct learners when they engage in a conversation in Kven, or even make fun of the way learners speak. Such experiences are also found in other contexts, as described by King and Hermes (2014):

> She paid a heavy cost for bucking these norms as she was "bullied" (in her words) and belittled by more advanced learners of Ojibwe when she attempted to practice speaking. These speakers made her feel anxious, insecure, and unworthy of the language – and like an inauthentic speaker. (p. 277)

The authors point out that the emotional aspects of language learning seem to be particularly strong in indigenous contexts, where identity politics and

[1] Language barrier is also a common concept in studies of language learning (e.g., Lambert et al., 1959).

social control over who has the right to claim the role of an authentic speaker run deep. These speakers sometimes evaluate negatively the language used by learners, making them feel embarrassed about their language skills (Abtahian & Quinn, 2017). In Kven and Sámi communities, speakers who correct learners are described as *the language police*. Even though those who correct may not at all constitute the majority of traditional speakers, a few negative experiences may suffice to silence learners or lead them to fear that they will encounter language policing. A consequence of this is that learners, like Ivar, may feel unsure when talking with more proficient speakers and resort to silencing themselves. Often what speakers fear is a perceived language police, that is, they construct possible scenarios and encounters with perceived better speakers and imagine feared consequences (Juuso, 2009). Such fears and anxiety then lead to self-criticism and avoidance of the language.

The language barrier also has a strong *inner* dimension, deeply connected to issues of identity and belonging. Recently, emotional aspects of language learning have received increased attention in studies of language revitalization, second language acquisition, and heritage and indigenous language[2] maintenance (Abtahian & Quinn, 2017; Huss & Stångberg, 2018; Sevinç, 2020). Emotional experiences are prominent in reclamation processes, as is evident in the following examples of challenges people had faced when they started speaking Kven. As discussed earlier, most use the term 'Kven,' but some prefer 'Finnish,' often modified as 'our Finnish.' Thus, Eli refers to her ancestors as Kven but calls the language 'Finnish.' Eli said that even though she had studied Finnish for several years (at a time when only standard Finnish could be studied), she still found it difficult to speak the language:

I find that this was a lot more difficult than I had expected and and if I had [.] noticed that I have a bit of this barrier to speak Finnish find it is difficult. (my translation)

The interviewer supports this by stating that language is difficult, and they both laugh. Eli says that she speaks Finnish with tourists who visit Bugøynes, and she does not mind making mistakes when talking to them, but contrasts this to speaking Finnish with friends. She juxtaposes these experiences by the use of the prepositional phrase *i forhold til* 'relative to/in comparison with':

[2] In this context I see both heritage languages and indigenous languages as minoritized languages that are or have been used in the family and/or local community, often alongside and in a weaker position than the national language. Heritage languages may be transnational languages or languages used by migrants, such as Turkish in Germany, whereas indigenous languages have become minoritized due to the development of nation-states and changes in or establishment of national borders.

I speak I s- I speak Finnish some times when I m- eh meet tourists and such in such [.] then I can [.] it doesn't matter if I make mistakes and such but in comparison to eh [.] we do have Finnish friends and my husband speaks fluent Finnish [.] and but with them the eh I just struggle [.] I don't manage [.] I find it scary, plain and simple [.] and this was a new experience because I've never been scared of talking lots [.] in yes Eng- yes English is ok. (my translation)

In this excerpt, an opposition along two axes may be identified: Eli states that speaking Finnish with tourists or strangers is easier than talking with her husband or friends. Though not using the term *sperre* [barrier], she describes speaking as scary, underscored by the phrase *rett og slett* [plain and simple], an expression that may be used for emphasis or to underscore something unexpected. In Eli's case, the expression seems to serve both functions; she repeats that she finds speaking Finnish difficult and then underscores that this was unexpected, "this was a new experience." Finally, she contrasts this to her experience with speaking English, of which she has never been afraid. Interestingly, she employs the term *redd for*, which could be translated as 'afraid of' or 'scared of' (see Lane (forthcoming) for further analysis). Implicitly, she links this to her previous statement on speaking Finnish by the choice of lexemes: scary, difficult, and scared of; thus, an emotional undercurrent may be identified. Interestingly, a woman from a different village, where Kven, Sámi, and Norwegian are spoken, voices the same concern about Sámi:

I didn't start speaking Sámi until when when I became an adult [.] then I dared to like starting speaking [.] but I have never been afraid of lang- speaking other languages. (my translation)

Like Eli, she says that she has never been afraid of speaking foreign languages, such as English and German. Their accounts resonate with my own experience of having reclaimed Kven as an adult; I felt that Kven was a language I ought to speak, and preferably should speak fluently, whereas English, German, and French were languages we were not expected to know but could learn from scratch.

These observations lead to a key question: Why is speaking Kven and Sámi experienced so differently from speaking a foreign language? Researchers investigating second and foreign language acquisition[3] have long been interested in the role of emotions in the learning of new languages. Initially there was an emphasis on cognitive aspects, and an important variable was anxiety, defined by MacIntyre (1999) as "the worry and negative emotional reaction

[3] In this context both second language and foreign language refer to languages acquired outside the home, usually in a school setting. The term second language indicates that the language acquired is used in a social domain outside the home or immediate social circle.

aroused when learning or using a second language" (p. 27). Subsequent research in the field of Second Language Acquisition (SLA) called for more attention to affect, emotions, real life outside the classroom, and power relations (Block, 2013; May, 2013; Norton, 2000; Wetherell, 2013). The response has been an affective turn in the field of SLA (Pavlenko, 2013) that explored the role of emotions, identity, and self-image in the learning process (e.g., Busch, 2012; Kramsch, 2009; Ortega, 2013) and a new understanding of language acquisition as socially situated and embodied, with the shift of the focus from the "*experimental* to *experiential* side of human language and life" (Prior, 2019, p. 517, emphasis in the original).

Emotions, including anxiety and insecurity, have also been investigated in the studies of maintenance and revitalization of heritage and indigenous languages, but there is still a need for more investigation of personal experiences and emotions when reclaiming such languages (Abtahian & Quinn, 2017; Sevinç, 2020). The difference between foreign language acquisition and language reclamation lies in the fact that indigenous languages are connected to people and the land and deeply steeped in its history. Intrinsically linked to this is the fear of being corrected by more 'authentic' speakers, as discussed earlier in this chapter. Reclaiming a minoritized language also brings to the fore issues of authenticity and legitimacy as we are expected and may even expect ourselves to speak 'our language' as a native speaker, which in turn places a burden of authenticity on those who strive to reclaim an indigenous language. This is closely intertwined with the third aspect, which I refer to as 'shadows of the past.' One of the main factors contributing to the tensions in reclamation processes, I believe, is the presence of the past and the reactions it evokes in us. The past reminds us of its presence, particularly when injustices, suffering, and the forgotten resurface and demand our attention, what Gordon (2011) describes as haunting:

> [H]aunting is one way in which abusive systems of power make themselves known and their impacts felt in everyday life, especially when they are supposedly over and done with . . . it is an animated state in which a repressed or unresolved social violence is making itself known, sometimes very directly, sometimes more obliquely. (p. 2)

Language reclamation forces us to face the hurts of the past, internalized by our grandparents and parents' generations and passed on to us. Though not talked about, or perhaps precisely *because* their experiences were not talked about and repressed, they haunt us. Embodied memories, though forgotten, may return and demand our attention, and the consequences of the oppressive policies of the past are present in our lives today (Lane, forthcoming). Often we are not even aware of how or when attitudes and feelings have been passed on to us and later materialized in practice, because time erases memory of learned practice, something Scollon and Scollon (2004, p. 3), drawing on Bourdieu (1977), refer to as 'genesis amnesia.'

Indigenous and heritage languages are often perceived as belonging to a specific group of people and a cultural context, and speakers may be portrayed as embodying this rootedness. In a sense, such speakers are expected to reclaim what they already have or ought to possess. This tacit expectation places new speakers of an indigenous minority language in a precarious position, which may lead to feelings of ambivalence and insecurity. The process of reclamation of indigenous minority languages may force speakers to face a sense of loss and shame resulting from oppression and stigmatization experienced by themselves or their parents, as the histories of indigenous and minority languages often are associated not only with positive belonging to place and family but also alienation, humiliation, and vulnerability, described by King and Hermes (2014) as 'the scars of colonization' (p. 279). The tension between emancipation and empowerment, on the one hand, and pain and anxiety, on the other, are prevalent in many Sámi and Kven communities (Todal, 2007). Reclaiming a language may make speakers vulnerable in several ways: they are faced with the burden, shame, and devaluation of the past, while becoming an authentic speaker seems unattainable because their ways of speaking are often perceived as less authentic when compared to those of traditional speakers. Busch (2012) and Kramsch (2009) draw our attention to the emotional and embodied dimensions of language learning, an aspect that is particularly relevant for the analysis of the lived experiences of minority language reclamation, when speakers often carry the load and expectations of authenticity. Such embodied experiences are important when analyzing personal experiences of minority language reclamation because it encompasses the bodily dimension of perceiving, experiencing, feeling, and desiring.

Learners have ways of facing and solving inherent tensions in revitalization processes. One strategy is to find or create safe spaces for speaking, such as attending a language course, finding a person one trusts, or talking with children or elderly people who do not feel comfortable speaking Norwegian (Rasmus & Lane, 2021). When studying Finnish, Tor decided that he would attempt talking with elderly people, trusting that they would not laugh at him:

> I thought I I will speak with the elderly [.] because they will not laugh they won't laugh at me [.] if I talked if I said something wrong.

Speakers' ability to find such safe spaces shows that, though reclaiming a language and becoming a speaker bring emotional challenges, speakers are able to find ways to overcome silence. If language revitalization is to have the desired outcome, there is a need to recognize that experiencing conflicting emotions when reclaiming an indigenous language is not an indication of weakness or failure, and to prepare those who embark on the journey of reclaiming a language for the challenges they might face.

Conclusion: Facing the Shadows of the Past

Language revitalization may be an emancipatory process through which speakers find and develop their own voice, identity, and belonging and experience some healing from the hurts of the past. However, revitalization does not come without a price, and becoming or remaining multilingual can be a costly and emotionally laden process for the individual. Therefore, it is essential to recognize the disparate and contradictory forces exerted on the individuals who engage in language reclamation. Facing shadows and specters of the past may be so challenging that those who embark on reclamation projects give up, often because they are not prepared for the emotional experiences they face. If language revitalization is to be successful, there is a need to recognize the challenges faced by speakers, support them on their language journey, and, perhaps most importantly, make them aware that they are not alone in experiencing conflicting emotions when reclaiming an indigenous language and that this is not an indication of weakness or failure.

References

Abtahian, M. & C. Quinn (2017) Language shift and linguistic insecurity. *Language Documentation & Conservation*, 13, 137–151.

Austin, P. & J. Sallabank (eds.) (2011) *The Cambridge Handbook of Endangered Languages*. Cambridge: Cambridge University Press.

Block, D. (2013) Moving beyond "lingualism": Multilingual embodiment and multimodality in SLA. In May, S. (ed.) *The multilingual turn: Implications for SLA, TESOL, and bilingual education*. New York/London: Routledge, pp. 54–77.

Bourdieu, P. (1977) The economics of linguistic exchanges. *Social Science Information*, 16, 6, 645–668.

Bull, K. (2012) Jordsalgslovgivningen i Finnmark 1775–1902 – en Oversikt. In Tuseth, B., Bugge, H., Voigt, C., Backer, I. & O. Fauchald (eds.) *Pro Natura: Festskrift til Hans Christian Bugge på 70-årsdagen 2012* [Pro Natura: Festschrift for Hans Christian Bugge on his 70th Birthday]. Oslo: Universitetsforlaget, pp. 108–119.

Busch, B. (2012) The linguistic repertoire revisited. *Applied Linguistics,* 33, 5, 503–523.

Comajoan-Colome, L. & S. Coronel-Molina (2021) What does language revitalisation in the twenty-first century look like? New trends and frameworks. *Journal of Multilingual and Multicultural Development*, 42, 10, 897–904.

Connerton, P. (1989) *How societies remember*. Cambridge: Cambridge University Press.

Costa, J. (2017) *Revitalising language in Provence: A critical approach*. Hoboken, NJ: Wiley Blackwell.

Dorian, N. (1987) The value of language-maintenance efforts which are unlikely to succeed. *International Journal of the Sociology of Language*, 68, 57–67.

Duchêne, A. & M. Heller (2007) *Discourses of endangerment: Ideology and interest in the defence of languages*. London/New York: Continuum.

Fishman, J. (1965) Who speaks what language to whom and when? *La Linguistique,* 1, 2, 67–88.
(1991) *Reversing language shift: Theoretical and empirical foundations of assistance to threathened languages.* Clevedon: Multilingual Matters.
Gordon, A. (2011) Some thoughts on haunting and futurity. *borderlands,* 10, 2, 1–21. Retrieved from http://averygordon.net/files/GordonHauntingFuturity.pdf June 26, 2018.
Haugen, E. (1953) *The Norwegian language in America: A study in bilingual behavior.* Philadelphia: University of Pennsylvania Press.
Hinton, L., Huss, L., & G. Roche (2018) Introduction: Language revitalization as a growing field of study and practice. In Hinton, L., Huss, L., & G. Roche (eds.) *The Routledge Handbook of Language Revitalization.* New York: Routledge, pp. xxi–xxx.
Hornberger, N. & K. King (1996) Language revitalisation in the Andes: Can the schools reverse language shift? *Journal of Multilingual and Multicultural Development,* 17, 6, 427–441.
Huss, L., & S. Stångberg (2018) The yoke and the candy bowl: Beliefs and emotions in South Sami revitalisation. In Roche, G., Maruyama, H., & Å. Kroik (eds.) *Indigenous efflorescence.* Acton: ANU Press, pp. 129–150.
Juuso, J. (2009) *Válddán giellan ruovttoluotta/tar språket mitt tilbake* [Take my language back]. Vuonnabahta: Isak Saba guovddáš.
King, K. (2009) Language loss and revitalization: Ten things we know. In Lindgren, A., Niemi, E., Hauan, M., Niiranen, L. & T. Thuen (eds.) *Kvener og skogfinner i fortid og nåtid* [Kvener and Forest Finnis in the past and present]. Tromsø: Speculum Boreale, pp. 9–23.
King, K. & M. Hermes (2014) Why is this so hard?: Ideologies of endangerment, passive language learning approaches, and Ojibwe in the United States. *Journal of Language, Identity & Education*, 13, 4, 268–282.
Kirke- og undervisningsdepartementet [Ministry of Church Affairs and Education] (1898). *Instruks angaaende brugen af lappisk og kvænsk som hjælpesprog ved undervisningen i folkeskolen, hvor dette af kirkedepartementet er tilladt i henhold til landsskolelovens § 73, 2 led. 18. april 1898.* [Regulation concerning the use of Lappish and Kven as supportive languages in primary education, where this by the Ministry of Religion is allowed according to the National Education Act § 73, 2 section. 18. april 1898] Retrieved from https://www.norgeshistorie.no/kilder/industrialisering-og-demokrati/K1540-Spr%C3%A5kinstruks-for-samiske-og-kvenske-skolebarn.html October 12, 2021
Kjeldstadli, K. (2006) En norsk kultur. Ja. Én norsk kultur. Nei [A Norwegian culture. Yes. One Norwegian culture. No]. In Engen, T., Kulbrandstad, L. & E-A. Syversen (eds.) *Monokultur og multikultur. Nasjonsbyggende diskurser 1905–2005* [Mono-culture and multi-culture. Nation-building discourses 1905–2005]. Oplandske: Bokforlag, pp. 31–44.
Kramsch, C. (2009) *The multilingual subject: What foreign language learners say about their experience and why it matters.* Oxford: Oxford University Press.
Lambert, W., Havelka, J., & R. Gardner (1959) Linguistic manifestations of bilingualism. *The American Journal of Psychology*, 72, 1, 77–82.
Land Sales Act (1902) *Lov om Afhændelse af Statens Jord og Grund i Finnmarkens Amts Landdistrict av 22. mai 1902 nr. 7 – Jordsalgsloven av 1902* [Act on Sales of

National Land and Ground in Finnmark County District of May 22 1902 n. 7. Land Sales Act of 1902].
Lane, P. (2010) 'We did what we thought was best for our children': A nexus analysis of language shift in a Kven community. *International Journal of the Sociology of Language,* 202, 63–78.
(2017) Language standardisation as frozen mediated actions. The materiality of language standardisation. In Lane, P., Costa, J., & H. De Korne (eds.) *Standardizing minority languages. Competing ideologies of authority and authenticity in the global periphery*. New York: Routledge, pp. 101–117.
(forthcoming). The South in the North: colonialisation and decolonisation of the mind. In Deumert, A. & S. Makoni (eds.) *From Southern theory to decolonizing sociolinguistics – voices, questions and alternatives*. Clevedon: Multilingual Matters.
Leonard, W. Y. (2017) Producing language reclamation by decolonising 'language'. *Language Documentation and Description,* 14, 15–36.
Lindgren, A.-R. (2014) Litt før den etniske renessansen – feltarbeid blant kvener på slutten av 1960-tallet [A little before the ethnic renaissance – fieldwork among Kven at the end of the 1960s]. *Ottar*, 5, 34–40.
MacIntyre, P. (1999) Language anxiety: A review of the research for language teachers. In Young, D. (ed.) *Affect in foreign language and second language teaching: A practical guide to creating a low-anxiety classroom atmosphere*. Boston: Mc Graw-Hill, pp. 24–45.
May, S. (2013) Disciplinary divides, knowledge construction, and the multilingual turn. In May, S. (ed.) *The multilingual turn: Implications for SLA, TESOL, and bilingual education*. New York/London: Routledge, pp. 17–41.
McCarty, T. (2008) Language education planning and policies by and for Indigenous peoples. *Encyclopedia of Language and Education*, 1, 137–150.
Moore, R., Pietikäinen, S., & J. Blommaert (2010) Counting the losses: Numbers as the language of language endangerment. *Sociolinguistic Studies*, 4, 1, 1–26.
Niemi, E. (2003) Regimeskifte, innvandrere og fremmede [Regime change, immigrants and strangers]. In Niemi, E., Myhre, J., & K. Kjeldstadli (eds.) *Norsk innvandringshistorie. I nasjonalstatens tid 1814–1940* [Norwegian immigration history. In the time of the nation state]. Valdres: Pax forlag, pp. 11–47.
Norton, B. (2000) *Identity and language learning: Gender, ethnicity and educational change*. Harlow, England: Longman/Pearson.
Ortega, L. (2013) Ways forward for a bi/multilingual turn in SLA. In May, S. (ed.) *The multilingual turn: Implications for SLA, TESOL, and bilingual education*. New York/London: Routledge, pp. 42–63.
Pavlenko, A. (2013) The affective turn in SLA: From 'affective factors' to 'language desire'and 'commodification of affect'. In Gabrys-Barker, D. & J. Belska (eds.) *The affective dimension in Second Language Acquisition*. Bristol: Multilingual Matters, pp. 3–28.
Pietikäinen, S. (2008) Sami in the media: Questions of language vitality and cultural hybridisation. *Journal of Multicultural Discourses*, 3, 1, 22–35.
Pietikäinen, S., Huss, L., Laihiala-Kankainen, S., Aikio-Puoskari, U., & P. Lane (2010) Regulating multilingualism in the North Calotte: The case of Kven, Meänkieli and Sámi languages. *Acta Borealia*, 27, 1, 1–23.

Prior, M. (2019) Elephants in the room: An "affective turn," or just feeling our way? *The Modern Language Journal*, 103, 2, 516–527.
Rasmus, S. & P. Lane (2021) New Speakers of Sámi: From insecurity to pride. *Linguistic Minorities in Europe Online* at https://doi.org/10.1515/lme.12818309
Romaine, S. (2006) Planning for the survival of linguistic diversity. *Language Policy*, 5, 4, 443–475.
Ruija Corpus https://tekstlab.uio.no/glossa2/ruija
Ruijan Kaiku https://www.ruijan-kaiku.no/vil-inspirere-flere-kvenske-kids/
Scollon, R. & S. Scollon (2004) *Nexus analysis: Discourse and the emerging internet.* London: Routledge.
Sevinç, Y. (2020) Anxiety as a negative emotion in home language maintenance and development. In Schalley, A. & S. Eisenchlas (eds.) *Handbook of Home Language Maintenance and Development.* Berlin/Boston: De Gruyter Mouton, pp. 84–108.
Sicoli, M. (2011). Agency and ideology in language shift and language maintenance. In Granadillo, T. & H. Orcutt-Gachiri (eds.) *Ethnographic contributions to the study of endangered languages.* Tucson: University of Arizona Press, pp. 161–176.
Todal, J. (2007) Språkleg vitalisering - faktorar som vi ikkje skriv om [Language vitalisation – factors we do not write about]. In Bull, T., Kusmenko, J., & M. Rießler (eds.) *Språk og pråkforhold i Sápmi* [Language and language issues in Sápmi]. Berlin: Humboldt-Universität, pp. 201–210.
Wetherell, M. (2013) Affect and discourse: What's the problem? From affect as excess to affective/discursive practice. *Subjectivity*, 6, 4, 349–368.

14 Historic Reenactments in Contemporary Spain: *Fiestas de moros y cristianos*

Yasmine Beale-Rivaya

In recent years, Spain has experienced an influx of immigrants from Arab countries and a rise of nationalist discourse (Eurostat, 2021; Vampa, 2020). The anti-Arab sentiments aren't new and neither is the adoption of language as an indicator of 'otherness.' Spanish historiography, argues historian García-Sanjuán (2012), has been dominated by the nationalist discourse that systematically distorts the past to construct a 'Spanish' and an 'Andalusian' identity predicated on the exclusion of anything associated with Islam and the Arabic language (all the while the tourism sector commodifies the 'exotic' Arabic past). One of the key settings that distorts and reinvents the past are the festivals of Moors and Christians, *moros y cristianos*.

Claiming to be true and faithful retellings of history, these festivals invoke a popular memory of the imagined past, while interlacing and mixing events from multiple time periods, from the Muslim conquest of the Iberian Peninsula in 711 to the so-called Christian reconquest, presented as an essential battle between Christianity and the Muslim invaders. By verbally enacting the tensions vivid in popular memory and in relations with Muslims today (Rogozen-Soltar, 2012), these festivals offer the means to interpret present-day immigration as a form of invasion and to reaffirm Spanishness constructed around an essentialized core of the Arab Other and ahistorical tropes that maintain their hold on the popular imagination. In the past fifteen years, the popularity of these festivals has grown exponentially, transforming small idiosyncratic events with half a dozen local participants into huge affairs involving whole villages. All festivals are based on a common script that supposedly originated in Granada. Variations in the celebrations stem from efforts to include historical content relevant to locations where the festivals are enacted.

In this article, I analyze one of the more popular and historically significant of these festivals, celebrated in the outpost village of Carboneras, established in 1776 in the province of Almería, northeast of Granada. The Carboneras festival is recognized as one of the most continuously celebrated festivals in the region. Additionally, the organizing committee from Carboneras regularly 'exports' the festival to other coastal villages, from Andalusia to Alicante, by training locals to put on similar celebrations. The committee also helps local organizers to appropriately include regional historical content, language, and landmarks. The analysis will begin with a brief history and explanation of the circumstances surrounding the creation of the festival and then move to the festival itself. Special attention will be paid to the language deployed in the script and the ways in which reenactments of historical multilingualism reveal anxieties brought on by immigration and promote an identity based on exclusion of the Other and a negation of a complex multilingual and multicultural past.

14.1 Festivals: History, Context, and Purpose

The tradition of the festivals, popularly known as *función(es)*, goes back to the late eighteenth century when the province of Almería – an area that once upon a time had a dense Morisco population – founded a series of coastal outpost villages to defend the coastline against Muslim invaders from North Africa (García-Arenal, 2015). The *función* was originally designed as a military exercise to keep the soldiers stationed at the outposts occupied and trained during the long solitary hours. It also functioned as community theater, performed by the villagers to bring the history of the region to life in a community that would have been mostly illiterate.

The events were – and are – reenacted in the emblematic spaces: the village center, the beach, the watchtower, the castle, and the church. The landmarks become as important as the play, as they serve as a visual complement to performances and lend further credibility and historicity to the events portrayed. Finally, and most pertinent to this study, the language they use is purposeful. Elevating the Christian identity while denigrating the Muslim one, it reveals an ongoing unease with the figure of the Morisco, reminiscent of the tensions with Moriscos in the sixteenth and seventeenth centuries. *Morisco*, at the time, was a common label for former Muslims converted to Christianity and their descendants.

The festival, which occurs over three days, alludes to, mixes, and conflates historical events that would be vaguely familiar to a local audience. These events range from the 711 crossing of Muslim forces into the Iberian Peninsula in what would mark the beginning of the Muslim hegemony to the 1492 fall of Granada, the last Muslim kingdom, to the Catholic monarchs in the process termed the *Reconquista*, reconquest. Modern historians find the term to be highly problematic as it presumes the legitimacy of one community, namely Christian, over another, namely Muslim (for an in-depth treatment, see Chalmeta, 1994; O'Callaghan, 2003; Quiroga & Lovelle, 1997; Safran, 2013; Vallvé-Bermejo, 1989).

The festival treats the period between 711 and 1492 as occupation of al-Andalus, the geographical area under Muslim control (not to be confused with

Andalucía, a contemporary region of Spain). In this period Arabic – more specifically, Andalusí-Arabic – became the dominant language of administration coexisting with Romance (Romance, in this context, refers to a cluster of languages that evolved from Latin but had not yet become modern-day Castilian, Catalan, French, Italian, etc). The level of bilingualism varied across time and space (Giménez-Eguibar & Wasserman-Soler, 2011), and even after cities, such as Toledo, came under Christian rule in 1085 and Romance became the language of politics, Andalusí-Arabic was maintained by the local community well into the thirteenth century (Beale-Rivaya, 2012).

The *función* celebrated in Almería alludes to the events leading to the conquest of Granada by the Catholic monarchs, and the historical events surrounding the establishment of the modern city of Almería. Located east of Granada, Almería was founded in the tenth century by the Umayyad Emir Abd Al-Rahman III. Over time, it became an active port city and the center of overland and maritime commerce of the Caliphate of Cordoba (Escobosa et al., 1998). In 1489, Almería was subjugated by Christian forces, three years before the fall of Granada. As the Christian monarchy sought to exert influence over their southernmost conquered lands and their Muslims, Moriscos, and Jews, tensions led to conflicts.

The most famous conflict invoked by the festival is the Rebellion of Alpujarras, aka the Morisco Rebellion (1568–1570). A long and bloody war, it was triggered by royal decrees, inspired, in turn, by a council of religious leaders, whose aim was to suppress covert practice of Islam and erase any vestige of Muslim identity within the Morisco population (Jiménez-Estrella & Castillo Fernández, 2020). The decrees marked a momentous departure from the initial period of Christian domination of Granada, when Muslims were allowed to practice their religion and "Christians who had converted to Islam under Islamic rule were not forced to return to their original faith" (Giménez-Eguibar & Wasserman-Soler, 2011, p. 230). Hernando de Talavera, the archbishop of Granada, had even "advocated preaching in Arabic" (Giménez-Eguibar & Wasserman-Soler, 2011, p. 230). The fact that the guiding council for the assimilation decrees was a Christian theological one only added to the conflict.

The distrust of people with 'hybrid' identities on the part of the political hierarchy and members of the Church is a recurring theme in the history of al-Andalus and Christian Iberia at large. For example, in the twelfth and thirteenth centuries, language maintenance and choice were affected by political, socio-economic and geographic factors (Beale-Rivaya, 2012). As time went by, however, in cities like Toledo bilingualism in Romance and Andalusí-Arabic became a sign of 'otherness' and an excuse to marginalize Muslims, Moriscos and Jews politically and to exclude them from desirable residential areas (Beale-Rivaya, 2016; Hitchcock, 2008).

The monitoring of language use was one of the key tools used to determine compliance among the Moriscos of Granada and the Alpujarras. By the 1560s, Arabic language was considered to have been eliminated from common usage, although it may have survived in non-formal and intimate spaces (García-Arenal, 2015). The decrees put the Morisco population in an impossible predicament because Church officials presumed that a Morisco could never really assimilate. As a result, "efforts to convert Jews and Muslims . . . led to the production of a considerable number of polemical texts . . . and gave rise to crypto-Muslim and crypto-Jewish groups" (García-Arenal & Wiegers, 2018, p. 2). Multilingualism, something that had previously been typical in al-Andalus and continued in the Alpujarras region of Granada and Almería, became an indicator of belonging to an un-assimilable community. As the conflict deepened and widened from Granada to Almería, extending all the way to Valencia, Moriscos faced further pressures, such as confiscations and higher taxes, that pushed them further to the margins (Benafri, 2011) and created a climate of terror and an atmosphere of mistrust of anyone with an affinity or association with the Morisco, Andalusí-Arabic, or Muslim identities. In the sixteenth century, in the Alpujarras, the mountainous region separating Granada and Almería, incipient mastery of Arabic became an indicator of covert affinity to Islam and a presumed contempt for Christianity.

In 1609, the Crown decided that it was necessary to issue formal decrees with the purpose of expelling the Moriscos. These decrees represent the final stage in the progressive degradation of relations between the Morisco population and the Crown. Where once there had been varying levels of cohabitation and tolerance, the decrees were the embodiment of overt antagonism (Deardorff, 2018, 1). The standardization of Castilian that began in the fifteenth and sixteenth centuries culminated with the promotion of Castilian as the official language during the reign of Philip V (1700–1746) (Giménez-Eguibar & Wasserman-Soler, 2011; Plann, 2009). The festivals of *moros y cristianos* examined here were born out of this hostile linguistic context, where Andalusí-Arabic had become associated with the Moriscos and Islam.

14.2 The Festival of Carboneras: A Three-Day-Long Celebration

The festival in Carboneras is based on a script entitled *La fiesta de moros y cristianos en la Villa de Carboneras procedente de una noticia histórica* [The festival of Moors and Christians in the Village of Carboneras coming from a historical note] (Cala y López et al., 1993; all translations of the text are by the author). Different versions of the script can be traced to a text published in 1918 in Cuevas, presumed, in turn, to be a local version of an eighteenth-century script produced in Granada (cf. Fernández-García, 1980). Even before the performance begins, the title declares that the events portrayed are grounded in historical fact, that is, a historical note. The prologue, read aloud, offers a brief context:

La historia comienza en 1559, o sea después de la reconquista, en plena época de sublevaciones musulmanas en Granada cuando Felipe II hizo entrega de estas tierras al marqués de Carpio con el mandato de edificar el Castillo de San Andrés. Esta [sic] 'defendería esta costa ante la sublevación de los moriscos' y además de eso, consiguió que la población se organizase en torno a este monumento. Más tarde en el siglo XIX pasó a formar parte de la Casa de Alba.

[The story begins in 1559, that is to say, after the reconquest, during the period of the Muslim revolts in Granada when Philip II entrusted these lands to the Marquis of Carpio with the mandate to build the Castle of San Andrés. This would 'defend this coast from the revolts of the Moriscos,' and furthermore, he [the king] made the population organize around this monument. Later in the 19th century, [the lands] would become part of the Casa de Alba.]

The introduction places the events after the Andalusí era (711–1492), during the Rebellion of the Moriscos, even if the date is off by nine years. The figure of the Marquis is familiar to the locals as is the castle that stands as the main, although modest, architectural feature of the town.

14.2.1 Act 1: Recalling the Rebellion of the Alpujarras

The festivities are kicked off with a mass and a procession of San Antonio, the patron saint of the village, from the Church, around the main streets of the village, to the local castle, the fort, or the outpost surveillance tower. The saint remains at the entrance of the castle until the closing events on the final day. The opening narration reads:

cuenta la historia, que sublevados los moriscos en la Alpujarra, invadieron nuestra costa otros moros, que procediendo de Argel y al mando de Caracas en su ayuda se aprestaban
[The story tells us that once the Moriscos of the Alpujarra rebelled, our coast was invaded by other Moors that came from Algeria and were under the command of Caracas and offered them [the Moriscos] their help.]

The use of the terms *otros moros* [other Moors] and *invadieron* [invaded] immediately place the Moriscos – who were, in fact, locals – as outsiders. The group is excluded from belonging to *nuestra costa* [our coast]. Being a *moro* or a *morisco* is juxtaposed to being Spanish, which by exclusion of this group, means 'not *moro*.' In the text, the terms *moro*, meaning Muslim, and *morisco*, a Christian of Muslim heritage, have been subsumed under one identity. The different religions have been erased. What matters is their perceived origin and the idea that a supposed Christian convert is, in fact, always a crypto-Muslim. This resonates with the ingrained notion that Moriscos only nominally converted to Christianity (Paego-Ruzafa, 2020). In the reenacted period, anything that could be associated with the Islamic past, including the Arabic language, was used against Moriscos to accuse them of maintaining a crypto-Islamic identity (García-Arenal, 2009).

The inclusion of the name of the General Caracas lends the reenactment its flair of historicity as he is a familiar local historical figure. General Caracas was a general of Turkish origin who participated in the coastal raids prior and during the Morisco Rebellion in support of the Morisco community in Granada and Almería (Cabrera-Sánchez, 1999). The fact that a general supposedly of Turkish origin supported the Morisco community further plays into the popular idea that the history of Spain, and therefore of the local peoples, is essentially a history of Christian–Islamic conflict. It also lends more credibility to the idea that the Moriscos have other loyalties, which is why they are supported by foreign powers.

14.2.2 Act 2: Conquest and Reconquest

The script continues:

> dos partes tiene esta historia: esta mañana, los cristianos derrotados; esta tarde, con la ayuda del Patrón, los moros serán conversos y después serán bautizados
> [There are two parts to this story: in the morning, the defeated Christians; in the afternoon, with the help of the Patron, the Moors will be converted and then baptized.]

The audience is told the sequence of events. First, the Christians will be defeated, just as they were in 711. Then, with the help of the patron saint and their strong faith, the Christians will regain the lands, just as it supposedly happened in the reconquest. Finally, there will be mass conversions. The Moors will become Christians. This detail glosses over the fact that the Morisco population was already Christian and serves as an example of how the figure of the Morisco dangled on the border between tolerance and intolerance (Novikoff, 2005). The contrast between the supposed Christian and Muslim characters cannot be clearer. The Christian general describes the scene as follows:

> A este humilde Alcázar que la nobleza cristiana eligió para dar culto a la persona sagrada de San Antonio, que es su patrono, hoy con fervor se le aclama ... Pues la malicia y soberbia de la nación mahometana puede intentar sorprendernos.
> [Upon this humble castle that the Christian nobility chose to venerate the sacred person of San Antonio, who is its patron, today, with fervor we acclaim ... Because the malice and the pride of the Mahometan state can try to surprise us.]

Christians are humble and dedicate themselves to the saint. People of the Muslim faith are proud and malicious.

Once the patron saint has been brought down from the church in a procession that includes only those dressed as Christians, the action begins.

A lookout, supposedly a Christian, rides to the town castle to tell the Christian in charge that there are *moros a la vista*, Moors on the horizon. Just like its close cousin *moros en la costa* [Moors on the coast] his expression is used to "warn Spaniards of the presence of someone who may be dangerous or who should not overhear what is said" (Plann, 2009, p. 376). It roughly corresponds to the English "speaking of the devil" and is used to alert their interlocutor that the subject being spoken about is arriving and one should change topic. The section reads:

Al ver unos moros llegar a la costa, van corriendo al castillo para contarle al cristiano lo que vieron.
[Upon observing some Moors arriving at the coast, they take off running to the castle to tell the Christian what they saw.]

On his way to the castle, the Christian lookout encounters a person that volunteers what he knows:

¿Sois Centinela de España? ... Y respondió ... has de saber que esos que se desembarcan son los moros argelinos que vienen aquesta playa como lo han hecho otras veces a llevarse la sagrada imagen.
[Are you a sentinel of Spain? ... and he replied ... you must know that those who are disembarking are the Moors from Algeria who come to this beach as they have done other times to take away the sacred image.]

This passage conveys the idea that the Moors are intent on plundering. Most importantly, the concept of Spain is employed anachronistically, as it had not yet solidified and the peninsula was still comprised of independent kingdoms that addressed the Morisco issue via different methods. The same can be said about the term 'Spanish,' used later in the text by the ambassador for the Moors, who greets the junior officer with these words:

Bizarro Marte español que con tu trompa la fama publica el valor constante que de tu pecho resalta; pues con el oscurecisteis la singular arrogancia de Héctor, de Aníbal y Jerjes; de Julio César; la audacia de Alejandro.
[O gallant Spanish Mars! With your horn you proclaim the constant valor that your chest radiates. With it you darkened the unique arrogance of Hector, of Hannibal and Xerxes, of Julius Caesar, and the audacity of Alexander.]

These grand names invoke a shared feeling of belonging and stress the heroism and bravery of the Spaniards, which even the ambassador must acknowledge. Once at the castle, the lookout describes what he has seen and describes the enemy in highly derogatory terms:

Yo que los reconocí, y sé que a uno le llaman el Talón y al otro el cojo el Cacho... y es que traen plagadas los moros de piojos sus cabezas aún más que la vista alcanza.
[I, who recognized them, know that one of them is called the Talón (the heel) and the other one who limps, the Cacho (the little bit) ... and the thing is that the Moors' heads are plagued with lice even more than the eyes can see.]

The lookout recognizes his adversaries and identifies them by their nicknames. One is named 'the heel,' the back part of the foot below the ankle. The other is identified first by a physical ailment, 'a limp.' Then, he is called Cacho, which refers to 'a little bit of something,' as in *pásame un cacho de pan* [pass me a little bit of bread]. The implication is that he is physically impaired and short or insignificant in stature. To round out the unflattering description, the Moors are plagued with lice, with the potential of bringing a plague upon the locals.

Upon hearing the news, the generals in the castle order their soldiers to follow them to the beach to witness the Moorish boats disembark. Upon disembarking, the ambassador for the Moorish troops explains that his purpose is to conquer these lands in the name of Mohammad and that he is supported by Musa's troops. Ibn al Musa was the general who led the conquest of the Iberian Peninsula in 711, but this passage refers to the events of May 1570 when supposedly, a group of 25,000–30,000 people on Turco-Berber boats clandestinely landed on the shores to aid the Morisco plight (Benafri, 2011). The effect is to confound, confuse, and merge the events of 711 with those of the sixteenth century until the two time periods become indistinguishable. The raid is framed as a process of religious and cultural invasion of Islam against Christians, of foreigners acting against the true and legitimate residents of the land. The implication is that the rightful residents of the region are Iberian Christians, and particularly families with a long-standing Christian heritage. Moriscos or recent converts to Christianity automatically become suspect and associated with the eighth-century invader.

The junior ranking officer, the Christian Alférez, replies to the ambassador:

> ¿No comprendes imbécil, que ahora mismo están, sin más, vencidas tus quimeras? ¿No recuerdas infiel, que el rey Fernando fue un héroe en mi Patria?
> [Don't you understand, you fool, that now your fantasies are defeated? Don't you remember, infidel, that the king Fernando was the hero of my homeland?]

Diplomatic protocol would require that a person of the same rank respond to the ambassador's statements. The fact that a junior officer responds to the ambassador's threats implies that the ambassador is seen as a person of lesser importance, or of lesser social status, than the Christian general. The Christian dignitaries unilaterally take the liberty of deciding that a protocolary response is not necessary in this case. To add insult to injury, the Moorish ambassador is again referred to in derogatory terms. He is a fool and an infidel. As these celebrations were originally created to keep the troops trained, they would have been familiar with the general protocol and the extra-protocolary exchange would not have been lost on the participants.

What follows is a second instance of anachronistic historical references that, again, draw upon general popular knowledge and a somewhat precarious memory for dates. The Christian continues the exchange:

¿Han oído sarraceno al Alférez cristiano?... ¿Qué se diría en Europa, América, África y Asia, que son las partes del orbe...
La intención de esos bárbaros es vencernos en batalla.
[Have you heard, Saracen, the junior Christian officer? What would they say in Europe, America, Africa and Asia, that together are the parts of the orb (earth)?
The intention of these barbarians is to defeat us in battle.]

The inclusion of the concepts of Europe, America, Africa, and Asia demonstrates that the script was written for an audience that would have at the very least been aware of the so-called 'discovery' and colonization of the American continent and the 'barbarians' found there. By calling the Muslims 'barbarians,' the Christian general is creating a significant juxtaposition. Having already represented Moriscos as indistinguishable from Muslims, they are made by extension uncivilized – thus, they have no claim and do not belong to the area in which they reside. In contrast, Christians are civilized and have legitimate claims. The inclusion of Europe, America, Africa, and Asia alongside 'barbarians' helps underscore the idea that the Moorish raiding army depicted in this reenactment has no legitimate claim and, by extension, questions the legitimacy of the Morisco claim to be considered part of the community in the land where they live. Any attempt of a claim would be rebuffed literally by all corners of the world.

The pejorative Muslim imagery continues as follows:

asquerosos reptiles, hora de esclavos viles ... árabe traidor, secta ruin, cobardes, forastero, fiera canalla, lagarto
[disgusting reptiles, hour of vile slaves, traitor Arab, contemptible sect, cowards, strangers, scoundrel beast, lizard]

The term *forastero* [stranger] defines Muslims and Moriscos, even those who had been for many generations in the land, as outsiders. To emphasize the disdain, Muslims are described as crawling animals associated with evil or foreboding. The reference to the hour of vile slaves alludes to the much longer time of a slave's labor, twice as long as a regular servant's time. Christians, by contrast, are referred to with the terms *bravura* [bravery], *fuerte* [strong], *fiel* [faithful], and *el mas importante león* [the most important lion] (the lion, considered a brave and noble animal, is one of the symbols of the Spanish monarchy). These brief but visually vivid descriptions feed the popular imagination and cement the idea that the Arab is a member of a sect, unacceptable, and unpleasant to look at or be around. The reference to 'slaves' also implies that they are of lesser economic/social class. In contrast, those Christians who reside in the area observe true faith and are noble and valiant.

14.2.3 Act 3: Conversion

Once the introductions are concluded, the Christians and Moors engage in a battle on the beach. Just as in 711, the Moors win. The conquerors head to the castle and put up their colors. Their victory, however, is ephemeral. The next day there are several celebrations devoted to the local saint, San Antonio, in the town square in front of the castle and on the beach where the battle had ensued. Amazed by the faith of the Christians, the Moors repent. At the end of the day, the Moorish and Christian armies return to the castle in a grand procession and the Moorish general declares:

> Amigo me has convencido y llenado es esperanza y con esta confianza voy a pedir humillado. Con vergüenza me presento a vuestros pies San Antonio, ya sabéis que en esta hora de mis culpas me arrepiento.
> [Friend, you have convinced me and filled me with hope and with this confidence, I will ask in humility. Ashamed I present myself at your feet, Saint Antonio, and you know that in this hour my faults I repent.]

The event ends with the return of the saint to the church by the Moorish general and his troops. The narrator explains: *puesto que siempre fueron creyentes devolvieron al santo a la capilla* [since they had always been believers, they returned the saint to the chapel].

The Rebellion of the Alpujarras had been likened to civil and religious wars that led to the radicalization of positions (Jiménez-Estrella & Castillo-Fernández, 2020). The festivals of the Christians and Moors encapsulate the sentiments of hate and distrust between 'old Christians' and 'new Christian' Moriscos that were at the root of the rebellions. The intent of the 'Old Christians' was to intimidate those crypto-Muslims who may have slipped through the cracks. This becomes clear in the closing portions of the ceremony when the statue of the saint is returned to the church. To prove their repentance, the Moors put their hands on the saint, a common test used in the Inquisition to prove that a Morisco, a former Muslim, had truly converted to Christianity and was not merely claiming a cursory conversion. Distrust is at the basis of this step of the ceremony. The act of touching the saint has the purpose of confirming conversion not just in words but also in action. The vocabulary chosen serves to reinforce the mono-religious identity and the language used becomes the external performance and confirmation of the very same. Finally, the figure of the Morisco, to be incorporated, is transformed from 'fake Christian' into 'new Christian.'

Conclusion

In his recent paper on Spanish historiography, García-Marsilla (2020) recalls a famous debate between the cultural historian and philologist Américo Castro and the historian Claudio Sánchez Albornoz about the essence of Spanish identity. Américo Castro considered the Spanish essence to lie in the coexistence of the three 'casts,' the people of the three Abrahamic faiths. For Sánchez Albornoz, the period of al-Andalus and Islam in the Iberian Peninsula represents only a passing chapter in Spanish history (García-Marsilla, 2020). The reenactments of Christians and Moors embody the same debates. Today, when Spain is facing a growing immigrant Muslim population, the growing popularity of the reenactments has taken on a new significance. The purpose of this chapter was to trace the ways in which the scripts create links between past events and the present unease.

The festival of Carboneras, held to be the model for other villages trying to recapture their historical roots, was born out of the events surrounding and following the Rebellion of the Moriscos in 1568–1570. In the eighteenth century, the festival was devised as a strategy to maintain the troops trained and keep them mindful of their mission. The propagandist language drew the line between the legitimate identity, language, and religion and the illegitimate ones.

The language and the structure of the festival presupposes that only a specific community, the self-defined Christian, has an authentic legitimate claim of belonging in the land and that the eight-century-long coexistence with Muslim communities was a parenthesis in that history (for more on the coexistence debate, see Castro, 1948, 1965; Catlos, 2004, 2014; García-Sanjuán, 2018). One of the purposes of the festival is to emphasize the continuity of the Roman-Christian heritage in the region (Beale-Rivaya & Busic, 2018; Corbera & Utrilla-Utrilla, 1998; Porres Martin-Cleto, 1985). By extension, the language of the script legitimizes abusive behavior toward and the expulsion of 'invaders' and 'outsiders' (García-Sanjuán, 2012). The term *Morisco* is transformed and recast from its original meaning to refer to a complex set of events and to affirm one narrow and distorted vision of the past. Likewise, the word 'Spanish' did not originally refer to a language but to a people. It was only after the thirteenth century that this term began to appear in place of or alongside names given to the inhabitants of different regions of Spain, that is, *gallegos*, *leoneses*, *castellanos*, *navarros*, and such.

The use of 'Spanish' to refer to the Castilian language appears only toward the end of the fifteenth century, when the Catholic monarchs, Isabel of Castille and Fernando of Aragón, conquered Granada (Rivarola, 1978) and precipitated the series of events that would eventually lead to the creation of the festivals examined here. Until then, there had never been a particular language associated with a national identity. Andalusí-Arabic and Romance had, to varying degrees, at different times, and in different locations, shared spaces throughout the peninsula (Rivarola, 1978). Afterward, language became a means to confirm an identity and to exclude those who do not neatly fit into the supposed in-group.

While there were variations in the extent one or another language were used at different times, the pursuit to codify the Castilian language and the shift in the meaning of the specific term *español*, Spanish, to indicate a preference for a particular Romance language over Andalusí-Arabic was in many ways radical. Andalusí-Arabic went from being a language that was spoken by the locals to an index of crypto-Muslim activities. This, in turn, was used to marginalize the Morisco community. Suddenly, to be considered Spanish one had to speak a Latin-based language. Multilingualism, common in the thirteenth century, was harnessed punitively to exclude complex 'problematic' identities, such as that of the Morisco. The festivals of *moros y cristianos* help engrain the legitimacy of nationalist ideas that seek to generate a specific hegemonic identity grounded in an affirmation of the Roman-Latin-Christian vision of the past.

Add to this the specific local history of Almería, where the 'natural' state between Moors and Christians was war (Giménez-Soler, 1904), and one begins to see how these festivals, which are often ignored and underestimated as a quaint local tradition, are a visual and aural reflection of historical tensions emblematic of the Rebellion of the Moriscos, a site of commodification of the exotic Other and a means of promotion of distorted historiography and popular memory. Their language is purposefully selected to elevate and justify the actions and attitudes of the Christians and to amalgamate the identity of Moriscos, whose families had lived in these lands for centuries, with that of *Moros* from across the Mediterranean. While the Iberian Peninsula was and is a society of many languages, it had redefined its identity through the exclusion of Arabic. The reenactments that skillfully play with, confuse, and obscure several periods in Spain's history are a theatrical mirror of a real process of linguistic and social exclusion that reaches from the past to the present day.

References

Beale-Rivaya, Y. (2012) The written record as witness: Language shift from Arabic to Romance in the documents of the Mozarabs of Toledo in the twelfth and thirteenth Centuries. *La Corónica*, 40, 2, 27–50.

(2016) At the crossroads of languages: The linguistic choices along border communities of the Reconquista in the eleventh and twelfth Centuries. In Klassen, A. (ed.) *Multilingualism in the Middle Ages and Early Modern Age: Communication and Miscommunication in the Premodern World.* Mouton de Gruyter, pp.127–44.

Beale-Rivaya, Y. & J. Busic (2018) Introduction. In Beale-Rivaya, Y. & J. Busic (eds.) *A Companion to Medieval Toledo: Reconsidering the Canons*. Leiden: Brill, pp. 1–14.

Benafri, C. (2011) La posición de la Sublime Puerta y de la Regencia de Argel ante La Rebelión de los moriscos granadinos (1568–1570): Entre esperanza y decepción [The position of the Sublime Porte and of the Regency of Argel in the face of the Rebellion of the Moriscos of Granada (1568–1570): Between Hope and Disappointment]. *AREAS. Revista Internacional de Ciencias Sociales*, 30, 141–146.

Cabrera-Sánchez, M. (1999) El Señorío de El Carpio en el Siglo XV [The Estate of El Carpio in the 15th century]. *Aragón En La Edad Media*, 14–15, 227–242.

Cala y López, R., Flores González-Grano de Oro, M., & J. Grima Cervantes (1993) *La fiesta de moros y cristianos en la villa de Carboneras: Precedida de una noticia histórica* [The Festival of the Moors and Christians in the Town of Carboneras: Preceded by a Historical Note]. Almería: Ayuntamiento de Carboneras Instituto de estudios almerienses.

Castro, A. (1948) *España en su historia: cristianos, moros y judíos* [Spain and its history: Christians, Moors, and Jews]. Buenos Aires: Editorial Losada.

(1965) *Los españoles: Cómo llegaron a serlo* [The Spanish: How they came to be]. Madrid: Taurus.

Catlos, B. (2004) *The victors and the vanquished: Christians and Muslims of Catalonia and Aragon, 1050–1300.* Cambridge: Cambridge University Press.

(2014) *Muslims and medieval Latin Christendom, c. 1050–1614.* Cambridge: Cambridge University Press.

Chalmeta, P. (1994) *Invasión e islamización: La sumisión de Hispania y la formación de al-Andalus* [Invasion and Islamization: The submission of Spain and formation of al-Andalus]. Madrid: Mapfre.

Corbera, C. & J. Utrilla-Utrilla (eds.) (1998) *De Toledo a Huesca: Sociedades medievales en transición a finales del Siglo XI (1080–1100)* [From Toledo to Huesca: Medieval societies in transition at the end of the 11th Century (1080–1110)]. Zaragoza: Universidad de Zaragoza.

Deardorff, M. (2018) ¿Quién es morisco? Desde cristiano nuevo a cristiano viejo de moros: Categorías de diferenciación en el Reino de Granada (siglo XVI) [Who is Morisco? From new Christian to old Christian Moors. Categories for Differentiation in the Kingdom of Granada (16th century)]. *Forum Historiae Iuris*, 1–27.

Escobosa, F., Muñoz-Martín, I. & M. Lirola-Delgado (1998) Las producciones de un alfar islámico en Almería [The productions of an Islamic potter in Almeria]. *Arqueología y Territorio Medieval*, 6, 207–239.

Eurostat (2021) Asylum and first time asylum applicants: annual aggregated data. [https://ec.europa.eu/eurostat/databrowser/view/tps00191/default/table?lang=en. Date accessed June 21, 2021].

Fernández-García, J. (1980) *Función de moros y cristianos dedicada a San Antoni de Pádua patrón de Carboneras: Texto Corregido* [Festival of the Moors and Christians dedicated to Saint Anthony of Padua, Patron of Carboneras. Corrected Text]. Cuevas.

García-Arenal, M. (2009) The religious identity of the Arabic language and the affair of the Lead Books of the Sacromonte of Granada. *Arabica*, 56, 6, 495–528.

(2015) The converted Muslims of Spain: Morisco cultural resistance and engagement with Islamic knowledge (1502–1610). In Tottoli, R. (ed.) *The Routledge Handbook of Islam in the West.* New York: Routledge, pp. 38–54.

García-Arenal, M. & G. Wiegers (2018) Interreligious encounters in polemics between Christians, Jews, and Muslims in Iberia and beyond. *Medieval Encounters*, 24, 1–13.

García-Marsilla, J. (2020) Leyenda negra, medievo rosa: Reflexiones sobre el mito de La 'España de las tres culturas.' [Black legend, pink medieval: Reflections on the myth of the 'Spain of the Three Cultures']. *Pasajes*, 60, 29–42.

García-Sanjuán, A. (2009) El fin de las comunidades cristianas de Al-Andalus (Siglos XI–XII): Factores de una evolución [The end of the Christian Communities of Al-Andalus (11th–12th centuries]. In de la Peña, J. (ed.) *Cristianos y musulmanes en la Península Ibérica; la guerra, la frontera y la convivencia* [Christians and Muslims in the Iberian Peninsula; the war, the frontier, and coexistence]. Ávila; Fundación Sánchez-Albornoz, pp. 257–287.

(2012) Al-Andalus en la historiografía del nacionalismo españolista (Siglos XIX–XXI). Entre la reconquista y la España musulmana [Al-Andalus in Spanish nationalist historiography. Between the Reconquest and Muslim Spain]. In Melo Carrasco, D. & F. Vidal Castro (eds.) *A 1300 Años de la conquista de Al-Andalus (711–2011): Historia, cultura y legado del islam en la península ibérica* [1300 years after the conquest of Al-Andalus (711–2011): History, culture and legacy of Islam on the Iberian peninsula]. Coquimbo-Chile: Centro Mohammed VI, pp. 65–104.

(2018) Rejecting Al-Andalus, exalting the Reconquista: Historical memory in contemporary Spain. *Journal of Medieval Iberian Studies*, 10, 1, 127–145.

Giménez-Eguibar, P. & D. Wasserman-Soler (2011) *La mala algarabia*: Church and the Arabic language in 16th-century Spain. *The Medieval History Journal*, 14, 2, 229–258.

Giménez-Soler, A. (1904) *El sitio de Almería en 1309* [The siege of Almeria in 1309]. Barcelona: De la casa provincial de caridad e montealegre.

Hitchcock, R. (2008) *Mozarabs in medieval and early modern Spain: Identities and influences.* Cornwall: Ashgate.

Jiménez-Estrella, A. & J. Castillo-Fernández (2020) *La rebelión de los moriscos del Reino de Granada y La Guerra en época de los austrias: Estudio para un debate abierto* [The Rebellion of the Moriscos of the Kingdom of Granada and war in the times of the Austrias: Study for an open debate]. Granada: Universidad de Granada.

Novikoff, A. (2005) Between tolerance and intolerance in medieval Spain: An historiographic enigma. *Medieval Encounters*, 11, 1–2, 7–36.

O'Callaghan, J. (2003) *Reconquest and crusade in medieval Spain.* Philadelphia, PA: University of Pennsylvania Press.

Paego-Ruzafa, J. (2020) Huestes, milicias y soldados en la rebelión de las Alpujarras. La estrategia de Abén Humeya [Troops, militias, and soldiers in the Rebellion of the Alpujarras. The strategy of Aben Humeya]. In Jiménez Estrella, A. & J. Castillo (eds.) *La Rebelión de los moriscos del reino de Granada* [The Rebellion of the Moriscos of the Kingdom of Granada]. Granada: Universidad de Granada, pp. 79–94.

Plann, S. (2009) Arabic: Another 'other' Spanish language? *International Journal of Multilingualism*, 6, 4, 369–385.

Porres Martin-Cleto, J. (1985) *Historia de Tulaytula (711–1085)* [History of Tulaytula (711–1085)]. Toledo: Instituto provincial de investigaciones y estudios toledanos.

Quiroga, M. & M. Rodríguez-Lovelle (eds.) (1997) *La invasión árabe y el inicio de la 'Reconquista' en el noroeste de la península ibérica (93-251/711-865)* [The Arab invasion and the beginning of the 'Reconquest' in the North-East of the Iberian Peninsula]. Turnhout: Brepols.

Rivarola, J. (1978) El español medieval: algunos aspectos de la formación del español como lengua literaria [Medieval Spanish: Some aspects of the formation of Spanish as a literary language]. *Revista de la Universidad Católica*, 4, 31, 321–331.

Rogozen-Soltar, M. (2012) Managing Muslim visibility: Conversion, immigration, and Spanish imaginaries of Islam. *American Anthropologist*, 114, 4, 611–623.

Safran, J. (2013) *Defining Boundaries in al-Andalus: Muslims, Christians, and Jews in Islamic Iberia*. Ithaca, NY: Cornell University Press.

Vallvé-Bermejo, J. (1989) *Nuevas ideas sobre la conquista árabe de España, Toponimia y onomástica* [New ideas about the Arab conquest of Spain: Toponymy and onomastics]. Madrid, Spain: Real Academia de la Historia.

Vampa, D. (2020) Competing forms of populism and territorial politics: The cases of Vox and Podemos in Spain. *Journal of Contemporary European Studies*, 28, 3, 304–321.

15 Multilingual Ghost Signs: Dissonant Languages in the Landscape of Memory

Aneta Pavlenko

The Ukrainian city of Lviv is the world capital of multilingual *ghost signs* – signs that no longer serve their original purpose. Every time prewar buildings are renovated – or when paint or plaster crumble off from old age – more ads for forgotten brands, obsolete goods, and defunct businesses come to light. Andriy Pavlyshyn, a Ukrainian translator and journalist, once described his native city as "this beautiful place where one could always find lots of strange things.

Fig. 15.1 Ads in Polish and Yiddish for Halpern's fabric store and warehouse, *Skład towarów bławatnych*, on Nalyvaiko Street, 13 (at the turn of the twentieth century the street – then known as Rzeźnicka – was inhabited primarily by Jews). Lviv, September 2019. Photo by the author.

For their insightful feedback on this chapter I am very grateful to the three anonymous reviewers and to many scholars who participated in the crowd-sourced peer review on Academia.

Old bits and pieces in the attic written in an unknown language; walls where the plaster peeled off and names made up of foreign words appeared – later I learned that it was Polish, Yiddish, German" (in Lewicka, 2008, pp. 214–215). The tacit agreement in the city is to let them be. On the surface, so to speak, the consensus is not surprising: All cities cherish their heritage, right?

"Ghost signs," explains William Stage (1989) in a book that launched the term, "are the most interesting of all wall signs. Faded to the point of illegibility, they linger on old buildings, echoing the robust commerce of times past" (p. 71). For some building owners they are an eyesore, but the ephemeral signage has long had a dedicated fan base: eagle-eyed ghost sign hunters who scout the streets to spot new apparitions, hang from rooftops and fire escapes to capture their spectral outlines from the right angle in the best light, and share their treasured finds via social media, websites, online forums, walking tours, and glossy books about the fading ads of Dublin and London, Montreal and Detroit, Philadelphia and New York.

Scholars who study ghost signs have identified several reasons behind their popular appeal: the sense of continuity with the past, nostalgia for the bygone era, fascination with history, the retro cool of vintage aesthetic, fondness for quality handicraft (Schutt et al., 2017). Sign spotters have their own rationales: the thrill of the quest, the joy of discovery, the giddiness of being "transported back to an earlier time" (Passikoff, 2017, p. xvi). Pavlyshyn adds a new perspective that highlights the difference between Lviv signs and their counterparts in Australia, the USA, UK, and France (cf. Schutt et al., 2017): in Lviv, their languages are 'strange,' 'unknown,' and 'foreign' because its residents are not the descendants of people who created the ads.

Lviv is one of Europe's 'repopulated' cities, alongside Breslau/Wrocław, Danzig/Gdańsk, Königsberg/Kaliningrad, or Czernowitz/Chernivtsi: in the wake of World War II, Polish Lwów became Ukrainian Lviv (for an in-depth discussion of such cities, see Blacker, 2019). The drastic rupture turned its built environment into *dissonant heritage* (Tunbridge & Ashworth, 1996) and its former languages into *dissonant tongues.*[1] The discontinuity raises an interesting question: If Ukrainian history is not a factor, what are the signs in Yiddish, Polish, and German doing on Lviv streets? More generally, what do urban authorities do with dissonant heritage?

15.1 Dissonant Heritage in the Landscape of Memory

After the fall of the Berlin Wall and creation of the European Union (EU), dissonant heritage came into prominence in discussions of a common

[1] Other 'repopulated' cities also display dissonant ghost signs: In Wrocław in 2021 a team of enthusiasts published a map of over 200 ghost signs in German.

European identity and the voids left by World War II. Many Polish, Czech, German, Hungarian, and Slovak towns are still struggling to overcome mutual resentments and memories of deportations (cf. Kurnicki & Sternberg, 2016) and in some places, silence and erasure are the only responses to the troublesome past (Bartov, 2007). Acknowledgment of dissonant heritage is also fraught with ambivalence, as seen in the case of the Jews. In the 1990s, many European cities opened Jewish museums, erected Holocaust memorials, restored Jewish cemeteries, placed plaques on former synagogues, and organized festivals of klezmer music and exhibits on Jewish history. Several joined a project, initiated in 1992 by the German artist Gunther Demnig, where brass plates with the names and life spans of Nazi victims were embedded in the streets as *Stolpersteine* – stumbling stones. Gruber's (2002) brilliant analysis revealed the complexity of this commemoration, where sincere desire for atonement intersected with political calculation and commercial exploitation, as in Krakow's Kazimierz, an old Jewish quarter redeveloped as a tourist Yiddishland with Jewish-themed cafés and souvenir stalls selling hook-nosed, side-curled toy Jews (see also Burdin, 2021).

The studies to date highlight four trends in the management of dissonant heritage: (a) invention of a 'noble past' that foregrounds positive events and erases or downplays events that shed negative light on patriotic 'national' history; (b) commodification of the past as a spectacle or 'historytainment'; (c) exoticization and stereotyping of vanished 'others'; and (d) exclusion from the decision-making process of the very people whose heritage we are invited to celebrate (Bartov, 2007; Bechtel, 2016; Blacker, 2014, 2019; Boll, 2020; Burdin, 2021; Calderwood, 2014; Corsale, 2021; Flesler & Pérez Melgosa, 2008; Godis & Nilsson, 2018; Narvselius, 2015).

Burdin (2021) adds a new dimension to this work by highlighting the role of the newly made – and often ungrammatical – signs in Yiddish and Hebrew that index Jewishness and add faux 'authenticity' to Krakow's Kazimierz. In what follows, I will extend this exploration to other dissonant signs that (re-)appeared on European streets. Some are still dilapidated, others restored, yet others manufactured anew but all have one thing in common: their languages are long gone from local repertoires. At first glance, their roles are similar to those of Kazimierz signs – just another way to commemorate lost 'others' and add 'authenticity' to visitor experience and 'historicity' to the urban façade. My aim in this chapter is to show that multilingual ghost signs are also multitasking in ways that are less obvious, benign, or banal.

In what follows, I will examine the roles of dissonant signs in four cities designated by the United Nations Educational, Scientific and Cultural Organization (UNESCO) as World Heritage sites. Primary data comes from my fieldwork, which included site visits, participation in tours in relevant languages, interviews with tour guides and foreign visitors, and analyses of UNESCO reports, tourist guides, media, and travelogues. The aim of the critical discourse analysis was to compare academic histories with city marketing narratives, where "the urge to remember and commemorate is tightly bound with the need to suppress and forget" (Bartov, 2007, p. 173). Politicians, business owners, architects, historians, activists, and tour guides are seen in this analysis as *memory actors* and restoration and installation of signs as *practices of collective remembrance* that promote, contest, or erase certain versions of the past (Huyssen, 2003; Lähdesmäki et al., 2019; Tunbridge & Ashworth, 1996). Drawing on my findings and on published research, I will try to answer four questions: Who are the memory actors behind dissonant signs? What images are they trying to project? What historic and linguistic realities do the signs conceal? And what does the resurrection of the multilingual past say about us?

15.2 Toledo

In 2018, a new plaque was affixed in a little Toledan alley Callejon de San Pedro: a list of its previous names, most of them Arabic, going back to 1187 (Fig. 15.2a). The plaque is the latest addition to the growing number of signs that invoke the city's Islamic and Jewish past. Local museums display Hebrew and Arabic inscriptions, the boundaries of the *Judería*, the old Jewish quarter, are identified by tiny tiles with menorahs and the Hebrew word *Sefarad* [Spain], and the historic center abounds in Spanish-English signs that clarify

(a) (b)

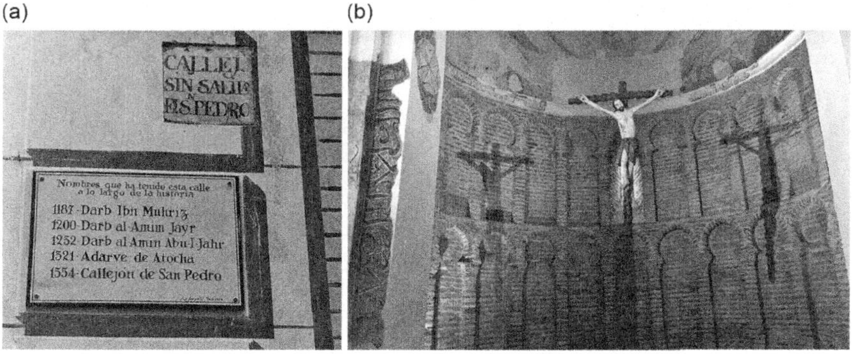

Fig. 15.2 Arabic in Toledo: (a) Street plaque with former street names, installed in 2018. (b) A Kufic sign on the apsidal arch of the church Cristo de la Luz, offering a formulaic blessing *al-yumn wa al-iqbal* [fortune and prosperity]. Toledo, September 2019. Photos by the author.

the origins of place names like Alcántara, Arabic for bridge, and Zocodover, once a cattle market, *suq al-dawab*.

The city's exotic heritage long fascinated curious foreigners, like Albert Calvert (1907), whose poetic guide to Toledo features 500 photographs, including Hebrew inscriptions of the Ha-Levi synagogue and the Arabic frieze of the ibn Hadidi mosque converted into the church Cristo de la Luz (Fig. 15.2b). Regular visitors were scarce – Spain wasn't on the Grand Tour. Genteel Europeans snubbed it as a bigoted, ignorant, and intolerant backwater ever since the 1492 expulsion of the Jews (indignant Spaniards dubbed the libelous image the Black Legend).

In the mid-twentieth century, historian and philologist Américo Castro (1954) proposed an alternative view: Spanish culture was a hybrid shaped by centuries of *convivencia*, a peaceful coexistence of Christians, Muslims, and Jews. In academia, the idea triggered a heated – and still ongoing – debate but tourism authorities sensed an opportunity: in the wake of Franco's death, Spain was rebranded as the cradle of medieval tolerance. Following the renewal of diplomatic relations with Israel (1986) and facing the 500th anniversary of the expulsion (1992), several Spanish cities unveiled Jewish heritage sites and in 1995 formed a network, *Red de Juderias de España* (Flesler & Pérez Melgosa, 2008; Lacave, 2004). International exhibits promoted *convivencia* to the general public (e.g., Mann et al., 1992), and Muslims were offered tours of al-Andalus with Islam-friendly services, featuring halal food (Boll, 2020; Calderwood, 2014).

By the twenty-first century, Spain had become one of the leading destinations for Jewish heritage tourism, 'halal tourism,' and urban visitors at large. This tourism, argue Flesler and Pérez Melgosa (2008), solved a national riddle: Why care for dissonant heritage in a country whose very identity is predicated on the erasure of Muslims and Jews? Among the greatest beneficiaries of the multicultural turn was the city of Toledo, designated in 1986 a World Heritage site:

> All of the civilizations which contributed to the grandeur of Toledo left there amazing masterpieces which expressed both the original beauty of a highly characteristic style and the paradoxical syncretism of the hybrid forms of the Mudejar style which sprang from the contact of heterogeneous civilizations in an environment where for a long time the existence of three major religions – Judaism, Christianity and Islam – was a leading feature. (UNESCO, 1986, pp. 1–2)

Ever since, municipal authorities have made impressive efforts to restore medieval buildings, open museums in former mosques and synagogues, and market Toledo as *La Ciudad de las Tres Culturas* – the city of three cultures. Endlessly recycled in promotional materials, the story begins with the 'Reconquest' of Muslim Tulaytula in 1085 and celebrates its conqueror,

Alfonso VI, as the Emperor of Two Religions, who respected all faiths, "giving rise to a cultural interchange of great importance"[2] (see also Pérez Monzón & Rodríguez-Picavea, 2001). The reality was more prosaic: Tulaytula surrendered without resistance after a symbolic siege and an offer of a new kingdom for its ruler – Valencia. Most Muslims followed the king and so did some Christians and Jews. Shortly after, the Great Mosque was converted into a Christian cathedral (Beale-Rivaya & Busic, 2018). Still, Alfonso VI did grant *fueros*, self-governing privileges, to 'Old' Christians, and later on to Castilians, Franks, Muslims, and Jews (Garcia-Gallo, 1975).

Missing in the guidebooks and the tours are linguistic aspects of *convivencia*, including the fact that 'Old' Christians, nicknamed Mozarabs, refused to give up 'the tongue of the oppressor' – they were equally proud of their resistance to Islam and their mastery of the language of the Quran. For two centuries after the 'Reconquista', Toledo's Mozarabs maintained their native Arabic and so did its Muslims and Jews. Archival records also retain the names of Franks, Gascons, and Galicians who learned Arabic and adopted names, like Abd Allah bin Gilbert (Moreno, 2012). Medieval Toledo was a city where Kufic writing had pride of place in the churches and synagogues, dual names were par for the course, and transactions between the Catholic church and Mozarabs, Muslims, and Jews were documented in Arabic, according to Islamic notary manuals, complete with the *bismillah* "In the name of Allah, the Merciful, the Compassionate" (Beale-Rivaya, 2012; Beale-Rivaya & Busic, 2018; Witcombe, 2018).

Mozarab reluctance to relinquish Arabic does not fit well with the popular narrative of 'the triumph of Castilian' perpetuated by patriotic Spanish scholars and by popularizers who follow in their stead. One recent 'biography of Spanish' denies Mozarabs spoke Arabic at all, even under Islamic rule. "Despite their name – which suggests the opposite," contend Nadeau and Barlow (2013), "Mozarabs spoke a form of Ibero-Romance, not Arabic" (p. 39). Popular histories also erase Mozarabs as a group. Nowadays, Toledo still has a Mozarab community with two parishes, but if you think the heirs to the city's oldest Christian tradition feature prominently in the booklets and the tours you would be wrong. Not only tourists, "some people in Toledo don't even know anything about us or that we even exist," complained a local Mozarab. "Some think we are the Moors"[3] (see also Beale-Rivaya's chapter in this volume).

You also won't find an explanation of how Arabic came to an end. The 1492 expulsion of the Jews is familiar to all – its 500th anniversary witnessed a public apology by King Juan Carlos and a joint prayer with the Israeli

[2] www.lacerca.com/noticias/turismo/toledo-ciudad-tres-culturas-23725-1.html.

[3] https://ordoromanusprimus.wordpress.com/2008/02/07/rediscovering-the-mozarabs-of-toledo-the-defense-and-survival-of-mozarabism-depends-basically-on-us/.

president Chaim Herzog. In 2015, a parliamentary act made it easier for descendants of Jewish exiles to obtain Spanish citizenship. In contrast, the 1609 expulsion of Moriscos – the forcefully baptized Muslims and their offspring – was never mentioned in the tours I followed and neither was the campaign to eradicate Arabic described in the introduction to this volume (see also Giménez-Aguibar & Wasserman Soler, 2011). As of this writing, no apology has been issued to descendants of Moriscos – in Spain, Islamophobia still runs deep (Beale-Rivaya, this volume; Boll, 2020; García-Sanjuán, 2018).

The list of Arabic names in Callejon de San Pedro (Fig. 15.2a) isn't an apology but it is not a regular touristy sign either – San Pedro is a blind alley off the beaten visitor path. Paid for and installed by a prominent local artist and historian Fernando Aranda Alonso, the plaque endows the neighborhood with a memory of its Arabic-speaking past.[4] The dates and names, derived from old charters, are a reminder that Arabic was in use long after the 'Reconquista'. The juxtaposition of crucified Jesus and Kufic writing in the museum-mosque-church Cristo de la Luz (Fig. 15.2b) is meant to be educational as well: the formulaic blessing was painted *in* and *for* the church, on the apsidal arch added after the conversion of the mosque (Hutcheson, 2014). Foreign visitors I talked to missed these subtle hints – they left Toledo with the prepackaged image of three cultures, 'separate but equal,' interacting in shared Castilian.

15.3 St. Petersburg

St. Petersburg is a destination that doesn't need marketing. The designation of the city as a World Heritage site in 1990 was a recognition of its magnetic appeal. Municipal authorities are eager to preserve the charm – new construction is banned in the historic center but restoration is welcome, as seen in the case of two elite department stores – *Passage*, reopened in 2012 (Fig. 15.3), and *Au Pont Rouge* [At the Red Bridge], reopened in 2015 (Fig. 15.4).

Passage, an elegant shopping arcade on the Nevsky Prospect – St. Petersburg's answer to the Champs Elysées – was first opened by Count Essen-Stenbrock-Fermor in 1848. Covered by glass and steel, the gallery was a novelty – one of the world's first shopping malls, alongside London's Burlington Arcade and Parisian Passage du Caire and Galerie Vivienne.[5] What the visitors took for granted were the French signs announcing its boutiques, cafés, and pâtisseries. *Français* was *de rigueur* on the Nevsky, and Russians, Germans, Estonians, and Finns also advertised their tailor shops as *à la mode* and their hair salons as *de Paris*. "All of the shop signs on the Nevsky Prospect

[4] https://realacademiatoledo.es/los-sucesivos-nombres-del-callejon-de-san-pedro/.
[5] https://passage.spb.ru/o-passazhe/.

(a) (b)

Fig. 15.3 French in St. Petersburg: (a) *Passage* in 1902. Wikimedia Commons. (b) Restored French sign. *Passage*, Nevsky Prospect 48, St. Petersburg, September 2018. Photo by the author.

(a) (b)

Fig. 15.4 (a) *Au Pont Rouge* in 1913. Wikimedia Commons. (b) Restored bilingual signs. *Au Pont Rouge*, Moika Embankment 73. St. Petersburg, September 2018. Photo by the author.

are in French and rarely, here and there, with translations into Russian," grumbled Yegor Rastorguev, author of a popular guide *Strolls along the Nevsky Prospect* (1846):

It's doubtful that in Paris there is even a single sign in a foreign tongue, while in the Russian capital, not only on the Nevsky but on all the main streets of Petersburg, all signboards, all inscriptions are in French, as if Petersburg were not a Russian city. (Rastorguev, 1846, pp. 40–41, translated from Russian by A.P.)

By the time Belgian businessman Stefan Esders and his Dutch nephew Karl Scheefhals opened *Au Pont Rouge* in 1907, laws demanded translation and that's exactly what the shoppers saw on the Art Nouveau façade: gilded signs in Russian and French. Russia's first multistory department store, in the grand tradition of Selfridges and Galeries Lafayette, *Au Pont Rouge* was so chic that even empress Alexandra was among its clientele.[6] The 1917 revolution brought the business to an abrupt end. *Au Pont Rouge* was taken over by a garment factory, and *Passage* reopened as a Soviet department store. French signage was stripped – alien tongues were of little use behind the Iron Curtain and their mastery aroused suspicions of espionage and sabotage.

After the collapse of the USSR (1991) and in anticipation of the 300th anniversary of the city's founding by Peter the Great (2003), the imperial past came back in vogue, as seen in the name change from Leningrad to St. Petersburg. As visitor numbers went up, the city's tourism industry expanded its offerings from museums and theaters to tours of German, French, Italian, English, Muslim, and multinational St. Petersburg. The highlights of the multinational tour include one of Europe's largest synagogues (opened in 1893), the Tatar mosque (1913), and Nevsky Prospect, where an Orthodox cathedral stands in close proximity to a (former) Dutch church, a German Lutheran church, a Catholic church, and an Armenian church.[7]

The itineraries also feature the city's historic tongues. On the French tour, you may see the restored *Français* of Passage and Au Pont Rouge and on the German tour the headquarters of the city's first newspaper, *Sankt-Petersburgische Zeitung* (1727–1914), the city's first school, *Petrischule*, the first Lutheran church, *Petrikirche*, bilingual street signs installed in 1768 on the orders of Catherine the Great, and German tablets commemorating the flood of 1824 (Fig. 15.5).

What you don't hear about is the Russification campaign. By the 1880s, the dependence on Baltic German officials and foreign tongues became a source of embarrassment for imperial authorities, and Russification expanded from Poland and Western provinces to Baltic provinces and St. Petersburg, where the brunt was borne by the city's German colony (Henriksson, 1993). After the 1917 revolution, out-migration, purges, and deportations of Germans and Finns in the 1930s and 1940s eliminated the remaining diversity (Rozanova, 2012). In 2010, Russians constituted 92.5 percent of St. Petersburg's population and Russian speakers 99.7 percent.[8]

6 https://aupontrouge.ru/en/history/. 7 https://eduvpiter.ru/2020/1204.
8 https://petrostat.gks.ru/VPN2010.

(a) (b)

Fig. 15.5 German in St. Petersburg: (a) Russian–German sign for Dvortsovaya Street, installed in 1768. Dvortsovaya Embankment 34. (b) Flood tablet in German "The height of water on November 7, 1824," Grazhdanskaya 19. St. Petersburg, September 2018. Photos by the author.

It is all the more surprising then that in 2008, municipal authorities adopted a law to protect the rights of the Russian language.[9] Articles 4–6 require all signs to be in correct Russian. Foreign languages, accompanied by translations, are allowed in special cases. Cultural heritage is one such case – hence, the gilded French. The threat to the Russian language is unnamed but isn't hard to guess: in 2006–2008, the city saw a spike of labor migration from Uzbekistan and Tajikistan and an upswing in anti-migrant demonstrations, campaigns, leaflets, and graffiti (Rozanova, 2012). The municipal response was twofold. In 2006, city authorities, headed by Valentina Matviyenko, unrolled the Tolerance-1 (2006–2010) initiative, followed by Tolerance-2 (2011–2014). Both programs featured well-intentioned round tables and public events but tolerance for accented Russian and migrant languages wasn't on the table – instead, the city tightened restrictions, as seen in the 2008 language law, signed by Matviyenko.

Not surprisingly, studies of the city's linguistic landscape reveal a uniformly Russian façade and negative attitudes toward migrants' 'unintelligible mumbo-jumbo' (Baranova & Fedorova, 2019, 2020). The only exceptions are the ads in English and Chinese, aimed at foreign visitors, and historic signs in German and French. Their restoration may invoke imperial nostalgia, but it is not a nostalgia for being surrounded by foreign tongues.

15.4 Lviv

In 2012, Lviv, a cohost of the European soccer championship, was spruced up in preparation for an unprecedented influx of visitors (for analysis of the city's

[9] www.assembly.spb.ru/ndoc/doc/0/706137974.

Fig. 15.6 Café Sztuka, with restored Polish and Yiddish ads for groceries and haberdashery. Kotlyarska Street 8. Lviv, September 2019. Photo by the author.

marketing campaign, see Godis & Nilsson, 2018). The famous ghost signs also received a new coat of paint, including at Café Sztuka [Polish for 'art'], opened in 2009 in a former Jewish store (Fig. 15.6). "The signs in different languages illustrate not only a wide selection of goods," explains its website, "they are evidence of the tolerant coexistence of Ukrainians, Poles and Jews and show the multinational character of old Lviv"[10] (translated from Ukrainian by A.P.).

The city's leading ghost sign hunter and blogger Areta Kovalska, an expat from the USA, couldn't agree more. "Ghost signs are lovely," enthuses Kovalska (2020):

> They add charm to the city, help us feel the city's old atmosphere. They are a reminder of a different era – not only of when the landscape was void of neon lights and bulky plastic signs, but of the city's multicultural and multilinguistic past.

The signs, in other words, create a welcoming and cosmopolitan atmosphere, as do Viennese-style cafés that invoke the city's Habsburg past. Sztuka,

[10] https://shtuka.net.ua/history/.

for one, has become a popular stop on the tours of Jewish and multicultural Lviv.[11] Yet the equation of multilingual signs and tolerance is not as unproblematic as it seems – the first thing you notice is the absent Ukrainian.

Founded by a Rus prince, Daniil of Halych, in the fourteenth century, Lviv was taken over by Polish kings and remained in Polish hands until 1939. For most of its history, Lwów was a Polish city, where Jews and Rusyns (modern Ukrainians) were a minority, at times restricted to a single street, and Cossacks a terrifying enemy force. Jews first appeared in the city records in 1348 (Bartov, 2007) and, as time went by, their numbers grew, despite the periodic pogroms. In the 1930s, the era many ghost signs come from, 50.4 percent of the city's population was Roman Catholic (what we see as 'real' Poles), 31.9 percent Jewish, and 15.9 percent Greek Catholic (a confession common among Rusyns). Language-wise, 63.5 percent declared Polish as their mother tongue, 24.1 percent picked Yiddish or Hebrew, and 11.3 percent Ukrainian or Rusyn/*Ruski* (not the same as Russian/*Rosyjski*, also in use) (Główny Urząd Statystyczny Rzeczypospolitej Polskiej, 1937).

The interwar Lwów had some Ukrainian ads, but Ukrainianization began in earnest in 1939 when the Red Army annexed the city to Ukraine under the Molotov-Ribbentrop pact. Ukrainians became the titular nationality and their language the official tongue. To celebrate the 'reunion' of east and west, the authorities put up a monument to Stalin's constitution in front of the Opera House inscribed in Ukrainian, Polish, and Yiddish. This wasn't what the Organization of Ukrainian Nationalists (OUN) had in mind: their dream was an ethnically pure Ukraine, and their hopes for making it happen were pinned on Hitler. In preparation for the German invasion, on June 30, 1941, OUN plastered Lviv with posters "Ukraine for Ukrainians," leaflets calling on Ukrainians to destroy Poles, Muscovites (Russians), Hungarians, and Jews (Himka, 2011; Mick, 2011) and banners glorifying Hitler and OUN leader Stepan Bandera (Fig. 15.7a).

These banners are a poignant reminder that bilingual signs do not invariably signal tolerance. The Nazi takeover of Lviv was followed by the cold-blooded Jewish genocide, perpetrated by German troops, with the help of Ukrainian militia and the Ukrainian battalion Nachtigall. Ukrainian veterans of Nazi troops vehemently deny participation in anti-Jewish activities but documentary evidence, films, and photographs speak to the contrary (Himka, 2011; Mick, 2011). By the time Waffen-SS Division Galizien was formed in 1943 with Ukrainian volunteers, OUN leaders had a new goal – to cleanse 'Ukrainian lands' of Poles. The division took part in the ethnic cleansing of Galicia and Volhynia led by the Ukrainian Insurgent Army (UPA) (Snyder, 2003). When the Red Army retook the city in 1944 Yiddish was no more.

[11] https://wildeast.blog/en/jewish-lviv/.

(a) (b)

Fig. 15.7 (a) German–Ukrainian banners in the city of Zhovkva, near Lviv, in 1941: "Heil Hitler! Glory to Hitler! Glory to Bandera!" Wikimedia Commons. (b) Monument to OUN leader Stepan Bandera (1909–1959), erected in 2007. Lviv, September 2019. Photo by the author.

Polish disappeared shortly after, when remaining Poles were deported to Poland as part of the Soviet-Polish population exchange. Ironically, many refugees from Lwów ended up in Breslau, emptied of its German inhabitants to become Polish Wrocław. Lviv, stripped of most of its prewar population, was repopulated with Ukrainians from the surrounding countryside, repatriates from Poland, and newcomers from eastern Ukraine and other regions of the USSR. Ukrainian and Russian became official languages; Polish, German, and Yiddish signs were painted over; streets were renamed; and all but four Polish monuments removed. Alongside the inevitable Lenin statue (1952), the authorities installed monuments to Ukrainian writers Franko (1964), Stefanyk (1971), and pro-Soviet Halan (1972), assassinated by Banderites in 1949.

When I first visited Lviv in 1980, it was a Ukrainian-speaking city, where Russian was official but unwelcome. Nationalist Ukrainians treasured the memory of Bandera and his dream of independent Ukraine, and when it did come true, Lviv was promptly de-Sovietized: Russian signs were stripped with alacrity, streets renamed, Soviet monuments taken down, and public space repopulated by a pantheon of Ukrainian heroes, among them the national bard

Taras Shevchenko (1992), the founding father of Ukrainian history Mykhailo Hrushevsky (1994), medieval founder of Lviv Daniil of Halych (2001), soldiers of the UPA and SS Division Galizien (2008, Lychakiv cemetery), and Stepan Bandera (2007), viewed as a national hero by western and diaspora Ukrainians and as a Nazi collaborator by eastern Ukrainians, Russians, Poles, Jews, and western scholars (Amar, 2011; Blacker, 2019; Rossoliński-Liebe, 2014). Russian speakers responded by leaving the city: between 1989 and 2001 the proportion of Ukrainians jumped from 79.1 percent to 88.1 percent, while that of Russians dropped from 16.1 percent to 8.9 percent and Jews from 1.6 percent to 0.3 percent.[12] No one was sorry to see them go, said my Jewish interviewees.

Eerily Leninesque, the Bandera monument symbolizes the replacement of Soviet myth-making with a new political and ideological project, conspicuous on the city's website: the reinvention of Lviv as an ancient Ukrainian stronghold, victimized by "the Polish authoritarian regime" and "Soviet totalitarianism" and free at last as "an indisputable capital of Ukrainian culture, spirituality and national identity"[13] (as opposed to Ukraine's actual capital, Russophone Kyiv). Yet savvy politicians realized that nationalizing public space wasn't enough: to gain political goodwill in the west and become a tourist destination, Lviv had to be Europeanized. The Habsburg past, quintessentially European, became an asset in this pursuit and so did Polish and Jewish heritage, insofar as it didn't interfere with the patriotic narrative and implicate Ukrainians in morally reprehensible activities (Amar, 2011; Bartov, 2007; Blacker, 2019). The efforts paid off – in 1998 old Lviv was designated a World Heritage site, in part thanks to its past 'diversity':

> The political and commercial role of Lviv attracted to it a number of ethnic groups with different cultural and religious traditions, who established separate yet interdependent communities within the city, evidence for which is still discernible in the modern townscape. (ICOMOS, 1998, p. 111)

Multilingual ghost signs are part of this discernible evidence – hence, the tacit agreement to keep the best ones on display. They also help with public relations. When two experts on Lviv's Polish inscriptions, Ksenya Borodin and Ivanna Gonak (2012), created a tour of the city's ghost signs, their goal was to challenge Lviv's reputation as a fascist and nationalist Banderstadt:

> Some try to present Lviv as a "Bandera" city, where other nations are not respected and loved. This is not historically true and the signs show this to us.[14] (translated from Russian by A.P.)

[12] http://2001.ukrcensus.gov.ua/eng/results/general/nationality/Lviv/.
[13] https://lviv.travel/en/lviv-history.
[14] www.primetour.ua/ru/company/articles/-Lviv-po-polsku–zberezheni-napisi-polskoyi-dobi-vistavili-u-Lvovi.html.

The exploitative nature of appropriation of Jewish heritage was evident in the restaurant At the Golden Rose. Opened in 2008 next to the ruins of the eponymous synagogue, it was advertised as Jewish with the term *zhydivsky*, seen as a slur by Russian-speaking Jews, and offered its customers a full immersion experience. The visitors were greeted with *Shalom*, given price-free menus, and invited to haggle over the price of their (non-kosher) meals and to dress up as Jews with black hats adorned with fake sidelocks (Bechtel, 2016; Blacker, 2014; Narvselius, 2015). While many visitors were offended by the perpetuation of anti-Semitic stereotypes (as seen in Tripadvisor reviews), Ukrainian owners called their approach humorous but respectful and remained in business until the COVID pandemic forced them to close the doors in 2020.[15]

In noncommercial contexts, financial responsibility for dissonant heritage is less clear. Interviews conducted in 2019–2020 with heads of Lviv's cultural institutions, administrators, managers, educators, and artists revealed that for many of these memory actors, Jewish, Polish, and Russian/Soviet legacy is "not our heritage" (Otrishchenko & Kozlova, 2020; for similar findings, see Corsale, 2021). Jewish memorials in Lviv are the work of its Jewish community and US, Israeli, and German groups, Polish signs are frequently vandalized, and when a gallows with a star of David was painted over a Yiddish sign in 2015 no one bothered to clean it up. When I visited the city in 2019, the anti-Semitic graffiti was still in place (Fig. 15.8).[16]

The reinvention of business ads left over from Polish Lwów as an emblem of Ukrainian tolerance and the emphasis on the city's Austro-Hungarian past serve three city-marketing goals: to downplay historic antagonisms between Ukrainians, Poles, and Jews; to interrupt the continuous narrative of Lviv as a Polish city; and to direct attention away from the inglorious birth of Ukrainian Lviv. More importantly, while Lviv authorities are content to display Polish and Yiddish as a symbol of tolerance and love, the same courtesy is not extended to Russian, the language of the city's largest linguistic minority, including its present-day Jews. Having roamed the streets for a week, I found plenty of Yiddish signs but of Russian there was no trace.[17]

The thoroughness of the erasure of Russian and Russians in the city's linguistic landscape can be seen in the monument to Cossack Ivan Pidkova, Ivan Horseshoe, erected by Soviet authorities in 1982 (Fig. 15.9). The Ukrainian inscription on the plinth celebrated Pidkova as "the hero of the joint struggle of Russian, Ukrainian and Moldovan peoples against Turkish

[15] https://lviv.vgorode.ua/news/dosuh_y_eda/a1139578-ne-perezhila-karantinu-u-lvovi-zakrili-populjarnu-halitsko-zhidivsku-knajpu-.

[16] For discussion of anti-Semitism in Lviv politics of memory, see Blacker (2019, pp. 113–117).

[17] On conscious erasure of Russian language, spoken by Russians and Russophone Ukrainians, from Lviv's literary palimpsest, see Blacker (2019, pp. 32–33).

(a) (b)

Fig. 15.8 Anti-Semitic graffiti, Kulish Street 1. Lviv, September 2019. Photos by the author.

Fig. 15.9 Monument of Cossack Ivan Pidkova with a small horseshoe plaque covering up the word 'Russians.' Lviv, September 2019. Photo by the author.

invaders, executed by Polish nobles of Lviv on June 16, 1578" (my translation). After the dissolution of the USSR, local authorities concealed the mention of Russians with white paint and then covered it up with a tiny, elegant horseshoe smack in the middle of text.

The contradiction between the absence of Russian and the abundance of Yiddish, no longer understood even by local Jews, suggests that Europeanization of Lviv may be one paint layer deep. The aim of the city's administration was to attract foreign tourists and EU funding without adopting EU values, such as minority language rights (for discussion of Ukrainian language laws, see Csernicskó & Márku, 2020; Fiala-Butora, 2020; for a prescient analysis that linked compulsory Ukrainianization to the threat of war with Russia, see Lieven, 2022).

15.5 Palermo

Palermo was once a popular stop on the European Grand Tour, but by the twentieth century, the decaying city, ruled by the mafia, scared off visitors. The turnaround began with the Maxi Trial of 475 mafiosi (1986–1992) and the election of a new mayor, Leoluca Orlando, a law professor known for his anti-mafia stance. His five terms (1985–1990, 1993–2000, 2012–2022) ushered in the Palermo Renaissance. "Before I was elected mayor," recalls Orlando, "people living in Sicily had no respect for the time, no memory of the past, no hope for the future" (in Majeed, 2012, p. 4). His aim was to restore the sense of hope and civic pride. Cutting the ties between the city government and the mafia, Orlando's administration revitalized business and cultural life, paved roads, fixed sewers, built schools, planted gardens, reopened the Opera House, and renovated the historic center with the help of school children, given 'adoption' certificates for monuments they helped research, restore, and maintain (Bacon & Majeed, 2012; Orlando, 2001).

At the heart of the historic narrative is the Norman kingdom of Sicily that functioned in Arabic, Latin, and Greek (Johns, 2002). The UNESCO nomination dossier, signed by Orlando, opened up with one of its famous artifacts – a memorial plaque, commissioned in 1148 by the royal priest Grisandus, to commemorate his mother in Latin, Greek, Arabic, and Arabic in Hebrew script. The trilingualism was fairly short-lived, like the Norman kingdom itself, but the kings did leave behind an impressive artistic legacy, recognized by UNESCO in 2015:

> Arab-Norman Palermo... bears witness to a particular political and cultural condition characterized by the fruitful coexistence of people of different origins (Muslim, Byzantine, Latin, Jewish, Lombard, and French). This interchange generated a conscious and unique combination of elements derived from the architectural and artistic techniques of Byzantine, Islamic, and Western traditions. (UNESCO, 2015, p. 239)

(a) (b)

Fig. 15.10 (a). Street sign in Italian, Hebrew, and Arabic in the historic Jewish quarter, *La Giudecca*. Via Divisi, Palermo, April 2017. Photo by the author. (b) Defaced trilingual sign on Via dei Martiri. Photo posted on Facebook by mayor Leoluca Orlando, on April 3, 2017.

And when a scholar of Jewish history Titta Lo Jacono proposed to mark the Jewish quarter with trilingual signs (Fig. 15.10a), Orlando eagerly supported the initiative.[18] For Orlando, these signs are not just a form of commemoration but a symbol of cultural change and a harbinger of things to come. When he was growing up in Palermo, diversity wasn't a part of life – the mafia kicked out everyone who was different. "Until I was 30," confessed the mayor,

> I had never seen a migrant on the streets. There were no people of color, Asians, Africans. The only migrants in Palermo were the distinct German ladies who were the governesses of children of the well-to-do families of Palermo. I too had a German governess, for me she was a migrant. (in Bercioux, 2017)

His new goal is to make the city a safe haven for migrants and to bring lost diversity back to the streets. Orlando's (2015) Charter of Palermo calls on the EU to abolish residence permits and recognize migrant mobility as a human right. The Global Parliament of Mayors he founded promotes the vision worldwide. The link between the vision of Palermo as a sanctuary city and trilingual historic signs is hard to miss: When on April 3, 2017, vandals spray-painted over Hebrew and Arabic (Fig. 15.10b), Mayor Orlando and civic organizations publicly decried the action as an expression of racism, intolerance, and hatred of migrants fueled by the media, and organized a cleaning campaign.[19] When I arrived in Palermo on April 21, the signs were sparkling clean.

[18] https://ricerca.repubblica.it/repubblica/archivio/repubblica/2004/04/28/noi-gli-ultimi-figli-della-giudecca-di.html.

[19] https://palermo.meridionews.it/articolo/53647/ballaro-tolta-la-vernice-dai-cartelli-vandalizzati-i-media-alimentano-intolleranza-verso-migranti/

Conclusion

On the surface, Toledo, St. Petersburg, Lviv, and Palermo have little in common, other than their status as World Heritage sites. A closer look, however, reveals a common thread. Once upon a time, all four cities had been ethnically and linguistically diverse and then underwent traumatic unmixing: Toledo and Palermo in the Middle Ages, St. Petersburg at the turn of the twentieth century, and Lviv during and after World War II. By the turn of the twenty-first century, homogeneity created a challenge for urban marketers, eager to promote their cities as 'cultural capitals' and 'multilingual hotspots' and to engage in 'celebrations of diversity' encouraged by UNESCO, the EU, and the Council of Europe (cf. Sokolovska, this volume).

Luckily for promoters, 'multilingual' is an ambiguous term. Luxembourg and Montreal are 'multilingual' because their inhabitants share two or more of the same languages, while London, Melbourne, New York, and Sydney vie for the designation of 'the multilingual capital of the world' based on the number of languages their residents speak and despite the fact that they rely on English as a lingua franca and are ruled by an unapologetically monolingual elite. In Toledo, Palermo, and Lviv, municipal authorities mobilized past diversity to achieve present-day aims, including the desired status of the UNESCO World Heritage site.

Nowadays, in all four cities, dissonant signs perform multifaceted identity work oriented toward the past, present, and future. When it comes to history, they help promote the appealing narrative of harmonious past diversity or, in the case of Lviv, appropriate someone else's semi-tolerant past. The job of pseudo ghost signs in this context is to write Ukrainian language into the mix (Fig. 15.11). The present-day role of dissonant signs is to recontextualize the cities as 'welcoming,' 'multilingual,' and 'cosmopolitan' and to deflect attention from current suppression of minority languages, be it Uzbek in St. Petersburg or Russian in Lviv. Palermo reminds us that some signs are also oriented toward the future, and it is this orientation that elicits the greatest tensions and anxieties today, as seen in Vilnius, the capital of modern-day Lithuania.

In 2016, the city's liberal mayor Remigijus Šimašius unveiled bilingual street signs in Yiddish, Hebrew, Tatar, German, Russian, and Polish that commemorated these communities on the streets where they once lived. "All these plaques are to celebrate our diversity," said the mayor to the Reuters correspondent, echoing the Council of Europe discourse.[20] Not everyone was eager to celebrate: the Russian sign was smeared with paint within hours. The

[20] www.reuters.com/article/us-lithuania-streetsigns-idUKKCN11R1UC.

(a) (b)

Fig. 15.11 Lviv's faux ghost signs with added Ukrainian: (a) Pawn shop with Polish terms for 'gold,' 'silver,' and 'watches' on the left and Ukrainian words for 'pawn shop' and 'money' on the right. Corner of Shpytalna and Koptyarska Streets. (b) Dairy store with a Ukrainian word for 'groceries' alongside ill-fitting cognates in Polish and German and a Hebrew term. Kulish Street 1. Lviv, September 2019. Photos by the author.

government's representative in the Vilnius county, Vilda Vaičiūnienė, had a bigger concern: historic signs might encourage Polish and Russian minorities to demand bilingual signage, made illegal in Lithuania. To stop them in their tracks, Vaičiūnienė filed a claim in court, arguing that the signs violate the Law on the State Language and may incite hatred and discord. When the lower court rejected the claim, she appealed to the Supreme Court. In 2019, the Supreme Administrative Court of Lithuania made a binding ruling that the signs do not violate the law because they are decorative and not official.[21]

The stark contrast between the multilingual policies of the Grand Duchy of Lithuania, discussed in the introduction to this volume, and aggressive monolingualism of modern Lithuanian, Russian, and Ukrainian language laws shows that linguistic nationalism has made us less pragmatic and rational and more ideologically driven and emotional and is, unfortunately, proving hard to unthink.

P.S. This is how I planned to end this chapter until President Putin ordered an invasion of Ukraine on February 24, 2022, days before this volume went

[21] www.baltictimes.com/lithuanian_court_rules_that_bilingual_street_signs_in_vilnius_do_not_breach_law/.

into production. In his speech, Putin justified the invasion by national security concerns and the need to protect Russian speakers in Ukraine against violations of their linguistic and cultural rights. This rhetoric made me think twice about the Lviv part of this chapter. The intolerance of Ukrainian language laws adopted between 2014 and 2021 (cf. Csernicskó & Márku, 2020; Fiala-Butora, 2020; Lieven, 2022) does not justify Russian aggression. Nothing does – the invasion of Ukraine is a violation of international law and a horrific war crime. Upon further reflection, however, I decided to leave the chapter unchanged for the sake of future scholars trying to understand the everyday workings of petty ethnic chauvinism and linguistic intolerance, weaponized by Putin's government with disastrous consequences for all Ukrainians, regardless of their mother tongue.

References

Amar, T. (2011) Different but the same or the same but different? Public memory of the Second World War in post-Soviet Lviv. *Journal of Modern European History,* 9, 3, 373–396.

Bacon, L. & R. Majeed (2012) *Palermo Renaissance Part 1: Rebuilding civic identity and reclaiming a city from the mafia in Italy, 1993–2000.* Princeton University: Innovations for Successful Societies. Retrieved on March 3, 2022 at https://successfulsocieties.princeton.edu/publications/palermo-renaissance-part-1-rebuilding-civic-identity-and-reclaiming-city-mafia-italy

Baranova, V. & K. Fedorova (2019) 'Invisible minorities' and 'hidden diversity' in Saint-Petersburg's linguistic landscape. *Language and Communication*, 68, 17–27.

(2020) Overcoming aggressive monolingualism: Prejudices and linguistic diversity in Russian megalopolises. *Open Linguistics*, 6, 672–689.

Bartov, O. (2007) *Erased: Vanishing traces of Jewish Galicia in present-day Ukraine.* Princeton/Oxford: Princeton University Press.

Beale-Rivaya, Y. (2012) The written record as witness: Language shift from Arabic to Romance in the documents of the Mozarabs of Toledo in the twelfth and thirteenth centuries. *La Corónica*, 40, 2, 27–50.

Beale-Rivaya, Y. & J. Busic (eds.) (2018) *A companion to medieval Toledo: Reconsidering the canons.* Leiden: Brill.

Bechtel, D. (2016) Remembrance tourism in former multicultural Galicia: The revival of the Polish-Ukrainian borderlands. *Tourism and Hospitality Research,* 16, 3, 206–222.

Bercioux, L. (2017) Was an "Asshole Mayor" Just What a Free Palermo Needed? Orlando Speaks Out. *La Voce di New York,* September 10, 2017. Retrieved on March 3, 2022 at www.lavocedinewyork.com/en/people/2017/09/10/was-an-asshole-mayor-just-what-a-free-palermo-needed-the-words-of-orlando/

Blacker, U. (2014) Urban commemoration and literature in post-Soviet L'viv: A comparative analysis with the Polish experience. *Nationalities Papers*, 42, 4, 637–654.

(2019) *Memory, the city and the legacy of World War II in East Central Europe: The ghosts of others*. London/New York: Routledge.
Boll, J. (2020) Selling Spain: Tourism, tensions, and Islam in Iberia. *Journal of Intercultural Communication*, 20, 2, 42–55.
Borodin, K. & I. Gonak (2012) *Львів po polsku. Ім'я будинку та інші написи* [Lviv in Polish. House names and other inscriptions]. *Львів: Коло.*
Burdin, R. (2021) Hebrew, Yiddish and the creation of contesting Jewish places in Kazimierz. *Journal of Sociolinguistics*, 25, 81–102.
Calderwood, E. (2014). The invention of al-Andalus: Discovering the past and creating the present in Granada's Islamic tourism sites. *The Journal of North African Studies*, 19, 1, 27–55.
Calvert, A. (1907) *Toledo*. London: John Lane.
Castro, A. (1954) *The structure of Spanish history*. Princeton, NJ: Princeton University Press.
Corsale, A. (2021) Issues and changes related to dissonant heritage: A case from Jewish and Polish heritage in the small towns of Western Ukraine. *Tourism Planning and Development*, 18, 4, 479–487.
Csernicskó, I. & A. Márku (2020) Minority language rights in Ukraine from the point of view of application of the European Charter for Regional or Minority Languages. *Alkalmazott Nyelvtudomány*, XX. évfolyam, 2.
Fiala-Butora, J. (2020) The controversy over Ukraine's new Law on Education: Conflict prevention and minority rights protection as divergent objectives? *European Yearbook of Minority Issues*, 17, 233–261.
Flesler, D. & A. Pérez Melgosa (2008) Marketing convivencia: Contemporary tourist appropriations of Spain's Jewish past. In Afinoguénova, E. & J. Martí-Olivella (eds.) *Spain is (still) different: Tourism and discourse in Spanish identity*. Lanham: Lexington Books, pp. 63–84.
Garcia-Gallo, A. (1975) *Los fueros de Toledo* [Toledan charters]. Madrid: Instituto Nacional de Estudios Juridicos.
García-Sanjuán, A. (2018) Rejecting al-Andalus, exalting the Reconquista: historical memory in contemporary Spain. *Journal of Medieval Iberian Studies*, 10, 1, 127–145.
Giménez-Aguibar, P. & D. Wasserman Soler (2011) *La Mala Algarabia*: Church, monarchy and the Arabic language in 16th century Spain. *The Medieval History Journal*, 14, 2, 229–258.
Główny Urząd Statystyczny Rzeczypospolitej Polskiej [Head Statistical Agency of the Polish Republic] (1937) *Drugi Powszechny Spis Ludności z dn. 9.XII. 1931 r., miasto Lwów* [Second General Census from December 9, 1931, the city of Lwów]. Warsaw.
Godis, N. & J. Nilsson (2018) Memory tourism in a contested landscape: Exploring identity discourses in Lviv, Ukraine. *Current Issues in Tourism*, 21, 15, 1690–1709.
Gruber, R. (2002) *Virtually Jewish: Reinventing Jewish culture in Europe*. Berkeley, CA: University of California Press.
Henriksson, A. (1993) Nationalism, assimilation and identity in late imperial Russia: The St. Petersburg Germans, 1906–1914. *Russian Review,* 52, 3, 341–353.
Himka, J.-P. (2011) The Lviv pogrom of 1941: The Germans, Ukrainian nationalists, and the carnival crowd. *Canadian Slavonic Papers*, 53, 2–4, 209–243.

Hutcheson, G. (2014) Contesting the Mezquita del Cristo de la Luz. *La Corónica*, 43, 1, 201–229.

Huyssen, A. (2003) *Present pasts: Urban palimpsests and the politics of memory.* Stanford, CA: Stanford University Press.

International Council on Monuments and Sites (ICOMOS) (1998) *Lviv. Advisory body evaluation.* Retrieved at http://whc.unesco.org/en/list/865/documents

Johns, J. (2002) *Arabic administration in Norman Sicily: The royal diwan.* Cambridge: Cambridge University Press.

Kovalska, A. (2020) Ghost signs of Lviv: A look into the city's faded past. Retrieved on March 3, 2022 at https://forgottengalicia.com/ghost-signs-lviv/

Kurnicki, K. & M. Sternberg (2016) Arrested conflict: Transnational place-making in Polish-German border towns. *Space and Polity*, 20, 3, 263–279.

Lacave, J. (2004) *Guia de la España Judía* [Guide to Jewish Spain]. Cordoba: Ediciones de Almendro.

Lähdesmäki, T., Passerini, L., Kaasik-Krogerus, S., & I. van Huis (eds.) (2019) *Dissonant heritages and memories in contemporary Europe.* Cham, Switzerland: Palgrave Macmillan.

Lewicka, M. (2008) Place attachment, place identity and place memory: Restoring the forgotten city past. *Journal of Environmental Psychology*, 28, 209–231.

Lieven, A. (2022) Ending the threat of war in Ukraine: A negotiated solution to the Donbas conflict and the Crimean dispute. *Quincy Paper 6*, updated January 2022. Retrieved on March 3, 2022 at https://quincyinst.org/report/ending-the-threat-of-war-in-ukraine/

Majeed, R. (2012) Interview with Leoluca Orlando. Retrieved on March 3, 2022 at https://successfulsocieties.princeton.edu/interviews/leoluca-orlando

Mann, V., Glick, T., & J. Dodds (eds.) (1992) *Convivencia: Jews, Muslims and Christians in medieval Spain.* New York: George Braziller/The Jewish Museum.

Mick, C. (2011) Incompatible experiences: Poles, Ukrainians, and Jews in Lviv under Soviet and German occupation, 1939–1944. *Journal of Contemporary History*, 46, 2, 336–363.

Moreno, A. (2012) *Arabicizing, privileges, and liturgy in medieval Castilian Toledo: The problems and mutations of Mozarab identification (1085–1436).* Ph.D. dissertation, University of California Los Angeles.

Nadeau, J. & J. Barlow (2013) *The story of Spanish.* New York: St Martin's Griffin.

Narvselius, E. (2015) Spicing up memories and serving nostalgias: Thematic restaurants and transnational memories in East-Central European borderland cities. *Journal of Contemporary European Studies*, 23, 3, 417–432.

Orlando, L. (2001) *Fighting the mafia and renewing Sicilian culture.* San Francisco: Encounter Books.

(2015) *International Human Mobility Charter of Palermo: From the migration as suffering to mobility as an inalienable human right.* Retrieved on March 3, 2022 at www.iom.int/sites/default/files/our_work/ICP/IDM/2015_CMC/Session-IIIb/Orlando/PDF-CARTA-DI-PALERMO-Statement.pdf

Otrishchenko, N. & I. Kozlova (2020) (Not) our heritage: Cultural milieu and urban space of Lviv. In Mihaylov, V. (ed.) *Spatial conflicts and divisions in post-socialist cities.* Cham, Switzerland: Springer, pp. 151–170.

Passikoff, B. (2017) *The writing on the wall: Rediscovering New York city's "ghost signs."* New York: Skyhorse Publishing.
Pérez Monzón, O. & E. Rodríguez-Picavea (2001) *Toledo y las tres culturas* [Toledo and the three cultures]. Madrid: Ediciones Akal.
Rastorguev, Y. (1846) *Progulki po Nevskomu prospectu* [Strolls along the Nevsky Prospect]. St Petersburg: Karl Kray.
Rossoliński-Liebe, G. (2014) *Stepan Bandera, the life and afterlife of a Ukrainian nationalist: Fascism, genocide and cult.* Stuttgart Verlag.
Rozanova, M. (2012) *Migration processes and challenges in contemporary Russia: St Petersburg case study.* Washington, DC: Woodrow Wilson International Center.
Schutt, S., Roberts, S. & L. White (eds.) (2017) *Advertising and public memory: Social, cultural and historical perspectives on ghost signs.* New York/London: Routledge.
Snyder, T. (2003) *The reconstruction of nations: Poland, Ukraine, Lithuania, Belarus, 1569–1999.* New Haven/London: Yale University Press.
Stage, W. (1989) *Ghost signs: Brick wall signs in America.* Cincinnati, OH: ST Publications.
Tunbridge, J. & G. Ashworth (1996) *Dissonant heritages: The management of the past as a resource in conflict.* Chichester: Wiley.
UNESCO (1986) *Toledo. Advisory body evaluation.* Retrieved on March 3, 2022 at https://whc.unesco.org/en/list/379/documents/
(2015) Decision 39 COM 8B.28 "Arab-Norman Palermo and the Cathedral Churches of Cefalú and Monreale, Italy". Retrieved on March 3, 2022 at https://whc.unesco.org/en/decisions/6378
Witcombe, T. (2018) Maurice and the Mozarabic charter: A cross-cultural transaction in early thirteenth-century Toledo. *Journal of Medieval Arabic Studies*, 10, 2, 234–256.

Index

Printed in Great Britain
by Amazon

60757716R00178